A Journal of the
English Civil War

A Journal of the English Civil War

The Letter Book of Sir William Brereton, Spring 1646

William Brereton

Edited and with an Introduction by
Joseph McKenna

McFarland & Company, Inc., Publishers
Jefferson, North Carolina, and London

Also of Interest

The Irish-American Dynamite Campaign: A History, 1881–1896,
by Joseph McKenna (McFarland, 2012)

Guerrilla Warfare in the Irish War of Independence, 1919–1921,
by Joseph McKenna (McFarland, 2011)

British Ships in the Confederate Navy,
by Joseph McKenna (McFarland, 2010)

Library of Congress Cataloguing-in-Publication Data

Brereton, William, 1604–1661.
A journal of the English Civil War : the letter book of Sir William Brereton, spring 1646 / Sir William Brereton ; edited and with an introduction by Joseph McKenna.
p. cm.
Includes bibliographical references and index.

ISBN 978-0-7864-7269-7
softcover : acid free paper ♾

1. Great Britain—History—Civil War, 1642–1649—Personal narratives. 2. Brereton, William, 1604–1661—Correspondence. 3. Cheshire (England)—History, Military—17th century. 4. Staffordshire (England)—History, Military—17th century. I. McKenna, Joseph. II. Title. III. Title: Letter book of Sir William Brereton, spring 1646.
DA419.B74A4 2012
942.06'2—dc23 2012038039

British Library cataloguing data are available

Manufactured in the United States of America

McFarland & Company, Inc., Publishers
Box 611, Jefferson, North Carolina 28640
www.mcfarlandpub.com

To my former tutor,
Professor Malcolm Wanklyn

Acknowledgments

My grateful thanks go to my former colleagues in the Local Studies and Archive Department of Birmingham Public Libraries in England. I would also like to thank the staffs of Staffordshire and Lichfield Record Offices and those of the British Library.

Table of Contents

Preface

This letter book of Sir William Brereton was bought by Birmingham Public Libraries in England in December 1948 from a Mr. Gibbs for £18. It measures 11½ inches by 7¼ inches and contains 264 pages. Its catalogue number is 595611. In addition there are known to be four more Brereton letter books in existence. The British Library possesses three (Add MSS 11331–3) and Chester City Library one (Earwaker MSS). There is evidence of two others. Add MSS 11331, folio 45, refers to "the last booke," and Stebbing Shaw in his *History of Staffordshire* (vol. 1, p. 54) writes of a "2nd Book during the Warre, endinge in Julie 17, 1643." In 1795 this second book was in the possession of a Mr. J. Wright of Stafford. Since then it has been apparently lost. As each letter book covers only two months of the year, it would have required twenty volumes to have covered the entire war. Such is the scale of the loss.

This particular letter book is written in three distinct hands. One of the writers appears to be Richard Elcocke, possibly Brereton's secretary (see folio 177 in the letter book). The spellings are idiosyncratic, and consists of letters to, from, and of interest to Brereton. In particular the letter book deals with the sieges before Dudley, Tutbury and Bridgnorth Castles, and the Cathedral Close of Lichfield. The book covers the period from 4 April to 29 May 1646. Interwoven with details of the sieges is the daily life of both besiegers and besieged. Details of supplies, both food and armaments, and the constant need for pay for the soldiers, are included, as are the intrigues of the King with the Scottish army before Newark. Mutiny among the troops, applications for advancement and even a love letter appear in this letter book.

In support of this work I have used seventeenth century pamphlets collected in the British Library as the Thomason Tracts. In addition I have used the Civil War Collection in the Arts, Language and Literature Department of the Central Library in Birmingham, England. They are propaganda newsletters, and therefore biased, in favor of either King or Parliament. There are exaggerations, and sometimes there is confusion when a skirmish or battle is given different names by the two sides. Somewhere in between the two accounts, though, is to be found the truth. I have used later Victorian histories of the war, and books from the 1970s when interest in the Civil War was reactivated with the formation of re-enactment societies such as the Sealed Knot, and the Cromwell Association. Of all these later accounts C.V. Wedgwood's *The King's Peace* and *The King's War*, are particularly outstanding.

I have not changed the spellings of words used in Brereton's journal. It would have been possible, but I feel that more would have been lost than gained. Words and terminology over 360 years have changed, so the reader must expect certain idiosyncrasies. In those days unlike today, there were no hard and fast rules regarding spellings. Sometimes if the words are read out loud, one's ear will detect the word being used. For the more odd spellings and abbreviations, as well as military terms, I have supplied an explanation of terminology, which I hope will prove useful.

Explanation of Terms

Seventeenth Century English and Abbreviations

Abbreviate—a short list.
Accompt/acco't—account.
Agst.—against.
Alderman/men—a senior town councilor.
An:—an abbreviation of Andrew.
Andiron—metal furniture around a fireplace.
Birmincham/Bermincham—Birmingham.
Burgess—a man entitled to vote.
Burthen—burden
Cautilous—cautious.
Chirugeons—surgeons.
Comicon—commission.
Complices—accomplices.
Close—cathedral grounds, usually surrounded by ecclesiastical houses.
Cozin—cousin. A title which may also relate to a brother-in-law or other non-nuclear family member.
Cyprus—cypress pine, a chest of drawers made of cypress.
Diaconal—additional.
Die Sabathi—the Sabbath—Sunday.
Dyostacie—dystrophy, wasting away of issues.
Exa'ed—examined
Exaint—a person who has exited, or left.
Exigenses—needs.
Fadom—fathom, a depth of six feet.
ffr.—an abbreviation of Francis
Gent—gentleman/men.
Habitcons—Habitations, homes.
Hundred—"Peerhill Hundred," a county division which in ancient times was obliged to supply 100 soldiers for the King's army.

Imprimis—Latin—among the first.

Inegm't—engagement.

Intymason—intimation.

Kitterminster—Kidderminster, a bedspread made in Kidderminster. Kitterminster can also refer to carpets and curtains.

L—£., i.e., 100L = £100.

Lad:p—Ladyship.

Lecister—Leicester, the county town of Leicestershire.

Leisters're—Leicestershire, an English county.

Ltre—letter.

Maisters—masters.

Malignant—a derisory term for a Royalist.

Marty/Martii—the month of March.

Medietie—dispute

Mencond—mentioned.

Mocons—motions.

Munnes—moneys, money.

Nampywch—Nantwich

Palyis—palliasse, a mattress

Papist, Popery—a derisory term relating to the Roman Catholic Church.

P'ceding—proceeding

Peticon—petition.

P'fected—perfected

P'posicon—proposition.

Press/ p'ss'tt—present.

P'sonall—personal.

q'ter—quarter.

Quushens—cushions.

Race—Royal stable of horses.

Relacon—relation.

Resti'con—restitution.

Saweth—sayth.

Sd—said.

Sequestracon—a fine based on domestic wealth levied against Royalists.

Ser't—servant.

Sr.—Sir.

Standish—a stand for pens and ink.

Stoud coaltes—stud colts, horses for breeding.

Ten'ts—tenants.

30s.—30 shillings.

Voyees, voues—vows.

Wch—which.

Wth — with.
Ye — the.
Yt — that.

Military and Parliamentary Terms

Clks.—clerks.
Colours—company or regimental flags. Many of them had biblical inscriptions.
Commission of Array — the Royalist equivalent of the Committee of Both Kingdoms.
Committee of Both Kingdoms — A Parliamentary committee made up of both English and Scottish members, which directed the course of the war. There were also county committees answerable to the main committee.
Composicons—compositions, negotiations for paying sequestrations.
Cornet — the lowest rank of a commissioned officer.
Dragoons — mounted infantry who rode to battle, but fought on foot.
Drake — a small canon.
Drum — a drummer, used to carry messages.
Ensigne — a flag bearer.
Firelock — a musket with a priming mechanism ignited by a spark.
Foot—foot soldiers (infantry).
G'rall — general.
Granadoes — hand grenades.
Horse — horse soldiers (cavalry).
Leauger — siege.
Lift. — lieutenant (pronounced "leftenant").
Lockes—firelocks, musketeers.
Lo'ps. — Lordships.
Maior — major.
Match — treated string, which when set alight burnt slowly. It was used to ignite and fire muskets.
Ma'tie / Ma:ts — Majesty, his Majesty Charles I.
Parlyamt — Parliament.
P'oll. — parole.
Portcullis — an iron or wooden grating suspended vertically in grooves in the gateway of a fortification, that could be raised or lowered to bar an entrance.
Powther — powder, gunpowder.
Quarterm:ts — quartermasters
Qu'tringe — quartering of troops.
Reformado/reformader — troops from a regiment, which because of losses in former battles were placed in other regiments.

Sallie port—sally port, an opening in a fortified place from which the defenders can launch an assault against their besiegers.

Sconce—an earthwork fortification.

Self Denying Ordinance—an act of Parliament whereby politicians were excluded from holding military commissions. Realizing that some politicians were very capable soldiers, some exemptions were made at Parliament's will.

Sodyers/soldyers/souldiers—soldiers.

Train—a procession of people, munitions and equipment.

Trained Bands—The local county militia.

Introduction: A Brief History of the English Civil War

In order to understand the context of the Letter Book of Sir William Brereton, it is important to understand what was happening in England at the time. Civil war was raging. It was a war for democracy; albeit a limited democracy, fought by an elected Parliament against a king who believed that he was king by Divine Right—a King chosen by God to rule. The struggle was set against the religious wars of the seventeenth century then raging throughout Europe. In Britain it was not so much a war between Catholics and Protestants, but rather a war between Protestants themselves. There was the State Church which still retained some of the trappings of Catholicism, linked to the monarchy, versus the numerous Nonconformist sects, linked to Parliament, who wished to take the Reformation further, and in the process eradicate the Church of England. The successful prosecution of the war by Parliamentary supporters such as Brereton eventually helped shape the evolved democracy that exists today, not only in Britain, but also in the United States of America.

1625–1641

King Charles I acceded to the throne as King of Great Britain and Ireland in 1625. To curtail the new King's power from the start, Parliament failed to automatically renew customs revenues due to the king, in an attempt to gain concessions from him in exchange. The King resorted to collecting them himself, by royal prerogative, which was within his right, though this right was seldom used. The following year, with Parliament still at odds with the King, they impeached his favorite, the Duke of Buckingham, who was seen as a malignant influence. Rather than see him convicted, and possibly even executed, Charles dissolved Parliament.

In 1627 in an attempt to fund his foreign policy the King began collecting "forced loans" to compensate for the Parliamentary subsidies lost when Parliament was dissolved. In the case of five knights imprisoned for non-payment of forced loans, the judges found only partially for the King. With his right to raise taxes limited by the judgment, Charles was forced to recall Parliament. Once recalled, they responded by further attempting to curb the King's power. Parliament passed a Petition of Rights, a legally binding contract prohibiting forced loans, the trial of civilians by military courts and the billeting of soldiers on civilians. The King agreed to their demands in return for a quid pro quo—the restoration of Parliamentary subsidies. In 1629 Parliament complained about the Crown's continued collection of customs revenues without its consent. The Puritanical element within Parliament also complained of innovations in religion, within the Church of England, which they saw as "Romish." Matters were coming to a head over who ruled. The King, who was also Head of the Church of England, dissolved Parliament, amidst angry scenes. Seven Members of Parliament were imprisoned by him. Thus began eleven years of personal rule by the King.

Without a Parliament Charles was obliged to introduce a raft of royal prerogative powers in order to raise money. One such was the fining of all gentlemen with incomes over £40 a year who had not asked to be knighted at the time of his coronation in 1626. Other money-making schemes were also adopted which were widely unpopular with what today we would call the middle-class—the people who formed the backbone of the House of Commons in Parliament.

Further religious controversy followed. In 1633 William Laud was consecrated as Archbishop of Canterbury. He advocated a bureaucratic centralism in religion, basically outlining the ceremonial order of Sunday service. The importance of the pulpit was replaced by the communion table as the central focus of worship. Laud also proscribed many Puritan practices. In the same vein the King made a controversial visit to Scotland where he was crowned in the Anglican rite, rather than the Presbyterian that was so widely practiced in that country. That same year Thomas Lord Wentworth, later the Earl of Strafford, was appointed by the King, without consultation with Parliament, as Lord Deputy of Ireland. He introduced a hardline authoritarian rule, with the religious emphasis being on Anglicanism. This brought him into dispute with Ireland's Roman Catholic majority, as well as the Puritans in England. Further reforms along Laudian lines were introduced into the Church of Ireland in 1636. The King was making enemies.

The most contentious of the arbitrary taxes of Charles' personal rule was Ship Money, introduced in 1634. It was introduced in coastal counties to raise funds for the navy. The following year Ship Money was extended to all counties, making it a national tax. The rate was paid by ten times as many people as those who paid Parliamentary taxation. This brought in a revenue of three times as much money as was previously raised by Parliament. The tax, widely unpopular, was collected annually until 1640.

The King now turned to Scotland. In 1637 he attempted to impose a new Prayer Book on the Presbyterian Scots. This met with widespread opposition and civil unrest. In 1638 the Presbyterians signed a National Covenant, pledging not to submit to any innovation in religion. In the following year, 1639, the King attempted to impose his will on the Scots by force. In this he was defeated and a truce was signed at Berwick. The truce was but a temporary move on the King's part. In April 1640 Charles recalled Parliament, in order to gain their support in financing an invasion of Scotland. For their support though, Parliament sought concessions. The King would not agree to their demands. He dissolved what became known as the Short Parliament in the following month. In May there were religious riots in London following attempts to impose new rules for the government of the Church. Two rioters were killed.

In June the King made further plans for an invasion of Scotland. The Scots pre-empted him, though, and invaded England. By and large the people in northern England supported the religious inclinations of the Scots and did not oppose their invasion. The King sent an English army north to check the invasion. The motivated Scottish army surprised and defeated the largely pressed men of the English army at the ford at Newburn, a few miles west of Newcastle. On 30 August the Scottish army entered Newcastle, which had been abandoned by the English, and held it. In October negotiations between English and Scottish lords were held at Ripon in Yorkshire. The Scots refused to leave England until an English Parliament ratified a settlement. The King was forced to call a new Parliament to allow negotiations to occur. Very astutely the English commissioners transferred their discussions to London. This very clever stroke enabled the King's opponents from both sides of the border to work out a common policy against the King to limit his power.

In November 1640 the Long Parliament, as it became known, first met. From the start it set out to curb the King's power. Lord Strafford was impeached by them and imprisoned. In December Archbishop Laud was imprisoned in the Tower of London. In February 1641 Parliament passed an Act ensuring its own continued existence. It required Parliamentary elections to be held every three years. Lord Strafford was put on trial in March. Despite the abandonment of the trial, Strafford was sentenced to death under an Act of Attainder. He was beheaded in May 1641. From February through to May 1641 important debates were held on the future government of the Church. A Protestation Oath was introduced against Popery, to be taken by those in positions of influence. The following month, in June, important debates were held on Church government. Attempts were also made by the Commons to remove the Anglican bishops from the House of Lords. This failed to get the support of the Lords temporal, and the bishops remained as a force within Parliament. In July a Bill was introduced in Parliament to reform Church government "root and branch." Acts abolishing the Star Chamber and High Commission were also passed in July. The Court of Star Chamber was a particularly pernicious organization—a court with no jury or right of appeal, which had by 1641 developed into a political weapon, leading to abuse by the King. In August King Charles signed the Treaty of Edinburgh which normalized relations between the two countries and led to the withdrawal of the Scots from England.

Parliament recessed from 9 September to 20 October, but before it did so it issued instructions to churchwardens throughout the country to remove what it referred to as "monuments of idolatry and superstition." A fury of iconoclasm followed. At Canterbury Cathedral soldiers tore up the illuminated prayer books, slashed the tapestries, broke the stained glass windows and fired their muskets at the crucifix over the South Gate. The Lords had opposed the move, but the Commons, elected by the people, acted unilaterally, thereby setting a precedent as to who really ruled.

In late October in Ireland, the majority Catholic population rose up in rebellion against everything that was Protestant and alien, everything that had been forced upon them, from the theft of land to compulsory Anglican worship. Thousands of Protestants were massacred in a killing frenzy that followed. On 4 November Parliament responded. An Impressment Bill was accepted, to raise an army to suppress the Irish rebellion.

On 22 November 1641, the Commons passed the Grand Remonstrance. It catalogued the ills of Charles' reign and listed remedies. Measures were also called to end arbitrary government by the King. Very much hand in hand now, politics and religion, measures were also called to hinder the spread of Popery within the Anglican church. On 25 November the King returned to London from Edinburgh. Some sort of confrontation now seemed inevitable.

On 7 December, in Parliament, moves were made to empower the government in the appointment of the county Lords Lieutenants and those who controlled the local militias. If it came to war, and it was looking increasingly like it might, control of the militias by Parliament was essential. On 15 December the House of Commons decided to print the Grand Remonstrance for general readership, without the approval of either the King or House of Lords. In the Lords itself twelve bishops were prevented from taking their seats when important decisions were being made. They declared that all business conducted in the Upper House during that period should be declared null and void. For opposing the transactions of Parliament, the bishops were impeached by the Commons. Largely orchestrated by Nonconformist Members of Parliament, county petitions were now presented calling for the abolition of the episcopacy and the abolition of the Book of Common Prayer, the authorized Anglican prayer book.

1642

On 1 January news reached the King that the Commons intended to impeach the Queen. This was too much to bear. On 4 January the King with an armed escort entered the House of Commons in an attempt to arrest five leading Members of Parliament, John Pym, John Hampden, Arthur Haslerig, Denzil Holles, William Strode, and in the House of Lords, Lord Mandeville. Forewarned, all the birds had flown, as the King discovered. There was tumult in London. The Trained Bands (the city militia) were mobilized in support of Parliament. The city's apprentices, mariners and others offered to live and die for Parliament. Matters were edging towards war. The King left London. On the following day, 11 January, the five M.P.s boarded a barge and sailed up the river to Westminster to the acclamation of the people. The Trained Bands, with drums beating and colors flying, marched on the Houses of Parliament in support of the Commons.

On 13 February an Act was passed in Parliament for the removal of the bishops from the House of Lords. All clergy were also excluded from any secular employment.

On 23 February the Queen sailed to the Netherlands, taking her daughter to meet her new husband, Prince William of Orange. The Queen appealed to him for military supplies, and if possible, Dutch assistance for the King. On 5 March, despite the King's refusal to sign it into law, the Commons passed a militia ordinance giving Parliament control of the Trained Bands and local militia. The country, now much alarmed at the prospect of war, sent peace petitions to both the King and Parliament. The King rode north to Hull on the north-east coast, the point at which he expected Dutch aid to arrive. The gates of the city were closed to him. Hull had declared for Parliament.

In London, in the King's absence, Parliament sought once more to limit his power and bring about greater accountability. They agreed the "19 propositions," which were designed to make the King's ministers and counselors answerable to Parliament. A step was also taken to abolish the episcopacy of the Church of England, and an end to the Book of Common Prayer. As summer approached and the likelihood of war increased, the King issued commissions of array to reclaim his control over the county militias. Parliament

The English Civil War

reasserted its claim. By October 1642 Parliament had control of the militias of 22 counties, and the King just half that number. Possibly playing for time, the King published his reply to the "19 propositions." He renounced his right to an absolute monarchy. Meanwhile on 15 July the Earl of Essex was appointed Captain-General of Parliament's forces. One week later the King fled his capital and raised his standard at Nottingham. He called in all his loyal subjects to form an army. The English Civil War had begun.

The King began his march, zigzagging south to London, gaining fresh recruits as he did so. The Earl of Essex marched northwards with his Parliamentary army. The first major clash of the war was at Powick Bridge in Worcestershire. On 23 September the King's nephew, Prince Rupert, and some of his chief officers were reconnoitering between the rivers Severn and Teme. They received word that a party of forward scouting Parliamentary Horse had crossed the Teme at Powick Bridge with the intention of cutting them off. The Prince drew up his troops in a large field and awaited his adversaries. The Parliamentary troops advanced along

Top: **The Earl of Essex, Parliament's military commander.** ***Bottom:*** **The King raised his standard at Nottingham, declaring war on his Parliament.**

a narrow lane prior to entering the field. As they did so, and before they had the chance of deploying, Rupert launched a full cavalry charge against them. The untried Parliamentary troops were driven back into the lane, and retreat turned to rout. First victory had gone to the King.

By the time the King arrived at Shrewsbury he had an army of six thousand infantry, fifteen hundred dragoons and several thousand cavalry, commanded by his nephew, Prince Rupert. The King proceeded south-eastwards towards London. At Wolverhampton he was joined by Welsh levies, bringing his army strength up to over thirteen thousand men. Down through Birmingham, and onto Kenilworth into the heart of Warwickshire, the Royalists marched. Lord Essex's Parliamentary army was at Warwick, barely five miles distant. The Royalists side-stepped the Parliamentarian army, and for a time both armies marched along parallel routes, barely two miles distant from each other. Eventually they came together at Edgehill near Kineton, on 23 October. It was an indecisive battle, but 1,500 men were killed. The following morning the Earl of Essex drew off towards Warwick. The King continued his progress towards London. Regrouping his army, Essex set off in pursuit of the King and eventually succeeded in placing himself between the Royalists and London. The London militias came out to join Essex. The Royalists' approach was stalled. There was to be no battle that day. The King and his army withdrew to Oxford, and there the King set up his headquarters. As the weather worsened, and the roads became impassable for wagons, both sides retreated to winter quarters. Scouts were sent out to watch for any enemy movement. Castles were seized and garrisoned. There were skirmishes and lootings, but effectively the campaign season carried out by large armies had come to an end until the spring.

1643

There was heavy snowfall in January 1642–3.[1] On 2 February 1643 the Royalists struck first. Prince Rupert captured the Parliamentary garrisoned town of Cirencester in less than two hours. Seeing the half-naked, starved and frozen prisoners being driven through the streets of Royalist Oxford brought home to all the horrors of a civil war. In the last week of February the Queen, with a ship laden with arms, landed at Bridlington on the northeast coast of England. In Lancashire the Royalist Earl of Derby sacked the county town of Lancaster and put it to the torch. He captured Preston and sacked Blackburn. It was savage and deliberately designed to be so, to teach the rebels a lesson.

In March the Parliamentarians seized the Royalist garrison at Lichfield, in mid–Staffordshire. Lord Brooke, commanding Parliament's forces, was killed, but his successor, Sir John Gell, succeeded in capturing the stronghold in the cathedral close. With Lichfield as a base, Sir John was now able to link up with Sir William Brereton in the next county of Cheshire, creating an extensive area in central England under Parliamentary control. Alarmed, the King sent the Earl of Northampton to the Midlands to break the Parliamentary hold. The two armies clashed at Hopton Heath near Stafford. It was a narrow victory to the Royalists, but in the process the Earl of Northampton was killed.

In the southwest, Prince Rupert was unsuccessful in his attempt to capture the very important port of Bristol. Parliament's Major-General for Gloucestershire, Sir William Waller, put in more troops to forestall any further attempts. Waller then launched an assault on Malmsbury, driving the Royalists out. The Parliamentary garrison at Gloucester appealed to Waller for help when a Royalist army of Welsh soldiers under Lord Herbert arrived before the city. The Royalists were inexperienced, and Waller, crossing the Severn estuary over an improvised bridge of boats just below Gloucester, took them quickly unawares. The garrison in Gloucester came out as reinforcements and rather ignominiously the Welsh surrendered without a shot being fired. Some fourteen hundred prisoners were taken.

In East Anglia Oliver Cromwell captured the two Royalist towns of Lowestoft and King's Lynn, securing south-eastern England for Parliament. Southern central, and south-western England were loyal to the King, as was the northwest, but cutting them off from each other was the West Midlands, a great swathe of Parliamentary controlled countryside.

That March, Parliament sought to end the war. It sent Commissioners to the King at Oxford to negotiate a peace. Their terms, both civil and religious, were unacceptable to the King. The war continued on for a further three years. In Ireland, Charles attempted to bring the rebellion there to an end, with a view of bringing over Irish troops to help him. The King attempted the same with the Scots, but they were opposed to him making peace with the Catholic Irish. For the moment the Scots remained neutral, but their sympathies lay with their Puritan neighbors south of the border.

At the end of March, concerned that the passage between Oxford and the north was now blocked by Parliament's occupation of Lichfield, the King dispatched his nephew, Prince Rupert, to recapture the cathedral city. The Prince had an army of 2,000 Horse and Foot and six small canons. On Easter Monday, 3 April 1643, the Royalists arrived at Birmingham. Its two river bridges had been blocked up by the townspeople, and a force of some 200 Parliamentary soldiers under the command of a local man, Captain Richard Greaves of Lord Brooke's regiment. After being refused entry, the Royalists, after two repulses, successfully gained entry to the town. In the process four-

Prince Rupert and his dog, Boy. Marching to Lichfield, the Prince put the town of Birmingham to the torch, burning down 80 houses.

teen townspeople were killed, including two women. The town was looted and eighty houses were burnt before the Royalists left the next day. A new brutality had entered the war. Three days later Rupert and his army arrived before Lichfield. The Parliamentarians retreated into the fortified cathedral close. After a bombardment and a mine exploding against the walls, a breach was made through which the Royalists entered. They were eventually repulsed, and the breach was blocked up. The Parliamentarians were in a sorry state though. Their powder was all but expired, and with no hope of relief, they agreed to parley. The Prince agreed to let Lieutenant-Colonel Russell and his men leave, with their arms and colors flying. They marched away to the Parliamentary garrison of Coventry. Garrisoning Lichfield for the King, Prince Rupert returned to Oxford.

The King's main concern was his garrison at Reading, which controlled the road from London to Oxford and guarded the passage through the Chiltern Hills. It was now besieged by a sizeable Parliamentary force commanded by the Earl of Essex, complete with batteries of canon. Several attempts were made by the Royalists to break through and relieve their garrison, but without success. In the end they marched away and left Reading to its fate. Acting garrison commander, Richard Feilding, with no hope now of relief, surrendered his charge to Parliament.

In the West Country Sir William Waller established a number of Parliamentary garrisons. His nemesis, Sir Ralph Hopton, was ambushed in a nighttime assault near Okehampton, and his army was temporarily scattered. The victorious Parliamentary force under James Chudleigh captured a thousand muskets and five barrels of powder.

Parliament now appointed regional commanders. The Earl of Manchester was appointed general of the Eastern Association, with Oliver Cromwell as his colonel. Lord Grey, son of the Earl of Stamford, was appointed to the Midlands and the south-west, Sir William Brereton was appointed General of Cheshire and the Welsh border, Lord Fairfax, assisted by his son, Sir Thomas Fairfax, was appointed to the North, and Sir William Waller to the South. The Earl of Essex retained control of the main army, with special responsibility for the protection of London. Parliament which had seized all the principal stores and county arsenals before the outbreak of the war, extended its control, particularly in the industrial regions where arms were manufactured.

Sir William Waller, Parliament's General in the West Country.

Sir Ralph Hopton, with his Royalist army of Cornishmen, crossed the border into Devon. On 16 May 1643 they caught up with the Earl of Stamford at Stratton. The Parliamentary army was defeated and scattered. James Chudleigh, who had bested Hopton near

Okehampton, was captured, and promptly changed sides, as did his father. Hopton then captured the market town of Totness. In a co-coordinated campaign, Prince Maurice, the King's younger nephew, and the Marquis of Hertford proceeded out of Oxford to link up with Hopton. Under orders, Sir William Waller abandoned his siege of Royalist Worcester and marched south in a bid to prevent the junction of Maurice and Hertford with Hopton. Waller was too late to prevent them though. The Royalist armies joined together at Wells in Somerset. Now they marched unhindered, Waller's force was too small to confront them.

Prince Rupert with about 1,000 Horse and 800 Dragoons and some Foot, left Oxford on 17 June, and in what appears to have been a diversionary tactic, raided into the Parliamentary-controlled Chiltern region. At Thame, acting governor Sir Philip Stapleton, raising troops from Parliament's nearby garrisons, set out after him. Prince Rupert fell back towards Oxford, drawing his pursuers after him. At Chalgrove, Rupert made a stand. As Stapleton's men drew up for battle, Rupert's cavalry charged and routed them. Rupert returned to Oxford without further incident. Other successful hit and run forays were launched from Oxford by the Prince. His men drove off cattle and sheep from the neighboring villages and towns, taking them back to Oxford to feed the garrison.

In the North, in Yorkshire, Lord Fairfax and his army, drawing out men from the Parliamentary garrisons at Halifax and Leeds, marched towards Bradford in an attempt to relieve a siege of that town. They then discovered that Royalist general, the Marquis of Newcastle, and his army were marching to aid the besiegers. On 30 June, the Fairfaxes, father and son, were halted by a Royalist army twice their size on Aldwalton Moor. The Parliamentarians had some initial success, but the Royalists managed to outflank them and fell upon the Parliamentary rear. The Parliamentarians broke and ran. Sir Thomas Fairfax managed to get most of the cavalry away, but all their artillery pieces were lost. The younger Fairfax fell back upon Bradford, then under partial siege. As further Royalists joined the assault, Fairfax attempted a breakout, which was only partially successful. He lost a number of men. Fairfax withdrew with all speed, drawing out the remains of garrisons of Halifax and Leeds, all the time being pursued by Royalist cavalry. He attempted to cross the river Ouse but was prevented by a larger Royalist force waiting for him. Moving down the river, he eventually got passage across for his cavalry, to the Parliamentary garrison at Hull, and temporary safety. From Hull Fairfax and his men crossed into Lincolnshire and joined with Oliver Cromwell of the Eastern Association. Very soon Hull itself came under siege from the Royalists, and Yorkshire fell under almost total Royalist control.

In the South-west, Sir William Waller withdrew to Bath in Somerset.

Here he received a letter from his opponent, Sir Ralph Hopton, whose army was fast approaching the cathedral town. In earlier times they had been good friends. Hopton asked for them to meet and talk. Waller knew that nothing could come of a meeting, for both men were sincere in their beliefs. In a return letter Waller declined, adding,

> That great God, which is the searcher of my heart, knows with what a sad sense I go upon this service, and with what a perfect hatred I detest this war without an enemy.... We are both upon the stage and must act those parts that are assigned us in this tragedy.

Hopton kept on coming. Waller left the town and found favorable ground, and waited the approach of the Royalist army. Hopton's Cornish army crossed the river Avon at Bradford-on-Avon, effectively cutting Waller off from London. Scouts came back reporting Waller's position. The Royalists swung around to the north of Bath and rested for the night. Waller's scouts reported back to him, and during the night he moved his smaller army to the higher ground of Lansdown Ridge. The position was particularly good, for the Royalists would have to attack up hill, negotiating lanes and marshy ground in the process. Waller lined the approaching hedges with musketeers. The next morning, 5 July, the Royalist Horse advanced in a preliminary skirmish, but were checked by the musketeers, swiftly followed by a Parliamentary cavalry counter-charge. The Royalist Horse fell back. The Royalist Foot, however, engaged the enemy, giving their Horse time to recover and rally. The Cornish foot soldiers drove the musketeers from the hedgerows, forcing them back up the hill. Twice the Cornish foot soldiers almost reached the top of the ridge but were beaten back by Waller's canon and the Parliamentary Horse. The third time they reached the ridge with sufficient numbers and formed a square. They drove off Waller's Horse but could not secure the advantage, for their own Horse were still not mustered. As the light began to fade Waller withdrew his men and sought the protection of a nearby stone wall. Throughout the night there was sporadic firing, but in the morning as dawn broke, the Royalists discovered that Waller had withdrawn. Waller had withdrawn to Bristol with all speed, raised more troops and arms, and on 7 July marched out again to face Hopton. The Royalist Horse by now were scattered about the countryside. The Foot were short of powder for muskets and cannon. Hopton himself was wounded following the accidental explosion of a powder wagon. The Royalists withdrew. Waller set off in pursuit. His forward Horse caught up to the rear of the Royalists. Prince Maurice rallied the Royalist Horse, and they kept off the Parliamentarians until the Royalist Foot could be got off to safety to the town of Devizes. Waller and his army came on after them. He seized the height of Roundway Down, a position from which his batteries commanded the unwalled town. The Royalists decided that their Foot would have to hold the town, while part of their horse would ride to Oxford to summon reinforcements. Waller wrote to the Earl of Essex for assistance. At Oxford, Prince Rupert had greatly depleted the garrison, when he had left a few days earlier to meet the Queen and the arms she had brought from the Netherlands, at King's Norton near Birmingham. Nevertheless eighteen hundred Horse from the Oxford garrison were available, led by Henry, Lord Wilmot and Sir John Byron. They arrived before Devizes on the afternoon of Thursday, 13 July. They were just in time. Waller's men had penetrated the town' s hastily thrown up outer defenses. Parliamentary scouts now warned Waller of their approach, and exposed as he was between the besieged and the relief armies, he began the withdrawal of his men to the safety of Roundway Down. Lord Wilmot was quickly upon the Parliamentary flank before it could be brought into some sort of order. Byron led a second charge against the Parliamentary Horse who broke and fled. Now exposed, Waller's Foot came under a heavy attack from the Royalist Horse and Foot. They broke, threw down their arms and scattered. The Royalist victory was complete. Waller's remaining men, now few in numbers, fled to the safety of Bristol. From there Waller moved to Gloucester then Evesham, before making the long and dangerous journey down to London to confront the Earl of Essex, who he believed had let him down in not coming to his aid once summoned.

Ten days later on 23 July, Prince Rupert and an army from Oxford rendezvoused with the Royalist Western Army, two miles outside of Bristol, then garrisoned for the Parliament. Bristol's strategic importance was as a port to the west, enabling fresh troops to be brought in from Wales and Ireland. A summons was sent in to surrender the city for the use of the King. Its governor, Nathaniel Fiennes, refused. The Royalists lay siege to this well-defended garrison built along the river Avon. A battery of Royalist guns was placed on the other side of the river. Further batteries were placed to the south and east. On 24 July the Royalist guns opened fire on the city's defenses. While the city was well-fortified, its garrison was badly depleted after Waller had drawn out men for his army. In the fullness of time the garrison would have been compelled to surrender out of starvation, but Prince Rupert was impatient.

Shortly before dawn on the morning of 26 July, the Royalists moved forward to storm the city from the north, where a breach had been made in the walls. After an initial resistance by the defenders, the Royalists managed to capture the breach and brought on their cavalry. The outer defenses had been carried, but within lay an inner defense formed by the river Frome. Beyond this was the fortress of Bristol castle. On the south side a simultaneous assault led by Prince Maurice had been halted, but the defenders were badly stretched. They were also lacking in ammunition to withstand a prolonged assault.

Prince Rupert's men, now assisted by 500 Cornish Foot, were over on the other side of the Frome. Only the fort still held out. The townspeople feared the destruction of their city and appealed to Fiennes to surrender. Fiennes asked for a truce to parley. The result was the surrender of Bristol. The defenders, deprived of arms and ammunition, were allowed to march away. Other Parliamentary garrisons in the West now fell to the Royalists: Poole, Dorchester, Portland, Weymouth and Melcombe.

Anxiety grew in Parliament. They responded with an ordinance calling for the raising of a further 7,000 Horse. Control of the war passed from a loose committee called the Committee of Safety to a smaller but more dedicated group called the Council of War. Moves were made to remove the Earl of Essex as Parliament's military commander. He had failed to assist Waller and had become tainted by family ties to the peace movement. Better news came when the Scottish Covenanters made a proposal of a formal alliance with Parliament. This came in the face of rumors of an invasion of Scotland by Irish forces loyal to the King. A deputation from Parliament was sent to Scotland.

Meanwhile the Royalists were on the move. The Earl of Newcastle advanced into Lincolnshire and laid siege to the Parliamentary garrison of Gainsborough. The town fell, and panic grew as to what would happen next. Oliver Cromwell attempted to raise a fresh army to defend East Anglia. With the Southwest in Royalist hands, and with Newcastle triumphant in East Anglia, London looked vulnerable. The King's advisors, though, urged caution in not attacking London quite yet. Gloucester on the river Severn would be their next objective. The city was important in that as a Parliamentary stronghold on the river Severn, it blockaded the river, cutting off Royalist Shrewsbury, Worcester, and the iron foundries of the Forest of Dean from access to the sea. In early August the Royalists, led by the King himself, marched on Gloucester, arriving before the town on 10 August. The King demanded access to his city. Parliament's Governor, Colonel Edward Massey, refused. The Royalists began to make preparations for a siege.

When word was received in London, the siege of Gloucester became a pivotal moment in the war. She had to be saved at all costs. Townsmen and apprentices flocked to join the Trained Bands. Five new regiments of Foot were raised alongside one thousand Horse. Parliament voted £30,000 to pay them. Though suspect, the Earl of Essex was commanded to lead them to Bristol's rescue. On 22 August, Parliament's new army began its march to the west. Bristol had already been under siege for twelve days as the Royalist batteries bombarded her walls. Impulsive as ever, Prince Rupert wanted to take the city by assault, but fearing a heavy loss of life, the King refused his nephew. The freshwater supply was cut off to the city, but Massey organized supplies to be taken from the Severn. Gaps in the walls were filled with earth and turf, and sacks of wool. Then the Royalists succeeded in laying mines beneath the outer walls. On 24 August they gave Massey one last chance to surrender his charge. He responded by strengthening his inner defenses. He was not going to surrender. Just before dawn it began to rain and continued so throughout the day. The mines were flooded, and the explosives could not be fired. News reached the besiegers that a relief army had left London The King sent parties of Horse to hinder their progress.

On 5 September the relieving army reached Prestbury. Down below was the Severn valley and in the distance, Gloucester. Essex fired off a cannon to alert the defenders he was near. Massey fired an answering shot in acknowledgment. It was late now and Essex halted his advance until morning, in the sure knowledge that Massey would hold out. In the pouring rain the relieving army approached Gloucester the next morning, only to discover that the Royalist army had withdrawn during the night. Gloucester had been saved. But as they rejoiced word reached them that Exeter had been captured two days earlier.

With the city safe, Essex withdrew from Gloucester and began the long march back to London in the continuing rain. Early on the morning of 16 September he was surprised but managed to drive off a force of Royalists out of Cirencester. He also seized a convoy of wagons loaded with provisions bound for Royalist Oxford. Unbeknown to Essex, as he progressed slowly eastwards to London, the King's army were in pursuit, eager to bring him to battle, once they had discovered his true strength. On the morning of 18 September Prince Rupert and his Horse fell upon the rear of Essex's army. The Parliamentary musketeers drove them off, but skirmishing continued throughout the day, slowing down Essex's army in its progress. Meanwhile the main body of the Royalist army had succeeded in getting ahead of the Parliamentarians and reached Newbury barely two hours before the approach of Essex's men. Though the King's army was superior in numbers, its ammunition and powder were low. If the King committed to battle it would have to be short and decisive. It was now dark; Essex and his men remained on the alert, camped in the fields outside Newbury for the night.

The next morning, knowing that a battle was inevitable, both sides sought favorable positions. The Parliamentary army advanced towards the Royalist position, making made good use of hedges and ditches, keeping them safe from cavalry charges. Essex directed John Hampden's veteran regiment to secure Bigg's Hill to prevent being outflanked from open ground. The Royalist infantry and musketeers now came on and soon were engaged in close battle. As has been said the Royalists were very low on powder, and soon that was used up. They made a strategic withdrawal. The pikemen had great

Seventeenth century foot soldiers: A musketeer and a pike man.

difficulty maneuvering with their eighteen feet long pikes. The Parliamentary Foot pushed on, and victory seemed secure. At this point Prince Rupert launched a cavalry attack on the exposed other wing. This enabled the Royalist Foot to withdraw to safety. Seeing the danger, Essex sent men to reinforce that wing. Amidst the hedges it was impossible for Prince Rupert's Horse to build up any momentum, and as they moved from field to field, were forced to bunch up. The Parliamentary musketeers wreaked havoc among the enemy cavalry. The Royalists were forced to pull back and retired into the town. While the Royalists were driven from the field, it could not be truly said that the Parliamentarians had won the battle, nor indeed had the Royalists. The next day the Royalists remained in Newbury, and at noon, Essex resumed his march back to London. The army was led by the Horse, followed by the infantry, followed by another party of Horse to drive off any Royalist marauders who might follow. There were skirmishes throughout the day, but at dusk, the Parliament's army reached Reading, a Parliamentary garrison. Here they remained for the night, and on the following morning abandoned the garrison, withdrew its men and artillery and proceeded on to London. The King gave up the pursuit and returned to Oxford.

On 25 September 1643 members of the House of Commons, alongside the Commissioners from Scotland, signed a Solemn League and Covenant. It was a political and religious agreement, linking the two nations in their war against Charles I. Though there remained differences they now shared a common threat. The Marquis of Ormonde was on the point of arranging a truce with the Catholic Confederation in Ireland, which would enable English troops loyal to the King to be brought home. As the Presbyterian Scots saw it, any King doing deals with the Catholic Irish was their enemy. Following the truce, the English soldiers based in Ireland began arriving home at the Royalist secured ports of Bristol and Chester.

In the autumn of 1643, the Royalists continued their advance upon London. From the West Country, Sir Ralph Hopton pushed into Surrey and Sussex—counties bordering the Capital. Prince Rupert raided into Parliamentary territory in the Chiltern Hills, to the northwest. On 6 October the Royalists took the Parliamentary garrison of Newport Pagnell in Buckinghamshire. It was strategically important in that it controlled the roads and river into London from the eastern counties. In King's Lynn, in Norfolk, an ancient port on the river Ouse, the people now proclaimed for the King.

From East Anglia, Oliver Cromwell and Sir Thomas Fairfax linked up with the Earl of Manchester at Horncastle, in Lincolnshire, to meet the growing threat of an approaching Royalist army consisting of eighty companies of Horse and Dragoons, under the command of Sir John Henderson. If Henderson could defeat them, then East Anglia would fall to the King. Manchester's combined army was barely half that of his opponent. The Parliamentarians confronted Henderson at Winceby, on the edge of the open rolling countryside of the Lincolnshire Wolds. Cromwell and his well-disciplined cavalry, soon to become the backbone of Parliament's New Model Army, launched a fierce attack upon the enemy. In the charge Cromwell's horse was shot from under him, but even though their leader was temporarily indisposed, his well-disciplined men continued on into battle. The Royalist line was shattered and broke. Fairfax now launched a second cavalry assault on the Royalist flank and completely routed them. The battle was won and East Anglia was saved. Following on from this victory, a Parliamentary army under Sir John Meldrum relieved Hull, and the Royalist garrison of Lincoln now surrendered to the Earl of Manchester upon demand. On 27 October the Royalist garrison at Newport Pagnell, which guarded the roads to the east of London, was abandoned when supplies ran out, and news reached them that a Parliamentary army was on its way to besiege them. In the eastern counties things were turning Parliament's way once more.

In Hampshire Sir William Waller's attempt to capture Basing House proved disastrous. It was late autumn, the weather was cold and windy. Then the rain began to fall and continued for days on end. His men were short of

Sir Ralph Hopton, the King's General in the West Country.

supplies and food, unprotected from the elements, and they had not been paid for some time. They refused to soldier on and began to drift back home to London. Here was a noticeable difference between the undisciplined and uncommitted soldiers from London and those of Cromwell's Eastern Association. There had to be commitment, there had to be discipline, if Parliament was to win.

In the Welsh Marches—those counties that border England and Wales—Sir William Brereton captured Wrexham. It was a town of strategic importance in that it guarded the approaches of the expected "Irish" Royalist troops that might come by this shortest route from Dublin. But now it was late in the year, the roads were becoming impassable, and the campaigning season came to a close. Behind closed doors an agreement was reached by the Parliamentary Commissioners with the Scots. The Scots agreed to send into England an army of 18,000 Foot and 2,000 Horse, with artillery to match. Parliament agreed to pay this army for the duration of the war and to include the Scots in any peace negotiations with the King.

With both armies in winter quarters, the news that Hopton and a Royalist army were on the move came as a surprise. Hopton outflanked Waller and his men, who were bivouacked near Alton in Hampshire, and proceeded into Sussex, thus threatening London. Hopton had left a strong force under Lord Crawford at Alton itself, to keep watch on the Parliamentary commander. Foolishly Crawford drew attention to himself in correspondence with Waller, urging him to consider his position. Waller used the opportunity to survey the Royalist defenses, which were poor. He attacked Alton and took the town. In fright, Crawford rode off with the Horse, abandoning his Foot soldiers. They made a brave stand before their young officer, Captain Bowles, was killed. Thereafter the others surrendered. Waller took more than 500 prisoners, of whom at least 100 changed sides. The remainder were sent as prisoners to London. Waller now set out in pursuit of Hopton. At Arundel, Hopton established a garrison within its formidable castle. Reaching the town, Waller quickly drove its Royalist defenders from the town into the castle. Leaving sufficient men to blockade the castle, Waller proceeded on along the muddy roads, shadowing Hopton's army, the rain falling continually. The Royalist army had lost impetus though, and Hopton, seeing no future in continuing his foray into Sussex, fell back on Winchester, which he made his winter quarters.

1644

In January 1643–4, the Scottish army, financed from English coffers, set out from Dunbar under the command of Lord Leven, with David Leslie, a veteran of the Thirty Years' War, as General of the cavalry. They had sixty cannons, under the command of Alexander Hamilton. With them they took their Presbyterian ministers and lay preachers. As they set off, snow began to fall in the north, and the advance of the Scottish army was soon halted. They were forced to seek shelter and weather out the storm. South of the border in England, Fairfax, who had been marching towards the Welch Marches to intercept the return of the "Irish" regiments, had also been halted by the bad weather, at Manchester. Across the county border in Cheshire, Lord Byron, the King's general, met the first of the "Irish" regiments as they landed in England. Byron, now with an additional army, began a cruel purge of Parliamentary supporters in the county. At his approach, the villagers of Barthomley fled into the parish church in fear. Without any justification, for they had offered no resistance, Byron set the church on fire, forcing the villagers out, where a goodly number were murdered.

As the ground hardened under a frost, Fairfax, aware of Byron's atrocities, left Manchester and marched south into Cheshire in pursuit. Byron by then had begun a siege of the Parliamentary garrison of Nantwich. He had divided his force on either side of the river Weaver, which bisected the town, in order to more perfectly encompass it. When the frost lifted and the ground thawed out, the river turned into a torrent, and the bridge was swept away. It was at this point that Fairfax and his army, now joined by Sir William Brereton and a force of Cheshire troops, arrived. Byron's army was split in two. His men on the other side of the river were obliged to march six miles to the next crossing over the river. But before they could join, the Parliamentarians attacked. After a brief skirmish Byron and his cavalry ran off, leaving the

Left: **Edward Montague, Earl of Manchester, Parliament's General in the North of England.** ***Right:*** **William Cavendish, Earl of Newcastle, The King's General in the North of England.**

infantry to their own devices. Heavily outnumbered, they surrendered. The majority of them agreed to join Parliament's army. The men that made up this "Irish" regiment turned out to be Shropshire men who had served in Ireland.

With the improvement in the weather in early February, the Scottish army crossed the border into England. They marched down the east coast to Newcastle, a Royalist town. Their demand that it be surrendered to Parliament was rejected, and a siege was begun. This was not what Parliament wanted. Their intention was that the Scots would be a field army, not locked up in a prolonged siege. Sir Marmaduke Langdale, a Yorkshire Royalist, launched a series of hit and run raids against them, further bogging them down as they had to divert more troops to ward off these assaults. In the east Midlands Sir John Meldrum denied entry into the Royalist garrison of Newark, whose Governor was the brother of the notorious Lord Byron, set down to what looked like becoming a long siege. But, on 24 March Prince Rupert struck. The besiegers were caught unawares and suffered the consequences. Rupert's triumph was complete. Meldrum sued for terms of surrender. He was forced to give up his thirty cannon and all his fire arms, including 4,000 muskets and a similar number of pistols. Disillusioned, many of his men changed sides. Meldrum, with barely 2,000 unarmed men, was allowed to march away to the Parliamentary garrison at Hull.

The month of March, and with an improvement to the weather, a new Royalist campaign got under way. The defeat of Meldrum left the Midlands largely under Royalist control. Now the plan was to capture the South. On 27 March 1644, Lord Forth, with an army drawn from the garrison at Oxford, joined with Lords Hopton and Wilmot at Alresford in Hampshire. Their combined strength was about 5,000 Foot and 3,000 Horse. Their intention was to seek out Waller and his army and defeat him. Waller received this intelligence with some alarm. He had just received orders from the Committee of Both Kingdoms to send most of his Horse to join with Essex's army to secure the northern approaches to London. Once his Horse had gone he would be too weak to risk a battle. Things were moving at a pace, the Royalists were fast approaching. Waller decided to disobey orders, or at least delay his response. He kept his Horse with him. On the night of 27 March Waller and his men took up a position near the village of Hinton Ampner. Just across the marshy valley, on the ridge of Alresford opposite, were camped the Royalist army. As they settled down for the night the Parliamentarians could hear the Royalist sentries talking. Throughout the next day the Parliamentarians awaited a Royalist advance which did not come. On the morning of Friday, 29 March, soldiers drawn from Parliament's London regiments, moved forward into Cheriton wood to sound out their opponents. The woods were full of Royalist musketeers who with sustained fire-power drove them off. Without awaiting orders, a section of the Royalist cavalry charged at the fleeing Parliamentary Foot as they broke cover from the wood. After some initial hesitation Sir Arthur Haslerig counter-attacked with his heavy cavalry. His men struck the Royalist cavalry in the flank, doing considerable damage. The remaining Royalist cavalry now responded, but were greatly hindered by the narrow lanes, thus making it difficult to maneuver. Waller now committed his Foot, who advanced up hill on the Royalist Foot. The King's men were forced back, moving from hedge to hedge. On the other wing the Parliamentary Horse under Sir William Balfour charged the opposing Horse, driving them back on their retreating Foot. There was total chaos, the Royalist Foot being trampled under the hooves of their own cavalry. The Parliamentarians pushed on, not giving the Royalists a chance to regroup. Victory to Waller was complete. The Royalists, totally defeated at the battle of Alresford, retreated back to Winchester. Lord John Stuart, the King's young cousin, later died of his wounds received during the battle.

With an improvement in the weather the Scots army was also on the move once more, having left an adequate force to blockade Newcastle. In a series of sharp skirmishes on 24 and 25 March, they drove off the smaller Royalist forces that attacked them and proceeded on south. By the 8 April the Scots were within two miles of Durham, a Royalist cathedral town. Three days later, on the 11 of April, Parliament's English army in the North, led by Lord Fairfax and his son, Sir Thomas, attacked Royalist General Sir John Bellasis at Selby in South Yorkshire, capturing his cannon, ammunition and most of his infantry. By their capture of Selby the Fairfaxes had secured the main road south for the Scots. As the Scots approached the outskirts of Royalist Durham, the Marquis of Newcastle rode out of the town, and made for York, the King's Northern capital. Durham might fall, but York had to be held at all costs. While a few regiments were detailed to blockade Durham, the main Scottish army followed after Newcastle, and on 20 April they arrived at Wetherby. Here they were joined by the Fairfaxes who had proceeded along the other side of the river Ouse to York. The allied armies, now numbering about 16,000 Foot and 4,000 Horse, invested the ancient walled city, and set up their camps less than a mile from the city walls. The great cannon that had accompanied the Scottish army south was brought up and soon began a bombardment of the Royalist defenses.

Prior to his departure from Durham, Newcastle had sent an urgent letter to Prince Rupert asking for help. At Shrewsbury, Prince Rupert assembled a combined army of English, Welsh and "Irish" soldiers and prepared to march on York. But then he received orders to attend the King at Oxford, and all plans for the relief of York had to be put on hold. The King was concerned about the defense of Oxford. Days later, the conference at Oxford over, Prince Rupert returned to Shrewsbury with all haste. On 26 May he began a planned march to York, through Lancashire, with the intention of capturing Liverpool on the way. This Lancashire port would provide a further safe landing place for fresh troops from Ireland. As Rupert marched north, over in East Anglia Lord Manchester and the Army of the Eastern Association stormed the cathedral city of Lincoln. East Anglia was now firmly in Parliamentary hands. Then Manchester, with 6,000 foot and 1,000 horse, and 12 cannon, marched north to join in the siege of York. Unbeknown to Rupert he would be facing three Parliamentary armies. At Chester Rupert was joined by Lord Byron, bringing their combined army up to a total of 14,000 Horse and Foot.

While at Oxford Prince Rupert's advice had been to strengthen the garrisons that surrounded the university town. Now with him gone the King's advisors urged him to strengthen the army in Oxford at the expense of those surrounding garrisons. The King pulled out troops from Reading and Abingdon, and no sooner had he done so than these two vital towns were occupied by Parliament. The southern approaches to Oxford were now exposed. The Earl of Essex moved his army rapidly north, then veered to the eastern side of Oxford, making Islip his headquarters with outposts at Cowley and Headington. In conjunction Sir William Waller put his men across the Thames on a bridge of boats and occupied territory to the west of Oxford. The Royalist capital was threatened on three sides. Rather than be boxed in King Charles marched most of his Horse through the gap, making for Burford, then on to Worcester. There was now a second Royalist army in the field. The hope was that if Oxford was attacked the defenders would hold out until the King could return. As they approached Evesham the King heard that Tewkesbury had been taken by a Parliamentary force from Gloucester. At Pershore he broke down the town bridge to prevent the Parliamentarians from crossing. By the opening of June the King was in Worcester. Here he discovered that Lord Essex was in pursuit, with Waller and Lord Denbigh closing in upon the city.

Prince Rupert in the north country thrust into Lancashire. He took Stockport and Bolton in his progress. The Prince was joined by Lord George Goring, who brought in 5,000 men, increasing the Royalist army to 19,000. Later they were joined by Lord Derby who brought in an unspecified number of men — but men who were untrained. The Royalists entered the open towns of Preston and Wigan, then it was on to Liverpool. The Prince was unstoppable. He bombarded Liverpool for five days, then stormed the town. When his men entered, the town was all but deserted of soldiers. The majority of the defenders, complete with most of their cannon and gunpowder, had managed to escape by ship. Rupert established his headquarters here, then sent to Oxford for further supplies. While he waited, he trained up Derby's men and brought in as many men from the surrounding countryside as he could find to add to his army.

With the two Royalist armies in the field concentrating on the Midlands and the North, the Earl of Essex, without fear of interruption, went to the relief of Lyme Regis, a Parliamentary town on the south coast then under siege by Prince Maurice. Sir William Waller was sent to track the King, and if the opportunity should arise, then to combine with another Parliamentary army and attack him. When Waller arrived at Stourbridge, in Worcestershire, he discovered that he had outraced the King's army, which was at Bewdley, between him and Oxford. The King, discovering that Waller's army was shadowing his, moved off eastwards and across the Cotswolds by Broadway Down. As they proceeded they drew in foot soldiers from the Royalist garrisons along the way. By 21 June 1644, the King arrived at Woodstock, just a few miles north-west of Oxford. Here he was met by an additional 5,000 Horse and 6,000 Foot, as well as cannon from Oxford. Waller was still in pursuit. From Waller's intelligence, the Committee of Both Kingdoms ordered London-based Major General Browne to march north into Oxfordshire, in the hope of trapping the King's army between the two Parliamentary armies, and then bringing him to battle. Royalist scouts informed the King both of Waller's proximity and the approach of Browne. The King resolved to turn on Waller and destroy him before Browne arrived. On 28 June the King's army was about Banbury. Waller's army was but a few miles away on the other side of the town. The next day the King's army marched north towards Daventry in Northampton, keeping to the left bank of the river Cherwell. Waller's army was on the other side of the river marching in parallel with the King. While the King was looking for an advantageous position, Waller was hoping that Browne would catch up. Increasingly, though, it looked as if Waller would have to fight alone.

Concerned at the fast approaching Parliamentary army of Browne, the King sent a sizeable group of Horse and Foot off to check his advance. In the process he created a dangerous gap in the Royalist forces. Waller sent a party of Horse on ahead to secure the bridge across the river at Cropredy. At the bridge they found a party of Royalists already in occupation to prevent Waller from crossing. Without much difficulty the Parliamentarians cleared the bridge of Royalists, and 1,500 Horse, 2,000 Foot and a battery of light cannon poured across. A smaller force waded across the river a mile or so downstream to take the Royalists in the rear. The Parliamentary troops across the river sought out the detached group of Horse and Foot waiting for Browne and engaged them in battle. The Royalist musketeers, having the protection of a wagon, opened fire at the Parliamentarians, checking their assault. Lord Cleveland, who commanded the King's cavalry in the rear, received word of the Parliamentarians who had waded across the river and were now behind him. Without hesitating he ordered his brigade of Horse to attack them, which they did successfully. Waller was now trapped between the two sections of the King's army. Fortunately Colonel Birch still held the Bridge for Parliament, and after an afternoon of skirmishing Waller was able to get his men back across the bridge to safety. The Royalists did not pursue their adversaries; their mission was the relief of York. From the other side of the river Waller continued to shadow the Royalist army throughout the next day. At Aynho, in Northamptonshire, the King's army veered away. The King's march north to York was abandoned. Waller, whose forces were still scattered following the previous day's skirmish, was unable to follow.

With word that his uncle the King would not join him, Prince Rupert continued his march on York. The northern capital had now been cut off for two months. Forces under Lord Manchester had breached the Royalist's outer lines. Though the Parliamentarians were in the outer suburbs, the city's ancient walls were still intact. But powder and ammunition was low, and food was being strictly rationed. There were three Parliamentary armies surrounding York: the Scots under Lord Leven, the Northern army under Fairfax, and the Eastern Association under Manchester. In total the three armies comprised 25,000 men. On the way to the relief of York Rupert was joined by a further 1,000 cavalry from Cumberland, bringing his total strength up to 15,000 men, Horse and Foot. Hearing of his approach, the allied generals prepared to receive him.

On 14 June the Royalist army was at Knaresborough, barely fourteen miles west of York. Leven ordered men from the north side of the blockade to proceed to the west to block the road from Knaresborough to York. In a rapid response, Rupert turned north, crossed the river Ure at Boroughbridge, early on 1 July, and keeping the river between himself and the Parliamentarians, entered the city by the unguarded northern gate. As the Allies pulled back from the city to prepare for battle, the garrison troops poured out of York to loot the former Parliamentary camps. With few provisions left within York, not enough to sustain the Prince and his army, they camped for the night outside the walls in the nearby Forest of Galtres. Rupert sent word for the garrison to join him the next day. At four o'clock the next morning, with no sign of the garrison reinforcements, he set off impetuously without them. His troops crossed the river Ouse by a pontoon of boats and marched towards Long Marston, the last known position of the Parliamentarians. By that time though, the Parliamentarians had moved to a stronger position on Marston Moor. It was not until nine o'clock that morning that Lord Newcastle and the cavalry from York garrison joined with Rupert, and it was four o'clock that afternoon before the infantry under Lord Eythian arrived.

Now the two opposing armies were drawn up. The Parliamentarians were on slightly higher ground; the Royalists were on the open moor. Between them ran a hedge and ditch. The Parliamentary army was extended for a mile and a half, between the two villages of Marston and Tockwith. Oliver Cromwell with the Eastern Association cavalry, some 3,000 strong, were on the left wing, Sir Thomas Fairfax with the Northern cavalry, about 2,000 strong, were on the right. The Scottish horse, 1,600 in number, were divided into two wings providing a reserve behind the English. The Foot, Scots and English were in the center, under Lord Leven and Lord Fairfax.

The Royalist front was a little longer than the Parliamentarians, depth having been sacrificed for width. Rupert's cavalry, split up into squadrons, was on the right, facing Cromwell. Between each squadron Rupert placed musketeers to break up Cromwell's charge. Rupert intended to provoke Cromwell into charging his lines. On the Royalist left wing, opposite Fairfax, was George Goring and Charles Lucas with the Northern horse. In the center were the infantry, with the newly arrived York garrison troops as a reserve. It was half past four, with just under four hours before sunset. Neither side wished to attack at a disadvantage, the hedge and ditch would halt any momentum. By half past seven Rupert decided that there would be no battle that day and allowed his men to break ranks and to eat supper. He himself moved off to the rear. Cromwell watched and calculated. Could he descend the rise, cross the field, and get over the ditch and in amongst the enemy cavalry before they could reassemble? He decided he could, and charged. Byron, left in control of Rupert's first line, got his cavalry in order, and as Cromwell's Horse cleared the ditch, he moved his Horse forward. But in so doing he put his own Horse in line of fire from their own musketeers. As Cromwell and his Eastern Association cavalry crashed into the royalists, they broke. Rupert, warned of what was happening, rode up to the Royalist second line and took charge. As they moved forward they had to move between the shattered first line and again blocked the view of the musketeers. The Scottish reserve now came on and moved to the left of Cromwell's Horse, thus extending the width of the line and thereby hitting the Royalists in the flank. Rupert had no reserve Horse to meet this new challenge, and his Horse broke, fleeing the field. In the center, the Foot made short work of most of their opposition, most of whom were untrained pressed men. They threw down their pikes and surrendered. On the other wing Lord George Goring and his Northern Horse had launched an assault against Fairfax. The Parliamentarians broke under the fierce assault. Fairfax managed to rally a small group of Horse about him, but the others fled. The Royalists failed to capitalize by pursuing, and instead gathered in a grand melee on the ground where Fairfax had originally stood. At this point the Scottish Foot under General Baillie moved toward them. Having driven Rupert's Horse from the field, Cromwell became aware of what was happening on the other wing. He wheeled his Horse around and came racing back, taking Goring's Horse by surprise. They broke and fled. Victory was almost theirs, only a group of Yorkshire Royalists remained. They stood, refusing to surrender, trading shots with the Parliamentary musketeers. It was midnight before the last few of their number surrendered.

Having fled back to York, the Royalists abandoned the city on 4 July. Rupert still possessed a formidable force of near enough 6,000 Horse, though they were woefully deficient in arms and powder. The Royalist intention was to proceed west into Lancashire. The following day at Richmond, Rupert was joined by fresh troops from Cumberland and soldiers from Scotland under the command of the Marquis of Montrose. They formed a rear guard for Rupert's retreat into Lancashire. On 16 July, York surrendered. The Royalist defenders were allowed to march away with full military honors. The allied armies now dispersed. The Scots marched on Newcastle to continue their siege, Fairfax began a purge of the remaining Royalist garrisons in Yorkshire, and Lord Manchester and Cromwell turned south.

Waller returned to hover about Oxford, but in his temporary absence formidable earthworks had been created under the direction of Sir Henry Gage, a veteran of the Thirty Years' War. In the West of England, after relieving the Royalist siege of Lyme Regis, the Earl of Essex and his Parliamentary army captured Taunton and Dorchester. Essex now found himself approaching the Royalist controlled peninsular of Cornwall. Behind him, as he discovered, was a Royalist army commanded by the King. Essex realized that he was in danger of being trapped. Waller, with whom he was at odds, had failed to follow up his pursuit of the King's army, leaving Essex outnumbered and exposed. Essex dispatched a message to the Earl of Warwick, whose Parliamentary fleet was in the English Channel, to evacuate his army. Essex then moved his army to Lostwithiel, along the Fowey estuary, to wait. The King proceeded into the West Country. On 6 August while at Boconnock, just outside of Lostwithiel, the King sent a message to Essex, offering him terms. Essex refused and moved his army further away towards Fowey. Contrary winds prevented the Earl of Warwick from coming to his aid. To prevent a sea-borne evacuation, the Royalists outflanked Essex and seized the outposts above Fowey harbor, preventing the Earl of Warwick from reaching Essex by sea. Essex was now well and truly trapped. The Committee of Both Kingdoms ordered the Earl of Manchester to march to his rescue, but Manchester's army was still in the North. On the night of 31 August Essex and his cavalry very daringly managed to escape through the Royalist lines. Further down the coast Essex was able to board one of Warwick's ships and escaped by sea. He had abandoned his infantry. Philip Skippon was left in command. He considered an attempt to cut through the encircling Royalists, but his fellow officers were firmly opposed to the proposition. The Parliamentarians sued for terms. On 1 September, Skippon and his men were allowed to march away, after abandoning all their arms, ammunition, powder and cannon. They left thirty-six cannon, ten thousand muskets and pistols, and several wagons of powder and match.

Upon hearing of the bad news from Cornwall, the Committee of Both Kingdoms, based in Derby House in London, sent orders for Lord Manchester to join with Waller and proceed to the West Country. The King, after leaving Prince Maurice to besiege the coastal town of Plymouth, was by then marching eastward towards Dorset, with a view to relieving the sieges before Basing House in Hampshire and Donnington Castle in Berkshire. With a serious shortage of Horse though, his army was far from effective. The Earl of Essex, who had been landed at Southampton, took charge once more of his wretched little army—an army without arms, his Horse exhausted. Waller's ill-equipped army, then at Farnham in Surrey, were mutinous through lack of pay, and in London there was division and fierce debate in Parliament between the Independents and the Presbyterians as to what form the Government should take.

On 15 October the King entered Salisbury and began recruiting men into his army. Waller, with his mutinous troops, was still shadowing him. He begged the Committee to order Essex and Manchester to join him. There was serious dissent in these two armies though. Manchester was in almost continual dispute with his cavalry commander, Cromwell, over how to proceed. Essex, who had issues with Waller, and in command of a raggle-taggle, poorly armed army, was reluctant to march to Waller's aid. Before anything was decided, the King acted. He sent a force against Waller, who, receiving word of their approach but not knowing the exact number, withdrew to Basingstoke. Here at the little Hampshire town on 17 October, having been ordered by the Committee, and with the autumn rains lashing down, Manchester joined with Waller. Shortly after, Essex's Horse commanded by Sir William Balfour arrived. Two days later they were joined by Essex himself and the infantry. With the King having departed Salisbury, the allied armies then proceeded to the nearby Royalist garrison of Basing House in Hampshire. It was a massive and well defended mansion, which had withstood four months of siege. In an ill-organized assault the forces of Essex, Manchester and Waller were beaten back and forced to abandon the siege. Leaving a force to keep the garrison blocked up, they marched away.

The King meanwhile had moved his army to Newbury, not far from Donnington Castle, where he daily expected the arrival of Prince Rupert. While waiting, he heard the good news that his general in Scotland, the Marquis Montrose, had taken Aberdeen. This was balanced by the news that the Scottish

Covenanters had finally taken Newcastle-on-Tyne on 19 October. While the King waited for his older nephew he dispatched a troop of 1,500 cavalry to raise the siege of Banbury in Oxfordshire. The town had been besieged for three months. Things were desperate. Twice Banbury's defenses had been breached, but twice the attackers had been driven off. Ammunition and gunpowder were extremely low. They were short of water and food. All their horses but two had been eaten.

Putting their differences to one side the Parliamentary generals now acted as one. They marched towards Newbury with the intention of bringing the King to battle before Rupert, and the troops sent to Banbury could join with him. They reached Thatcham, a short distance north-east of Newbury, on 25 October. Here they encountered a body of the King's army drawn up and ready for battle. The Parliamentarians launched a probing attack but were driven off. As night descended the Royalists withdrew to the edge of the town. The following morning 26 October, long before dawn, the Royalists were drawn up on Speen Heath, north-west of Newbury, partly under the protection of the guns of Donnington Castle. Their intention was not to attack but to hold the ground in the knowledge that Prince Rupert was marching toward them with all speed. The Parliamentary generals decided to attack the Royalist army on Speen Heath on two fronts. Early on the morning of 27 October, Essex, Waller and Cromwell with most of the Eastern Association cavalry made a circuitous march until they arrived to the west of the heath. Manchester, with the other armies and the remainder of the Eastern Association, faced the Royalist front. Though it was not part of the plan, Manchester sent some of his force to attack Shaw House, a Royalist stronghold on the edge of the heath, as a diversionary tactic, while Waller and Cromwell attempted to outflank the Royalist army. It was a half-hearted attempt, and his men were soon driven back. They lined up once more for battle. The flanking Parliamentarians to the west discovered that entry to the heath was blocked off by hedges and ditches. They had to get through these before they could line up for battle. As they did so they came under fire from the Royalist musketeers, as well as the guns of Donnington Castle. It was four o'clock in the afternoon before they gained the heath and skirmishing commenced. Manchester by then had launched his frontal assault, achieving some success. It was getting dark, and nothing more could be achieved without endangering the flanking Parliamentary troops. The attacks were called off and the Parliamentarians withdrew to regroup. The Royalist army under the cover of darkness withdrew to Oxford by way of Wallingford. The Parliamentarians were too exhausted to follow.

Now the King with a dedicated bodyguard left his army and rode east to meet Prince Rupert's forward relieving column. Unaware that the King had left, the next morning Waller and Cromwell set off in pursuit of the Royalist army, with Manchester agreeing to follow later. The Royalists had too great a start on them, and just before the Royalist garrison at Wallingford, Manchester, now with them, insisted that they halt the pursuit. The King met up with Rupert at Bath, then the two of them proceeded back to Oxford. Here the King heard the good news that Banbury had been relieved. He knighted its young Governor, William Compton. The King, with an army of 15,000 Horse and Foot returned to Donnington Castle, where watched by a small Parliamentary force who were too weak to interfere, he retrieved his cannon. Thus ended the indecisive first battle of Newbury.

The battle was overshadowed by serious dissention in Parliament as to whether they should open peace negotiations with the King. This spilt over into the Parliamentary armies as was witnessed in the rows between Lord Manchester, a Presbyterian, and Oliver Cromwell, an Independent. Manchester had declared,

> Gentlemen, I beseech you let's consider what we do. The King need not care how of the fights.... If we fight a hundred times and beat him ninety-nine times, he will be King still. But if he beat us but once, or the last time, we shall be hanged, we shall lose our estates, and our posterities be undone.

Cromwell responded angrily, "Why did we take up arms at first?" By and large the nobles, with some notable exceptions, seemed to favor a negotiated peace. More radical men like Cromwell did not trust the nobles, fearing that they would secretly negotiate with the King, looking after their own selfish interests in the process. Cromwell certainly did not trust Manchester. He expressed the wish, "to live to see never a nobleman in England." With Parliament and its armies so divided, something had to be done to resolve the issue. In the end, without the full backing of Parliament, a delegation did go to see the King at Oxford. Only one concession was required for him to return to his throne. The King must reject the Church of England in favor of Presbyterianism. The King treated the delegates with utter contempt and gave his response in a sealed letter to be taken back to London.

The Committee of Both Kingdoms summoned Cromwell and Manchester to appear at an enquiry into the failure to stop the King at Donnington, when he had led off his cannon. When called, Cromwell condemned Manchester's lack of commitment. This antagonized Manchester's Presbyterian supporters, who sought to bring about Cromwell's downfall. Witnesses were brought forward to testify that Cromwell wished to see the House of Lords disbanded, while others claimed that he was prepared to fight the Scottish Covenanters rather than see Presbyterianism established in England. Cromwell, they maintained, championed the cause of the common man, preferring common men, and men of mean parentage as his officers, rather than gentlemen. He also favored New England men who had returned to fight in Parliament's cause. Though they attempted to discredit Cromwell, it was difficult for the Presbyterians like Manchester and the Earl of Essex to take any further action against him because he had such strong support in the House of Commons. In a bid to end this dissent, Zouch Tate, Member of Parliament for Northampton, put forward a motion that no member of the Lords or Commons should hold any military or naval command. This he believed would purge the army of political and religious faction. This notion developed into the Self-Denying Ordinance which was passed into law. It received the backing of both sides in the Lords and Commons. It meant that Manchester would lose his command, but so also would Cromwell. But, and it was an important but, Parliament had written into the Ordinance that it could make exceptions under special circumstances. There was also another important fact; members of the House of Commons could resign their seats to take up military command, whereas the position of the Lords was hereditary. They could not resign. Meanwhile the peace negotiations with the King proved a failure. He still believed that he could win.

1645

Though the campaigning season had finished for another year, military activities did not cease. The King wanted to capture Gloucester in the spring. To that end he established Royalist garrisons at Chipping Campden and Cirencester, effectively blocking off routes to and from the city. Rupert planned to recapture Abingdon from the Parliamentarians. There were rumors that its garrison were mutinous for want of pay. Some had even deserted. The garrison commander was General Richard Browne. In the early hours of 11 January 1644–5, Rupert, with the assistance of Sir Henry Gage, sent men forward in a surprise attack, advancing on the southern side of the town. They crossed over Culham Bridge and entered into the ruined abbey on the edge of the town. At this point they were discovered, and an alarm was sounded. Browne had men encamped on the other side of the river, and regardless of the freezing water, they waded across in numbers and attacked the unsuspecting Royalists in the flank. They were taken completely by surprise and broke under the onslaught. The Royalists were forced to withdraw with heavy losses. Henry Gage was mortally wounded in the exchange.

The King suffered another check at Plymouth. Sir Richard Grenvile, who had been blockading the Parliamentary town since the autumn, now launched an assault. His forces were thrown back with serious casualties. Unbeknownst to them since the siege had begun, the Parliamentarians had been strongly reinforced with arms and men, by sea.

As part of its great reform Parliament passed an ordinance for the creation of a New Model Army. Existing regiments were to be re-modeled, and new troops were recruited to create a unified national army of twenty-two thousand men in eleven regiments of Horse, twelve regiments of Foot, and ten companies of dragoons. The Presbyterians in the Lords and Commons insisted that names for the commander-in-chief must come before Parliament for approval. Philip Skippon, who had been in command of the London Trained Bands, was universally accepted as Major General. The Presbyterians put forward the names of Essex and Manchester for Commander-in-Chief. But, both men would be disqualified under the Self Denying Ordinance. They were also tainted with appeasement. The Commons summoned Sir Thomas Fairfax to appear before them. He had no pronounced religious views, had never been involved in Parliament's infighting, and perhaps more importantly, he was a professional soldier. Fairfax was appointed to the new position.

As Parliament debated the formation of its new army the war continued. Along the south coast the Royalists seized the Parliamentary garrison of Weymouth. On the other side of the bay was another Parliamentary garrison at Melcombe. While Parliament held it, the bay could not be used by Royalist shipping. The Royalists resolved to capture it too. A night-time assault was undertaken, and with the support of some Royalist sympathizers within the town, they gained entry. The defending Parliamentary garrison, though taken by surprise at this treachery, fought back bravely and drove the Royalists out of the town, causing them serious losses. Parliamentary reinforcements were swiftly sent to enlarge the garrison. With Melcombe still in Parliamentary hands, and therefore unable to use the bay, the Royalists at Weymouth withdrew to Dorchester.

Sir Thomas Fairfax, Commanding General of the New Model Army.

Parliament's soldiers were also on the move. In the Welsh Marches, under the cover of darkness, Colonel Mytton with 1,200 men launched a successful attack on Shrewsbury early one February morning. The town was an important staging post and recruiting center for men coming in from Wales to serve the King. Prince Rupert had been based there for a number of months in the previous year. With his departure, Prince Maurice then used it as an occasional base in the border country. Its governor was the aged Sir Michael Ernle. In the absence of Rupert the garrison became ill-disciplined, and Shrewsbury's defenses had become lax as a consequence. The townspeople were openly hostile to the Royalist garrison. They were hostile to the extent that they assisted Mytton in capturing the town. When Maurice departed on an expedition, taking with him a proportion of the garrison, some of the townspeople sent word to Mytton. A plan was made, and a small advance party of Parliamentary soldiers rowed across the river Severn and entered the town by a little-used gate in the walls. These men surprised the guards at the bridge, opened its gates and allowed in their awaiting comrades. By four o'clock that morning Shrewsbury was in Parliamentary hands. Those Royalists within Shrewsbury Castle, the inner bastion, surrendered on terms. The English and Welsh members of the garrison were allowed to withdraw to the Royalist garrison of Ludlow. They left behind them the entire magazine and stores, fifteen cannon, and all the soldiers who had recently come out of Ireland. Whether they were Irishmen, or more probably Roman Catholic Englishmen born in Ireland, is debatable, but what happened next was inexcusable. Colonel Mytton hanged thirteen of them the next day, purely because he believed they were Irish. Rupert responded by hanging thirteen Parliamentary prisoners, which caused the barbarity to cease. The loss of the garrison was keenly

Oliver Cromwell, Commander of Horse in the New Model Army.

felt. Shrewsbury was on the direct route between Oxford and Chester. Its capture also threatened the Royalist garrisons of Worcester and Hereford.

Cromwell and his army marched westward, linking up with Waller. They launched a surprise attack on Devizes in Wiltshire, capturing the Royalist Sheriff of Wiltshire in the process, as well as 300 of his soldiers. They then pushed into Dorset and marched into the town of Dorchester. Lord George Goring succeeded in driving them out, but the raid had shown how vulnerable the west was to a future well-planned Parliamentary expedition. An added complication, for both sides, was the rise of the "clubmen," so-called because in the absence of real weapons, these were what they used. They were country people, farmers in the main, led by the lesser gentry of their counties. They banded together against both sides, to physically protest against the looting, local taxation and billeting of troops on farming communities. In many cases their cattle had been driven off and crops seized to feed the various garrisons; their horses had been requisitioned for the cavalry. This "official" robbery was leading to ruin and starvation. Rather than see them joining with the opposition, both sides, Royalist and Parliamentary, had to compromise with them. To a degree the problem was resolved by greater discipline of the garrison troops of both sides. It was a timely warning not to neglect the people who were becoming war-weary.

On 3 April 1645 the Lords passed the Bill that came into effect as the Self Denying Ordinance. Lords Essex and Manchester resigned their commands. Cromwell, who was on active service, as was Sir William Brereton, could not be removed at once. They were given temporary exemptions, which were periodically extended. Later in April, Cromwell was made General of the Horse in the New Model Army. Sir Thomas Fairfax was its commander in chief, with Philip Skippon appointed Major-General under him. The former armies of Manchester and Essex were recruited into the new army with promises of better and regular pay, food and clothing. Each man was issued with a copy of the "Souldiers Catechisme," a booklet which justified why they were fighting. They now had a reason for fighting.

In the spring of 1645 a new campaign season got under way. On 20 April the Committee of Both Kingdoms, as part of a master plan, ordered Oliver Cromwell to advance to the west of Oxford to cut the line of communication between the King and Prince Rupert, who was temporarily based at Ludlow on the Welsh border. As his army approached the river Cherwell at Islip, on 24 April, Cromwell encountered the Queen's regiment. There was never any doubt as to who would win. His men, members of the old Eastern Association, were better trained and better disciplined. The Royalists were driven off with casualties, and the Queen's standard was captured. That night Cromwell approached the outlying Royalist garrison of Bletchingdon House. It was practically undefended. The Governor, Francis Windebank, had been entertaining his friends and neighbors. Now in the early hours of the morning, he chivalrously surrendered his charge, rather than see his friends suffer the house being stormed. He, his garrison and friends were allowed to leave peacefully and proceed to Oxford and the Royal court. Windebank was arrested for cowardice, was court martialled, found guilty and shot.

Cromwell, now north of Oxford, turned west. His scouts reported back the approach of a body of Royalists commanded by Sir Richard Vaughan. They were Welsh levies making for Oxford. With the advantage of surprise he scattered the Welshmen and took some prisoner. The King responded by summoning Rupert and Lord Goring from the southwest. Cromwell meanwhile continued his campaign. At Farrington he summoned the garrison to surrender, threatening to put them all to the sword if they refused. They refused. Cromwell launched an attack, but it was repelled. His brief did not include getting involved in protracted sieges. He marched away. Orders now reached him to rendezvous with Fairfax at Newbury for discussions.

Lord Goring arrived safely in Oxford. The Prince and his younger brother Maurice reached Oxford on 5 May. Two days later the King left Oxford with Rupert, Maurice and Goring to begin his summer campaign. He had a sizeable army. On 8 May, having called for a general rendezvous of his troops, he reviewed his army at the Cotswold town of Stow-on-the-Wold, some twenty-five miles northwest of Oxford. His army now consisted of some 6,000 Horse and 5,000 Foot, with the prospect of adding to this by drawing out a goodly number of troops from the Royalist garrisons in the west. At a council of war many of the Royalists argued that the campaign should be in the west, and with the help of the Western army, to cut off Fairfax who was known to be marching to Taunton — the object being to trap and destroy him as they had trapped Essex in the previous summer. Rupert argued first of all for the raising of the Parliamentary siege of Chester. Chester had to be held if fresh troops from Ireland were to be brought over. The King misguidedly divided his forces. Lord Goring was consigned to the campaign in the west; Rupert set off to the north. Fairfax meanwhile had halted his march to Taunton upon hearing that the King and his army were in the field. He detached a relieving force to continue on to Taunton's relief, but with the main body of his army he changed direction in order to shadow the King's movements.

In Taunton the Parliamentary garrison were in sore straits. They were surrounded by a besieging army of 6,000 Royalists who were preparing to storm the town. Robert Blake, the Parliamentary governor, was having to improvise as stores and supplied ran low. Thatch was torn from the houses to feed the garrison's horses. Match for the muskets was being manufactured from whatever material that came to hand. On 6 May the Royalists attacked on the east side, driving the defenders back from their outposts and into the town by the East Gate, which was slammed shut in the face of the attackers. On 8 May the Royalists stormed the East Gate and gained entrance into the town. Their point of entry, East Street, is long and narrow, forcing the Royalists to bunch together. At the top of the street, which forms a gentle hill, the Parliamentary musketeers were able to wreak a deadly shower of shot, forcing the Royalists to retreat back beyond the East Gate. The next morning everything was quiet. Then at 12 noon the Royalists launched attacks on the two sides of the town. They entered by the East Gate, charged up the hill, setting fire to the houses on either side of the road as they did so. The defenders were forced back to a pre-arranged last redoubt, Taunton Castle, and the nearby stone-built parish church. Here they continued the defense of Taunton until night descended. Under a white flag a Royalist messenger approached the redoubt and called upon the defenders to surrender by daybreak. Blake refused. The attack was resumed the next morning. Then word arrived that a relieving force was approaching. The Royalists had known that a force was approaching, but assumed that it was Goring. Then word arrived that they were Parliamentarians, and their numbers were unknown. Fearing that it was a superior force, the Royalists chopped down trees and placed them as barricades along the approach road to Taunton. Then they withdrew to safety. The advancing force was indeed a relieving force. It was a detachment of Fairfax's Horse. The siege was raised.

Rupert, on his march north now heard that Fairfax had halted his march to the West and was returning to the Midlands. He summoned Goring, whose army had failed to make contact with the Parliamentary army, to meet him at Market Harborough in the East Midlands. The King was also informed, and he turned his army towards Leicester in the East Midlands. Rupert's plan was to trap Fairfax between the Royalist armies, bring him to battle and defeat him and his untried New Model Army. Fairfax for his part was marching to join with Cromwell as per his instructions from the Committee of Both Kingdoms. They joined just outside of Oxford. Fairfax had been ordered to increase the siege of Oxford, while Cromwell was set the task of shadowing the King. Meanwhile Sir Marmaduke Langdale and the Northern Horse, obeying the royal summons, rendezvoused with Rupert at Ashby-de-la-Zouch, increasing the Royalist numbers. The King's army, approaching Leicester, were joined by local levies under the command of Lord Loughborough. On 29 May the King arrived before Leicester. A scouting party from the garrison was taken completely by surprise by the advancing Royalist army. A few shots were exchanged before the Parliamentarians made an orderly retreat. Later that evening Prince Rupert arrived. On the following morning the Prince drew up his cannon, and after two well directed shots at the town's defenses, called upon the garrison to surrender. They refused. Rupert now directed a battery on the south side of the town to open fire. By the early evening a substantial breach had been made in the defensive wall. From within the defenders brought up their cannon to cover the breach should any assault be launched. At midnight the Royalists launched a combined assault on three sides of the town. While the main body broke through the breach the other two attacking forces scaled the walls by ladders. The city gates were seized and opened to the Royalist cavalry waiting outside. By one o'clock Leicester had fallen to the King. There was an initial blood lust, but this soon gave way to looting.

When Fairfax heard the news of the capture of Leicester he left off the siege of Oxford and marched north into the East Midlands. Scouts were sent out to make contact with Cromwell. By 12th June the King had moved out of Leicester and was at Daventry. Fairfax was barely five miles away. But where was Cromwell? Fairfax could only hope that he would join him soon. The King marched to Market Harborough to hold discussions with Rupert. The war council put forward the case for battle. That night Rupert led a small detachment to reconnoiter Fairfax's position. The main body of the Royalist army marched southward to confront the Parliamentarians. Earlier that same night Cromwell joined with Fairfax, to much cheering, and the combined army of about 14,000 men marched to Guilsborough, six miles south of Market Harborough. Between the two armies lay the village of Naseby sitting on a ridge that dominated the surrounding countryside. Under the cover of darkness the generals of both armies sought high ground, and just before dawn moved their armies accordingly. They found themselves, come eight o'clock that morning, facing each other on opposing grassy ridges with a shallow dip between them.

Oliver Cromwell and his old Eastern Association cavalry were placed on the Parliamentary right wing. Opposing him on the King's left wing was Sir Marmaduke Langdale and the Northern Horse. On the Parliamentary left Commissary-General Henry Ireton faced Prince Rupert. The infantry, pikemen and musketeers in Parliament's center, were commanded by Major General Skippon. Facing them was the Royalist Infantry, divided into three sections, commanded by Lord Astley. Cromwell, surveying the enemy disposition, discovered that Ireton was facing Prince Rupert's Horse. Clearly, given the Prince's reputation, this was the wing that needed strengthening. There was a long double hedge, an old parish boundary, running at right angles alongside Ireton's line, extending across the battlefield almost as far as Rupert's position. He dispatched Colonel Okey's regiment of dragoons to line the hedge, in order to fire at Rupert's cavalry, and thus break up the impetus of their charge across the field. Seeing this Rupert sent Royalist musketeers to try and drive Okey off.

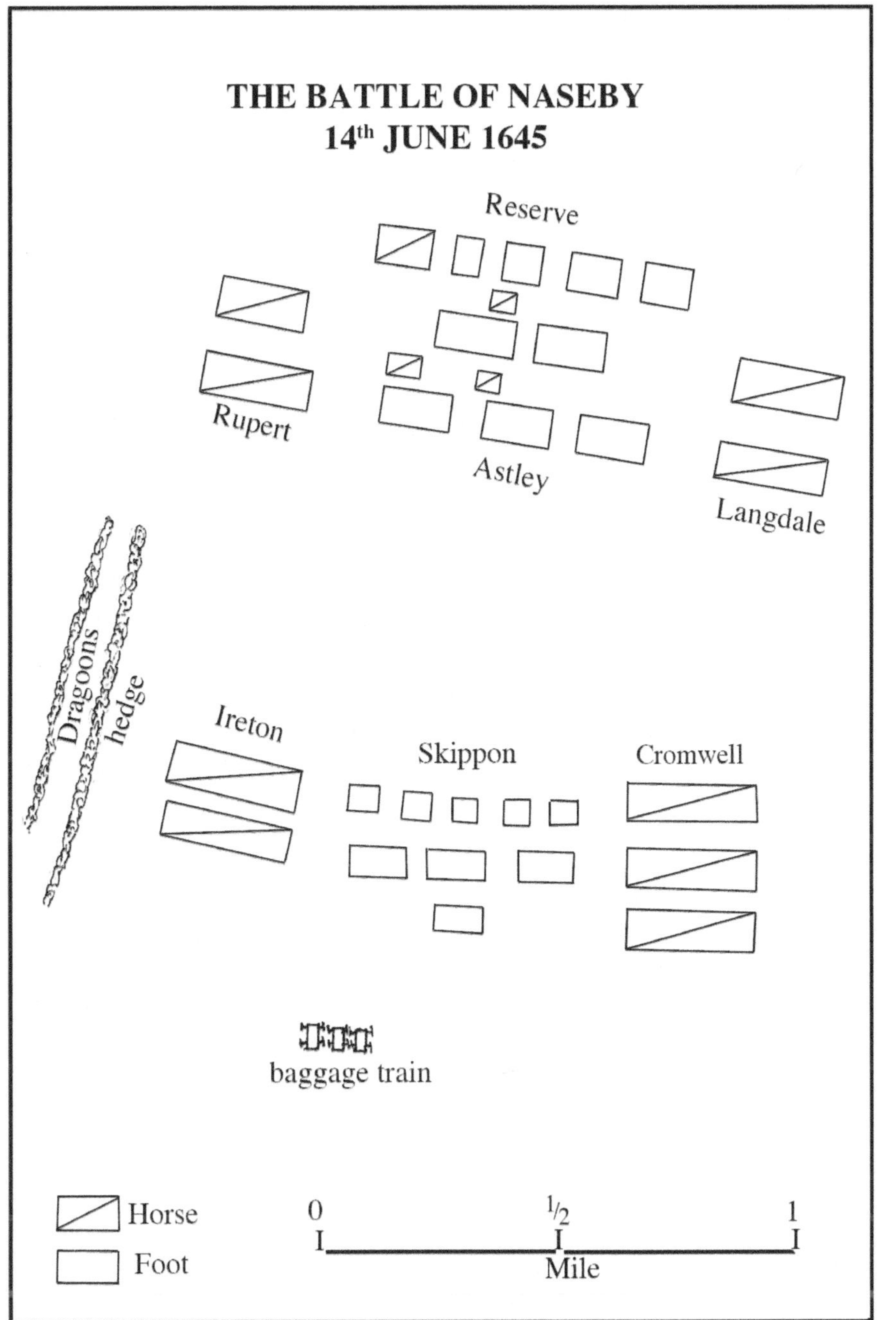

The Battle of Naseby

As was expected, Rupert's Horse began the battle. They swept down the gently undulating hill to the low ground, then up the opposite hill to the Parliamentary lines. They fired off their pistols. In the process Ireton was hit by a pistol ball, and command was lost on the Parliamentary left wing. Coming on now at speed, the Royalists then drew their swords. Under the impact of the Royalist charge Ireton's first line of Horse broke and fled. Rupert charged after them, but in the process left the Royalist infantry on that wing exposed. The Royalist musketeers opened fire, then their Foot advanced. In the firing, Skippon, who was on horseback, was also wounded. Nevertheless he continued to direct the Parliamentary Foot. Cromwell now led the first line of his Horse against Langdale's Northern Horse. Though they did not break, they did give ground, much to the dismay of the Foot on that wing. As it now stood Cromwell's second line was still unused, as was Ireton's second line. Ireton's Horse then attacked the infantry in the flank. Rupert's Horse, now badly blown, returned to the field in an attempt to protect this exposed wing of the infantry. On the other wing Cromwell's second line of Horse now charged and broke Langdale's Horse completely. They fled the field. While a section of the Parliamentary Horse pursued them, Cromwell reined in the main body, and swinging around to the other wing, returned to the field to attack Rupert's Horse in the rear. In the center the largely untried Royalist pikemen were no match for their Parliamentary opposition, and exposed to a cavalry assault, threw down their weapons and surrendered. The battle was lost. The King and his body guard departed the field; the retreat was covered by the few Royalist Horse under Rupert that remained. The better disciplined New Model Army had succeeded. In the battle the King had lost all his infantry, who were either killed or captured, as well as his guns and baggage train. Three days later the newly won Royalist garrison of Leicester was surrendered to Parliament. All the remaining magazine of powder and arms and 500 horses were handed over to Parliamentary use.

In retreat the King traveled by way of Lichfield, Wolverhampton and Bewdley to Hereford. From there he and Rupert went to Cardiff in Wales. Fairfax and Cromwell followed on, making for the West Country. Prince Rupert left Cardiff and the King, and by boat sailed on to Barnstaple in Devon. Here he hoped to raise a new army based on the existing King's army in the West under Goring. At Blandford Fairfax was met by Colonel Edward Massey, Parliament's Governor of Gloucester. By 3 July Fairfax's army was at Crewkerne, and closing in on the King's Western forces. The New Model Army had marched 80 miles in five days. They rested on Sunday, then the following day they resumed their march looking for Goring. The King's General discerned Fairfax's plan, to swing round in an arc and cut him off trapping him with his back to the sea. With Goring, feigning to go towards Taunton, Fairfax detached Massey with about 5,000 cavalry to follow him. By such feints and the feeding of false information, Goring was able to elude the Parliamentary armies. He sent his guns and baggage to the safety of the Royalist garrison of Bridgwater. With the two Parliamentary armies divided Goring made plans to bring Fairfax to battle before Massey could rejoin him. At Langport, in Somerset, Goring raised more troops, but in insufficient numbers to defeat Fairfax. On 10 July Fairfax's scouts discovered Goring's army. Rather than face Fairfax, Goring retreated, leaving a small number of musketeers behind to hamper Fairfax's advance. They were insufficient to hold the Parliamentary army for long, and soon the chase was resumed. The lanes were narrow. It was not cavalry country, but eventually they caught up with Goring's cavalry. There as a short tussle, and the Parliamentarians were forced back. But then the Parliamentary infantry arrived and fired a round into the Royalist flanks, forcing them to retire, then retreat, to Bridgwater. In the battle of Langport, Cromwell reported that they captured 2,000 prisoners and at least 1,500 horses.

At the time of Goring's defeat, the King was still in Wales attempting to raise an army. Rupert was attempting to stabilize the Royalist garrisons in the West Country. Bristol was decided upon as the new Royalist headquarters in the West, and plans were made to strengthen its defenses. Fairfax and Cromwell remained in the West Country, nibbling away at Royalist support. The garrison town of Bridgwater was surrendered to them after a brief bombardment. Its capture had two consequences: the considerable stores of arms and ammunition placed there for safety fell into Parliamentary hands, and the line between Bristol and the Western Army in Devon and Cornwall was cut. In the North the Royalist garrisons of Carlisle, Pomfret and Scarborough were captured. A great swathe of northern England was now in Parliamentary hands effectively cutting off Montrose and his Royalist army in Scotland from any of the King's armies surviving in England. Things were turning very much in Parliament's favor. The only problem in Parliament was the increasing division between the Presbyterians and the Independents. While the Presbyterians had the support of the Scottish Covenanters and the Scottish army in England, the Independents had control of the New Model Army. Tentative feelers were put out by certain Scottish Lords for an alliance with the King against the Independents. Charles also vainly hoped that troops would arrive from Ireland. As he saw it his cause was not yet lost.

In Wales, Parliament's forces under General Laugharne were clearing the Principality of Royalist support. His army scattered the Royalists at Colby Moor on 1 August. He drove them out of Haverfordwest, then marched on Carew Castle. The King meanwhile, with his Life Guard, was on the march into northern Wales, with the intention of making a dash for Scotland.

In the West Country, Lord Hopton had managed to raise a new Western Army, 6,000 strong, which he claimed he would use to drive Fairfax into the sea. Fairfax and Cromwell, meanwhile, continued their campaign unabashed. At Bath in Somerset, the citizens and indeed the soldiery were mutinous following Prince Rupert's last visit. While brooking no argument, he had taken whatever he needed to strengthen the garrison defenses. As a mark of their anger towards the Prince, when Fairfax appeared before the town they surrendered it without a shot being fired.

The King reached Lichfield, and from there, seconding men from the garrison. He and his little army of about 2,000 cavalry, then continued northwards. He was checked at Doncaster in South Yorkshire by the approach of the Scottish Covenanting army. He diverted eastwards into East Anglia, now largely unprotected. Its army, the former Eastern Association of the New Model Army, were fighting in the West Country. The King's men scattered a small force of Parliamentarians at Stilton, then marched on to Huntingdon, where the garrison fled in fear. Here the Royalists took full advantage of the arms, armor, gunpowder and provisions left by the former garrison. Then the Royalists fell to looting, and whatever goodwill had been built up was lost. Hearing that the Royalist garrison of Hereford was under siege by a section of the Scottish army, Charles and his army marched westward to relieve it. Traveling by way of Oxford and Worcester, the King, drawing out troops as he did so, reached Hereford on 4 September, only to discover that the Scots, their troops mutinous for want of pay and food, had abandoned the siege. The Scots had marched away to the Parliamentary garrison of Gloucester.

At the opening of September 1645, the Royalists in the West Country were in some degree of disorder. Goring was inactive, his men were deserting, while Hopton was still raising troops. Prince Rupert was at Bristol, in Somerset. Two weeks earlier, in mid–August, Fairfax laid siege to Sherborne Castle, the last Royalist garrison in Dorset. Sir Lewis Dyve, its governor, refused to surrender his charge. On 14 August the heavy guns that Fairfax needed for the siege arrived by sea. Fairfax summoned Dyve once more to surrender, but he refused. The outcome was inevitable. The castle walls were bombarded, causing great gaps in the defenses. That night the Parliamentarians successfully stormed the castle. Dyve was sent prisoner to London. The arms and ammunition captured more than equaled the losses sustained during the brief siege. Fairfax, leaving the disorder in the West Country for another day, now turned his attentions toward Bristol, and his principal opponent, Prince Rupert.

For more than a month Prince Rupert had strengthened Bristol's defenses against a siege. He had nearly 100 cannon and a great store of powder. He had brought in corn and cattle to feed his garrison troops. The garrison strength of about 1,500, mainly comprised the Bristol Trained Bands and new recruits raised in Wales. They were largely inexperienced soldiers and were insufficient to protect the city's defenses, which were five miles in length. Prince Rupert was relying on his artillery to keep off the besiegers. He had brought in his own cavalry, and these he intended to use to sally forth and attack the besiegers. Fairfax, with his heavy artillery, arrived before the city on 21 August. He demanded the surrender of the city and was expectedly refused. As he dispersed his troops into their siege positions they were harried by Rupert's cavalry as planned. Fairfax now brought his own cavalry into play, and when next the Royalist Horse sallied forth the Parliamentary troops were waiting. They not only drove them back, but with infantry support over-ran the city's outer defenses. Now protected from Royalist cavalry, the Parliamentarians, about 12,000 strong, encircled the town on both sides of the river Avon and built a bridge over the river to link up the two forces. A flotilla of Parliamentary ships sailed up the river to re-supply Fairfax with provisions and reinforcements. On 3 September, with everything in place, Fairfax sent in a further summons to the Prince. Rupert asked to be allowed to send a message to the King. Fairfax refused. Rupert then offered to negotiate. This Fairfax agreed to, but after six days with no return, he realized that Rupert was just playing for time, hoping that a relieving army would arrive and lift the siege. On 9 September Fairfax unleashed his assault upon Bristol. Early on the morning of 10 September, Fairfax turned his largest siege pieces on the Prior's Hill Fort, the most formidable part of the city's defenses. Within an hour they had created two breaches in the walls. The Parliamentary soldiers assaulted the gaps, and after a fierce fight, but with superior numbers, captured Prior's Hill. The Royalists began to withdraw to their inner defenses. The Parliamentary Horse under Cromwell rushed in through the gaps and captured, or isolated, the fleeing defenders. By eight o'clock that morning, in order to save further loss of life in a pointless gesture, Rupert appealed to Fairfax for terms. The terms for surrender were generous. Prince Rupert and an army of 1,500 Horse and Foot were allowed to march away to Oxford. The infantry were allowed their pikes and colors, but not their guns; the cavalry were allowed their horses and swords. Left behind for the victorious Parliamentarians were the 100 cannon, powder, arms, corn and cattle. The King was shocked and felt betrayed at the surrender of Bristol. Blaming Prince Rupert, he revoked his commission and ordered him to leave the country.

There was better news from Scotland. The King's general, the Marquis of Montrose, was enjoying considerable success. The King resolved to join him. With his remaining cavalry he began the march northwards. News now reached him that Chester, besieged by Sir William Brereton, was on the point of surrender. The King diverted his march to go to the garrison's aid. On 23 April the King and his men entered Chester on the Welsh side, which had not been blockaded. On the following day the Royalist Horse under Sir Marmaduke Langdale sallied out of the besieged city to attack the Parliamentary forces from their works at Rowton Heath. The Parliamentarians had been warned of the assault, presumably by a spy within Chester, and a strong party of Horse under General Poyntz was waiting. Langdale was hopelessly outnumbered and the Royalists were driven back into the town with heavy losses. Among the dead was the King's cousin, Lord Bernard Stuart. The King now left Chester in a night-time dash. Upon his departure the King advised the mayor of Chester that if he could not send relief to the city within a reasonable time, there would be no shame nor recrimination if he were to surrender the city. With that he withdrew with his Horse into Denbigh. With the real possibility that Oxford, now closely besieged, might fall to Parliament, the King sought out an alternative safe garrison. Worcester was considered, but in the end the King chose his castle at Newark on the river Trent, in Nottinghamshire. From Wales the King and his cavalry rode to Bridgnorth in Shropshire and from there to Lichfield, and on to Newark.

On 26 September Berkeley Castle in Gloucestershire surrendered to Fairfax. Cromwell, acting independently, cleared Wiltshire and Hampshire of Royalist garrisons. He captured Devizes, and on 5 October, Winchester fell to him. Then on to Basing House in Hampshire, the home of the Marquis of Winchester. The house was possessed of formidable ramparts and had withstood a half-hearted siege of two years. Cromwell and the New Model Army were a new breed of soldiers. They began their all out siege on 8 October with heavy cannon. By 15 October, the outer walls were breached. An assault was launched, and amidst terrible slaughter, the house was captured. A number of civilians, including a woman, were killed by the fanatical Puritans of the New Model Army once they entered in. Then the soldiers fell to looting.

Newark had a garrison of 2,000 men. A fair proportion were officers, who having surrendered their own garrisons, had sought shelter here. There were tensions amongst them. They all had to be paid salaries commensurate with their rank. As a consequence, not only within the town, but also in the surrounding countryside, the people were severely taxed. Prince Rupert, who felt that he had been unfairly treated, was at Belvoir Castle in the neighboring county of Leicestershire with his brother Maurice. Accompanying them were but 100 Horse. The Royal party arrived at Newark on 16 October, and Rupert gave the King his personal account of the fall of Bristol. It was at odds with the account given by the King's advisor, Lord George Digby, no friend of Rupert's. At a council of war in Newark, it was decided that Rupert was not guilty of any failure and was restored to favor.

Royalist control in England and Wales was diminishing. In South Wales General Rowland Laugharne captured Carmarthen for Parliament, Thomas Morgan took Chepstow and two weeks later captured Monmouth, after undermining its defenses. Fairfax took Tiverton in Devon, capturing its 12th century castle. The remaining Royalists fled into Cornwall, where they were effectively trapped. In addition to Cornwall, the King still held Oxford, Newark, Worcester, Hereford, Exeter, North Wales and a number of garrisons in central England including Bridgnorth, Dudley and Lichfield. Late at night on 3 November, protected only by his Life Guard, the King left Newark, and after a hard ride arrived at Oxford two days later on 5 November, having dashed through the weakened Parliamentary line at this point.

Parliament's triumphs in the field continued. Beeston Castle in Cheshire was starved out; Lathom House near Wigan in Lancashire, a family home of Lord Derby, surrendered to Parliament in December. At Denbigh in North Wales, Sir William Brereton defeated a Royalist force commanded by Sir William Vaughan, who were attempting to raise the siege of Chester. Colonel John Birch, gathering together an army drawn from the Parliamentary garrisons of Bristol, Gloucester and Bath, marched on Hereford. Early on the morning of 18 December the Parliamentary soldiers gained the town by subterfuge. As they dashed through the town making prisoners of the soldiers of the garrison, its Governor, Sir Barnabas Scudamore, and 50 of his men made good their escape over the frozen river Wye, leaving the rest of his men to their fate. To add to the King's woes Lord Goring, commander of his Western Army then in Cornwall, pleading illness, left for France, deserting his men. King Charles wrote secretly to David Leslie, commander of the Scottish Covenanting army in the north of England, asking for a parley. He wrote back that he would be willing to receive him. Word got back to the Independents in Parliament of these tentative negotiations. Were the Scots going to change sides?

1646

On 15 January 1645–6, Lord Hopton was given command of the King's Western Army. He found himself with less than 2,000 infantry and about 800 cavalry. With Goring's departure to France, Lord Wentworth was given command of the depleted cavalry. With a reduced army Hopton, rather than risk a battle, opted to relieve the besieged city of Exeter. Fairfax and the New Model Army were at Dartmouth, where on 19 January his men stormed the town and secured it for Parliament. Very cleverly he gave every man in the defeated garrison half a crown if he agreed to go home and live peaceably. He offered three shillings to every man if they would join the New Model Army. On the one hand he prevented a new Royalist army being raised, and on the other he reinforced his army. The new recruits realized that pay and food would be on a regular basis, rather than the hit and miss basis of the Royalist army. About this time a Royalist ship was captured at sea, which was carrying correspondence from the Queen. She was attempting to raise a foreign army in France. More interesting perhaps were details of correspondence between the Scottish Commissioners within the Committee of Both Kingdoms and the King, carried on through the mediation of the French Ambassador. Here was proof positive of intended Scottish treachery.

When news of Dartmouth's capitulation reached Hopton, he realized that the relief of Exeter was impossible. Further Parliamentary reinforcements would undoubtedly be sent there from the captured town. He turned his army north and made for Torrington, which he made his base. As he undoubtedly expected, perhaps sooner than he had hoped, Fairfax and the New Model presented themselves before the town and demanded its surrender. Hopton refused, but on 16 February Fairfax attacked and his men gained access to Torrington. Hopton was wounded in the assault, but having the presence of mind, he blew up his own arsenal to prevent it from falling into Parliamentary hands. Hopton asked for terms for surrender. Fairfax allowed the Royalists to leave and march to one of the King's garrisons not under siege without guns or baggage. Hopton and his men marched to Stratton, near Bude, in northern Cornwall. Fairfax continued on in his subjugation of the West Country. He captured Launceston and Bodmin, then Padstow.

Previously on 3 February 1646, with a starving and hostile population, low on ammunition and powder, Lord Byron surrendered Chester to Sir William Brereton. With Bristol also in Parliamentary hands, any longed for reinforcements from Ireland would have to be landed in Scotland. Meanwhile in the West Country Hopton was on the move once more. He marched his men to Truro in central-southern Cornwall. He faced a mutinous garrison who wanted to surrender to the approaching Sir Thomas Fairfax. Regaining some control Hopton moved the garrison's cannon into nearby Pendennis Castle. Before long Fairfax arrived and demanded the surrender of Truro. As Hopton negotiated terms, his men deserted in droves. They were unwilling to continue. Hopton agreed to disband whatever remained of his army, and for himself to go into exile. From the captured garrison Fairfax now turned his attention to Pendennis Castle and called for its surrender. John Arundel, its Governor, refused with defiance. Analyzing the situation Fairfax, rather than assaulting it, decided merely to block it up with sufficient men, and wait for its surrender through starvation. He then marched back to Exeter to reinforce the Parliamentary siege.

At Worcester Sir Jacob Astley, the King's last commander in the field, assembled an army of about 2,000 infantry and some horse, and in mid–March 1646 he set out for Oxford to join with the King. As he progressed south-easterly, he sought desperately to avoid the attentions of the Parliamentary scouts from the garrisons of Gloucester, Evesham and Warwick. In this he failed. Scouts from Gloucester found him. Colonel Morgan, with insufficient troops of his own, sought the assistance of Sir William Brereton who was then in the Midlands. Brereton sent back word that he was on his way. In the meantime Morgan must do all he could to hamper Astley's progress. Morgan's cavalry skirmished with the Royalists on a daily basis. Bridges across the Avon, a river Astley must cross to get to Oxford, were seized and held. Nonetheless, at a suitable point Astley's men waded the river. By the night of 20 March, Astley was near Stow-on-the-Wold. At 9 o'clock that night Brereton and his cavalry joined Morgan. Aware of their presence, Astley took up a strong defensive position on a hill just south of the town and waited for dawn. On 21 March 1646 Morgan and Brereton attacked him. Astley's raw recruits, mainly drawn from Wales, put up a brief resistance before surrendering en masse. The few that fought on left a trail of bodies all the way into Stow. The Royalist Horse, heavily outnumbered, fled to Oxford, leaving their comrades to their fate. Defeated, Astley surrendered, and was taken into custody.

From Oxford, the King now sought to make peace with the Independents who held the reins of Government in the Commons and largely controlled the New Model Army. He wrote to Sir Henry Vane, Member of Parliament and a leading member of the Committee of Both Kingdoms. Vane did not even reply to the King's entreaty for a negotiated peace. Charles then tried once more to join with the Scottish Presbyterian army, in the hope that they would co-operate with the Royalist Marquis of Montrose to help him against his English enemies. The King had reason to believe that the Scots would aid him. The Covenanters were then at odds with the English. The Scottish army had been welcomed into England as saviors, but once the danger had receded, pay had become erratic, and food and lodgings were far from adequate. Jean de Montreuil, the French envoy at Westminster, agreed to act as the King's secret messenger to the Scots who were besieging Newark. Their response was that the King must first accept, without reservation, Presbyterianism.

As the King attempted to negotiate, word reached him that Sir John Berkley had sued for terms at Exeter. On 13 April, Exeter was surrendered to Parliament. Under the terms of surrender the Royalist garrison marched out, and the men were allowed to return to their homes unmolested. The Princess Henrietta who was resident there when the siege was begun, was taken prisoner to London. Within the week of Exeter's fall, Barnstaple,

Dunster, and St. Michael's Mount, the castle that stood atop a 250 foot high summit, surrendered to Parliament. Pendennis Castle still held out, but there was no hope of relief; no Royalist army would come to their aid. For the King, the only good news was that the Prince of Wales, the future Charles II, had escaped from the West Country to the Scilly Isles and from there to the safety of the Channel Island of Jersey, off the coast of France.

Fairfax, after his triumphs in the West Country, now returned to the siege of Oxford. Its surrender to Parliament was now only a matter of time. Meanwhile, in the West Midlands Sir William Brereton was mopping up the isolated Royalist garrisons who still placed their loyalty and trust in the King.

Now we must look at the life of Sir William Brereton—how his ideas and beliefs were formed, and of his part in that most tragic of events, a war without an enemy.

1

The Early Life and Military Career of Sir William Brereton

"Here is a good report," wrote Walter James to Sir Francis Ottley, Royalist Governor of Shrewsbury, "Sir Will. Bruerton is either slain or dangerously shott at Delamere; if its not so I would it were."[1]

William Brereton, hated yet respected by the Royalists, was one of Parliament's most gifted, yet underrated military commanders. He came to the war not as an experienced soldier — a veteran of the Thirty Years War, but as an inexperienced civilian. In many ways he was like his contemporary and friend, Oliver Cromwell, and yet because he won no great battles, he remains in obscurity. He is like a back-cloth to the victories of Parliament's other generals.

Brereton's greatness as a military man was his ability to interpret intelligence. Not only do we see him gathering information, but also imparting it. The Earl of Clarendon, by no means a friend, readily acknowledges that Brereton had the willing assistance of the common people. They supplied him with intelligence, "and the difference in the temper of the common people of both sides was so great, that they who inclined to the Parliament left nothing unperformed that might advance the cause."[2] Brereton also drew intelligence from armies in the field, and from the various County Committees. Captain Stone at Stafford, and Sir Richard Skeffington (Brereton's brother-in-law) at Coventry, both reported to him any Royalist movements, whether they effected Brereton or not. Even at Westminster he had a source of intelligence in the shape of William Ashurst, an old and loyal friend.

As a soldier Brereton had the trust and respect of his men. The author of *Shropshire's misery and Mercie*,[3] records that "Sir Will. Brereton who commands in cheife in Cheshire, and is a Colonel in, and hath a tender care of, and interest in the affections of Staffordshire souldiers." He was not wasteful of human life. The trade-mark of his military career was the dawn attack, when resistance was lowest. That is not to say that all his victories were easy victories. Thomas Middleton praises his victory in the field. Raising the siege before Montgomery Castle, Middleton writes:

> Sir William Brereton with the Cheshire foot did most bravely behave themselves that day, and did beat the best Foot in England, as they the very enemies confesse, being all Prince Rupert's foot, and the chosen foot out of all their Garrisons.[4]

Brereton is constantly introduced as "that active and faithful patriot,"[5] or "that most famous and successful pious Patriot."[6] Praise received, but also given. He is not stinting in his praise of others: "Adjutant Louthiane performed gallant service," while "Lieut.-Col. Jones led on the horse with much judgment, valour, and success," while "Capt. Zanchie ... is a very valiant man."[7] Perhaps the greatest of all praise is reserved for God; "that God which heareth prayers, and giveth successe to those that seeke him, and make their dependence upon him."[8] Brereton deeply believed that he, and like-minded men such as Cromwell, were instruments of God's intent, "That God who is most glorified by working by the weakest and unworthiest interests."[9] Cromwell in a letter to Brereton wrote, "God has sett the way and tyme of putteing a period to the miseries of this distressed Kingdome. It is good for us to waite upon God, and to seeke his face which I am persuaded you doe."[10]

William Brereton was born in 1604, the son of William Brereton of Handforth in Cheshire, and Margaret, the daughter of Sir Richard Holland of Denton in Lancashire. Both his parents died when he was five years old, and it is probable that part of his upbringing was spent at Denton. The register of Brazenose College, Oxford, where he was educated, records him as of Lancashire.[11] Brereton's maternal grandfather was a zealous Puritan, and the grandson's bias towards Puritanism was greatly accentuated by his association with Sir George

Sir William Brereton, 1604–1661.

Booth, his future father-in-law. Clarendon writes that Booth had "absolute power with the Presbyterians."[12]

In 1627 Brereton received a Baronetcy, and the following year at the age of 24 became a Member of Parliament. The grant of Baronet came about because of Brereton's agreement to maintain 30 foot soldiers in Ireland for three years. "Like most Cheshire landowners [he] was enthusiastic for the Protestant domination of Ireland, both for economic and religious reasons."[13]

Brereton traveled quite extensively before the war, both at home, and on the Continent. In 1634 he traveled through the United Provinces and the Spanish Netherlands. He visited Paris several times, and in 1635 toured through Scotland and Ireland. His journals[14] give minute details of institutions, dress, manners, husbandry, industry, commerce, food and lodgings. Throughout he makes comparisons with England. In Ireland, while deploring the Roman Catholic Church, he admires the pride of its adherents. In Scotland, while praising the Presbyterians, he condemns the citizens of Edinburgh as "most sluttish, nasty and slothful people." Though Puritan in upbringing his journals do not reveal him as a religious bigot. He is shown to have an enquiring mind. He talks to men of all religious persuasions, and even visits a Jewish synagogue. Wherever possible on his tours he visited universities and libraries. One which was to interest him later during the war, was that of Archbishop Usher. The library, "although there be not very many books, yet those that are, much used and employed. Herein," wrote Brereton, "he showed me the whole books of the Wildness, which are very rare; but I left mine with him, which was more ancient and orthodox than his."

Running through his journals are references to duck decoys. Part of Brereton's income was drawn from duck farming. He sedulously collects information upon the subject in Holland, and contrasts it rather unfavorably with his own decoys. At the outbreak of the war, when the two factions were attempting to secure magazines, the Royalist, Sir Thomas Aston, teasingly writes of Brereton's interest, "You know what a spirit he is of. Having a company of Roundheads about him, may be of much advantage to him about Chester. He is near unto his decoys, that he may send out his ducks every way to fetch in others."[15]

Thus in Brereton we have the very epitome of the Renaissance man. He is interested in everything. With the coming of war his education was complete. Clarendon writes:

> it cannot be denied but Sir William Bruerton, and the other gentlemen of that party, albeit their education and course of life had been very different from their present engagements, and for the most part were very unpromising to matters of courage and therefore were too much contemned enemies, execute their commands with notable sobriety, and indefatigable industry (virtues not so well practised in

the King's quarters) insomuch as the best soldiers who encountered with them had no cause to despise them.[16]

With the approach of war Brereton began actively recruiting for Parliament's cause in his native county of Cheshire. Appointed Major-General, his first military action occurred on 28 January 1642–3. With a troop of Horse and a regiment of Dragoons, Brereton marched from London to Cheshire. From Congleton he advanced towards Nantwich. Hearing that the Royalist Commissioner of array, Sir Thomas Aston, aided by Sir Vincent Corbet and his Shropshire soldiers intended to garrison the town, Brereton sent a party ahead at full gallop to secure Nantwich for Parliament, while he himself remained with the body of his men, bringing up his carriage and guns. The Parliamentarians got there first. At three o'clock that afternoon, with the approach of dusk, the Royalists arrived before the town. It was open on all sides, without any trenches or banks. Emergency barricades of carts and whatever lay close to hand had been thrown up by Brereton's forward troop. Five times the Royalists assaulted the town, and five times they were repulsed. Darkness had descended as Aston called off the attack. News had reached him that Brereton with an unknown number of men and ordnance were advancing on Nantwich. The Royalists, nearly 400 in number, assembled for battle. It was now nearly six o'clock as Brereton, with barely 150 men, approached the Royalists. "They discerned them more by the enemies own whispering, then by their own eyes," Vicars narrates[17] Quickly Brereton drew his men up, and prepared for battle should it come. In the darkness they were assembled. A short way off they could see the light of the Royalist match, glowing like so many fire flies. All of a sudden the Royalist ordnance opened up. The Parliamentary guns responded. As Vicars reports, Brereton's guns "wrought more terrour then execution among them.... But the enemy on a sudden cried out, let us flie, for they have great peeces of Ordnance." To add to the confusion, Parliamentary Captain Gouldsgay dismounted his dragoons and drove the un-mounted horses towards the enemy. In the dark, panic set in amongst the untried Royalists. Brereton's men now gave fire, and advanced towards the enemy foot, making as much noise as possible to add to the confusion and fear of their opponents. They fell on the Royalists using their pistols and carbines as clubs. The enemy broke and fled, pursued by Brereton's men. Sir Thomas Aston "fled away on foot (as we are credibly informed) at least three miles, and then got a horse on which he fled to Whitchurch," wrote Vicars. Nearly 200 Royalists were taken prisoner, and the next morning a number of dead soldiers were discovered in the fields and lanes about. In triumph Brereton marched that night into Nantwich, which he made his headquarters.

Over the next few months Brereton fortified Whitchurch, a small market town on the river Weaver. The winter snows and quagmire roads prevented further military excursions until the coming of spring. The terrible conditions did not prevent Brereton from sending out small bands to reconnoiter during the winter months though. He made preparations for the forthcoming campaign season. In February Brereton applied to the Commons for 1,500 muskets, swords, bandoleers and helmets. In addition he requested 30 barrels of gunpowder, and whatever stores that could be spared.[18]

On 13th March 1642–3, with the approach of spring, Brereton acted. In a dawn attack he afflicted a second defeat on Sir Thomas Aston, who had garrisoned nearby Middlewich. In a sharp engagement the Parliamentarians captured the town and took prisoner Sir Edward Mosely, Colonel Ellis, several Lieutenant-Colonels and Majors, as well as 600 soldiers, two pieces of ordnance, and all the arms and baggage of the garrison.

That same spring, Lord Brooke, Parliament's commander in Warwickshire went on the offensive. "Lord Brooke," it was reported, "having taken Stratford-upon-Avon, and settled that town and the county of Warwick in peace, marched with his forces against the Earl of Chesterfield and M. Hastings, which were with some considerable forces at Lichfield."[19]

At the outbreak of the war Lichfield had been garrisoned for the King by the Earl of Chesterfield. Its inner bastion was the Cathedral Close. The walls were strengthened and the Close was encompassed by a deep and wide moat. Mounds were thrown up on the inner banks and double wooden doors were erected at the gates. Portcullises and drawbridges were constructed and loopholes pierced in the outer walls.

With an army of 3,000 men Lord Brooke broke down the town gates, the defenders fleeing to the inner bastion of the Close. As he approached Brooke demanded use of the Close for King and Parliament. Chesterfield refused, and before Brooke could complete his encirclement, he sent out a message for assistance in raising the siege. Hearing of the assault on Lichfield Lord Northampton wrote to Prince Rupert:

> Sir,
>
> I have just now received intelligence that my Lord Chesterfield is besieged in the close at Lichfield, by an express messenger from his lady, and that Sir William Brereton's forces, and Sir John Gille's lie so close between his lordship and Colonel Hastings that he cannot possibly come to his aid. I have a messenger of my own that confirms it, and informs me that my Lord Brook's forces are between a thousand and fifteen hundred men. And that his intention is (if he effects this business) to march to Stafford.[20]

The Prince ordered Northampton to relieve Lichfield with all speed. Meanwhile at the Close, Brooke ordered his artillery to be brought up before

Left: **Parliament's Midland Commander, Robert, Lord Brooke, was killed at the siege of Lichfield Close, 2 March 1643.**

the garrison's gates in Dam Street. Anxious to see "what execution was made against the walls, or gates,"[21] Lord Brooke proceeded from his headquarters at Michael Biddulph's house. Through the house of Richard Newbole he passed, and then by an entry into the garden, and so passing safely behind the houses to Dam Street. "Having passed safe threw, he came unto one Walter

Francye's house ... which house had a very long entry, and just opposite unto the piece of ordinance, where his lordshipe was willing to see his gunner give fire, once or twice; after which shoots,[22] Lord Brooke raised the visor of his helmet so that he could see better. High up in the cathedral steeple, so legend has it, Sir Richard Dyott's younger son, "Dumb" Dyott (so called because of his affliction), espied the Parliamentary leader. Taking careful aim with his flintlock, he fired. Lord Brooke fell to the ground, a bullet through the head.[23] He died on 2 March, the feast day of St Chad, to whom the cathedral was dedicated. Upon his approach to Lichfield, Lord Brooke had prayed out loud, "that if the cause in which he was engaged was unjust, he might presently be cutt off." One Royalist observed that it was, "A judgment, for mark you he prayed to be enabled to destroy St Chad's church on St Chad's day, and he was smitten with a bullet made from the lead that covered St Chad's Church."

Fearing mass desertion the news of Lord Brooke's death was kept from his soldiers. Brooke's senior officers[24] sent to Derby for Sir John Gell to take command of the siege. "Captain Fox[25] came post from Lichefield, and brought the sadd news of the noble Lord Brooke's death, whereupon our Colonell went immediatelie with the captain to Lichfield and kept together those forces ready to disband," one of Gell's junior officers recorded.[26] Gell and a small entourage rode to Lichfield. That same day Colonel Henry Hastings and a small party of Royalist horse set out from Rushall, bound for Lichfield. They entered the town by Sandford and St John's Streets. The arrival of the Royalists alarmed the besiegers, but not knowing the Parliamentary strength, Hastings prudently withdrew back to the safety of the King's garrison at Rushall.

On 3 March the besiegers, now under Gell's command, made two attempts at storming the Close. Pitch, rosin, tar, hemp, and flax were brought up in an attempt to burn down the west gate. The attackers came under heavy fire and were forced to retire with loss. An attempt was also made to storm the Close on the northern side. Carts and ladders were assembled, but the carters were afraid of the Royalist snipers and refused to drive their carts beyond Gay Lane. At this point the Royalists sallied forth from the Bishop's Tower, routing the besiegers. They returned safely into the Close with only minor casualties.

Realizing the probability of a protracted siege Gell sent to Warwick for a mortar. It arrived on Saturday, 4 March, much to the horror of the besieged garrison. Mortar shells, with a fuse attached, were fired from a canon. When the fuse burnt down the shell exploded, scattering death-dealing shards of metal in all directions. The next day following a petition by the women in the Close, the Earl of Chesterfield, much to his dishonor in Royalist eyes, agreed to surrender his charge. An officer was sent out of the Close to negotiate articles for its surrender. He was immediately blindfolded so that he should not see what military changes had taken place in the town. The negotiator was then led to Mr. Biddulph's house, where, still blindfolded, he was brought before Gell and his officers. Chesterfield had proposed that the Close would be surrendered if he, his officers and the gentlemen volunteers be allowed to march away to any of his Majesty's garrisons. Further, that the churchmen be allowed to carry out their functions as before, and that all townsmen living within the Close be free from pillage. Gell, having the measure of Chesterfield, rejected all his terms, and offered only free quarter to all those who threw themselves on Parliament's mercy. Failing this Gell proposed to take the Close by assault.[27] The Earl agreed to Gell's terms and surrendered the Close. Had he but held out for ten days more the siege would have been raised. At that moment the Earl of Northampton and a strong party of Horse were riding to Lichfield's relief.

Now too late to be of assistance Northampton with between 800 and 900 Horse, rode to Stafford, where Chesterfield and his men had marched, following the surrender of Lichfield. On 19 March, after having sent word to Sir William Brereton, asking for his assistance, Gell with a small army, including some 240 Horse from Brooke's Warwickshire "Purple Coats," advanced upon Stafford Castle.

At Haywood, not far from Shugborough Park, a force of 200 Parliamentary soldiers on their way to join Gell, quartered for the night. On Friday, 17 March, two days before Gell left Lichfield, news of the presence of this group was brought to Lord Northampton. He dispatched a force, commanded by Major Skudamore, to enter Haywood, while he and Colonel-General Hastings waited above the town to cut off the fleeing Parliamentary soldiers. In the subsequent skirmish, taken completely by surprise, and unaware of the number of their attackers, the Parliamentary force fled. Their Horse managed to escape across the fields, leaping hedges and ditches, but the Foot were either captured or killed. Eighty of them were taken prisoner. That night Northampton and his men camped in and about Haywood. The next day they continued in their march to Stafford.

The Battle of Hopton Heath

About 11 o'clock on the morning of Sunday 19 March, intelligence reached the Earl of Northampton that Sir John Gell and a small army were on Hopton Heath. Unbeknown to the Earl, Sir William Brereton had joined with Gell. The combined Parliamentary army consisted of:

Foot: Pikemen	500[28]
Musketeers	
Horse: 6 troops[29]	400[29] (240 of which were reformado troops of Lord Brooke's Regiment)
Dragoons: 5 companies[30]	300
Total	1,200[31]

Artillery: "8 Drakes and 3 greate peeces [of cannon]."

It was almost 3 o'clock before the Royalist army was assembled. They marched out of Stafford by the East Gate, and along the Weston Road to Hopton Heath. There they found the Parliamentary army drawn up and ready for battle. Being first in the field the Parliamentarians "had the advantage of choosing the ground which they did soe that they had not only hedges and old walls which served them for breast works and were by them lyned with musquetteeres,"[32] but also the main body were placed behind "a warren full of cunny [rabbit] holes where horses could not charge without great danger and hazard." Gell drew up his Foot who stood ten deep.[33] "They had 8 Drakes and 3 greate peeces all upon the advantage of a hill which to come unto had Moorish ground to hinder," the Royalist approaches. Brereton's Horse were placed on the two wings. "Both our horse and foote were unhappily disposed [and] divided into small bodyes," Brereton relates.

The Earl of Northampton and Colonel-General Hastings drew up their army on the Heath. The actual size of their army is contradictory. Gell gives a figure of 1,200, the same as Parliament's army. The Dunrobin MSS (A Royalist source) gives the figure as not "above 1,000 horse and foote." From other sources it is possible to arrive at an accurate figure:

Foot:	100
Horse: 25 troops[13]	800[34]
Dragoons: [?] 5 companies	300[34]
Total	1,200

Artillery: "One very good piece called 'Roaring Meg.'"

The Earl drew up his army "within halfe a cannon shot."[35] of the enemy. The Royalist dragoons were dispatched to clear the hedges and walls of the Parliamentary dragoons. A fierce engagement ensued. Captain Bromhall and his dragoons fought the Royalists "untill all their powder and bullet was spent. Afterwards they joyned, and fell to it pell mell. One upon another, with the stocks of their musketts."[36] The Royalists eventually succeeded in clearing the hedges. While this was going on, the Parliamentary guns opened fire. They did little damage to the Royalists, because due to the close proximity of the two armies, the Parliamentary canon fired too high. The Royalists with their one canon, "Roaring Meg," were more accurate. The first shot killed

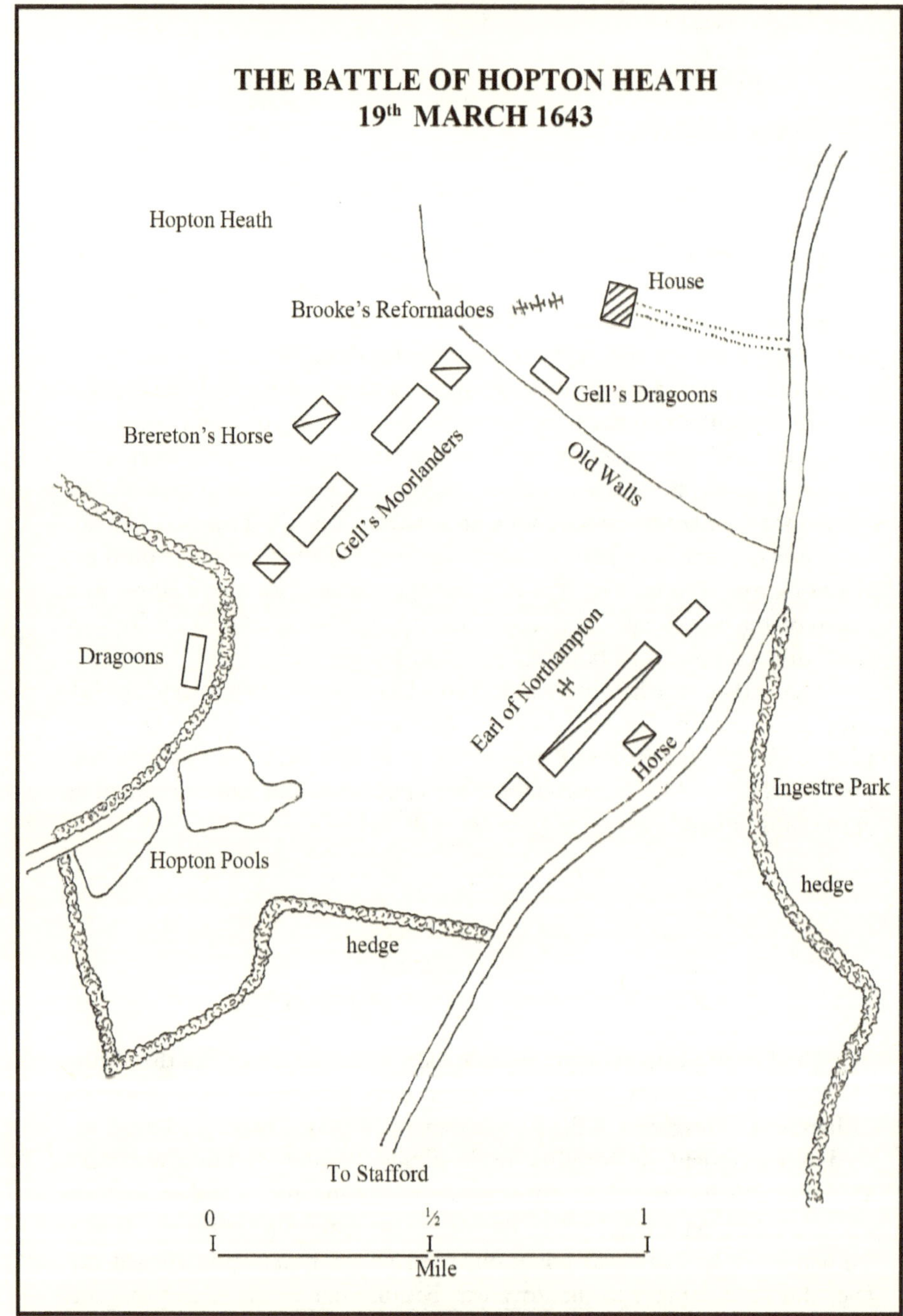

Battle of Hopton Heath

"six of their men and hurt four more and the next made such a lane through them that they had little minde to close agayne."[37]

With the hedges and walls cleared, Northampton's Horse moved up on a front of between 120 and 200 horse-men.[38] At a trot they proceeded, probably three deep. Gathering speed the Horse broke into a gallop as they neared the Parliamentary Horse. The Parliamentary musketeers "who by the discharge of their first volley of shott did perform mighty great execution" upon the Royalist Horse. They, nonetheless, succeeded in driving off the Parliamentary Horse after some fifteen minutes. The "greatest parte of our horse," Brereton records, "were disordered and routed." "All our horse fled," Gell confirms in his account, "except about 240 of the lord Brooke's reformader troupe, who behaved themselves all very gallantly." The remaining Horse were pulled back and interspersed with the Foot. "Our Colonel [Sir John Gell] quitt his horse, and went to the foote, being then in great feare and disorder, many of them readie to rune, and standing with theyre pikes advanced.2[39]

During the Royalist charge the Earl of Northampton was killed. His "horse received a shott but himself had not then received any hurt."[40] He was thrown to the ground, the horse was dead. The remaining Royalist Horse continued on. Picking himself up, the dazed Earl saw an enemy colonel of Foot making haste towards him. Northampton defended himself, killing the colonel and wounding a captain before being struck himself. His helmet was knocked off his head by the butt of a musket. Northampton was called upon to surrender, but refused, saying, "I scorn to take quarter from such base rogues as you are." Thereupon he was killed by a blow from a halberd on the back of his head.[41]

The Royalist Horse continued their rout of the Parliamentary Horse. "Wee gained their cannon and here Sir Thomas Byron left some few Dragooners and a guard of horse,"[42] the Royalist author tells us, but "he no sooner quitted (with the intention to fetch up some more to make a stand and to stopp the rest from further pursuite) but those horse came off and some of their Rebells reserve of horse [probably Brooke's men] came up and regained their cannon."

Colonel-General Hastings taking command of the Royalist army, led the Horse in a second charge against the Parliamentary Foot and the remnants of the Horse. The musketeers gave them a fierce "vollie of shott upon theyre chardge."[43] Brereton viewed the charge as "a most desperate attempt, which did produce and occasion their own destruction." Royalist, Sir Thomas Byron, was wounded twice; "the one with a carbine, the other with a sword and both towarde the lower part of his back, that of the carbine went thro his body from the bottome of his Armour and out at the groyne."[44]

While the Parliamentary Foot were thus engaged, the Royalists succeeded in dragging off the enemy's Drakes. The Parliamentary Foot doggedly resisted the Royalist Horse, being left without any support from their own Horse, which had been almost completely routed.

Hastings withdrew his men with the intention of charging once more. At this point in the engagement Captain Bowyer arrived with one troop of Brereton's Foot. If we are to believe Gell's account, only Captain Thomas Willoughby and his troop of Foot remained on the field. Bowyer's men joined them and the two troops now awaited the next Royalist charge. It was "with much labour," the Royalist Horse "were gotten together into a body and made a stande with intention to charge agayne."[45] But it "was soe late [in the day] that nothinge could bee done without hazard of great confusion in the darke." The Royalist army retired to the edge of the heath. Their great canon, "Roaring Meg," and the captured eight Parliamentary Drakes were sent off to Stafford with a guard of dragoons.

During the night the remains of the Parliamentary army withdrew. Brereton went off to Cheshire, and Gell, with the body of the Earl of Northampton, journeyed north to Uttoxeter. Viewing the body before he departed, Brereton observed, "I cannot perceive that he was knowne before he was dead, pillaged, and stripped, when though it was in the night, I viewed his body, lyeing naked upon the ground." Early the next morning the Royalists instigated a search for the dead Earl's body, but without success. A trumpeter was sent after Gell, to ask for the return of the body, but "they refused to returne itt without restitution of their 8 Drakes with their ammunition and prisoners."[46] The Earl's body was buried at All Hallows Church, Derby, on a shelf in the old Countess of Shrewsbury's vault. James, Lord Compton, who was wounded in the leg during the battle, succeeded to the title as third Earl of Northampton.

Of the Royalist army it was reported that as well as the Earl, Captains Cressitt, Bagot, Bidulph, Harvey and Baker were killed; as were Captain-Lieutenant Middleton, Lieutenant Greene, Cornets Spencer Lucy, Billing and Hall, and Ensign Bowyer. Nearly 600 bodies were taken away for burial. The largest common grave is in a wood high above Salt Railway Station. It is identified by a circle of trees, some now dead, and only their stumps remain. The circle is some two feet higher than the surrounding ground. Many others lie buried in the churchyard at Weston. One soldier, identified as a local man, was buried at Sandon. The parish register records that:

> John F. Marshall, a soldier mortally wounded at the Battle of Hopton Dy'd in this Pr'sh and was buryed March 20th 1642.[47]

There is no reference to which side he fought on; and perhaps that is best. Thus ended the Battle of Hopton Heath; a battle of Royalist cavalry versus Parliamentary infantry. It was a battle won by the cavalry.

Undaunted by the setback at Hopton, at the end of March 1643 Brereton marched out of Nantwich, bound for the Royalist garrison of Warrington. He had pre-arranged to rendezvous with a Parliamentary force from Manchester and assault the garrison held by the Earl of Derby. On Easter Monday, as Brereton's men were drawing up before the town, the defenders sallied forth and attacked them. In a short but bloody encounter the Royalists having the initiative, succeeded in capturing some of Brereton's colors, before retiring back to the safety of their garrison. With the arrival of the Manchester men Brereton drew up his combined strength before the town. As dusk fell the defenders sallied forth once more. This time though they were repulsed with losses, and retreated back to their lines. They set fire to the outbuildings of the town to impede Parliamentary pursuit. As night descended the Parliamentarians withdrew.[48]

On 21 April 1643 Lichfield was recaptured for the King by his nephew, Prince Rupert. It was a serious blow for Parliament's cause. In the process of capturing Lichfield the Royalists extended their territorial control east of the river Severn, effectively cutting the country in two. They held a bulging line from Worcester, on the Severn, to Dudley, Lichfield and Stafford. The Parliamentary garrisoned towns of Coventry and Burton-on-Trent lay threatened, as was Derby, now caught in a pincer of Royalist garrisons. In the early morning of 16 May, Brereton broke the stranglehold by capturing Stafford. With a small army of Cheshire and Staffordshire soldiers he entered the town at three o'clock in the morning. The townspeople "all being asleep in their beds," Stafford was captured without loss of life. The castle itself, under the aged Lady Stafford, put up a short defense before surrendering. Brereton now capitalized on his success by taking Wolverhampton, a town with Royalist sympathies. In a letter published in Shaw's *Staffordshire,* Brereton writes,

> We went towards Wolverhampton, which towne wee entered about three o'clock in the morneinge without any opposition or resistance, the greatest malignants were fled, those that remained were summoned and appeared, and theire armes whereof wee brought two or three cart-loades, and some cannon bulletts from Mr Folies forges; and the moulds which made these bullets, which they intended for Lichfield, all which were brought into Stafford; reserving the ransome and compositione of that towne for some more seasonable opportunity, when the grete and rich men were returned.[49]

While Brereton had been engaged about Stafford and Wolverhampton, the Manchester men before Warrington had been reinforced by both Horse and Foot, and with the addition of six pieces of ordnance. On 21 May Brereton "and all his horse ... and some considerable forces out of Cheshire" joined them.[50] For a week the Parliamentary guns played upon Warrington. Though the defenders put up a brave resistance, they knew how ill-prepared they had been for a resumption of the siege. Supplies of powder and food were low.

They now learnt that Lord Goring and his men, who were marching to their defense, had been engaged by Sir Thomas Fairfax's Northern Army, and had been defeated at Wakefield. All hope of relief was gone. Reluctantly the garrison surrendered on terms. Sir George Booth, the 73-year-old father-in-law of Sir William Brereton, was appointed Parliament's new Governor of Warrington. The *Perfect Diurnall* reports that the victors captured "14 peece of ordnance, 1100 prisoners, and a great store of armes."[51]

The Royalist Lord Capel, based at Whitchurch, unaware that Warrington had already surrendered, sent a message to the Royalist defenders, urging them to hold out for a day or two longer. He was on his way to relieve them. His messenger to the defenders was intercepted by some of Brereton's men. Realizing that Capel's quarters at Whitchurch would be virtually undefended, Brereton, after first ensuring Warrington's safety, by a circuitous route, bypassed Capel's advancing army and struck at Whitchurch. In the early morning assault 150 Royalists are said to have been killed before the Governor Sir Michael Woodhouse, surrendered his charge.

Brereton, the amateur soldier, was proving to be a skilled and able tactician. His specialty was the capturing of enemy garrisons, thus extending Parliament's territory. In July "that renowned and pious patriot Sir William Brereton," as Parliamentary chronicler Vicar's calls him,[52] captured Houghton Castle near Preston in Lancashire. At the end of August 1643, Eccleshall Castle in Staffordshire fell to him. Its capture had an element of farce. The siege was conducted by three of Brereton's subordinate officers, Captains Bowyer, Snow and Mason. It lasted eight weeks, during which time the Bishop of Lichfield and Coventry, whose house it was, died. For the remainder of the siege his body remained unburied within the castle. Lord Capel, since deprived of Whitchurch, hearing of the Parliamentary siege, hurried to the relief of Eccleshall. He occupied the town and after a brief skirmish drove the besiegers into the parish church, which he now besieged. Unbeknown to the Royalist besiegers, a Parliamentary soldier had escaped, and rode to Stafford for aid. Meanwhile back in Eccleshall the Royalists prepared to bury the dead bishop. He being dead for some time, and it being the height of summer, the body had developed a disagreeable odor. On the morning of 29 August a flying column of Parliamentary troops from Stafford, commanded by Colonel Leigh, approached Eccleshall. From the church tower, seeing relief at hand, the besieged troopers in the church sallied forth and attacked the besiegers. From the Bishop's Palace, seeing the break out of the besieged men, and not yet seeing Leigh and his men, the Royalists rode out to reinforce their comrades. The Royalists now found themselves in a pincer movement between the Parliamentarians formerly in the church, and Leigh's relieving force, who attacked them in the rear. They suffered heavy losses. The few Royalists remaining in the castle, a captain and ten men, slammed the gate closed in the face of the attackers, the body of the dead bishop on his way for burial was hastily abandoned out on the road. From the castle the defenders fired upon the Parliamentarians, who not knowing their strength, retired out of harm's way. The next day one of the captured Royalist troopers revealed the true garrison strength—just 11 men. An all out assault on Eccleshall Castle was launched. The drawbridge and the gate were captured, and eventually the tiny garrison agreed to surrender upon terms of free quarter. The Royalists marched out, the castle was occupied, and the bishop's body was hastily buried. Vicars reports briefly of the incident,

> Upon Wednesday, August thirtieth 1643, beeing the Fast-day of that month and therefore (as in many more of our victories) so much the more memorable, the brave and strong castle, called Eccleshall Castle, was taken by Stafford Souldiers.[53]

A few Royalists who had fled the skirmish before the church, at the arrival of Colonel Leigh, rode with all haste to summon aid from Colonel Hastings at Tutbury Castle. He gathered his men, many of them being former Cannock miners, and they rode to the defense of Eccleshall, not realizing that it had fallen. Parliamentary scouts observing this movement of Royalists, rode off to inform Brereton. He quickly assembled a party of Dragoons and Horse, and they rode to Eccleshall. "Sir William understanding the whole designe, made as speedy preperations to meet" Hastings, "and upon notice of his neer approach, placed his ambuscades very secretly behind hedges, and afterwards faced the Colonell with a small party of horse, skirmished a little with him, and then made a seeming retreat."[54] The Royalists set off in hot pursuit. Just past the place where Brereton had placed his dragoons, he halted his Horse. The Royalists came on at a gallop, right into the ambush. The Dragoons opened fire. Hastings and his men were "put to an absolute rout, about 100 of his horse slain in the place, and about as many were taken prisoners; himself wounded, and with a few of his ragged troops ... escaped, and fled to Tutbury Castle."[55]

With the plunder from Eccleshall, which amounted to £10,000, Parliament was able to finance an expedition into Shropshire. From Nantwich, Sir Thomas Middleton marched to rendezvous with Brereton and Colonel Thomas Mytton. With him were seven great pieces of ordnance, four cases of Drakes and above forty cases of ammunition. The three Parliamentary commanders resolved to garrison Wem, to the south-west of Nantwich, thus giving Parliament a seventeen mile corridor into North Wales. On 14 September, Brereton and Middleton rode to Market Drayton to muster soldiers for the Wem expedition. Such a venture into Royalist-controlled Shropshire by two such prominent Parliamentarians did not go un-noticed. Lord Capel sent 1,000 Horse against the Parliamentary Major-Generals. They however were now accompanied by a sizeable army. When the Royalists attacked them along the road, the Parliamentary army easily repulsed them, forcing them to flee back to Shrewsbury.[56]

Linking up with Mytton, the combined Parliamentary army marched towards Wem on 11 September. They entered the little market town unopposed. Colonel Mytton was installed as governor. Ditches were dug and earth works thrown up. Houses outside of the fortifications were burnt to prevent them being used by the enemy. Mytton then moved to protect his flank. He put a garrison of three companies of dragoons under Captain Broomer, into nearby Loppington Church which was fortified and surrounded by ditches.

Capel had no choice but to attack this new garrison, which had effectively completed a chain of Parliamentary

Top left: **Sir Thomas Middleton, Parliament's General in North Wales.** ***Bottom left:*** **Arthur, Lord Capel, The King's General in the Welch Marches.** ***Right:*** **General Thomas Mytton, Parliament's General in the Welch Marches.**

garrisons blocking the free movement of his troops. He raised an army of 4,000 men drawn from the neighboring Royalist garrisons. Owing to the presence of Brereton and a strong Cheshire force from Nantwich within the town, Capel decided against attacking Wem, and instead led his men again Loppington Church on 1 October. The garrison, hopelessly outnumbered, were forced from their outer works back into the church. The assault was begun; the defenders fought bravely, until the roof and porch caught light. They held out for as long as possible, but with the building burning they had little choice but to surrender. Meanwhile, Mytton hearing the gun-fire, dispatched 300 Horse and 200 Foot to assist Loppington garrison. As they arrived the Royalists, with their prisoners, were withdrawing towards Shrewsbury. The Parliamentarians fell upon them and succeeded in rescuing their comrades.

Capel now marched into Cheshire with the intention of capturing Nantwich, Brereton's headquarters. Though weakened in numbers the defenders put up a stout resistance. News reached the Parliamentary Major-General of Capel's attack. Brereton immediately raised his army and marched out of Wem towards Nantwich. Anticipating this the wiley Capel outmaneuvered Brereton and returned to the now weakened garrison of Wem, in an attempt to capture it before Brereton discovered the ruse. After a forced march to Nantwich, the Parliamentarians were too exhausted to return to Wem that night.

On 17 October Capel attacked Wem, which was defended by a garrison of barely 300 men. The Royalists captured the Parliamentary trenches, but could get no further, so stout was the resistance of the hitherto untried garrison. The women of Wem were as brave as their men folk, filling up the breaches in the defenses, though constantly under fire. Their heroism has been immortalized in the couplet:

> The women of Wem and a few musketeers
> beat the Lord Capel and all his Cavaliers.

The Royalists attacked again and again, but were beaten off with heavy losses. In one assault "one of Colonel Mytton's case of Drakes killed sixty of the King's party at one shot."[57]

Brereton, his men now rested, marched on Wem. They arrived on Wednesday 18 October. Trapped between two Parliamentary forces, Capel took the only course of action open to him — he withdrew. Brereton pursued the retreating Royalists as they quickly marched back towards Shrewsbury. He caught them at Lee Bridge. As night began to fall Capel withdrew his men over the bridge, fighting a rear-guard action as he did so. For the moment Wem was safe.

Throughout the remainder of October and into November Brereton and Sir Thomas Middleton had a string of successes. Holt Castle was taken; the drawbridge over the River Dee, Hawarden Castle and Wrexham were all captured. The Royalist garrison at Chester was thus deprived of any provisions out of North Wales, and the siege of Chester was just a matter of time.

Brereton's plans now suffered a severe setback. In September a cessation of hostilities in Ireland had been arranged, thus enabling a large body of troops to be released for the war in England. Loyal to the King, 2,500 "Irishmen" (in reality Shropshire soldiers who had served in Ireland) landed at Mostyn in Flintshire, Wales, on 18 November. On the 29, Lord Byron with an army of 1,300 Royalists, joined them. Taking command, Byron marched on Hawarden Castle. It fell to him on 2 December. Beeston Castle and Crew House were captured in quick succession. Brereton withdrew with all his forces to Nantwich to await an assault which must surely come. Nantwich was the key to the north-west. As Clarendon remarked:

> It cannot be denied the reducing of that place at that time would have been of unspeakable importance to the King's affairs, there being between that and Carlisle no one town of moment (Manchester only excepted) against the King: and those two populous counties of Cheshire and Lancashire (if they had been united against the Parliament) would have been a strong bulwark against the Scots.[58]

Not since the outbreak of the war had matters been so desperate for Parliament's cause in this region. Two Members of the Cheshire Committee, Andrew Lloyd and Robert Corbet, wrote to Humphrey Mackworth on 21 December:

> The enemy are potent in Cheshire. Nantwich is surrounded, the country round about plundered, 19 colours more of the Irish come over, and no considerable force to contend with the enemy [they entreated Mackworth] to represent our forlorn condition to ye Parliament, for whom we have desperately engaged our estates and lives. We hope they account us friends worthy of some consideration and pitty, and not to suffer us to perish in ye midst of merciless men.[59]

Brereton, with a small body of Horse, left Nantwich in the care of his brother-in-law, George Booth, and rode to Manchester to raise an army. By letter, he had arranged to rendezvous there with Sir Thomas Fairfax. Brereton's proposal was that the combined Parliamentary army should then return to strengthen the defense of Nantwich. In the meantime Parliamentary Colonel Ashton with his Lancashire regiment, in answer to Brereton's appeal for aid, was proceeding to the beleaguered garrison at Nantwich. Lord Byron however heard of Ashton's approach and prepared an ambush for the unsuspecting Lancastrians at Booth Lane near Sandbach. The *Perfect Diurnall* (No. 25, p. 199, 15 Jan.) briefly records the events that followed:

> You have heard, I doubt not, of the unhappy surprizal of part of Colonel Ashton's regiment from Lancashire, going to assist Sir William Brewerton, the truth of which businesse for your better satisfaction is thus related. That the said Colonell marching

> with his forces towards Midlewich, which place was appointed for a general rendezvous, the Lord Byron having private notice thereof, with about 4,000 horse and foote lay in wait to surprize them, and accordingly set upon them at a greate advantage by gaining of a passage, and after a very hott encounter, and many slaine (whereof Major Ferrer of the enemies, some other officers and many souldiers), our forces being so far overpowered by the number of the enemy, were put to the rout, but with great losse of men that I heare of.

The Royalists now moved on to Nantwich, and began preparations for a siege. When news was received of the combined Parliamentary army preparing to leave Manchester to relieve the pressure upon Nantwich, Byron dispatched a force to Shrewsbury for more arms and ammunition. At Wem, Colonel Mytton received intelligence of the approach of the Royalists, and of their mission. He permitted them to pass through Ellesmere (the nearest way open between Chester and Shrewsbury) unhindered. His intention was to await their return. On 12th January 1643–4, the returning Royalists, having acquired eight barrels of powder, seven hundred weight of match and other ammunition, camped for the night at Ellesmere. As darkness fell, Mytton and his men marched out of Wem. It was a wild and stormy night as they approached the enemy's camp. They fell on the unsuspecting Royalists, capturing the whole of the ammunition, and took prisoner Sir Nicholas Byron, Governor of Chester, Sir Richard Willis, Sergeant-Major General of the Horse, his brother Major Willis, Captains Offley, Hatton, Dixon and 100 inferior officers and men, with 250 horses and arms.

On 21 January 1643–4, Fairfax and Brereton marched out of Manchester to the relief of Nantwich. They had a combined army of 2,500 Foot and 28 troops of Horse. Brereton commanded the Cheshire forces in the expedition, while Ashton (so recently defeated near Sandbach), Booth and Holland, commanded the Lancashire regiments. The Parliamentarians arrived at Nantwich on the 25, and drove off the Royalist besiegers. In the skirmishing that took place, several notable prisoners were captured, including Major-General Gibson, Sir Michael Ernely, Sir Richard Fleetwood, Colonel George Monk, Colonel Warren, Sir Francis Button, Lieutenant-Colonel Sir Ralph Dove, and Major Hammond. In addition 14 captains, 20 lieutenants, 26 ensigns, 2 cornets, many non-commissioned officers, 1,500 common soldiers and 6 pieces of ordnance were also taken. On 13th February a day of thanksgiving was held for Nantwich's deliverance.

At the end of April 1644, Sir Thomas Fairfax and the Scottish Earl of Leven, with their two armies, moved from Tadcaster to York. They began an investment of the Royalist garrison. At the end of May, Fairfax and Leven were joined by the Earl of Manchester. York was now besieged on three sides. Only the north remained open.

On 16 May, Prince Rupert with 2,000 Horse and 6,000 Foot marched out of Shrewsbury. By-passing Nantwich, the Prince made for Stockport, which he took by storm on 25 May. Two days later he captured Bolton, and on 11 June Liverpool fell to Rupert. In less than three weeks Prince Rupert had destabilized the North-West. The capture of Liverpool meant that the King now had an extra port at his command for either importing arms or Irish troops. Holding Bolton and Stockport gave the Royalists extra hinterland, and also threatened the Parliamentary garrison of Manchester. Previously on 30 May Rupert had been joined by General Goring with 5,000 Horse and 800 Foot. A few days later 500 Derbyshire men arrived to swell the ranks of the growing Royalist army.

Alarmed by the Royalist successes, on 13th June, the Committee of Both Kingdoms, then sitting in London, ordered the raising of a new army. Under the command of the 2 Earl of Denbigh, it was to comprise of 200 Horse and 300 Foot from Lord Grey; 200 Horse and 300 Foot from Colonel Hutchinson, and 500 Horse and 500 Foot from Sir John Gell. Brereton and Middleton were ordered to join with Denbigh, bringing all the soldiers they could raise. Numerically smaller, Denbigh's army had orders "to hinder Prince Rupert's return out of Lancashire." At the time of writing, the Committee was unaware that Liverpool had fallen.

On 14 June the King, now at Bewdley in Worcestershire, wrote to the Prince, ordering him to march immediately to the relief of York. Rupert pro-

***Left:* James Stanley, Earl of Derby, the King's General in Cheshire. *Right:* Basil Fielding, Second Earl of Denbigh and Parliament's General in the Midlands.**

ceeded eastward to Preston, and then onto Skipton, which he reached on 26 June. He remained there for three days collecting together and organizing the many Royalist forces thereabouts into one army. On 29, Rupert marched to Knaresborough. Now convinced that it was the intention of the Prince to march to York's relief, the Committee of Both Kingdoms ordered Denbigh and Brereton to reinforce the allied Army before the city. With insufficient intelligence as to the strength of Rupert's army, the Allied Commanders broke off the siege, and concentrated their forces east of York, on the barren moor between the villages of Tockwith and Long Marston. The Prince meanwhile crossed the unprotected rivers Ure and Swale near Brafferton. Turning south-east his army marched to York, protected from the Allies by the river Ouse. At Nether Popleton he surprised some dragoons guarding a pontoon bridge. Rupert's army now crossed their third river and arrived at the outskirts of York. He had accomplished all that had been asked of him. As Clarendon was to write, "The Prince had done his work, and if he had sat still the other great army would have mouldered." But Rupert did not sit still. Despite lacking intelligence of the strength of Parliament's army nearby, Rupert impulsively gave battle on Marston Moor on 2 July—and lost. He himself was forced to hide in a bean field to escape capture.

Anxious to capitalize on Parliament's victory, the Committee of Both Kingdoms wrote to Denbigh and Brereton, who were at Nantwich:

> We have certain intelligence that the Scottish, the Earl of Manchester's and Lord Fairfax's armies fought upon Tuesday last with Prince Rupert's and the Earl of Newcastle's forces, and had a great victory. It is of great importance that this victory be improved. We therefore desire you to keep a constant intelligence with those armies, and to apply yourself to such resolutions as by correspondence with them you shall find most advantageous for the total suppressing of the enemy.[60]

Sir John Meldrum, a Scottish professional soldier and Parliament's commander in the South Midlands.

On 10 July, following the news that "Prince Rupert is returned again towards Lancashire," the Committee ordered Brereton and Sir John Meldrum to march into that county. Their orders were to follow him and secure any advantage that presented itself. Prince Rupert, with perhaps 6,000 men, marched north, joining with Colonel Sir Richard Clavering's force on 3 July. Onto Richmond, collecting stragglers as he went, the Prince crossed the Pennines and reached Chester on 25 July. From there by easy stages he marched south. One month later Prince Rupert and his army arrived unmolested at the Royalist garrison of Bristol.

On 21 August Brereton dispatched a party of Horse under Lieutenant-Colonel Jones, and a party of Foot under the command of Major Trevas, from Northwich to Freedsham, where it was believed that a force of Royalists were encamped. The Parliamentarians arrived too late. The Royalists had marched away. Jones and Trevas followed after them. Through the Forest of Delamere they followed the enemy, and onto Ashton, only to discover that their quarry was now at Tarvin, some four miles from the major Royalist garrisoned city of Chester. Resolute in their intention Brereton's officers set off in hot pursuit. Just outside of the village they met some Royalist scouts. Seeing the Parliamentarians they promptly turned tail and galloped off back to Tarvin, hotly pursued by Jones' Horse. The Parliamentarians had surprise on their side and totally routed the Royalist scouts. The Royalist Foot in the village sought the safety of the stone-built parish church, while the remaining Horse fled with all speed towards Chester. They were chased by Captain Zancky (who commanded Brereton's own troop of Horse) and his men, to within a pistol shot of Chester's walls. A gentleman in Zancky's troop, a Mr. Dury, killed one of the enemy close to the works before the city.

Back at Tarvin the fighting continued in earnest. Jones and his men rejoined Trevas, and attempted an assault upon the church. They were met by intense musket fire. Corporal John Cooper of Brereton's troop succeeded in capturing one of the Royalist horses, which they had been unable to get into the church. He pistoled the man who had been holding the horse at the church wall, and escaped with his prize, which was valued at £80. Jones was very much aware that the arrival of a large troop from Chester was inevitable. He ordered the withdrawal of his men. They took with them 40 prisoners and "about three hundred horse."[61]

Three days later Brereton was again offered the opportunity of capitalizing on Parliament's victory at Marston Moor. News reached him at Nantwich on the evening of Saturday, 24 August, that a large body of Royalists were nearby at Malpas, bound for Shrewsbury. The following evening a force of 800 Horse and Foot under Lt.-Col. Jones, marched out of Nantwich. It was typical of Brereton's strategic thinking, to have his men arrive just before daybreak and catch the Royalists still abed. But this time though the Royalists had been warned. They had drawn out all their "Horse and Dragoones in Battalia, consisting of about two thousand, and placed their Musketeers in hedges and places of advantage."[62]

Without hesitation Jones and his own troop charged the massed ranks of Royalists. His three remaining troop of Horse followed quickly after, and his Foot moved forward. Shook by this Parliamentary attack the Royalist lines wavered under the assault, but held. Jones pulled his men back to regroup. In the charge he had been wounded in the thigh by a musket bullet. Undeterred he and his men charged again. Under this determined second attack the Royalists broke and fled. With the Royalists scattered the day was Parliament's. Those Royalists who fled back to Chester were treated with scorn at having been beaten by a smaller force. In a letter to the Committee of Both kingdoms, Brereton confirmed what had happened. Those Royalists who "fled back towards Chester, where they could not be admitted, but were looked upon very scornfully, because they were beaten back by so inconsiderable a number, which they exceeded ten to one."[63]

One hundred Royalists were killed, including Colonels Conyers, Baines and Hesketh, and Captain Harris. Sir Marmaduke Langdale was dangerously wounded, but was carried off to safety by his men. About 140 horses were captured and many prisoners taken. The chief of these were Majors Murray, Cromwell (major to the Duke of York's Regiment), Grathorn and Captain Clavering. With his men safely returned to Nantwich with their prisoners and prizes, Brereton wrote to the Committee to tell them of the victory. In reply they wrote:

> We are much gratified by the good success of your army, and return you thanks for your constant care in advancing the public service. We have sent to the Earl of Manchester the information received from you of the access of 2,000 horse from Westmorland, and have required him to send a sufficient party to suppress the forces with Prince Rupert, which we assure ourselves he will carefully observe.[64]

Once more Brereton made plans for besieging Liverpool. It was a frustrating time as the Committee of Both Kingdoms made frequent requests upon him to supply men for other duties. On 30 August he was asked to spare 500 Foot to garrison Wem and Oswestry. Sir Thomas Middleton wanted to withdraw his forces from the garrisons to raise the siege before Montgomery Castle. Brereton eventually began the siege of Liverpool, a port essential to the Royalist cause. The Royalist Earl of Derby gathered what forces he could and marched to Liverpool's relief. Brereton was more than a match for Derby though, killing or capturing 500 of the Royalists and putting the rest to flight.[65] Across the Mersey, Birkenhead fell to Brereton on 22 September, thus increasing the stranglehold on Liverpool. By blocking up west Chester, Brereton prevented the garrison there from assisting the port. As if to frustrate his plans yet again, the Committee wrote to him requesting his assistance in helping Middleton at Montgomery, "he being there about service of very great importance."[66] Brereton dutifully obeyed the request. Joining with Sir John Meldrum and Sir Thomas Fairfax, the joint force of 3,000 Horse and Foot marched to Montgomery Castle, then under siege, arriving there on 17 September. Not knowing the Parliamentary strength, the Royalist besiegers retreated up the mountain that overlooked the castle. The following morning, perceiving the true strength of the enemy, the Royalists, 5,000 strong, came down from the mountain to give battle. Sir Thomas Middleton in a letter to the Committee of Both Kingdoms gives an account of the fight that followed:

> They marched downe in a body both Horse and Foot, being in number about 5,000 and came up to our ground, and gave us battell; wherein after an houres fight, it pleased god we obtained a glorious victory, having taken many officers, 1,400 Common Souldiers, slaine 400 and taken their Ammunition, with a great part of their Armes, and some few horse, the rest all flying away; the Lord Byron commanded in chiefe the enemies forces, and Sir John Meldrum the Parliament's forces, who behaved himself most bravely and gallantly; and Sir Thomas Fairfax, who had command of the horse did most valiantly set upon their horse and engaged himself so farre that he was taken prisoner, but presently fetched off by the valour of our men, but soe wounded; our men issued also out of the Castle, and fell upon the enemies in their trenches and tooke divers of their Officers, and Souldiers which they had left to keepe their Workes: Sir William Brereton with the Cheshire foot did most bravely behave themselves that day, and did beat the best Foot in England as the very enemie confesse, being all Prince Rupert's foot, and chosen foot out of all their Garrisons.[67]

The victory before Montgomery Castle was a joint victory. Middleton in his letter extols the bravery of all the commanders. Brereton writing briefly of the battle does not distinguish between individuals but writes of the bravery of the army as a whole, giving credit for their victory to God.[68] So it is rather surprising to read Sir John Meldrum's attempts at blackening Brereton's name. In a letter to the Committee of Both Kingdoms, published in the Calendar of State Papers (Domestic), he writes:

> I am very jealous that my last letters delivered to Sir William Brereton have not yet come to your hands. I have had some discourse with a Colonel, who tells me that he saw a printed diurnal at York, Giving Sir Wm. the whole praise of the victory at Montgomery Castle, whereof, I take God to witness, he was free and innocent either of contriving, ordering, or executing of that service, as [he was] standing by the cannon, whilst others were in the fight, at a very far distance from any danger. I have never studied much to get applause by popular airs, and should rather neither envy such counterfeit glory, nor pity my own infelicity, being so ranked with so worthy and noble a gentleman as Sir Thomas Fairfax who was served with the same measure in the victory before Nantwich. I have seen two printed diurnals; in the one Sir William Brereton is highly extolled for the overthrow given [to the enemy] at Ormskirk, when he was at least 30 miles from the place, and where there were none of the Cheshire forces but such as came to Ormskirk by my order and against his will; in the other the Earl of Derby is made to come to raise the siege before

Liverpool, but totally routed by Sr Wm. Brereton. In my former I enlarged upon the personal carriage of Sir William Brereton, wherein I desire not to be mistaken as that I meant otherwise than of his modesty and care in keeping those under his charge together in good temper.

What to make of it? Obviously there was some ill-feeling on Meldrum's part towards Brereton. Brereton had declined to assist him in the Ormskirk venture until pressure was brought to bear by the Committee. One can easily understand his annoyance when Brereton's men were given credit for the victory, and their victory in its turn reflected glory upon their commander. This is not a case of Brereton putting himself forward, but rather the work of the propagandist writer of the Yorkshire tract. In the same way Josiah Ricraft in his *Survey of England's Champions* writes:

> Sir William Brereton parted with Sir Thomas [Fairfax], and marched up towards Chester, and beat up the enemies quarters, and straightned the towne, the which Prince Rupert hearing drew all his forces upon Sir William and gave him battell near Tarum, who quickly made the Prince retreat with the losse of 450 men.

This is in fact the skirmish at Tarvin, where neither Brereton nor Rupert were present. Troops of the two forces in fact become the personification of their two leaders. How greater the victory for Parliament that a well-known commander like Brereton should defeat the arch-enemy Prince Rupert. Meldrum greatly wanted the glory from the conflict at Montgomery to offset an ignominious surrender some six months previous. On 24 March 1644, Meldrum, out-generalled before Newark had sued for terms from Prince Rupert. He was obliged to give up all his arms; four thousand muskets, a similar number of pistols, and thirty canon. Many of his men changed sides. He himself with two thousand Foot, was obliged to march away.[69] Now having redeemed himself before Montgomery, it was particularly galling for his subordinate in the venture, Sir William Brereton, to be given all the credit. But Brereton was just better known. It was assumed that he had been in charge. Hence the victory was his.

With Montgomery relieved, Brereton returned to the blocking up of Chester, while Meldrum marched on Liverpool. On Friday, 1 November, Liverpool fell. The first person to proclaim Meldrum's great victory was William Brereton.[70] Meanwhile at Chester Brereton had been joined by Sir Thomas Middleton. The force though was still inadequate for the job. Middleton wrote to the Committee informing them that the garrison was low on gun powder and ammunition. If only three or four regiments of Scots could be sent to them, "I doubt not," wrote Middleton, "but in a short time to give you a good account of that city, and also of North Wales."[71]

Brereton's shortage of men was due to the constant call on him to supply soldiers for other missions. He was, while engaged with Middleton in the blocking up of Chester, also besieging Beeston Castle. By January 1644–5 he had overstretched himself with his various commitments. In Chester, still far from being completely encircled, the Royalists resolved to break out with a sizeable force, and relieve Beeston. On 18 January, at about two o'clock in the afternoon, they issued out of Chester, intending to fall upon the besiegers' quarters. Some 800 Foot and 300 Horse had been assembled for the venture. Their preparations had not gone unnoticed however. Lt.-Col. Jones and Sergeant-Major Brookes having notice of the Royalist plan were waiting. As the Royalists poured forth out of the city, confined to a narrow exit, the Parliamentarians charged at them, forcing them back into the city with losses. Brereton takes up the narrative:

> We have taken more than 200 prisoners, amongst whom are two colonels, two lieutenant-colonels, and ten other officers besides a good store of horses and arms. The [Parliamentary] foot led on by Adjutant [major] Louthiane performed gallant service, they came on valiantly, bear the enemy from the ambuscades, slew many of them almost within range of their cannon, which saved them from being so totally taken and slain as otherwise they would have been. Lieut.-Col. Jones led on the horse with much judgment, valour and success. I do not hear of any of our commanding officers being slain, but Capt. [John] Blackwell is missing and Capt. Zanchie, who is a very valiant man and commands my own troop, being without his arms, was wounded, but it is hoped not mortally. This may have good effect upon Beeston Castle, and we will endeavour to improve time and advantage by all means in our power.[72]

Chester was now much weakened and Brereton was anxious to capitalize on that weakness. Once again though the Committee at Derby House requested his assistance. This time it was in reducing one of the Shropshire garrisons. He was given a choice of three; Tong Castle, Lindsill Abbey or Shrawardine. Perhaps out of desperation, before the troops left, on the morning of 27 January, he instigated an ill-conceived assault upon Chester. His men launched an attack on the Northgate Turnpike. Under heavy fire their scaling ladders were pushed against the city walls, and the Parliamentarians began what was a suicidal climb. Of the assault a Royalist eye-witness wrote, "they had also hot a breakfast as divers went with bullets for concoction — which hindered their drinking ever after."[73] Brereton ordered the withdrawal of his men in what had been a desperate venture. Cautiously, step by step, the siege was then continued in the accepted manner of siege warfare. The chief outer bastion at Beeston was blocked up, and a forward detachment were pushed up to Christleton on the edge of the eastern suburbs of Chester. As the noose grew tighter appeals for aid went out from the city. Prince Maurice, the younger brother of Rupert, was ordered to relieve Chester.

The Prince set out with a commission to raise levies in North Wales to

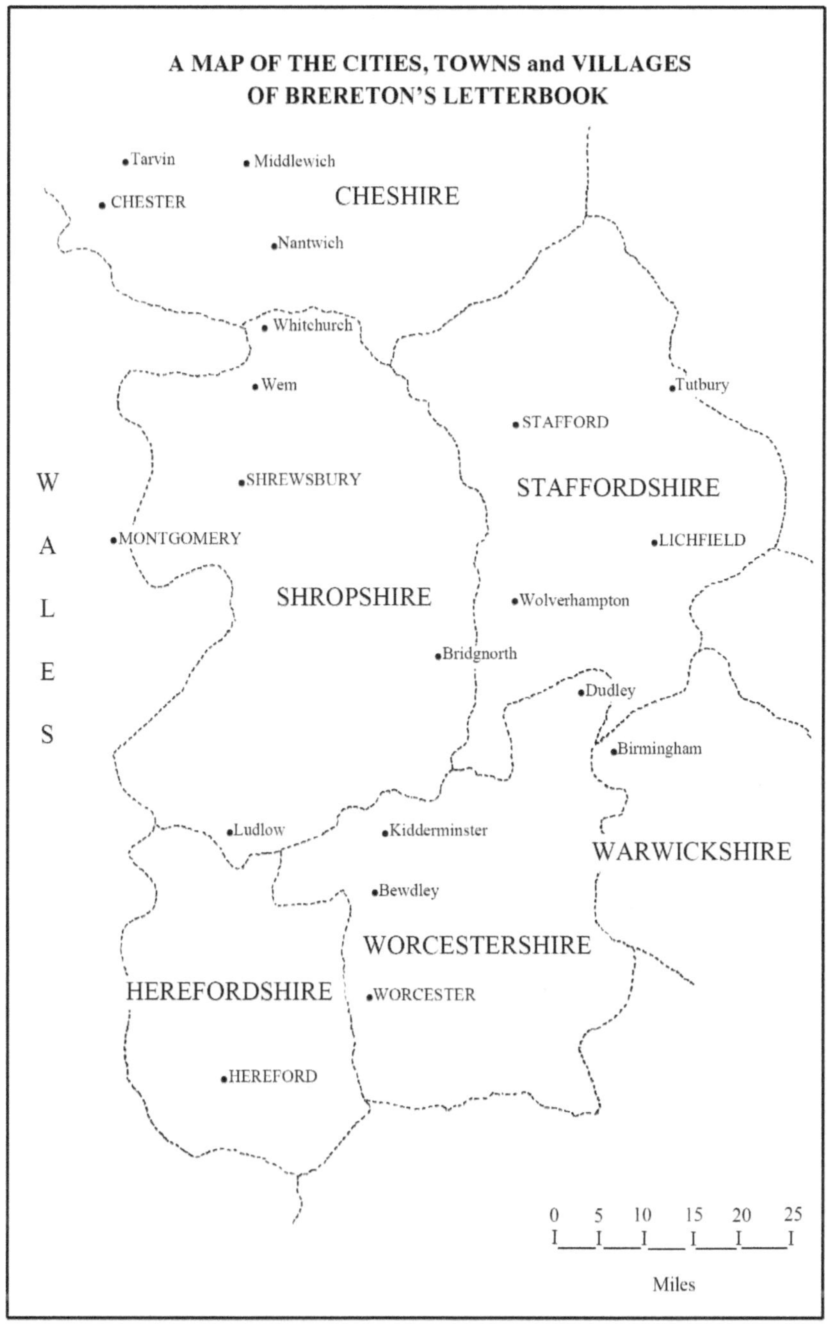

A Map of the Cities, Towns and Villages of Brereton's Letter Book

supplement his under- strength army. At Shrewsbury Maurice drew out part of the garrison and proceeded into Wales. Colonel Mytton, Parliament's vigilant commander received intelligence of the weakened state of Shrewsbury, and resolved to capture it. From the garrisons of Wem, Moreton and Stoke, he drew out 250 Horse and 250 Foot. Upon appeal Brereton sent a further 400 Horse of the Cheshire and Staffordshire Regiments, and 300 of the Staffordshire Foot, as well as a company of his own regiment, all under the command of Colonel Bowyer.[74] On the evening of the 22 February Brereton received the good news;

> We are possessed of Shrewsbury this morning. We entered Horse and Foot, and all in it, we are now staving off the soldiers from Plundering. We have not yet time to give you a list of the Prisoners, but many of quality, the Governor and Sir John Wylde and his son, with many more, we beseech you to consider how to improve this advantage, and the Destruction the Prince must needs receive by it.[75]

At five o'clock that morning the Parliamentary force had stormed the town near the castle wall. They proceeded into the Market House and captured the main guard. The Parliamentarians secured the castle's foregate and after a quarter of an hour the drawbridge was down and the gate opened to admit the remaining force waiting outside. Within four hours the castle was delivered up.

A short time later the Royalists suffered a further setback when Sir John Preen, one of Brereton's officers, launched a surprise attack upon Aply Park. The surprise was total and His Majesty's Commissioners of Array, the equivalent of Parliament's Committee of Both Kingdoms, then sitting at the house, were all captured.

Prince Maurice meanwhile, having had little success in raising the hoped-for Welsh levies, had arrived before Chester. His force was too weak to drive Brereton from Christleton or break the blockade of Beeston. He sent to his brother, Prince Rupert, for assistance in the venture. Concerned when Maurice embarked on the campaign to relieve Chester, the Committee of Both Kingdoms summoned assistance for Brereton. On 7 February they had written to Ferdinando, Lord Fairfax, as well as to the County Committees of Lancashire, Leicestershire, Warwick, Derby, Stafford, and Shropshire, to send men. When news reached them that Rupert was on his way to assist Maurice, they redoubled their efforts. On 13th March they wrote to Colonel Rossiter for assistance. That same day the Committee also wrote to Brereton to reassure him:

> We have been sufficiently informed of the forces marching against you both under Prince Rupert and Sir M. Langdale, and are sensible how far the public is concerned in your safety. We have consequently sent to your aid forces from the Lord General's and Manchester's armies who are coming to you under Major-

> General Crawford's command. We have like wise directed Col. Rossiter and Lord Fairfax to send you all the forces they can spare.[76]

In addition four regiments of the Scottish Horse and 2,000 Foot commanded by Lieutenant-Colonel David Leslie were also marching to Brereton's aid. In the request to the Earl of Leven, the Committee informed him that "Parliament has ordered the despatch of money to your army,"[77] as an inducement. While the County Commissioners were putting their orders into effect, Prince Rupert crossed into Cheshire. Completely unsupported, Brereton abandoned Christleton, and the blockade at Beeston, and withdrew to Middlewich. On 18 March Prince Rupert marched into Chester. The siege had been raised.

Slowly but surely the allied armies marched on Chester. Lt.-General Leslie's 5,000 strong Scottish army marched south from Yorkshire. By 22 March they were on the Cheshire Plain. Rossiter and Fairfax's Horse were on the heights above the city. With Brereton advancing from Middlewich, Chester had all the appearances of being caught in a trap. At this point the two princes rode out of the threatened city, not only with their own army, but also with 1,200 of the old "Irish" regiments that had once formed part of the garrison. Lord John Byron, the Governor, complained bitterly that he was left with only a garrison of citizens, his own, and Colonel Mostyn's regiments—barely 600 men to defend Chester. To add to his anxiety Mostyn's men were proud Welsh gentlemen who did not easily submit to discipline. They had become a liability, and Byron was obliged to dismiss them. In reality Chester had all been abandoned as a Royalist garrison.

David Lesley, general of the Scottish Army.

Ponderously the Scots pursued the retreating Royalist army as far as Whitchurch. Here Leslie received orders from Leven to return. Despite the entreaties of Brereton to assist him at Chester, Leslie continued on northwards. On 4 April

Brereton renewed the siege of Chester. Byron with a greatly reduced garrison, had less than ten barrels of gunpowder left.[78] Brereton on the other hand had been voted sixty barrels of powder with match proportionate.[79] He also had been able to retain a regiment of Lancashire Foot, two regiments of Yorkshire Horse, and some Staffordshire troops. On 21 April Brereton wrote to the Committee of Both Kingdoms:

> wee are soe neare to Chester on all sides and ye inhabitants therein are much pinched and yet so confident of speedy reliefe.... If at this tyme they be disappointed in their expectacons ... the City will before long be surrendered.[80]

As the siege progressed Brereton's constant worry was that Irish troops might land in North Wales, or that he might be surprised by a Royalist army from the Midlands. Left alone he knew that Chester must soon surrender to him. As before, with Chester almost within his grasp, the Committee of Both Kingdoms requested him to assist in a venture in Wales. On 12th April they thanked him for his former assistance in Shropshire, confirmed that his request for £5,000 to supply the needs of his troops was being dealt with, and reported, "We have just received information from [Sir William] Waller that the Princes [Rupert and Maurice] are marched westward, but should they return towards your parts we will give you timely advertisement and order supplies for you."[81]

Three days later they sent word to Brereton that Rupert and Maurice had turned north. From Gloucester a few days later, Major-General Massey wrote to Brereton to inform him that the Princes had left Evesham and were marching towards him. Brereton was at St. Asaph in Wales, directing a raid. The letter failed to reach him until the 24 April. He immediately returned to Cheshire. Leslie was at Leeds, and Brereton wrote to him for assistance. The Committee at Derby House had written to Leven on 15 April, urging him send Leslie to Brereton's aid. Leven was at Newcastle, and ordered Leslie to await his arrival. Fairfax was at Windsor, just outside of London, organizing the fledgling New Model Army. Oliver Cromwell, exempted from the Self Denying Ordinance for forty days, was ordered to assist Brereton by disrupting the Royalist communications between Oxford and the north. With a few thousand Horse he swept the area north of Oxford, bringing in all draught horses; the type used to pull field artillery. The King, whose intention was to rendezvous with his nephews prior to a campaign, was now obliged to summon them back to Oxford.

On 9 May, with a combined army, Charles began his march north. By the 11 he had reached Droitwich in Worcestershire. Brereton was informed by the Committee that the King's march tended towards Chester, and that he should "have an eye to the King's motions so as not to be surprised."[82] They also wrote to Lords Leven and Fairfax, urging them to assist Brereton. The following day Brereton received a coded message from Shrewsbury to the effect that the King and Prince Rupert were marching with 12,000 Horse and Foot to relieve Chester, and recapture York. That night Brereton wrote to Leven, Leslie, Montgomery, Lord Fairfax, Gell and Sir Henry Vane, urging their immediate assistance. Gell replied a few days later saying he had other work to attend to, but was given to understand that the Scots were coming to his support.

To add to Brereton's worries, the promised £5,000 had not as yet been sent to him. Both the Yorkshire Horse and the Lancashire Regiment were near to mutiny for want of pay.[83] By 17 May Brereton was obliged to raise the siege before Chester and Hawardine Castle. He had written to the Committee to inform them. Three days later they replied:

> We received yours of the 16th enclosing a copy of the Earl of Leven's letter. We thank you for your care and pains taken in the public service, and desire you to look to the security of your garrisons upon the approach of the enemy towards your parts. We have appointed Fairfax's horse which are with you to join with the Scottish army, and desire you to send your proportion of forces with them according to former orders to such rendezvous as the Earl of Leven may select. You may be pleased to notice that the Parliament has continued you in your former employment for 40 days.[84]

Temporarily like Cromwell, he too had been exempted from the Self Denying Ordinance that forbade Members of Parliament from holding military command. With his men now put into garrisons, Brereton wrote to Ferdinando, Lord Fairfax, offering him 1,500 men. All his plans to capture Chester had come to nothing. Two years had been wasted. Then Brereton received word that Cromwell and Major-General Browne were near Warwick. Leslie he knew was still with Montgomery at Leeds, while Lord Fairfax was at York. The King was in a potential trap. If he could be brought to battle and defeated, then the war was over. The disappointment over Chester faded into insignificance. Brereton wrote to Lord Fairfax informing him of Cromwell's march. Fairfax in his turn wrote to Leven urging him with all speed to march south. Leven though had heard of Parliament's defeat at Auldearn at the hands of the Scottish Royalist, General Montrose. With one Royalist army behind him in Scotland, and another approaching him, Leven was sure that the King's real intent was Scotland. He was reluctant to move his army south. He had to defend Scotland. Brereton wrote to Leven, Fairfax and Cromwell, imploring their assistance. Cromwell wrote back to him with good news. While his orders were to follow the King, he had written to Sir Thomas Fairfax urging him to join with them as soon as possible. "I thinke it were happy you were conjoined with the Scotts," Cromwell wrote, "and wee with Sir Thomas Fairfax and then wee were, having the King's Army betweene us, with the blessing of God to bring him into great straights."[85]

But again Brereton's plans were thwarted. Cromwell was ordered to leave off the pursuit of the King and return to London. As the King and his army approached Chester, Brereton discovered that his was the only Parliamentary army of any size within one hundred miles of the King. Under pressure Leven agreed to rendezvous with the English armies at Barlow Moor, just south of Manchester. Brereton rode to meet him. In London the Scottish Commissioners of the Committee of Both Kingdoms urged the sending of the New Model Army to join with Leven The Committee agreed to the sending of a mere brigade of 2,500 Horse and Dragoons under Colonel Vermuyden. The Independents, Parliament was beginning to fracture, had reserved the main body of the army for the capture of Oxford.

Arriving at the rendezvous on 22 May, Brereton discovered that the force gathered there was totally inadequate. There were barely 1,000 Foot and 300 Horse. Neither Leven nor Lord Fairfax had arrived. Brereton beseeched Leven to hurry. He wrote to the Committee to send Cromwell back, and to draw off Sir Thomas Fairfax from the siege before Oxford. The Scots were held to blame by Parliament, but Leven was fearful that without an army to defend it, Montrose would seize Scotland for the King. Their Commissioners in London blamed Parliament's refusal to send the New Model Army in pursuit of the King. Everybody was blaming somebody else, and nothing was being done.

Word now reached the King that Oxford was short of provisions, and could not hold out for long. He sent word that if they could hold out for six weeks he would continue northwards. If they could not, he would return to his capital. While he waited for a reply Prince Rupert persuaded the King to assault Leicester, the nearest Parliamentary-controlled town of any size.

Brereton's scouts brought him news that the King had turned east. He dispatched Colonel Bowyer and his Stafford Horse to observe the Royalist's movements. As news reached him Brereton passed it on to the Committee, to Leven, and to Lord Fairfax. The Royalists moved towards their garrison at Newark, drawing out as many men as could be spared, then on towards Ashby-de-la-Zouch. There was speculation as to the King's intent. Brereton believed that the Royalists were intending to attack the Eastern Association, Parliament's grouping of East Anglian counties. He informed the Committee of Both Kingdoms, who from other reports received, thought that he was right. They sent Cromwell to the Isle of Ely to raise the trained bands. Vermuyden's brigade and the Yorkshire and North Midlands' forces were ordered to rendezvous at Nottingham. The New Model Army though, received no orders to move from their siege before Oxford. It was the fall of Leicester by the King's forces that galvanized the Committee into action. On 1 June they instructed the New Model to march north. Their commander, Sir Thomas Fairfax, was given a free hand in his use of the army. On 14 June, Fairfax and Cromwell brought the King to battle at Naseby—and defeated him.

In accordance with Parliament's instruction, Cromwell and Brereton rode up to Westminster to lay down their commissions in accordance with the Self Denying Ordinance. However, on 16 June, the Lords agreed to waive the Ordinance for three months in respect of Oliver Cromwell, who was to be appointed Lt.-General of the New Model Army, Sir Thomas Middleton who was appointed Commander in North Wales, and Sir William Brereton who was appointed Commander in Cheshire.

In mid–September 1645, Colonel Michael Jones resumed the siege of Chester on Brereton's behalf. In a typical Breretonian maneuver Jones advanced under the cover of darkness with 500 Horse, 200 Dragoons and 700 Foot. At dawn on 21 September the Parliamentarians stormed the suburbs of Chester and seized the bulwark at Broughton. The entire suburb up to Eastgate was now in Parliamentary hands. As a tangible sign of their success the city sword and mace, the instruments of government, were also seized. With the fall of Bristol, Chester remained the last Royalist port where the much hoped for reinforcements from Ireland could arrive. But even as Chester's fate seemed sealed, news arrived that the King was advancing towards the city. By 22 September the King had reached Chirk Castle, barely 20 miles south of Chester.

Sir Jacob Astley, commander of the King's last army in the field, was defeated at Stow on the Wold.

Throughout that day, even in the knowledge that the King was close at hand, Jones continued the bombardment of the Royalist garrison. One of the defenders wrote of the assault, "the east side of our walls near the new gate received a visit from their artillerie ... thirty-two shots were made and by them a breach at which ten men abreast may enter."[86] That night Brereton's men tried unsuccessfully to storm the city through that breach. The next day the King, with Lord Astley, Lord Charles Gerrard and the Earl of Lichfield, with about a third of their army, entered Chester. Meanwhile Sir Marmaduke Langdale with about 3,000 Royalist Horse, crossed the river Dee by a bridge of boats, some eight miles below the city, with the intention of falling upon the besiegers. The Royalists were vaguely aware that Parliament's Major-General Sydenham Poyntz was advancing towards them, but they were completely unaware of his anxiety to bring them to battle. By the night of 23, Poyntz had reached Whitchurch. Here he was met by a rider from Jones. Instead of halting for the night, Poyntz continued his march. The following morning he halted at Hatton Heath, two miles from Rowton Heath. Here he briefly rested and fed his men. By an intercepted letter Langdale learnt of Poyntz's approach. He turned his Horse round to face this new enemy. From Rowton Heath Langdale espied the Parliamentary Horse drawn up opposite on Hatton Heath. Between the two armies was a narrow hedge-lined lane. Whoever attacked first would place themselves at a disadvantage. Progress across the lane would halt any momentum built up. Langdale refused to attack. Poyntz was therefore obliged to. His men moved forward and crossed the lane, initially pushing the first line of Royalists back. They regrouped, and counter-attacked, driving the Parliamentarians back onto the lane. Langdale did not follow up. Poyntz succeeded in rallying his men, and moved forward to the edge of the heath once more. Now Langdale faced them once more. It was a curious situation. Langdale could neither move forward nor back, being as he was between two enemy forces. Yet Poyntz could not join the besiegers because Langdale barred his way. Poyntz sent for reinforcements from the besiegers. Jones himself arrived with 500 Horse and 300 Musketeers. While Poyntz launched a frontal attack, Jones attacked Langdale in the flank. The Royalists were pushed back. Unable to regroup, the Royalists broke and fled back to Chester's walls. At Chester, the other Royalist commanders, Gerrard and Lichfield, were preparing to assault the Parliamentarian besiegers. At this point Langdale's men, closely pursued by the Parliamentary Horse, arrived. There was a grand melee, with close fighting. From the city walls the Royalist musketeers fired indiscriminately into the massed ranks, killing both friend and foe alike. At the end of the day 600 Royalist soldiers were dead and about 800 taken prisoner. The King dishonorably quit Chester, telling the Governor and Mayor to make the best terms they could. They had more stomach for the fight though, and refused to surrender. On 26 September a summons to surrender Chester was sent and rejected. Parliament's guns renewed their bombardment. Breaches were made in the walls, but just as quickly were filled in by rubble and whatever came to hand. On 16 November the Royalist garrison at nearby Beeston Castle fell after a year's siege. The news was sent to Chester, and with little hope of relief, a parley was agreed for the 19 of that month. Byron remained stubborn, believing that the King would not leave them to their own fate. So the talks came to nothing. With a certain amount of bravado 70 Horse sallied forth out of Chester to attack the besiegers on the Welsh side. Needless to say they were beaten back by superior odds. Brereton was determined to take Chester. After so long it was almost an obsession with him. Byron was equally fanatical that it should not fall. Brereton brought up mortars, which now began to play upon the city. The same eye-witness who had earlier written of the breach made in the wall, records that on the 10 December, "eleven huge grenadoes like so many demy-phaetons threatened to set the city if not the world on fire. This was a terrible night indeed."

Throughout Christmas the bombardment continued unabated. Much of Chester was in ruins, There were fires raging everywhere, and the inhabitants were now starving. On 7 January 1645–6, Brereton sent in a further summons to surrender. It was ignored. Brereton knew the sorry state that Chester was in, and was growing genuinely anxious not to waste more lives unnecessarily. He sent in a second and a third summons. A misguided loyalty to a morally bankrupt King, coupled with pride and obstinacy prevented Byron from replying. On 15 January Brereton received a letter from Chester's Mayor, Charles Walley. He had persuaded Byron that further resistance was futile. A week later as a mark of their confidence in him, Brereton received a letter from the Lords and Commons, circumventing the Self Denying Ordinance, and granting him continuation as Commander-in-Chief of all of Parliament's forces from the counties of Cheshire, Stafford, Lancashire, Shropshire, Derby, and North Wales, then engaged in the siege before Chester. The command was extended for a further four months. The city surrendered to Brereton. On 3 February Parliament's triumphant troops entered Chester. Surveying the ruins Brereton knew that it was a hollow victory.

From Chester Brereton now turned his attention towards Lichfield. In a raid that was typical of him, he arrived at the city on the night of 5 March. Under the cover of darkness, and with the loss of only three of his men killed, Brereton captured Lichfield. The defenders, said to have been 1,000 Horse and Foot, were driven into the fortified Cathedral Close. The Governor, Colonel Hervy Bagot, immediately opened up with his guns on the Parliamentarians. Two shots came perilously close to hitting Brereton, as a Parliamentary tract relates.[87] The next morning the besiegers erected blinds across the streets near the Close to prevent the Royalists from seeing their movements. As at Chester, Brereton's main concern now was that he should not be surprised by a flying column of Royalist Horse from Oxford. To prevent such a surprise he ordered his Horse to Coleshill, some ten miles south-east of the Cathedral city, on the road to Oxford.

At Derby House, in London, the Committee of Both Kingdoms received word that Lord Astley (formerly Sir Jacob Astley) had marched out of Worcester with 1,500 Horse and Foot. As he proceeded towards Oxford he drew out troops from the remaining Royalist garrisons. This looked like one last desperate effort to raise a Royalist army. On 7 March the Committee ordered Sir William Brereton, then the nearest Parliamentary general, to command a force to follow the enemy. They wrote to him accordingly:

> The House of Commons being informed that the forces of the enemy under Sir Jacob Ashley are drawing into the field, and will endeavour a conjunction with the forces at Oxford, and so attempt to raise recruits and make a beginning for an army, have ordered that those forces which were formerly ordered to come to Wolverhampton on the 18th shall forthwith draw together into a body and attend the motions of Ashley's forces in the field. Let the Cheshire forces appointed for this service march up to the others and hasten the march of the Shropshire forces, which we hear are not yet come up. We desire you to march up to those forces and take that party into your charge, and so endeavour to prevent the junction of Ashley's party with the rest of the enemy's forces, to hinder their recruits, and preserve the country from their plunderings and spoil.. We have appointed the regiment of Reformadoes under Col. Sanderson to come up for the same service, to whom we desire you to give orders accordingly. You are also to keep correspondence with Cols. Fleetwood and Whalley for better hindering the conjunction of the enemy's forces.[88]

Drawn out from the Parliamentary garrisons of Gloucester, Hereford and Evesham, Colonel Thomas Morgan led a small army with all speed westward towards the river Avon, in a bid to prevent Astley from crossing it. Astley marched south towards Droitwich and "endeavoured by all meanes to get by me," wrote Morgan, "which foyled my brigade to prevent, in marching from place to place, to secure the place upon the River Avon."[89] Astley succeeded in crossing the river at Bidford-on-Avon, on 20 March, watched by Morgan's scouts. Writing to Fleetwood, Whalley and Brereton for their immediate assistance, Morgan crossed the Avon at Warwick, and marched southwards towards Stow-on-the-Wold in a bid to place himself between Astley and Oxford.

Astley was ahead of Morgan, but by less than an hour. Throughout the 20 March, Morgan's forward troopers skirmished with the Royalists in a bid to slow them down until reinforcements could arrive. About nine o'clock that night Brereton arrived with 800 Horse. Astley was by now near Donnington. After resting, the Parliamentarians set off the next morning, 21 March, in hot pursuit. Morgan, commanding 400 Horse and 200 Firelocks, attacked Astley's rear. The Royalist commander was compelled to stand and fight. He drew up his army on high ground, about 1¾ miles north of Stow-on-the-Wold. Brereton now came up with the remaining soldiers, and the combined army charged Astley. Morgan commanded the central division consisting of approximately 2,000 pikemen, musketeers, and some Horse. Brereton's 800 Horse were on the right wing and the Gloucestershire men formed the left wing. In the initial charge the Parliamentarians drove the Royalist Horse from the field. Regrouping, Brereton's Horse plus some 200 Firelocks attacked again, totally routing the Royalists who remained. They fled back towards Stow, pursued by Morgan and his men. The killing and wounding continued right into the town square. Some 200 Royalists were said to have been killed. Thus was defeated the King's last army in the field. At this point Colonel Fleetwood and some 1,000 Parliamentary Horse appeared. Too late for the battle, but they helped round up the fleeing Royalists. Astley and all his Foot officers were captured, as were 1,600 common soldiers. Many were wounded, and Morgan eventually permitted them to return to their homes upon taking an oath never again to bear arms against Parliament. Dejected, Astley sat on a drum amidst Parliament's victorious officers. "You have done your work," the old man said churlishly, "and may go play, unless you will fall out amongst yourselves." Brereton took Astley as prisoner to London, duly receiving the nation's gratitude.

Brereton was now directed towards Worcester. He, Morgan and Col. John Birch marched the thirty miles to Worcester, arriving there on 26 March. Worcester was held for the King by Colonel Henry Washington (ancestor of a certain George Washington), with a garrison of just over 1,500 men. From Red Hill, to the east of the city, Brereton sent a trumpeter with a summons to Washington to deliver up his charge:

> Gentlemen,
>
> Our tender care and neighbourly affection to your welfare, and care to prevent that ruin that hath fallen upon other places which have obstinately refused good conditions and have had far greater hopes of relief than yourselves (there being now not any appearance of any Army in the west, or elsewhere within this Kingdom but what have submitted to the Parliament, or are already their prisoners) hath moved us to send you this summons, to let you know that you may prevent your houses from spoil, your estates from ruin, your persons from restraint, the effusion of blood, such other miseries as inevitably will fall upon yourselves, your wives and children (if the Lord have so great mercy for you and your city), by timely submitting to the two Houses of Parliament. In whose name we now require this from you, and that you deliver the city and forts into our hands for the use of the King and Parliament, which if you shall do, we shall willingly secure unto you any of your reasonable desires; but in case otherwise, and that misery follows, the cause of it may not be imputed unto those who desire your preservation, not your destruction. And (expecting your speedy answer) rest
>
> Your Servants,
> Willm. Brereton
> Tho. Morgan
> John Birch

March 25th 1646
To the Mayor, Governor,
of Worcester[90]

Governor Washington replied:

Gentlemen,

If the arguments you give us for the delivery of this City and Forts were true, in all likelihood we should (before this time) have received his Majesty's further pleasure. And until we do, we shall take no notice of any summons; but accordingly to our duty and the trust reposed in us we shall (God willing) keep this town.

Your Servants
Hen. Washington
Willm. Evett, Mayor
MartinSandys
John Knotsford
Tho. Hackett
Rich. Hemming

Worcester, this 26th of March 1646
For Sir William Brereton
Col. Morgan, and
Col. Birch.

Brereton wrote once more to Washington:

Gentlemen,

We know no cause you should question the truth of our intelligence, which we assure you is in every part thereof most true, and therefore to the end you may more fully inform yourselves therein, We will draw our Forces to such a convenient distance as that you may gain more certain Intelligence; and then we cannot doubt but that you will better understand yourselves, which if it be done within a few days you may expect the performance of what was tendered; if otherwise, whatever misery befalls your city must be inputed to your selves, and not to your Servants,

Willm. Brereton
Tho. Morgan
John Birch
William Lygon
Chudley Coote

To the Governor, Mayor
Aldermen and Citizens
of Worcester

In accordance with his promise, Brereton drew off his men, and marched to Droitwich. The next day he received orders to proceed to Lichfield. Washington then sent a messenger to Oxford, to speak to the King. Henry Townsend, a citizen of Worcester at the time, wrote in his diary:

28 [March] They marched away from Droitwich, Sir William Brereton, to the siege of Lichfield with some forces.[91]

This narrative now temporarily ends, and is taken up by Sir William's Letter Book which covers the two months of April and May 1646. But first, some details of siege warfare, which plays such an important part in the Letter Book.

2
Siege Warfare

The Brereton Letter Book is primarily concerned with siege warfare. While the siege lacks the glamour of a pitched battle, it too is a form of battle. It is a clash of strength, with a winner and a loser. At the outbreak of the Civil War, England lacked expertise in fortification and siege-craft. Its most modern fortifications, as at Southsea and Hull, dated from the Renaissance. On the Continent the Thirty Years War had brought about great innovations in fortifications to combat the mobile siege gun. The Dutch, while using the Renaissance-style fort, built their fortifications of earth. It was cheaper, easier, and quicker to erect, but more importantly it absorbed artillery fire. A cannon ball striking stone would shatter the masonry, sending death-dealing pieces like so much shrapnel, over a wide area. With palisades planted, and ditches dug, the earthworks were as formidable as any stone wall.

Continental engineers like Bernard de Gomme and John Dalbier were at a premium at the outbreak of the war, but gradually English and Scottish veterans of the European war returned with some knowledge of siege-craft. To aid them, handbooks were produced such as *The Art of Warre,* written by John Cruso. This book not only detailed the construction of fortifications, but also the best way to assault and capture them.

The Siege

As to an assault upon an enemy garrison, the besiegers began by digging a fortified position in order to defend themselves from sorties by the enemy within, or attacks by a relieving force. Gradually trenches and breastworks were constructed along what was called the "line of circumvallation." This was basically an encircling trench. An inner system of surrounding trenches known as the "line of Countervallation" was now dug. The besiegers were now secure (or as secure as they were ever likely to be), from attack from both the besieged and any relieving force. The besiegers now began constructing redoubts (small square earthworks enclosed on all sides) and from them cut zig-zag trenches towards the fortress. The idea of a zig-zag rather than a straight line was that if the enemy got into the trench their fire power only extended towards the next angle and no further.

Artillery

Meanwhile the gunners erected batteries. Earth-filled wicker baskets, or gabions, were set up to form a protective screen around siege pieces. The most common siege cannons were the demi-cannon and the culverin. The guns were grouped into batteries and placed anywhere between 200 and 500 yards from the enemy defenses. The list below gives the type of cannon available, its range and weight of ball.

	Weight of shot	*Caliber*	*Weight of Charge*	*Weight of Piece*	*Maximum Range*
Cannon Royal	63 lbs.	8 ins.	40 lbs.	71½ cwt	1500 yards
Cannon	47 lbs.	7 ins.	34 lbs.	62 cwt	1740 yards
Demi-Cannon	27 lbs.	6 ins.	25 lbs.	53½ cwt	1600 yards
Culverin	15 lbs.	5 ins.	18 lbs.	41 cwt	2000 yards
Demi-Culverin	9 lbs.	4½ ins.	9 lbs.	22½ cwt	1800 yards
Saker	6 lbs.	3½ ins.	6 lbs.	—	1760 yards
Falcon	2 lbs.	3 ins.	2 lbs.	—	1500 yards
Robinet	1 lb.	1¼ ins.	1 lb.	—	1000 yards

The smaller pieces of artillery, Falcon and Robinet would not have been effective as siege pieces, and would have been considered as anti-personnel weapons.

Even more feared than the siege canons was the mortar. Lord Chesterfield surrendered Lichfield Close to Parliament before the mortar which Sir John Gell had with him, was even fired. As with the canon, mortars varied in size as did their bomb, or "granado." The bomb was a cast iron sphere (about ¾ inches thick), packed with powder. It might vary from 12 inches in diameter (as supplied to the New Model Army), to nearly 15 inches (as used by Cromwell at the siege of Pontefract Castle). In weight the granado might vary from 500 lbs. up to 2 cwt. (as used by Ireton against Limerick). Use of the mortar greatly demoralized the defenders by its power of fire and destruction, as narrated by the diarist during Brereton's siege of Chester.

Another method of breaching the defenders' walls was by mining underneath them and blowing them up. If the defenders heard the besiegers tunneling underneath them they would counter-mine and destroy the enemy's tunnel. A breach having been made, the assault force charged from their

Top: A culverin, as shown here, fired an iron ball, 15 lb. in weight. ***Bottom:*** More feared than the cannon, was the mortar. When its bomb exploded, it shattered into deadly shards of iron.

trenches across open ground and to the breach. If the besieged place was defended by a ditch, wood was collected into faggots and thrown into the ditch to enable the besiegers to cross, and enter the town.

The besieged could now expect no mercy, for under the accepted rules of war no quarter was given when a place was stormed. This was thankfully very rare during the Civil War in England. Pillage was inevitable.

The principle sieges that occur in Brereton's Letter Book were at Dudley and Tutbury Castles, and the Cathedral Close at Lichfield.

Dudley Castle

Dudley Castle dates from the twelfth century. In 1530 it was rebuilt as a Renaissance palace by John Dudley. Prior to the outbreak of the Civil War, in late August 1642, it was seized for the King by Colonel Thomas Leveson, formerly a prosperous merchant from Wolverhampton. The event is recorded in a pamphlet published in London on 1 September:

> News is come out of Staffordshire that some Gentlemen have possessed Dudley Castle, and there is many Collyers and Naylors are come into them, and day and night they beat their Drums, and shoote off their musquetts, to the great terrour of the Countrey. They have taken some Iron-workes of Master Folies, where it is said they are casting of Ordnance, and making Iron Bullets.[1]

The castle formed a line of Royalist garrisons stretching from Worcester to Lichfield, effectively giving control of the West Midlands to the King. From Dudley, Leveson's men raided the surrounding countryside, and levied taxes for the upkeep of the garrison. In December 1643 Leveson, in an attempt at preventing Aston Hall from falling into Parliamentary hands, put 40 musketeers into Sir Thomas Holte's house, three miles north of Birmingham. The townsmen in Birmingham appealed to Coventry for assistance. Colonel Boswell and 800 Horse and Foot, along with some small field pieces, were sent to dislodge the Royalists, which they successfully accomplished on 26 December. At the beginning of February 1644, Leveson launched a night-time raid on Birmingham. Under the command of Sergeant-Major Henningham a party of 400 Horse and Foot marched from Dudley at about 11 o'clock at night. They surrounded the town, then keeping the townspeople in their houses, plundered the town at will. In response, in June 1644, a Parliamentary force commanded by the Earl of Denbigh, assisted by Sir Thomas Middleton and Colonel Mytton, besieged Dudley for three weeks, until the siege was raised by Lord Wilmot and the Earl of Northampton, with an army of one brigade of Horse and 1,000 Foot.

On 26 April 1646, Brereton renewed the siege. He had with him the Warwickshire and Leicestershire regiments of Horse, and the Staffordshire and Shropshire Regiments of Foot. At 11 A.M. the Parliamentary forces secured the town with a loss to themselves of just two troopers killed. As they retreated into the castle, the Royalists set fire to a number of houses in the town. These fires were put out and Brereton over the next few days created walls and breastworks of stone from the nearby church, torn down by Leveson's orders. The ruined Priory, adjacent to the castle, was seized by Brereton's men and fortified. As the troopers worked at their breastworks, the Royalists surged out of the castle in numbers and surprised the unprepared Parliamentarians. However, seeing the assault, Parliamentary troopers rushed to their comrades' aid, driving the Royalists back into the castle. Under a parley, Brereton sent in a summons for the surrender of the castle. Leveson requested that he be allowed to send a man to Oxford to speak to the King. Brereton readily agreed. On 5 May, still without a reply from Oxford, Leveson requested to send another messenger to the King. This time Brereton refused. Oxford, he told Leveson, was now under siege, and he could expect no help from there. Brereton demanded a positive response to his summons to surrender. Leveson agreed to discuss terms, and hostilities were suspended. On 10 May articles for the surrender were agreed upon, and on 13 May the castle was given up. A considerable amount of munitions and provisions were found within the castle. Of the surrender of Dudley, and other Royalist garrisons, Henry Townsend in Worcester was scathing. In his diary for 21 May he wrote:

> There were never 4 such Governors as Sir Michael Woodhouse of Ludlow, Col. Luseen of Dudley, Capt. William Sandys of Hartlebury, and Capt. Edward Ashton of Madresfield, which delivered up traitorously, cowardly, and basely 4 such strongholds, so poorly, so treacherously; places that the weakest would withstand against an Army (as they themselves confessed) for a quarter of a year. And some 3 of them an age if victuals would have lasted and ammunition.[2]

The true reality of the situation, confirming Townsend's assertion, is revealed in a Parliamentary letter which indicates that "the castle was yielded without any shott of the Parliament."[3]

Tutbury Castle

At the outbreak of the Civil War, Tutbury Castle in Staffordshire, was garrisoned for the King by General Hastings. Hastings proved to be an active soldier, drawing a response from Parliament in 1643, with a siege of the castle. Dissention within the Parliamentary ranks led to it being abandoned, but

Parliament established a garrison nearby at Barton Blount, to prevent Hastings from acting as freely as he had previously. Hastings was later replaced as Governor by Sir Andrew Kniveton. With the defeat of the King at Naseby, and Astley at Stow, the Parliamentary authorities now concentrated on the King's remaining garrisons. On 30 March 1646, Brereton began a second siege at Tutbury. Repeated sallies were made to disrupt the Parliamentarians before they could perfect their encirclement, but in the end it was futile. After three weeks, and with all hopes dashed of any relief coming from the King, Kniveton, in order to avoid further loss of life, agreed to surrender. Conditions of surrender were signed on 30 April 1646.

Lichfield Close

Lichfield Cathedral Close was besieged three times during the Civil War. At the outbreak of the war the Close was seized by the Earl of Chesterfield and Sir Richard Dyott, and garrisoned for the King. Other local gentlemen and townsmen joined them. Preparations were made in early 1643 to fortify the Close, with additional walls and bastions. The gates were given double wooden doors, portcullises, and drawbridges were erected. In addition trenches were begun. On 2 March 1643 Parliamentary forces under Lord Brooke assaulted the Close with a fierce bombardment. After three days, Brooke being killed during the siege, the Close was surrendered to Brooke's replacement, Sir John Gell. The Close was now garrisoned for Parliament with Lieutenant-Colonel Russell as Governor. The King's response was immediate. He dispatched Prince Rupert to retake the Close. Rupert arrived before Lichfield on 6 April, having fired the town of Birmingham along the way, Two days later, on 8 April, Rupert summoned the garrison to surrender. Being refused, Prince Rupert opened up with his canon, eventually creating a breach in the wall. An assault was launched, but repulsed with heavy losses. Rupert then drained the moat, and undermined the walls in four places. On 13 April, the fourth mine was sprung, destroying a tower, and creating a breach wherein six men might enter abreast. The Royalists poured in; one hundred defenders were killed, before Russell surrendered his charge. The remnants of the defeated garrison were allowed to march away to the Parliamentary garrison at Coventry.

The third siege, conducted by Sir William Brereton, lasted from March to July 1646. It was a very destructive siege in which the central spire of the cathedral was destroyed. Garrison commander, Sir Thomas Tyldesley, refused to surrender without the King's permission. The King, then in the hands of the Scots, wrote from Newcastle on 10 June 1646:

Charles R.

Having resolved to comply with the desires of our Parliament in everything which may be for the good of our subjects, and leave no means unassayed for removing all differences amongst us, therefore we have thought it fit the more evidence the reality of our Intentions of settling a happy firm peace To require you, upon Honourable Terms, to quit those Towns, Castles and Forts entrusted to you by us, and to disband all the forces under several commands. To our trusty and well beloved Sir Tho. Glenham, Sir Tho. Tyldesley, Col. H. Washington, Governors of our cities and garrisons of Oxford, Lichfield and Worcester, and all other commanders of any of our towns, Castles and Forts in our kingdom of England.[4]

3

The Letter Book of Sir William Brereton

The letter book is transcribed in its entirety in this chapter. Manuscript page numbers are included in the text, and the table of contents below refers to the manuscript page on which the item can be found. "Itm" is an abbreviation for "item," meaning a listing.

INDEX OF SUCH LETTERS AND OTHER PASSAGES CONTEYNED IN THIS BOOKE WHICH PASSED IN THE TYME OF THE LEAUGER BEFORE DUDLEY CASTLE AND TUTBURIE CASTLE & LITCHFIELD CLOSE BEGINNING THE 4TH APRIL 1646 AND ENDING THE [29 May 1646].

1

An Ordinance for Setling of the Government
Of ye Cittie of Chester.

Whereas ye Cittie of Chester hath beene from ye beginning of these unnaturall Warres under ye power of [the] Enemy and many Aldermen Sheriffes Peeres & Comon Councell men of ye sayd Cittie have taken upp Armes and otherwise beene violent Fomenters of these unnaturall Warres against Parliament And ye Cittie seeing now by ye Providence of God Reduced into ye Custodie of ye Parliament The Lords and Comons Assembled in Parliam:t Beeing informed by Divers well affected persons of ye sayd Cittie that Charles Walley Mayor of ye sd. Cittie and Sheriffe of ye same Cittie, Nicholas Ince, Randle Holme ye Elder, Randle Holme ye younger, Tho: Cooper, Tho: Chr---,[1] Will:m Ince, Sr. Tho: Smithe, ffrancis Gamull and Robt Brirewood, Recorder, Aldermen and Justices of ye peace: James Earle of Derby, John, Earle Rivers, Rich: Aroster & Tho: Savage Aldermen: Humphrie Phillips, Tho. Mattershead, Edw: Hutton, Wm. Whittle, Rich: Wright, Humphrie Lloyd, Rich: Taylor, Willm. Sutton & Arthur Walley, Sherriffs, Peere and Comon Councell men of ye sd. Cittie shall bee Removed & Discharged And hereby are Removed and discharged from theire Respective places of Mayor, Recorder, Sherrifes, Aldermen, Justices of ye peace, Sherrifes, peer, and Comon Councell of ye said Cittie and of any Assembly or publique meeting of ye same with ye Mayor, Aldermen, Sherrifes and Comon Councell. And as further Ordayned yt such other gvt of ye Aldermen, Sherrifes, Peeres and Comon Councell men who have taken up Armes or bene imployde agst. Ye Parliament shall be Removed and Discharged Severally from beeing Justices of ye, and Comon Councell Men of, ye sd Cittie or of any other publique meetinge as aforesaid. And bee itt Ordained yt: ------[2] shall bee Mayor for ye Cittie of Chester For ye yeare Ensueing Untill ye usuall tyme for Electing a new mayor according to ye Charter of ye sd. Cittie at yt. Ye sd. Mayor shall Call an Assembly of ye Aldermen, Comon Councell and Free Cittizens and there ye sayd Mayor shall take ye Severall Oathes wch usually ye mayor of yt. Cittie takes. And ye sd. Mayor having taken such oathes, Hee shall with advise of ye Assembly Ansring to ye Ancient Customs of ye sd. Cittie nominate and Elect five Sherrifs from ye sayde Cittie And ye Mayor shall give them ye usuall Oath wch ye Sherriffes there doe take and ye sd Mayor and assembly of aldermen and Comon Councell shall either ye same day or at some convenient tyme after Elect and make Choyce of Aldermen and Comon Councell men to make upp ye number of 24 Aldermen and 4 of ye Comon Counc:ll whereof ye sherrifs peeres are within ye Number of ye Comon Councell According to ye Charter of ye sd. Cittie and alsoe Elect and make Choyce of the jurors Corners Leavelookers and such officers and members as are usually chosen according to ye Cittisones and ye Charter of ye sd. Cittie and ye sd Mayor shall from tyme to time as duration shall require, Call and appointe Assemblies According to ye usage and Customs of ye sd. Cittie and Charter thereof. And ye Sd Mayor and Sherrifes shall keepe their several Courts at ye usuall-tymes. And bee it further Ordered and Ordeyned yt. Such free Cittizens of ye sd. Cittie who have beene Expelled ye sd Cittie, or been cautioned to depart thence by reason of their good affection to ye Parliament and Kingdoms shall bee, and are hereby restored to all such places, offices and privileges wch formerly they held and enjoyed wthin ye sd. Cittie any act of assembly declaration or order in ye sayd Cittie to ye Contrary notwithstanding: and it is further ordered & ordained yt such Iriesh and others as have beene made free of ye d Cittie while it was yet in Hostillitie agst. Ye Parliam:tt and have noe right there unto birth or service made, shall be and are herby disfranchised and shall not for themselves nor for their posterity have any benefit or priveled thereby. And it is Lastly ordered by ye Authority aforesaide for discoverie of other Aldermen, Sherrifes, Peeres and Comon Councell men: who have bene unyloyed agst ye Parliament and are not Expressed by name in this Ordinary & discharged and removed herby from their Respective place ye Mayor of ye sd Cittie for ye tyme being Sr. Willm. Brereton Barron:tt, Michael Jones Esqr., Robert Wright, Calven Bruen, Edw: Bradshaw, Rich: Bradshaw, Robt: Gregg, John Whittle, Willm. Compton, Rich: Golborne, Samuell Ratcliffe, Wm. Edw: Junior, Peter Leigh, John Harvey, John Wyn, sam: Bucke & Jefery Mallor, Citizen of ye sd. Cittie & or more of them shall bee and are hereby made a Committee for ye sd. Cittie of Chester and ye Countie of ye sayd Cittie and shall have as full power to put all ordinances of Parlt. On Execution within ye sd. Cittie and ye Countie of ye Sd. Cittie of Chester as is graunted by any ordnance unto ye Committee of ye Countie of Chester and ye sd. Committee shall Examine the miscarage of ye sayd Aldermen, Sherrifs, Peeres and Comon Councell as have taken upp Armes or been Vyolent Agents and imployed agst. Ye Parliam:t And to remove and discharge from their Respective places of Aldermen, justices of ye peace, Sherrifes, Peeres and Comon Councell and ye sd. Committee or any & or more of them have herby Authority from tyme to time to administer all such oathes and covenants to ye Inhabitants & others of ye sayd Cittie as are or shall bee apointed to bee taken by any orders or ordinance of both or Either howses of Parliam:t portrayed in this Ordinance nor anything therein Conteyned shall for tyme to come prejudice ye Charter of ye sd. Cittie nor any of ye Ancient Privilages, Liberties and Imunities thereof.

3

For Sr. Willm Brereton: Letter from ye Comittie of Both Kingdomes beefore Newarke touching ye Sumoning of Newarke

Sir,

Wee have received yors of ye 31st of March last and returne you thankes for ye Intelligence: For our Affaires in these parts they stand thus, On Saturday last wee sent Sumons into Newarke to which they returned an Answer. The Copie Whereof wee send you inclosed. And since they refuse ye Mercie offered them thereby wee shall Endeavor by such other Meanes as God and ye Parliam:t have put into our handes to reduce ye same. And I hope in a short tyme to give a Good Accompt thereof To which end Collonell Generall Points[3] hath dammd up an Arme of the River Trent yt rann close by Newarke and is turning ye course of ye river Smite into another Channell Wherby to make their Milles unisexual to them. The Scotts have lately taken a Sandie fforte from ye Enimy wch they had Built in ye Island within musquett shot of ye Castell Soe yt ye Northsyde of ye Towne by wch ye River rann. Having noe flanckers and ye Houses standing verrie close thereon will bee verie easye for attempt. And one ye South side wee are to beeginne our Approaches on Munday next that Syde of ye Towne beeing soe verrie strongly and soe regularly fortified yt ye Horse may ryde Tenn a Breast round ye line. The plague in ye Towne in many places wch will some what add to their other discouragements wee pray God add a Blessing to our Endeavours and to ye in yr Heartie prayers of

Yor Assured loving ffrende &
Servants

From Collonell Rosseters
Quarters att Balderton
This 4th Aprill
1646

Rutland
Edw. Monntagu[4]
W. Peerpointe Mr Wyn
Tho: Hatcher
Edw. Syswyche

The Earls of Dunfermline & Louthane, ye Lo: Balcaries, Sr. Tho: Ruthven, Sr. Tho: Kerr, Sr. David Hume, Mr. Glendoning & Mr Johnson, Com:rs of ye Parliam:t of Scotland came to Southwell on Fryday last and some of them have since beene with us at Lincolne.

4

A Sumons sent into Newarke by ye
Committee of both Kingdomes

Wee ye Committee of both Kingdomes beeing sent and Authorised to use our best Endeavours for reducing ye Towne and garrison of Newarke, doe Hereby in ye name of both Houses of ye Parliam:t of England and for the use of ye king and Parliam:t Demand of you yt you forthw:th surrender ye same into their hands. It is ye pious care of ye Parliament to prevent ye Effusion of C[h]ristean Blood, ye Wastening of ye Countrie and ye Distruction of Townes. Wee shall Esteeme our selves Happie in being Instrum:tl to avert those miseries and shall therefore to you ye Gent with you and ye Towne Honorable and faire Conditions wch if you shall now neglect And will lett noething but Experimentall Sufferings Declare unto you yor unavoidable Ruyne. You are to give an Accompt to God, to this press:tt age and to posteritie, for all ye Blood shall from henceforth bee shedd for ye wasting yor Native and neighbouring countries and distruction of soe considerabl a place you may not, nor can any in reason Expect and most Assuredly and on ye faith of honest men you shall not hereafter obtaine from us such tearmes as wee are now willing to affoard you. Wee sent noe summons untill you and all with you might see wee were able by force to attaine what wee much rather desire by Treatie. Ye Parliam:t have 16,000 Horse and foote at rest before yor towne. Soldiers of Experience, united and in health and Courage. This noe way menconed as if wee trusted in ye Arme of flesh, God ye Lo[rd] of Hosts have manifested yt wee fight his Battells. But to shew you ye vast Expences wch will be occasioned by ye Continuance of this Seige for wch yor Estates must answer and yt yor holdeing out may not further tempt ye Almighty and through you should not regard yor owne Ruyne, though some others should bee of yt yor opinion shall yet yt Welthye towne bee saved, and others perish with you yt see theire owne Miserye and would avoyde it. A prudent man a souldier cannot live or dye in reputacon or peace of Spirit to maintaine a place not soe longe tenable as till it can be redeemed of wch you cannot have ye least Hope. If eather not yor selves, reliefe is not to bee had. Chester was nearer succour and considerable Armies for them in ye West and in Wales now searse to bee seene. What remaines of Either. Was not ye stronge Citty of most greate importance were they not verrie often promised — did not all assurance to bee rescued come to them: they had none. That place is Surrendered. Yor Wealth if you rightly consider in what state you are proves yor Certain and sudden distruction. You are prepare in some things for defence, yet you knowe and wee knowe you are not for some other. Consider these things seriously, and you Cannot but through them see yor Ruyne to bee inevitable. If you doe not avoyde it by accepting what is now offered: Wee will Expect yor Answer on Monday next by 11 of ye clocke in ye forenoone att Balderton

Balderton 28 Marty
1646

Signed in ye name and by ye
Warr:tt of ye Comittie of both kingdomes
Rutland : Lothian

For ye Governor of ye Towne and
Garrison of Newarke, ye Gent. There
And ye Mayor, Aldermen and
Burgesses of ye towne

5

The Answ: to ye Sumons
Sent into Newarke by ye
Committee of both Kingdomes

Having received a paper subscribed by ye Committee of both Kingdomes directed to a Committee Governor, by putting ye Gentlmen and Corporacon in Equall comicon with mee through ye joyneing together, was with ye intencon to divide up, I shall in answere thereof desire you to reflect upon ye Kings letter of ye 23rd of March, sent to ye 2 howses of Parliament, wch I received from yor owne Quarters wherein a full complim:t with all their desires upon ye Most gracious conditions yt Ever a Prince propounded hee offers to disband his force and dismantle his Garrisons, to what End then doe you demand yt of ye Steward, wherof ye Lord and Maister makes a voluntarie Tender. I conceive it my Dutye to trace his Comands, not to outstrip them, soe that though honor and conscience would peermit ye deliverie of them, yet Civilitie would retard it, least his Majesties Act of grace be frustrated by my over hastie speed, I shall wave ye Arguments where with you Endeavour to evince my concent. I am neither to bee stroaked into dyostacie by yr mencon of faire condicons in a mistie notion, nor to bee frighted into dishonor by running devision upon ye fate of Chester, for as I doe not measure my Allegiance by my mistrost for ye former, soe I doe disdane yr povertie of spirit as by resemblance of Chester to suffer by example I can bee Loyall without yt Copie And I hope this Garrison shall never bee ye Transcript of theire calamitie, you may doe well to use yor fortune modestly and thinke not that God Almighty doe upplaude yor Cause by reason of yor Victories or yt hee hath not a blessing in store for ours. Wheras you urge ye expence of a seidge and ye pressures of ye Countrie in supporting e yor charge (since occasioned by yor selves) I am not concernd, yett in order to theire ease if you will graunt a pass for some Gent. To goe to ye king and returne I may then knowe his majesties pleasure whether according to his letter hee will winde upp ye busines in Generall or leave mee to steere my owne Course, then I shall knowe what to determine otherwise I desire you to take notice yt when I received my Comission for ye Government of this place I annexed my life as labell to my trust.

Newarke 31 Marty J. Belasisse[5]
1646

To ye Committee of both kingdomes

6

Letter from ye Deputie Lts & Committee
of Chester to Sr. William Brereton
touching Capt. Cleggs Company

Sr,

Wee have used our utmost Endeavors concerning ye March of Capt. Cleggs Companie and soe hath hee likewise, We have borrowed and ye soldiers one months pay. But cannot pay them any more. Neither will they march unless they have ye months pay p'mised upon surrender of ye Cittie. We therefore are necessitated to desire you to take course there for ye satisfying of yt Engagem't Accordeing to yor p'mise, soe you may have them readie to bee comaunded and obey yor orders wch otherwise will not (for anything wee are able to doe att press't) and soe leaveing it to yor consideracon wee humbly take leave and rest Remaining

Readie to bee comanded by
you to our power

Chester 4th Ap'll
1646

Hen: Brooke
Tho: Stanley
Phi: Manwaring
Edw: Hyde : Rog: Wilbraham
John Bruen : Jo: Wiknhall
James Garfsyde

Lett'r from Leveson Governor of Dudley
Castell sent to Sr. Tho: Tildesley,[6] Governor
Of Litchfield Close intercepted and sent
By Capt Tuthill to Sr. Willm. Brereton

Ever honoured Sr,

I have att this tyme received a Letter under Collonell Levesons hand directed to ye Governor of ye Close, ye orriginall I keepe till yor returne, beeing goeing to show it to ye Committee. Ye Letter follow'th.

Sr,

Cpll Devalleere is this day Come to Worcester with letter from ye king to ye Governor, Mayor and ye rest of ye Cittie to lett them understand yt Mountross is now in Westmoreland and Cumberland, wch Countries wholly rise with them and yt they are marching to joyne with ye Scots Armye aboute & before Newarke, who are come into ye King: SR I am ye rather induced to believe by reason thers a sudden press by ye Parliam't in all ye townes hereaboute us and yt I heare all theire Littl Garrisons about us to be sleighted. I have sent one other letter to ye same effect hopeing one or both will come to yor hands.

Tho: Leveson[7]

Sr This is all yt I have to pr'ss'tt into yor Honor for ye pr'ssentt. Yor Honor to ye utmost of my power

Robt. Tuthill

Munday 6th of Apll 1646
Past 6; in ye afternoone

7

Lett'r to Mr Ashurst & Mr Swinfen[8]
touching supplye of Moneye to ye Army

Sr,

Touchinge ye state of affaires in these partes you will receive an accompt att large by Coll: Bowyer, Mr Vernon and Andrew Miler, who all went from Tutburye on Tuesday last whence my selfe alsoe after I had setled ye Leaguer there, went, and am now returned back to ye Leaguer att Lichfield where wee are in verrie good forwardnes with our worckes and have not only erected severall mounts and sconces on each side. But if Pyoneeres come in shall finish our trench from mount to mounte and from ye Waren to ye water rounde aboute ye Close at a verrie neere distance soe as it will bee impossible for any to escape our masterpieces. Granadoes are also in as good forwardnes to bee played and now I am preparing a summons to send in within a day or two, wch I have forborne ye longer to ye End ye enemy may first bee ye more sensible of ye improbabilitie of releife and of escaping and if I receave not a satisfactory Answer, to pr'ceed to use of all meanes possible to reduce them otherwise. The Chester men are now come upp to ye number of 700 and are verrie willing to doe service. But I feare unless speedily prevented by supply of money, there may bee an evill president given, for those yt came upp first beginn to murmer and threaten to goe home if they receave not money. Money speedily, for they must have non oute of theire owne County for the service they doe here. I have here inclosed set a letter to ye Comittie of both Kingdomes to bee delivered if you think fitt and yt it mat availe for ye encurragmt of those who were in ye last Battell if our soldiers might receave ye encourage of some certaine constant pay it would much enable and encourage us not onely to carrie on this worke and yt agst Tutbury, but likewise the designe agst Dudley & Worcester wch service shalbe by noe man more endeavoured themn myself who am and will always remane

Yor Verrie faithful friend
to serve you
Willm. Brereton

Lichfield Apll 11th 1646

8

Letter to ye Committee of both Kingdomes
touching money for ye Horse for ye feight
at Stowe[9]

My Lords and Gent,

I am given to understand yt after such tyme as it pleased god to make us successful at ye Battell att Stowe, the Parliam't for encouragement of our Officers and soldiers was pleased to appointe ye sume of 6000L to bee distributed amongst them. This hath given mee the humble boldness to offer to yor honors Consideracon ye services done yt day amongst others by yor Warwicksh're, leisters're & Darbysh're Horse who to bee impartiall and speake sparingly, performed their parts with ye best. My humble request in theire behalf is yt yor Honors would bee pleased to proportion them such pay thereof as may bee suitable to theire number. Whereof I have sent a list by this bearer, Mr Swinfen, whereby yor honors may much encourage them and engage him who shall always approve himself,

Yor honors most faithfull &
most humble serv't
Willm: Brereton

Lichfield Apll 11th
1646

9

Letter to Mr Ashurst &
Mr Swinfen

Srs,

The inclosed will imparte unto you what ye soldiers here may expect out of Chester. And impossible it is obtaine soldiers to continue upon service w'thout money: Those that came first are not without cause impatient as may appeare by theire peticon. Capt. Clegg and Capt. Walleys men are in Chester but will not march without money. Had I not for ye Parliam'ts advantage husbanded ye last money sent downe as well to draw on and encourage ye soldiers to ye service as to discharge part of ye engagement of ye Chester Gent. there had beene noe Seige maintained here. I am sending to Coventrie upon my owne creditt to take upp some money upon bond wch I cannot doubt by ye Parliam't will consider, for you know well theire was 6000L ordered for this service and ye enimys strength and obstinaciousnes in ye Close wherein these are acknowledged to bee more then 1000 feighting men enlisted requires a suitable strength to bee appled to reduce them. This 6000L is otherwise disposed of but I cannot doubt yt ye Parliam't will bee wanting to make necesarie supplyes for us, who I hope may without abstention and offence affirme yt whr they have allowed my forces from the begininge of these Warres to ye end, hath not exceeded, nay I believe not Equalled yt chardge of yor traine of artillarie whereof alsoe wee have not beene unprovided nor unserviceable and unsuccessfull, Through God's blessing in ye use thereof, as I alsoe ye chardge of Newarke hath more then doubled ye chardge of Chester, and yett unreduced, and Banburye hath (ye tyme considered) cost you much more then double what Lichfield hath, and yett I beleeve they are much stronger in Lichfield then Banburye. These considered I cannot doubt but wee shalbee provided for and yt ye Horse who were with mee att Stowe Battell may p'take proportionably with ye rest, otherwise seeing they performed as good if not better service as ye rest, Dissaremeing and laying them asside might bee imputed rather to their misfortune in beeing under my Comand then to theire undeserving wch I am not willing to beeleave and have therefore ordered Mr Wirrall to take care of and convey downe what is appointed for them. I have appointed him to observe yor orders and desire yor assistance whereby you shall much engage

Yor Most faithful friend to
serve you
Willm. Brereton

Lichfield Apll. 11th
1646

10

A Copie of a peticon by Capt. Boothes[10]
& Captaine Leadbeaters Companies to
Sr. Willm. Brereton for Money

To ye Honorable Sr. Willm. Brereton, Generall

The Humble peticon of ye soldiers of Capt. Anthony Boothes and Capt. Leadbeaters Company now in ye Leauger att Lichfield Humbly Shewinge,

That whereas formerly yor peticoners had maisters from whom they received due pay according to the service they p'formed and now are is they understand by ye Committee in Chester taken from them and debarred yt privilidge, M. soe much yt now they knowe not where to demande one pennie, wch makes them bold to crave yor Honors Consideracon and loving assistance to yor Service, in this meane Condicon they are as unwilling to leave this Service or gain yor Displeasure as to loose themselves. Although in regarde of ye family charges manie of them bee tyde to mainetaine, they are forced to lett yor Honor knowe yt without a press'tt supplye of money they shall bee constrained to leave ye Service and Leauger, Whereof they beeing soe unwilling.

Humbly Intreat yor Honor as they have served you in love hitherto soe they may still Continue in ye same, And for ye press'tt Either receave pay here for theire late service, and an Assurance of itt for ye future, or ells a fuee Discharge according to theire voluntarie willingnes

And Yor Petitioners shall Ever praye

11

For ye Honorable Sr Willm. Brereton
A Letter from ye Committee of Salop:
Touching

Honorable Sr,

Wee returne yor many thanckes for sending yor messinger to give us notice of yor comeing to us. If yor more weightie affaires had not enforced you Backe, wee are (Blessed bee God) in good Condicon before this place, our Ordnance readie to play and wee doubt not but in shorte space wee shall be able to give both yourself and ye rest of our friends a good accompt of our Busines here. Wee returne thanckes for ye sending backe of our Horse to us who came verrie seasonably to ye assistance of our friends who have now fortifyed themselves w'thin a mile or less of Ludlow. Wee shall Communicate our affaires to you from tyme as occation shall bee offered us and shalbee glad to have ye like correspondencies may bee from you for wch as for all other labours we shalbee readie to approve our selves

Yor Humble servants
And: Lloyd
Robt; Harlston

Bridgnorth 10th of
Ap.ll 1646

Letter from Sr. Tho: Leigh
to Coll. Georg Booth[11] out of
Lichfield Close

Dear Cozin,

I receaved yor letter with as much affection as you writt of & wisht yt you had exprest it upon some other occasion wherin I might have mett you in yor desires. My beeing here was not accidental, beeing ever resolved not to avoyde any danger yt may happen either to my p'son or estate. I should bee verrie unfortunate yt any action or oppinion (But this) should ruyne as you Imagine our family, And happie yt all I have might bee a sacrifice for him who may or should comand all, upon this resource my Endeavors have beene Grounded, and I am Confident ye foundation is soe Rockye yt it's Imoveable, However I confess my self Infinitely obliged to you, and desire I were in a

Condicon to serve you. I did apprehend some danger of my ladies health when I heard yt one Mr Booth, of myne as hee sayd, had taken those things from my house wch my ladie had Intrusted mee with, but beeing Assured from you of her sicknes I am beyond expression greeved yt I cannot wayt upon her. I shall desire you when either write or send towards her, to present my most humble duty

Sr Yor verrie humble servantt &
affectionate kinsman
Tho: Leigh

Lichfield Close Apll. 9
1646

If you will mediate for a passe
For my wife to go to Ridware, She
Beeing not well, will oblige us both

12

Letter from Sr Willm. Brereton
to Sr Rich: Skefingham[12] touching
takeing upp of Money upon Bond

Sr,

That you may not thincke strange of ye carriage of busines att Tutbury the other day, I thought good to give you this shorte accompt of itt. That Sr John Gell after hee was by mee much charged to declare & p'duce what authoritie or comand hee had receaved from ye Parliam't for treating and concluding of any Articles with ye Enimy in Tutbury did after much waveing and shifting, fullie acknoweledge hee had received noe orders or comicon for yt purpose in writinge, But onely verball, yet had hee Treated and Concluded with them upon ye Strangest & most dishonourable Articles yt I have seene. I have sent you a copie of them—bearer Mr Hynde, whom I have sent again to you aboute ye moneye I have formerly wrote of. Hee can acquainte you with the Discontents and Mutinies of some of our Companies upon ye feild, of some Companies yt are marched parte of ye way and will not advance for want of moneys. Wherfore I desire you yt not onely yt you told of, but as much more as possiblye you cane may bee readie, and next weeke I shall come myselfe and bring some others wth mee, to take such Corse aboute it as shall give Content. Yor help and Assistance herein will much advantage our press'tt service here, and further oblige to you

Yor verrie faithful freind &
Brother-in-law
Willm. Brereton

Lichfield Apll. 11th
1646

13

Letter from Sr Peter Wentworth
touching ye Battell at Stowe

Noble Sir,

You have honored wth severall Letters to wch I have returned Answer but have not understood whether you have receaved them or noe. Sr. it is ye joy of my heart yt God hath made you (who I have always soe much honoured) soe great an Instrument of his Glorie, not onely in yor former greate and numerous successes but also in this last soe seasonable and soe compleat a victory neer Stow where you made hast to gaine honor by yor soe long and speedie march thither and great p'sonall Resolucon there, though others have not done you soe faire and full Right in relacons as you have done them, that defect must bee supplyed by those who wd truly honor you and have had a true Narrative of ye Gallantrie of yor currage there. I shall troble you noe further onely most Earnestly recommend unto ye Busines inclosed in this paper concerning one Georg Warner now in Lichfield Close and desire you to beeleave yt I Delight to doe you service wherby it may appeare yt I am; Sr

Yor humble & most affectionat
Servantt
Peter Wentworth

London 30th March
1646

The inclosed paper men coned in ye above
written letter from Sir Peter Wentworth to
Sr Willm. Brereton: touching Geo. Warner
now in Lichfield Close 1646: Apll.

Wheras there is one Geo. Warner of Wolston in ye Countie of Warwicke now in ye Close of Lichfield. I shall desire to advertise you yt hee is a most prodigious and malignant clowne, a Batchelor aboute 80 years old, who by Grasing hath gott 900L p:ann., the Greater part of it lyinge in Northamptonshire, ye rest in Warwickeshire, hee hath almost all his life tyme delighted in suites and therin to Grapple wth his Betters soe noe neighbour can live peaceably by him, But Glories how hee holdes theire noses to ye Grinston: hath Encountred Sr Hen: Yelverton ye Judge, ye Lo: Dunsmore, Sr. Christopher Yelverton & myself and three of us all at once, his aboade before these tymes was at Wolston wthin 4 miles of Coventrie, where I have a mansion Howse but tooke little Delight to live in itt Because yt over growen peasantt lived there and is Lord of ye Manor and a most Desperate Mallignant and hath halfe a Pope and halfe a B'pp in his Bellie having beene always reputed Papist call a Creature of Canterburies, and of Sr. Jo: Lambe and ye like. You may p'haps remember how att ye Begining of this Parliam't hee was on his knees att the Commons Barr and was fined 100L and Comitted to ye Tower for making a false returne of ye Lo: Compton instead of Mr. Comb: hee beeing Sherrif of Warwickesh're at ye beginning of these Warres, hee harboured ye plate of ye University of Oxford in his howse as itt went from Oxford to Yorke to ye King, wherby ye King was first enabled to raise forces since to shew ye rancknes of his malignity hee notwithstanding all his Estate, lyes now Quart'd and his great age and Constant Residence att Waleston Weston hath almost ever since these warres quitted his Habitacon and nested himself in ye Enimys Garrisons att Worcester, Lichfield or else where.

Hee is known to bee a most Bitter Enimy to Parliam't and to his utmost, hath Given assistance to ye Enimy, his Elder Brother is just of ye same making but too decrepitt to Craule out of ye Enimys Quarters. His Elder Brother hath 2 sonnes who depend on Georg theire uncle and are in Armes agst the Parliam't and now are both in Lichfield too. Ye second Will: Warner was furnish wth a Horse for ye Warr by his uncle & was maintained by him agst ye Parliam't and hee gave him 30L, at one hee is a Major of Horse, hee sent aboute 20 of his tenn'tts to Southam to ye Comicon of Array and forced one to goe thither threatening him if hee would not goe.

Sr the things considered I shall desire if fall into yor hands yt you will according to his Demerritt hold him to as hard Meate as you can, itts pittie but that his Estate should bee sold for ye Parliam'ts use. I hope such order will bee taken yt hee shall neaver bee suffered to live att Weston nore to animate his most Malignant tenants, but yt hee shall suffer according to his Demerritt. This Busines I humblye recommend to you & should bee glad to have yor advice how hee may bee p'r'mittd to purpose. You will doe mee a great favor to beestow an Answer upon mee to this Letter & Busines, this Warner is soe Cuning and Corrupt, that if theire bee any means to worcke upon any hee will fynde it out & use itt. I beseech you keep this to yourself and without discovering from whence you had it.

P: Went.

Hee sent his tenn'ts horse to ye
Earl of Northampton[13] to ye Comis'ers
of Array & assisted at ye Seige agst
Coventrie & as I credibly informed
was theer in person.

15

Letter from Mr. Swinfen to
Sr. Willm. Brereton touching:

Honorable Sr,

I desire yor pardon in yt I write not soe often as you may expect for my owne Busines concerning my Ellection doth take upp soe much of my tyme and the house hath sate of late soe much in ye Afternoones yt I have had of late verie little tyme to spare, and ye committee of both kingdomes sitt but once a weeke, or twice att ye most, soe yt I have not got soe quicke dispatch there, of amunicon and such other thing as yt worcke on wch you are requires, But my owne Busines I hope will be Concluded this next weeke, And then I shall be more free to serve you. In ye meane tyme I shall [not] neglect to use my utmost Endeavor in ye several particulars wch you have committed to me by yor Letters. 3,000L of 6,000L is assigned by ye Committee of both Kingdomes, to whom the whole was referred to apportion, And I hope itt will not bee verie longe before it bee borrowed, But in ye meane time I hope these forces wch come from Counties wch are cleared from ye Enimy will have satisfaction from thence to support them from Mutiny. I hope upon ye readings ye letter in ye Howse, wch came last from ye comittee of Stafford, more moneys may be p'cured. But ye Excise is soe deeply Charged and money comes soe heavily yt I desire you will use yor utmost Endeavors there to gett ye respective Counties pay theire forces, I know Warwickeshir pays theirs, and if ye rest would doe soe, ye moneys from hence would well discharge what Extrodinaries ye Countie shall bee put upon for provision or otherwise, and yt is all will bee borne out from hence. I much feare Coll. Jones[14] came to Towne last night. I have not yett seene him nor can heare wht his Busines is, But I will, soe soones as I can. By yor last and ye Copie of Coll. Jones to Major Zanckys,[15] he seemes to d'bate some things of his former heat, and if hee take Entertainem'tt under ye Lo: Lisle, I could wish you did parte fairely. This Evening I was att the Committee of Both Kingdomes with Coll. Bowyer and Mr. Vernon, who related the whole p'ceedings of the Treatie att Tutburie, And the Committee did ill resent the Articles wch Sr Jo: Gell[16] had agreed upon and the manor of his p'ceding for wch hee had noe Order hence that I can heare of. The Orders in that Busines wch are According to yor Desire Collonell will Bring who setts forth tomorrow.

This day a messenger from Exeter brings word ye Articles for ye surrender thereof are signed. The proposicons are not agreed upon yett by ye Scotts to bee sent to the King, nor will bee agreed a long time as I conceave: All yor Hopes there beinge by ye worckes of yor masterpieces I humbly offer it to you yt you bring them as neere as you desire have all matterialls readie, and as many of them as canbee gott. Possiblie you may have that from Belvoire wch shoots 200 lb Bullett, that soe you may Infest them severall p'ts, Espeshallie where they Lodge theire Amunicon and provision. Most att ye Same tyme for otherwise that Grounde is soe large and soe many stronge & Spacious Buildings standing att Distance, one from another yt there will bee securitie from 1 or 2 Granados for ye soldiers and for provisions. I have [no] more to add at press'tt, But I am

Yor Assured Servant
Jo: Swinfen

Aprill 10th 1646

16

Letter from Major Snowe to Sr Willm. Brereton
Touching Release of prisoners menconed in a
Letter from Capt. Rodes & alsoe touching ye
Castell of Tutburie[17]

Worthy Sr,

I have received yor Letter & Orders and God willing will Endeavor my best in p'formeing them. A Capt. of Sr Jo: Gells sent mee yt hee had Orders from his Coll., Jo: Gell, not to advance any further then their olde quarters, yet never ye less I have maintained ye Beerhouse Guarde. There is many clashings betwixt theire Officers and ours, yet for ye publique Good I have passed by manie Infirmities and kept unitie wth them, and ye rather because wee are soe verie weake. Sr. Jo: Gell hath beene Continuallie hear aboutes, hee was once at Burton wth Sr. And: Kniverton where I heard they were verie pleasant together. Sr. Jo: sayth hee is not to bee comanded by any but by ye Parliam'tt. Therefore I knowe not what may Ensue hereafter, If I offer any thing contrarie to theire likeing Sr. Jo: Gell likewise sath yt if any would come forth of ye Castell hee would give them protectione, they Behaveing themselves well. Nothwithstandeing you had graunted yor Order none should come forth. Sr. I have formerly written to ye Committee to send mee a Phisiscon, but they are verie slowe in p'formance. Manie of our soldiers sicke. I beseech you put them in remembrance of itt. I rest as I will doe ever,

Yor faithfull Dutifull
Servant
Wal: Snowe

Tutbury Ap'll 13th
1646

They of ye Castell & Sr. Jo: Gells men are very desirous to have trumpets to pass too & fro upon small occasions. But I will not give way, though my forces bee weake my hope is stronge. I hope ye End will bee well.

17

Letter from Sr. John Gell
to Lift. Coll. Kniveton

Sr.,

ffor ye release of some of yor soldiers names in ye List you sent mee were gone from Derby before you they came thither. Yor Letters to mee about them are att Derby, And I nowe doe not well remember ye Contents of them soe as I conceave ye Letters Cannott bee done by Letters but in regard I am verie willing to make good Coll. Bowyers and Capt. Rodes agreem'tt wth you, and to take of all Cause of exception if you please to send yor pass for Mr Hen: Tupton that hee may safe come and safe returne this afternoone, hee shall treat with you and Compleat ye Agreement and make upp ye number you wantt.

Yor Servantt
Jo: Gell

For Lift. Coll Kniveton, Governor
of Tutburie Castell

A Letter sent from
Capt. Rodes to Major Snowe

Major Snowe,

There was an Agreement made by Coll. Bowyer and my selfe wth ye Governor of ye Castell aboute ye release of prisoners. The Governor of ye Castell wants his number, doth much press upon mee to make good our Agree-m'tt. Sr. I have pr'valed wth my Gov'r Sr. Jo: Gell to give Mr Buxton leave to treate with Leift. Coll. Kniveton aboute ye p'fectening of ye agreem't and make good his number. Therfore I desire yor Concurrance & Consent herein yt noe blott may fall upon Coll. Bowyer or my selfe, and soe desiring two words in writeing from you, that this Accompt may Quietly pass. I remaine

Yor friend & Ser't
Will'm. Rodes

For his worthy friend
Major Snowe att his
quarters in Tutburye
Apll. 12th 1646

18

Letter from Mr Hen: Vernon to Sr
Willm: Brereton touching ye proceedings
att London agst Sr. Jo: Gells treatin'
at Tutbury Castell wth the Governor thereof

Sr,

Coll. Bowyer and myself Arrived att London on Thursday by 6 in ye morning but wee could doe nothing but advise wth and prepare our freinds till Fryday noone ye Comittie of both Kingdomes not sitting till that tyme but we weare then fortw'th called, and Mr. Swinfen went wth us into ye Committee. I made in ye first place a relacon wht wee had done in p'section of yt Comission wherein yor selfe and I were joined and how wee weare obstructed by Sr. Jo: Gell and delivered them a copie of his articles wch were read and much disliked. Coll. Bowyer made relacon of ye Seige and sessation and Mr. Swinfen verie definitely added what was further materiall. Shortly after our withdrawing Sr. Jo: Curson was called in and then wee were again called wch begate severall disputes to longe to relate concerning ye besieging of ye place wch came to ther heads on our part that ye Castle was in Staffordshire and Consequently under yor Comand yt Coll. Bowyer did comand there in horse under you, that ye Seige was not first made by ye Darbysh'r forces, But by both Counties at ye same time wth Divers other particulars. In conclusion our mocon was yt in Case ye Committee disliked Sr. John Gells Articles they would send by us theire Instructions to you wht further should bee done therein and yt Sr. Jo: Gell might bee sent for, ye later will bee again moved for in ye howse upon those grounds yt hee had noe Instrucons from ye Committee of both Kingdomes, And yt hee departed without licence from attending his busines, ye former I intend to send you a Copie of inclosed if I cann concerning ye writts of Ellection for our Counti. I understand yt ye vacancie of ye Chamberlaines place doth as yett Stopp it for yt ye Writt should bee directed to him and not to ye Sherriff as in other Counties, the Newse of ye fortes of Exeter beeing Delivered upp on Condicons came last night by a Messinger to ye Speaker, and ye Towne is to bee delivered upon Munday next.

Kings Daughter ther, is to bee at his Dispose, Sr. Coll. Bowyer and I intend this night to sett out of Towne towards you, And I shall make what speed I can to doe what service lieth in ye power of

Yor most Effectionat Cozin to
Serve you
Hen: Vernon

I have sent you here inclosed a coppie of ye Letter of ye Comittee of both Kingdomes to you and Sr. Jo: Gell, ye Originalls wee bring wth follow in ye next.

19

For Sr Willm. Brereton a Letter
from ye Committee of both Kingdomes
touching Tutbury Castell & Sr. Jo: Gell

denying yt they ever gave Sr. Jo: Gell
any power to treat wth ye Enimy in
Tutbury Castell.

Sr.

Wee have seene ye Articles sent upp by Coll. Bowyer & Mr. Vernon signed by Peter Kniveton the matter of wch wee altogether dislike and never gave any power to Sr. Jo: Gell to treate aboute yt place and have signified soe much to him, wee therefore desire you and Collonell Bowyer. Coll. Needham & Mr. Vernon or any two of you to treate wth ye Governor or any other for yt place according to the instructions wee formerly gave you wch wee desire you to pursue and certifye unto us yor p'ceedings therein

Signed in ye name & by ye warr'nt of
ye Committee of both Kingdomes
P. Wharton J. Henston

Ye 10th Apll. 1646
Derby House

Copie of a Letter to Sr. Jo: Gell from
ye Committee of both Kingdomes wherein
the Comand this force to Continue at ye
Siege at Tutbury set down by Col: Bowyer
& Mr. Vernon who went uppe Poste.

For Sr. Jo: Gell,

Wee have received yor letter of ye 6th of Aprill and the Articles yt have beene treated upon by you wth the Governor of Tutburye ye matter whereof wee wholly dislike, neither did wee give you any power to treate aboute it, wee had formerlye committed ye busines to Sr. Willm. Brereton and others. And have again recommended it to him and Coll. Bowyer, Coll. Needham and Mr. Vernon or any two of them to treate according to our former instructions. Wee therefore desire you to give noe interuption nor impediment to ye worcke, But leave it by them to speede in. And that ye Derbishire Horse and foote yt are there at the service may continue there for ye finishing of that service.

Signed in ye name by ye sev'll
of ye Committee of both Kingdomes
P. Wharton J. Henson

Derby House 10th Apll.
1646

20

Letter to ye Speaker of ye House
Of Comons and to ye Committee of
both Kingdomes, Sent inclosed in
A Letter to Mr. Swinfen by Mr.
Zanckye

Sr,

These lines may give you this accompt touching our further p'gresse in our engagement against Lichfield that now yt ye full number of Cheshire men are come upp. Wee have inclosed ye enimy on Bacon Streete side and have perfected 3 mounts upon ye same side & have sufficiently entrenched and secured our Chesh:re Campe wch I hope (by Gods assistance) will bee a strong reserve for them all, wee have also drawen a line and made a trench (wch is almost finisht) from Stowe poole to Bacon Street wch is intended to bee made good to ye poole over against Sandford Street where wee erected another mounte for ye securing of our men on that part of the towne.

Untill these works were finished I did not apprehend itt seasonable to summons them, but now that the same are brought into such forwardness this inclosed summons was this day (by ye advice of a Councell of War) sent into ye Close and an Answ'r returned wch you will likewise herewith receave. When wee have made tryall of all ye morter peeces yt wee could possibly p'cure though wee could not obtaine ye greate one from Belvoire nor yt from Shrewsbury the one beeinge imployed at Newarke, and the other at Bridgenorth. Wee shall bee able to give you a further accompt of the Effects thereof (those yt wee have beeing in readines to bee made use of) and noe other endeavor shall bee omitted yt may conduce to the shortening of this worcke wch is not more desired by any man then by

Yor Most humble servant
Willm. Brereton

Lichfield Apll. 13th 1646

21

A summons sent into Lichfield Close
by Sr. Willm. Brereton, Apll. 13th 1646
directed to Sr. Tho: Tyldesley &
Hen: Bagot.

Gent,

I have hitherto forborne to Sumon you to ye End you might as much Dispare of escape as of Releise and have not before, tender of mercye, put in execution any Destructive attempts knowing the Parliam't (whom I serve)

Sir Thomas Tyldesley was the Royalist Governor of Lichfield.

desires rather yor Reducem'tt then yor Ruine. It Canbee no newse to imparte to you ye totall defeate given to yor ONELY FFIELD ARMY in this Kingdome (laste under ye comand of Sr. Jacob Astley) wthin a shorte time after the Submicon of Sr. Ralph Hoptons army to Sr. Tho: Fairfax in ye west. Besydes the surrendering of Exeter wch (though p'haps unknown to you) is most true, whereof I make mencon not to seduce nor triumph over you, But to bring you to a right understanding of yor pres't condicon. I have now sent this Sumons to demand for ye use of the King and Parliam't, the Close of Lichfield wth all armes, amunicon and other warlike provisions, Yor speedie surrender whereof will prevent further Effects of Hostillitie and yor selves, and those Gent. of quallitie & others wth you may receave honorable Condicons. But if yor Obstinancie deprive you and them thereof, the guilt (wch must necessarily bee answered for) is yor owne & you must expect worser condicons hereafter yor positive answere is required by 4 a clocke this afternoone by

Yor servantt
Willm. Brereton

From our Campe
On Baconhill
Apll. 13 1646

The Answer to ye Sumons

ffor Sr. Willm. Brereton
Barronett

Sr,

Though yor Sumons hath beene long Expected ye Answ'r shal bee short. Wee will keepe this Garrison (God willing) wth our lives and fortunes for ye King our Leige Soveraing, By whom wee are intrusted, this is the Resolucon of ye Whole Garrison together wth

Yor Servants
Tho: Tildeslye
Her: Bagot[18]

Lichfield Close
Apll.13th. 1646

22

Letter on ye Behalfe of Sr. Tho: Smith
To ye Committee of Composicon

Gent,

Though I have bene verie modest and spareing in moving you in ye behalf of those yt are to Compounde wth you, Yet shall presume to bee an earnest suiter in ye behalf of Sr. Tho: Smithe, late one of ye Members of ye house of Comens concerning whom I take ye Boldness to certifie on his behalf that in ye beginning of these Warres when I was first commanded downe to settle ye Militia in Cheshire, hee being then in ye house, hee writt to mee testifying his willingnes to conforme thereunto and upon my late Entring Chester hee came and submitted him selfe Assureing mee wth soe much of serious protestation as I beeleeve itt to bee true. This hee came to his owne howse in Chester by leave of ye House onely for a short tyme of repose, and though hee had his horses in readines divers times to have returned, But could never gane the opportunitie, the cittie being garrisoned immediately after his comeing thither. And I have often heard and doe beleeve that hee never as'ted in ye Comission of Arraye, nor was in Armes nor Joyned wth them in any Councell of Warre. The greatest part of his estate hath beene in ye Parliam'ts power and Imployed to Maintaine our forces in Cheshire during thes Warrs. I Comend him and his Condicon to yor Grave Consideracon, And Beseech all lawfull favor on his behalf and give you the assurance that I am

Yor faithful friend to
Serve you
Will. Brereton

Lichfield Apll 11th
1646

23

Letter from Major Snow to Sr. Willm. Brereton touching Sr. Jo: Gells private Discourse wth ye Enimy in Tutbury Castell

Honorabl Sr,

Since I wrote you Sr. Jo: Gell hath been at ye Castell and had conference wth them wthout makeing mee acquainted. Hee came over ye Walles on ye Backe of ye Castell where our Guards could not discover him and Braught wth him Sr. Jo: Harper and there stayed till hee was Discovered from ye Woodhowses, And they beate them of, not knoweing who they weare, Likewise yester night hee gave a contrarie word unto his men, the wch I had given before yester night, there came one out of ye Castell who Braught to mee theise Inclosed Letters, who sayes they were to goe to Lichfield Close, And one Slake Gave him halfe a Crowne to bring them to Mee wch hee did Willingly. Yesternight there came 2 of 8 of Sr. Jo: Gells Capts. To me aboute 12 a clocke beeing in great Discontent, and sayd theire Coll. was much discontented because hee was opposed & Hindered from goeing to ye Castell. Upon this Discontent I gathered by theire discourse they Intended to Draw of theire companies yt they may not bee readie to ayde in case of Necessitie thus leaveing to yor honor'ble consideracon I rest & will ever bee

Yor faithfull & dutifull
Servant
Wal: Snowe

Tutbury Apll. 14th
1646

Another Letter from Major Snowe

Honorable Sr,

Just now two of Sr. Jo: Gells Capts came to mee And told mee they had orders from Sr. Jo: Gell to draw off forth both horse and foote. Theire foote to ye Woodhowses where they cannot bee serviceable to us. And their Horse to ffowdes. You knowe in what poore Condicon we are. I leave it to yor honour Consideracon.

Wal: Snowe

Tutburie Castell
Apll 14th 1646

Letter Intercept wch came forth of Tutburie Castell

Dear love let mee desire thee to lett mee hear two words from thee of yor health under yor owne hande what you desire, whether you desire to come forth of ye Close, or may adventure in: The Condicon of this place I hope will bee well. But reserve ye declares till God of his goodness send ye to mee, till wch tyme I comitt you and all our frends wth you to ye protection of ye Almightie, & rest, yor loving husband,

ffr. Ward.

Another Intercepted Letter

Dear Sonne, My longe Exsile from my dearest wife, yor selfe & freinds in soe great a Leaguer, a manner yt I must never [**blank**] ye left Requitall, but Comitt all to him yt I trust wilbee yor Protector, but if it had pleased god to have lett mee have beene among you, I had beene happie. But I hope itt was to preserve this, though it bee on condicons but honorable, And never to bee inhabited by ye Enimy, but demolished, and all Comanders and Souldiers to goe Either to ye King or to their owne homes wth a free Act of Oblivion, and all Sequestracons taken of theire Estates or howses till Death. The Author whereof you may Imagine, and I heartily Desire to you, see but two lines from you, & whether if I should get a ticket to procure my wife out of ye Close, and some other small things, whether it would bee granted or noe. The Newse here is from Derby yt Sr. Jo: Gell is comanded to draw forces towards Sallie ford to hinder ye King from his Joyneing with ye Scotts.

Yor ever loving fath'r
ffr: Ward

Tutburye Castell
Apll 14th 1646

Letter from Sr. Willm. Brereton to
Major Zanckye touching ye sending
Upp to ye Leauger at Lichfield
Sr.W.B. his troope & Capt. Breretons
Troope, all if wth Convenience

Sir,

Before ye Battell at Stowe (wherin it pleased God to give happie success), I not onely send unto you, but lett you knowe how serviceable ye Cheshire Horse might bee unto us by theire advance to us, But did alsoe send to Coll: Mytton[19] to acquainte him of the neccessitie thereof and how much theire service might have beene in order to ye service of Wales (wch noe man Endeavors nor desires more to promoat then myself), Because as much as ye safetie and welfare of these partes of ye Kingdome and of Wales depended upon ye event and success of ye Battell, wherein ye horse yt were wth mee Carried themselves much honor, It pleasinge god, After theire three or foure dayes and nights Almost Constant March to make them ye Instruments of Recovering ye day by wch victory theire is a faire way upon theire beeing noe Army in ye feild Against the Parliament, to put a period to ye Warre. And as Desireous thereof It is my Endeavor to improve yt opportunitie & advantage, for wch End I have received Comand from ye Parliam'tt to Drawe some forces towards Worcester, And am preparing for yt service. And for yt End would desire all ye forces that might bee possible should bee sett apart for itt. I here now ye Lancashire forces are comeing for Wales having received (as I have been Informed) theire Money due upon takeing of Chester (wch is yet unpayde to others who have since yt time beene upon Constant Duty in obedience to ye Parliam'tts Comands) Soe as though I beleeve there being noe Enimy in Wales able to Disturb ye Parliam'tts forces, and some Cheshire Dragoones beeing there, have beene spared to ye prejudice of the service here, out of my desire to advance that the 400 Cheshire Horse might bee spared from ye service in reguard they have remained and doe still continue in theire Quarters (Contrarie I beleeve to theire Desire), Yett I shall not as yett Order them all hither, but for ye Super Numorarie Number. I Cannott Conceave they Cann bee better imployed then to assist to ye Worcke for wch I have received Comand in these partes, and for Carrieing on whereof wee doubt not but ye Parliam'tt will make provission in competent measure for this end, therfor I desire yt my owne troope, wch I beleeve may bee spared (My Dragoones beeing in Wales) may bee sent unto mee, who will take a care of them, that they bee provided for as well as any, and shall not imploy them further then I shall goe wth them my selfe. And my Brothers troope likewise if it may bee spared, Both wch may bee returned as there may bee occation

Yor Loving friend
Willm. Brereton

Lichfield Apll: 13
1646

Postscript

Since I wrote these lines wthin, Coll; Birch, Governor of Hereford[20] is this night come post from London to advise wth mee for ye speedie carringe on ye Service. Comanded therefore I desire My troope will not faile to march accordinglie hither soe soone as Conveniently where they (whom I returne in greate respect and value) shall bee under my Speshall Care, and shall not faile to bee accommodated wth the best, And I doubt not but ye Parliam'tt largelie provide for such forces as they have appointed mee to call together upon theire Speshall Service.

Lichfiield 14th Apll Willm. Brereton
11 at night, 1646

26

Sr. Willm. Brereton, his Orders to Major Zanckie or his Officers for ye marching upp of his owne troope to ye Seige at Lichfield

Whereas there was formerly some Cheshire horse set aparte & left in ye Countie for ye service of Northwales, But have not beene there Imployed, but remained for a long space unserviceable in their Quarters (Nothwthstanding ye necessitie of theire assistance in these parts formerly as hath beene Intymated, and there beeinge noe Considerable Enimy in Wales) And for yt now some of ye forces here are by ye Committee of both Kingdomes comanded upon other service (much conduceing to ye service of Northwales) ther is a necessitie of a supplye of forces hither & for yt ye rest of ye Cheshire Horse Remaining in Cheshire, there beeing ye Cheshire Dragoones alreadie in Northwales in parte of ye number assigned, wch will make upp ye full number Appointed by ye Committee of both Kingdomes for ye service of Wales as there may bee occation. Thes are therfore to require and comand you forthwth to march wth my troope to this Leauger before Lichfield, where you shall receave further order. Given under my hand att Lichfield this 15th of Apll. 1646.

Willm: Brereton

To Major Zanckye &
in his absence to his officers.

27

Letter to ye Comittee of the House of Comons for plunderd Ministers in ye behalf of Capt. Swetneham

Gent,

Beeing desired to move you in ye Behalfe of Capt. Swetneham I can doe noe less then in ye first place to certifye you what I knowe of him, hee hath comanded a troope of horse belongeing to Derbyshire and hath beene under my comand for ye space of 18 months, and done verie greate service (in particular at ye Battel at Stowe his service was verrie considerable and successful) Besydes he hath exercised his ministrie (as convenient he served in ye regiment since his beeing Capt. wch hast beene aboute three years. And now yt it hath pleased God to bringe his owne worcke to such a forwardnes and to reduce these partes wherein hee hath formerly served as a faithful minister for ye space as I am informed, 18 yeares, and since ye beginning of these warrs as a Comander. It is desired yt hee might returne to his ministerie and his function of a minister and yet hee may bee setled in Darbishire. I know not any in yt Countie as I conceive, yt deserve a precedence of Preferm'nt, my humble suite on his behalf is yt wch will please upon consideration of his deserving & ye desires of ye Mayor and Burgeses of Derbye & ye Gentrie of ye Countie. Touching him you will afford him Such Engagem't as you shall thincke fitt, wherby in particular you shall much engage

Yor faithful friend and servant
Willm. Brereton

Lichfield Apll 15th
1646

Sr,

These lines may give you this Accompt touching ye condicons of this place before wch wee are engaged, yt having been constrained to resort unto ye use of ye last meanes for ye reducement of ye Close, wch was our masterpieces & herewith I hope soe good execution may bee done as yt may not be longe before a good accompt may bee given of this place, wherein ye meane tyme yor affaires are disadvantaged and wee are forced to send upp messengers on purpose because there is noe Postmaster, or if any hee calls not to give mee notice, for ye supplye of wch Defect I have taken ye boldnes to present unto you on[e] who is verrie fitt for yt Imployment, hath done you good service and is verrie well approved of by ye committee here, wch I leave to yor consideracon and Subscribe myself

Yor faithfull friend to serve you
Willm. Brereton

The man I mencon is this bearer
Andrew Miller, whose father lives neere
to this Cittie & who hath done you service
and brought you intelligence severall tymes
as I presume you may Remember
Lichfield Apll: 15th 1646

28

Letter from Mr Ash: to ye
Committee of Stafford touching
His seizement in Staffordshire

Gentlemen,

I have received yor letter of ye 20th past in Answear of Myne, formerly written to Capt. Stone.[21] I am Satisfyed that you have power to seaze Peerhill hundred for the maintenance of ye Garrison of Eclesall Castell, and doe alsoe beleeve yt all men, both Lords & comons doe pay According to the Rents of theire levie in that seazmentt: Wch in a moderate way I am willing to see seased as others are, yet I must Acquaint you yt heare in London noe members of Parliam't doe pay towards any taxe att all. Though by ye Ordinance of Parliam't any member may bee seazed, yet not levied upon them without the leave of ye howse, I was informed by some members of ye howse of Comons yt are yor Countriemen, that for ye maintenance of Eclesall Castell hee doth raise 82L a weeke, and that there was but 14 men in ye Castell. But I am justified wth what you write both of ye horse and foote belonging, wch if kept there for ye maintenance of yt Castell, those hundreds ought to pay them, but if taken away for any other service then I am not soe well satisfied yt those hundreds should pay those Rates. I must Acquainte you that I have always beene forward to advance the service in farre greater summes then the taxes of any Rents in Staffordshire. Soe shall not now looke att smaller matters not doubting but you will have that Respect unto mee as not to seize mee more then Gentlemen of the same Revenue, thus takeing leave shall Ever Remaine

Yors to Comand
Ed: Ashe

London ye 7th March
1646

29

Letter from Sr. Tho: Tildesley
to Sr. Willm. Brereton touching
Major Bywaters p'roll

Sr,

If you please to p'mitt Major Bywater to Come into this Garrison upon his p'roll I hereby Engage my selfe hee shall returne unto yor Quart'rs att ye tyme Limited by you.

Yor Servantt
Tho: Tildesley

Lichfield Close this
15th of Apll. 1646

Sr. Willm. Breretons Answ'r
To Sr Thomas Tildesleys Letter

Sr,

I have received yor letter that Major Bywater may bee p'mitted to come upon his p'roll to you, whereunto I shall give way this Afternoone, as also yt ye Govern'r of Stafford may come into ye Close to confer wth Sr. Richard Dyott aboute his Sonne who is a prisoner wthin, provided in ye meane tyme yt you send a suitatable to our Campe on Bacon hill wth yor Engagement for theire safe Returne unto

Yor servantt
Willm. Brereton

Apll 16th 1646

30

Letter from Capt. Whitworth to
Sr. Willm. Brereton, ye Goods att
Chester ye vallew of is sould &
What is unsould

Honored Sr,

Yors by Mr. Jo: Brereton of the press'tt I received, for goods there is betwixt ffoure & five thousand pounds worth of goods sould already & I beleeve is manie more to be sould as will make up eight thousand pounds, much of wch goods are Damaske, Dyaper, Haingeings Extraordinarie, Suites for Beds, heares, and Stockes, Vestm'ts & mens aparrell, onely Sr. ffrancis Gainills Goods wch wee have foreborne till now upon hopes of his byeing of them:

There is in towne onely five Trained bands & Major Daniells Companie, wch make about 600 men, for John's steeple nothing is yet done, ye Mount is in good forwardnes and ye worcke my ffather Langley hath beene houres some 14 dayes agoe, and is much lyen upon and I hope will bee prevealed wth but its verrie much adoe hee is go towards Camebridge and soe to London if you write two words to Mr. Done to London aboute itt might helpe to forward ye Worcke. The moneye I layd out at ye Leauger is 31L. 11s. 00d besides about 7L wch I am Engaged for to Mr. Greene & Mr. Evans wch they are verrie Earnest for. Its most layd downe for provission messengers and other things neere p'ticulers, if yor honor desire a p'ticuler you shall have itt. And I am much lyen upon for the money. I am much troubled, my last letter was soe longe in comeing to yor honor. It was p'mised to have beene wth you soone, you may doe well to write two words now, and then to Mr. Krue who is one yt truly honors you. I desire you will send mee word here I may have yt money wch is borrowed, wee are aboute to give ye Shropshire men some pte of Content by g. if it bee possible.

I feare Mr. L: hath beene a verrie greate Instrument to [**blank**] pp some Differences for hee taketh all Occations to vent his Spleene & Malice. The Lord direct yor honor to his Glorie, ye Churches Good, yor owne comfort, wch is ye Constant desire & prayers of him who is

Yor honors Most humble
Servant to Comand
Jo: Whitworth

Chester Apll: 13th 1646.

31

Letter to the high Sherrif of Cheshire
touching ye Battel at Stowe & touching
Ye Ordnance of Parliament placeing
Comand of ye forces in ye field yt followed
Sr. Jacob Ashley.

Sr,

Understanding yt some Envious Distrusting persons have taken ye Impudence to Contradict yt wch I did advertice in my letter touching ye success god gave us att Stowe as though I had not beene there but came after ye Battell and as though I had noe Comand there nor did noe service there, I have therefore sent you a Copie of ye Ordinance of Parliam'tt placeing the Comand of ye forces wth mee, and I could send you ye Comittie of both Kingdomes Letter wherein they acknowledge ye service done there. Its true indeed I did not over take ye partie yt was wth Morgan[22] & Birch untill about 4 howeres before the beginning of ye Battell, And its true yt Morgan desirede mee to give orders. I tould I liked well the way they were in, wch I desired might bee observed. I have made mencon to noe other End. But yt truthe may bee vindicated for ye whole honor & Glorys due to God alone, who was pleased to make those forces yt came wth mee and had a tedious march of itt, the Instruments of Recovering & Governing ye day & to stand Gallantly & charged when others Rune away as will bee acknowledged by all yt were there and as Sr. Jacob Ashley hath not onely Expressed but given it under his owne hande. I desire the honor and glory may asenyded to god alone giver of all victories and that wee may bee sufficiently thankful and study to bee desiring of ye continuance of his mercyes

Yor verrie Affectionate
friend to serve you
Willm: Brereton

Apll. 16 1646

The Ordnance of Parliam'tt placeing ye
command of ye Assotiated forces of
Stafford, Salop, Worcests. Warwicke, Derby
Hereford & Gloucesters. wth Sr. Wm. Brereton

Die Sabathi 7: Marty 1645

Ordered by ye Lords & Comons in Parliamentt Assembled that Sr. Willm. Brereton shall for three months have the Comand of the forces appointed to bee new drawen together for the following of the Enimy in the ffield.

Jo: Browne: Cler.

Dera Copia.

32

Letter from ye Committee of both Kingdomes
Before Newarke touching ye Kings Leaveing
Oxford & moving towards the northe

Sir,

Wee have intelligence from verrie good hands that the Kinge intends to leave Oxford and come northwards. Wee thought fitt to give you notice hereof yt you might use the best meanes you can to stopp his passage in case hee should come neer yor parts, and to advertise others yt they may doe ye like. Its thought hee will hazard his passage wth verrie few horse. Imagining by yt meanes to pass more safely securely. But if hee should stir wth any considerable number, Col: Fleetwood[23] and Coll: Ireton[24] willbee readie to attend his mocons, for they lye aboute Woodstocke and neare Oxford, that hee cannot stir wth any greate Bodie of horse but they must needs take ye Alurum. Wee desire to know how you speed in ye Seige before Lichfield Close, and whether Tutbury bee surrendered or noe, Since the finishing of our line before Newarke wee have beene verrie Busye in making our approaches on all sydes and appointing Batteries, Both for Ordinances and morter peeces. By ye End of this weeke we hope some of them will be readie to play. They contynue still obstinate in ye towne. The plague increases much among them, what ye Issue of our affaires wilbee you shall have notice from tyme to tyme as wee Desire ye like from you, and Rest

Henry Ireton, later a general in Parliament's army, married Cromwell's daughter Bridget.

Yor Affectionate friends to
Serve you

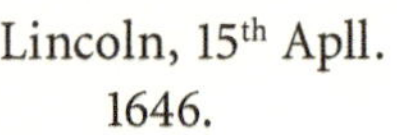

Lincoln, 15th Apll.
1646.

Edw: Montague
Wm: Pierepoint : Attorneye
Edw: Llycoghe
Antho: Arby Tho: Hatcher

33

Letter to ye Committee before Newarke
from Sr. Willm. Brereton

My Lords and Gentlemen,

Yors dated Apll. 15th at Lincolne I have Received & have Imployed my utmost Endeavors Accordingly. But wee are here soe much disabled from p'formeing that service yt might bee Expected by reason of the absense of the greater parte of ye horse Assigned mee as I doubt I may not bee able to give soe good an accompt of as otherwise as the most of the Warwicke Horse beeing now wth Coll. Morgan aboute Worcester, and some of them about Birmincham for securitie of those parts against Dudley Castell, the Regim'tts of Reformadoes beeing Ordered to mee are now with Coll: Fleetwood aboute Oxford, the Leicester horse beeing theire owne Countie and not wth mee as alsoe ye Gloucester, Hereford and Evesholme foote yt came wth mee from Stow are called backe, whereby ye Duty is much Encreased to ye rest, ye rather because there is soe powerfull and soe much Enraged Enimy in the Close against whom wee have Drawen and almost finished our Line on yt side wch was open and free to the Enimy, where we have alsoe placed three strong mounts and sufficiently fortified ye Chesh're Camp wch is a reserve to them all, which worcke were noe sooner in a good way of forwardnes and neere finished when the Enimy might bee as Hopeless of Escapeing out of the Close as receaveing releef into it. I sent them this Inclosed Sumons & received this Answer, And there upon resorted to our last Meanes for reducing thereof by ye use of our morter peeces, wch as I heare have done good execution, whereby wee cannot but looke upon ye Enimy as Enraged & rendered desperate and therefore beeing ye more to bee considered because theire strength of foote in the Close is neere as greate as ours in ye field and Cittie wthout whom it comes that wee are not able to spare forces for this service whereof ye advertise us, But have given order to soe many of our Horse as canbee possiblye soe imployed to have a watchfull eye and regarde thereunto, But unless ye Enimy move his Course neere unto Tamworth they will bee soe farre remoate from us as that they will bee cleare of our Distance: I know not any could bee more serviceable to this Designe then Sr. Jo: Gells forces who are imployed aboute Tutbury, where hee lately assumed to take upon him to make Condicons wth ye Enimy in ye Castell wch were after disclaimed and disallowed by ye Committee of both Kingdomes and ye former directions Given to mee and others. Confirmed however I beseech you not much to depend on him herein, But could rather humbly p'pose yt you would send some trustie & failthfull p'son from you, yor line beeing neere finished wth such a Considerable strength of horse and Dragoones as you thincke fitt to keepe ye passes over Trent aboute Weldon and Sawly ferries to whom I should bee willing to Contribute ye best of Intelligence & Assistance yt canbee Afforded. Hereof I have given Intelligence to ye Coventrie as alsoe to Warwicke and will not bee wanting to use my utmost Endeavors yt is in ye power of

Yor faithfull friend and humble
Sev'tt Will'm. Brereton

Lichfield Apll. 17th
1646

35

Sr. Will'm Breretons Letter to ye
Committee at Coventrie upon receapt
Of ye last letter ye Committee of both
Kingdomes at Lincolne

Gent, I have received a letter from ye Committee at Newarke imparting this much, yt ye King intends to leave Oxford and come Northwards and they desire I would imploy my Endeavours for the preventing thereof. My Request to you is yt you will lay out for Intelligence of any partie of horse yt may come towards Oxford and advertise Capt. fflowers & some other Darbish're Officers att Tamworth whom I have Ordered to use theire Endeavers to guard ye passes and Convenient places for ye King to make his way as also yt you will Acquainte us here att Lichfield of what you shall constantly heare Concerneing ye above writen & as occation shall serve to send to them at Tamworth, otherwise it will not bee possible to p'vent ye dangerous designe whereunto noe man desires to contribute more then my self thog I am much disabled in regard all yor horse are absent save two troops, And ye Lec'ster Horse in theire owne Countye the Gloucester, Worcester & Hereford sente wch occations harder Duty to ye Leauger notwthstanding what lyes in my power shall not bee wanting therein nor any thing els wherby I may approve myself

Gent, yor faithfull friend &
Servant
[**unsigned**]

From ye Leauger before
Lichfield Apll. 16th 1646.

Order for Capt. fflower & Capt. Hayfield
& Capt. Hope & Troopes to Attend

It is Ordered yt Capt fflower and Capt. Hayfields troops wth ye Assistance of Capt. Hope and ye Derbishire Troops do use theire utmost Endeavor to stopp all ye passes Betwixt Oxford and Newarke yt are neere unto Tamworth upon those Rivers and other plaices convenient thereabouts. Given under my hand at ye Leauger before Lichfield this 16th : of Apll. 1646

Will'm Brereton

For Capt. fflower & Capt. Hope.

Another Letter was sent to Coventrie to desire them to spare all ye forces they could towards Tamworth to joyne to p'vent ye Kings Designe & Informe ye Condicon of our Leaguer at Lichfield yt ye Herreford, Worcester, Gloucester foote beeing gone back ye Lecister forces in theire owne Countie, ye Warwicke not returned from Worcester & others of them aboute Birmingham to attend Dudley Castell & ye Enimy in ye Close beeing as strong almost as ye Leauger & Enraged, noe more would bespared.

A letter was likewise written to the Sherrif & Deputie Lift. Of Chesh're to send up Sr Willm Breretons owne troope & Capt. Shipleys & Carters, & a Letter to ye sequestrators to pay them for yt end & likewise to hasten ye Cheshire ffoot.

36

A Letter touching ye Governor of Chester Directed
Severall copies to ye Speaker Sr. Henry Vane[25] &
Solliciter Sr Wm. Strickland, Sr. Peeter Wentworth
Sr. Arth: Haslrige,[26] Coll. Risvilo & Col. Purefoy,[27] Mr.
Myles Corbett, Mr. Gordan Alderm'n: Hoyle, Mr. Ashurste,
Mr. Swinfen, Sr. Ralph Ashton & Coll. Ashton & Coll. Moore
Sent up by And: Miller to bee dd'd when Mr. Ashurst
& Mr. Swinfen thinke fitte.

Sr,

I understand my Lord Lisle Intends Coll. Jones now Governor of Chester for ye service of Ireland, if soe there must bee another Governor appointed for ye Cittie of Chester. Therefore seeing ye Condicon of yt place requires an able Souldier as well as a person of Integritie and partes and because there is noe many yt serves in Parliam'tt for ye Countie& Cittie but my selfe, I shall Humbly take ye Boldness to present unto you ye names of such as for whom I dare Engage Both for theire faithfullnes and Abillities viz. Colonell Robt. Duckenfield, Coll: Croxton Governor of Nampywch, Ajutant Gener'll Lothian & Left. Coll. Robt. Venable, late Governor of Tarvin. This is ye Reg. of Ireland and Comands all those partes of England and Wales wch Remaines yet much unsettled and in composed. And therefore Requires P'sons of larger Abillities and approved Integrities of these yt I have p'pounded. I have had large Experience and knowe them to bee fitt men, for this place as for this Comand & such as wilbee verrie Acceptable & gratefull to ye Countie & will Endeavor to Exact Gods honor & glorie as well to p'forme ye dutie of faithfull, able diligent Comander by wch choyce you will much rejoyce ye Hearts of all those yt serve God, And have Most faithfullie adhered to you in & about yt Cittie,

Sir Henry Vane was a senior member of the Committee of Both Kingdoms.

And noe man shall Exceed in thanckfulnes myself, who neither have nor will prefer nor Exalt any man further then may bee for ye Advantage of yor Affaires wherby I may Hope to confirme you in ye oppinion and beleeife yt I am & will always remaine

Yor most faithfull
Servant
Will'm Brereton

Lichfield Apll. 17th
1646

It. yt to ye Speaker was this Addicon:

Our line is now Roundaboute ye Close & almost finished & our mounts p'fected & our masterpieces have done some Execution (& our Cannons ready for batterie), But want of amunicon disables us for press'tt, Whereas when wee are supplied I hope wee shall you a good Accompt of this strong Holde.

37

Letter from Coll. Bowyer to Sr. Will'm Brereton
& ye Committee of Stafford touch: ye Affaires
of Tutburie Castell where inclosed is a
Letter of Mr. Vernon.

Gent,

I have this morning received this Inclosed Letter of wch I desire yor Serious Consideracon and your speedie result thereupon by this Bearer that soe I may bee ye better Informed to steere my course, the condicon of our Countrie I need not Informe you of. But shall desire you to write yor sence to ye Committee of Derbye, And likewise yor Instructions to mee in this case and Yt Concerneing our forces, you will settle such a parte of ye Countrie as may bee fitt and convenient for ye bringing of provision for theire maintenance for ye Sicknes Sr. Jo: mencons in his letter. I may have some Jelousies but can have noe grounded foundacon for ye same, Not knowing any p'son, place yt is infested. Derbyshire Officers come to require Amunicon as Conceiveing itt must bee found by us. Wee desire you to send our owne forces some Amunicon and to give leave yt Capt. Buckuhanna may come over tomorrow to sett out some works in case wee agree not soe desiring yor Answer in this p'ticulare I rest,

Yor Servant
Jo: Bowyer

Tutbury Castell
Apll 16: 1646

The Gentlmen of ye Castell have
promised to send out new Articles today

wch when I receave you shall have
further knowledge.
Jo: Bowyer

38

Letter from Mr. Vernon[28] to Sr. Will'm Brereton touching ye seige at Tutbury & ye Governor & ye Gent. In ye Castell meeting Coll. Bowyer & Mr. Vernon out of ye Castell & Conferring wth them.

Sr.

When I arrived at Tutbury I understood yt ye Quarterm'sters were gone to take upp new quarters for ye Darbishire forces and ye trumpets soundeing to Horse, Wherefore I immediately sent Capt. Gent & Mr. Humarsly wth ye letter of ye 10th and from ye Committee of both Kingdomes to Sr. Jo: Gell, then at Marston, his answer was that hee would obey Orders and those forces doe still remaine in theire olde Quarters and past upon ye same Dutye Except Capt. Greenes Troop wch removed to [**blank**] before I came and are Expected forthwith to returne to Sr. Jo: as wee are informed went last night to Derby and thence as is reported will goe to London.

Coll: Bowyer and I have sent severalties to ye Castell and have since mett with Sr. Jo: ffitzherbert and ye Governor betwixt ye Guards where wee showed them our Authoritie and a Copie of Sr. Jo: Gells letter and in conclusion agreed of tomorrow morning by 8 of ye clocke to receave p'posicons from them, afterwards they desired us to drincke in ye Castell, But at yt instant there began a mutinie in ye Castell, ye Gentlmen beeing all abroad with us, ye Bridges are Drawen against them and our friend yt sent ye Letter and p'posicons to Collonell Bowyer in ye Castell : and at this tyme Disputing Condicons wth ye Governor & Gent. Who are at our Guards Drincking wth us who desire yor further Instructions in this Business. And as soone as any more Considerable p' gress is made in this matter you shall have speedie Information thereof from

Yor most humble Servantt
Henry Vernon

Tutbury 15th Apll.
1646

39

Letter from Collonel Bowyer to Sr Will'm Brereton touching

Sr,

After ye receipt of these Articles I thought good to my thoughts wch oppinion I refer to yor serious consideracon it beeing my Intentions to act nothing without yor advice and approbacon it would bee more satisfying to us had wee yor Company wch wee Expect tomorrow, in ye meane tyme I rest

Sr.

Yors, Jo: Bowyer

Sr,

You sent mee word that Amunicon was comeing, as yett I have received none. My necessity is such yt I can scarse mounte ye Guards without itt, fayle not to expedite it hither wth all hast. Sr I have deferd to answer ye 10th Article by reason I was informed by an Officer in ye Castell who we Conceave hath great Intrest in ye Soldiers since ye last greate Mutinie yt ye matter of money willbee ye ting to bee stood on, all ye rest of ye articles will bee ye sooner declined then yt in ye least degree reverst. Mr. Vernon can tell you what sum ye soldiery (wch are to march away) will require. Sr, there is such private plotts and Contrivem'ts among ye Derbishire Officers & Souldiers wth them in ye Castell that I am informed yt some officers have stolen in privately wth some Letters of Sr. Johns: and answer backe the messengers beeing lett downe wth ropes, I dare not bee too forward in ye punishing of these least it should p'duce longer Breaches and discontents among us. But shall observe and put in execution when tyme serves. Sr, if it were as I conceave it is in yor power to draw away the Derbishire forces and give us others ye worcke will bee sooner expedited to all this I desire yor advice, and rest Sr,

Yor freinde & kinsman

Jo: Bowyer

40

Transacons betwixt Sr. Willm Brereton
& Sr. Tho: Tildesley touching Capt. Stones
Going into ye Close.

Sr,

I give you thanckes for yor p'mitting Mr. Bywater to come on his p'roll into this Garrison, but for ye other mocon of ye Governor of Staffords Comeing hither it is not thought fitting. But if you will send mee yor Engagem'tt for theire safe returne, I will desire Sr. Rich: Dyott & Coll. Snead to meet Capt. Stone & whom els you shall please this afternoone in ye field betwixt yor Leauger & this Garrison and I hereby Engage my honor you shall returne wth safetye, Sr I am

Yor Servant
Tho: Tildesley

16th Apll: 1646

Sr. Willm Breretons Answer to Sr Tho:
Tildesleyes Letter above written

Sr,

Capt. Stone & Capt. Daniell shall meete at yor Barracado before our Mounte in Bacon Street : on yor Engagem'tt for theire safe returne, And I doe hereby Engage myself for ye safe returne of Sr. Rich: Dyott & Coll. Snead, I have sent them wth yor Drume & Major Bywater wth them

Yor Servant
W. B.

Apll. 16: 1646

40

Another Letter from Sr. Tho: Tildesleye
to Capt. Stone.

Sr,

The performances of yor Engagement was never distrusted by mee either for Capt. or anything els and I wish it were in my power to declare my love to you wch shoulde be performed in ye highest way to diswade you from ye course you are in. But as you tolde mee in Eclesall Castell wee have fought to long now to dispute yor mocon of comeing into ye Garrison Cannot bee Accepted, you will see too much mischief done by yor Engines which wee now call Kingdome destroying Intencon, But if you please to p'cure Sr. Willm. Breretons Engagement for theire safe returne I will desire Sr. Rich: Dyott and Coll. Snead to meet you and whom else you please in ye field betwixt yor Leauger and our Garrison I have sent myne to Sr. Willm. Brereton yor speedie Answer is desired

by yor Servantt
Tho: Tildesleye

Aprill 16: 1646

Letter from Sr. Tho: Tildesleye to Sr. Willm.
Brereton touching Capt. Benets wife comeing
Into ye Close.

Sr,

I desired Capt. Stone yesterday to move you yt Mrs Bennett might come into this Close to see her husband and stay here one night. Since I have yet received noe answer I make bolde to Importune this suite yor answer is desired by,

Yor Servantt
Tho: Tildesleye

You will pardon our scarcity
of paper. Its one of our greatest wants.

41

Sr Willm Breretons Letter to Sr Tho:
Tildesleye.

Sr,

In satisfaction to yor desires and upon yor Engagm'tt for Major Bywaters Returne, I gave way yt hee should goe into ye Close. Hee is not returned wch is Expected this Afternoone. But I must desire to bee excused in not admitting M.B. into ye Close to returne backe

Yor Servantt
W. B.

By ye next I will send you some
paper & doe beleeve before it bee
longe you wilbee sensible of
Greater want then paper.

Another Letter from Sr, Tho: Tildesleye
to Sr. Willm Brereton.

Sr,

You will please to pardon all our wants, I had not detained Mr. Bywaters thus longe but presuming upon a p'miss from Capt. Stone to mediate his ransome at Tamworth I have now sent him a p'posicon if yt bee not accepted hee shall bee returned by

Yor servant
Tho: Tildesley

Apll. 18 1646

Sr Willm Breretons Answere to ye
Letter above written.

Sr,

Though I cannot allow myself to supplye all yor wants yet I have hearwth sent you some paper & when I have speaken wth Capt. Stone, I will returne an Answer to ye propos icon you make concerning Major Bywater And in this mean tyme I rest

Yor Servant
W. B.

18th Apll. 1646

42

Letter to Mr. Ashurst and Mr. Swinfen
Or either of them from Sr. Willm Brereton
touching writts for Cheshire.

Sr,

I have lately entertained into my thoughts the consideracon of ye Issueing of Writts for ye Ellecon of a knight of ye shire for Chesh're and doe begine to make a Scruple whether theire my bee any writts directed to ye Sherriffe for yt purpose for unless I bee deceaved the Ordinance enabling Mr. Broockes to execute as Sherriffe extends onely to writts betwixt partie & partie, wch if it reach noe further then there is a necesitie that there bee a Chamberlaine att Chester or els a speshall Ordinance enabling thereunto I pray you advise wth my Cozin Bradshaw and some other friends to bee satisfied in this choise noe more but that I am

Yor Most Assured friend
W. B.

18th Apll.
1646

Letter from ye Committee at Lecister
To Sr Willm Brereton touching theire
Sending forces to Lichfield to Sr. W. B.

Honorable Sr,

Wee received yor Lett. By this bearer and intend to send away all the forces wee can spare to you with all ye possible speed wee can, and rest

Sr,
Yor Affectionate Servtt.
Tho: Hesilrige
Jo: Browne
Jo: Swinfen

Liecestr. 16th: 1646

43

Letter from ye Committee of bothe
Kingdomes to Sr. Willm Brereton touching
the 3,000L for the forces before the Close
at Litchfield.

Sr,

The Howse of Comons haveing appointed six thousand pounds for the forces at Litchfeild and for those of the Countie of Gloucester, Hereford and Worcester yt lately followed Sr. Jacob Ashley and referred the desposeinge of ye said money unto us. Wee have thought fitt by ye advance of ye Gentlemen of these counties and such as are concerned in ye said forces to appoint three thousand pounds thereof for ye fforces before Litchfeilde, and some Gentlemen have here in source will take care for takeing of it up. And wee desire you that when ye money shall come to yor hand that those forces may be payd out of it for when there is noe other provision of pay.

Signed in ye name and by ye warrant
of ye Committee of both Kingdomes by
yor very Loveing friends
P. Wharton Lauderdaill

Darby House
15th Aprill 1646

Orders to ye Committee of both Kingdomes
for 60 barrells of powder for Litchfeild
& Match proporconable & 60 barrels
for Worcester

For Sr. Wm. Brereton,

Die Mercury 15 Aprill 1646

At ye Committee of both Kingdomes at Derby they ordered yt 60 barrells of powther be provided for ye forces before Worcester and 60 barrells of powder for ye force before Lichfield and Match and bullet proporconable and that Sr. Walter Erle be desired to provide it according to ye Order of ye Howse of Comons of ye 4th of Aprill.

44

Letter from Mr Swinfen to Sr Wm.
Brereton & ye Committee at Stafford
touching 3,000L for ye forces before
Litchfield and 60 barrells of powder
& match.

Gentlemen,

I have formerlie writt to you by two severall Messingers soe that by this bearer who is ready to take horse, I have noe tyme to adde anie thinge more onelie to let you knowe that the bearer brings you a ltre from ye Committee of both Kingdomes to informe ye 3,000L is assigned for ye support of that leauger, And because it may onely be payd where it is most necesarie other in provisione or forces not provided for and not upon a General Divident to all, which way it wilbe little serviceable to any ffor ye force not otherwise p'pounded for as you will understand by ye ltre, All I nowe desire is that you will send direcons to Mr. Worrall who is in Towne to contynue here and attend ye borrowinge of the money for ye present and returneinge of it to you so it can be gotton. If you please to order your forces according to my humble advise in my former lre soe that the money may supplie ye greatest Exigenses I hope wee may by ye strength thereof contynue till ye worke be ended or if it contynue longe our good Accompt of ye providence Husbandinge of this will procure us more. I have here inclosed sent you ye Copie of ye order of ye Committee of both Kingdomes wch I have procured for 60 barrells of powder and match proporconable. I am sure to have it in a fortnights tyme and till then I hope Coventrie will send you soe much as ye shall need to be repaid out of this Excuse my hast which allowes me not to write particulars to you, nor to add anie more but ye service of

Yor Servant
John Swinfen

Westminster Aprill 16, 1646

45

Letter from Georg Digby Esquire to Sr. Willm. Brereton touching the Race at Tutburie.

Sr,

His Majestie was pleased neare three yeares since in ye absence of Sr. Jo: ffremnike to command mee surveyor of his Race at Tutbury and I have since yt severall tymes receave orders to take speshall care of ye same, ye tyme is now yt stallions must bee procured for ye performance of ye service.

I shall therefore entreate you wilbe pleased to graunt yor tickett and safe p'tection for Martin Hughs and ffrancis Lodmore yt I may send them to ye Courte for 3 or 4 stallions for a Lese number will not serve ye turne for ye press't service and yt they may not onely come safe but likewise runne wth ye mares without molestacon and at ye end of ye season bee returned according to direction. I thought fitt in discharge of my duty to Acquaint you wth this much, not doubting of yor forwardness in a busines yt wilbee soe pleasing to his Ma'tie and soe generall a good to ye Comon wealth thus wth ye presentacon of my service I take my leave & rest,

Sr
Yor humble Ser'antt
Geo: Digby

Sandon this 14th Apll.
1646

A pass for Martin Hughes & ffran: Lodmore
To pass to Oxford & returne here wthin 30 dayes
Wth stallions for ye race of Tutbury, graunted
By Sr. Willm. Brereton.

Whereas I am moved by Georg Digby of Sandon Esquire appointed by his Ma'tie Surveiyor of ye Race at Tutbury to graunt a safe conduct for Martin Hughes and ffrancis Lodmore betwixt Oxford and London being sent for stallions for ye furnishing ye sayd race for this next season. Thes are to require you to p'mitt ye sayd Martin Hughes and ffrancis Lodmore wth theire horses to pass from Sandon to Oxford and thence to returne wthin 30 dayes next ensueing wth such stallions as shalbee sent for ye sayd service of Tutbury without molestacon or stopp, they behaving themselves inoffensively towards ye Parliam'ts proceedings. Given under my hand at our Campe on Bacon hill this 18th day of Apll. 1646

W. B.

To all whom these may come & concerne
in ye service of ye King & Parliam'tt.

Letter to Georg Digby Esquire from Sr. Willm Brereton

Sir,

According to yor desire I have herein closed you a pass & shall bee as ready to use my utmost Interest and power to preventt & restraine ye soldiers from committing any injury in ye Race and for yt and if any of ye Officers there have occasion to repaire unto mee I wilbee readie to give all possible reliefe and in ye meane tyme I add noe more but remaine

Yor Serv'tt
W. B.

Tutbury Apll. 20
1646

46

Letter to Capt. Greenwood & Capt Willars to take care of sleighting Tutbury Castell and after to March to Lichfield.

Gent,

The garrison of Tutbury beeing agreed upon to bee sleighted and made incapable of beeing made a garrison I desire yt you will contynue wth yor troops thereabouts and after Coll. Bowyers & Major Snows departure to make it yor care to see ye same Garrison sleighted sufficiently as aforesaid, and because there remaines nowe noe service to bee done by you in Darbishire I desire you will march to Lichfield after ye sleighting ye sayd Castell yt soe you may bee disposed of and assist in such service as ye Committee of both Kingdomes have appointe, Hereof I desire you will not faile as you respect ye carrieing on of this worcke Yor verrie loveing friend

W. B.

Tutbury Apll. 20th 1646

Letter from ye Committee of Derby to Sr. Willm. Brereton & ye Comittee of Stafford.

Gentlmen,

Wee received yors of ye 16th instant and wee must need justifye ye truthe that wee did to Coll. Bowyer wch is yt our Miserable Countrie is almost exhausted & yett wee are still enforces to contynue a great p'porcon of expence to ye Seige at Newarke. Besydes part of ye Scottish horse have for a long tyme, and are still amongst us, to ye exceeding damage of our poore Countrie. Ye Seige att Tutbury hath you knowe beene principally done by our forces and ye greatest parte of ye Charge by much hath hitherto beene borne by our Countie is already infected from thence, our forces and other Townes in exceeding great danger of yt infection wch may prove ye utter ruine of many. Wee therefore desire you again to help us to maintain our forces there, and yt you will joyne with us for ye reducing of that Garrison upon some reasonable condicons for ye good of both Counties, rather then linger that seige, as some endeavor thoe to ye greate Charge & hazard of our Countrie forces, this our reasonable request wee hope you will graunt to

Yor assured friends & servants

Geo: Gresley

Tho: Gell Jo: Wiglye

Jo: Winsfall Geo. Pole

Derby 17th of Apll.
1646

47

Letter to ye Comitty of Derby in Answ'r
To theires: sent from Sr. Willm. Brereton
& ye Comittie of Stafford.

Gent,

I have received yors of ye 17th of this instant, wherein you before Tutbury for ye foote of Staffordshire is double those of Derbyshire and some of yor horse are such as should have beene sent to Lichfield for yt ye number of them appointed by the Comittie of both Kingdomes hath not beene sent, but I have forbane hitherto to press that out of my earnest desire for ye speedy reduceing of yt place. Although I cannot omitt to acquainte you yt I am informed they have beene little observant'n to out orders or to keepe Guards as they ought and although yt contrarie to ye Comand of both Kingdomes, Capt. Greene & Capt Friths troopes are drawen of. Notwithstanding I shall not faile to Endeavor ye reduceing thereof according to ye trust reposed in mee and others by speshall Comicons for yt place and shall at yor desires bee more inclinable to grant larger condicons then otherwise I would, wch I must affirme will bee a great disadvantage to yor County and this of Stafford and therefore I doubt not but in reason you will thincke fitt both to assist us according to orders wth yor forces and wth maintenance for them out of yor owne cleared Countie dureing yt seige &ye rather because yt this county is much tasked for the maintaineing of ye Leauger att Lichfield wch is nothing but what may well bee desired & expected for a charitable fellow feeling neighbour Countie by

Yor friends & Serv'tts
W. B.
Jo: Bowyer
Hen: Vernon
Hen: Stone

Tutbury Leauger
Aprill 20th 1646

fforces in ye Leauger at Tutbury

Col. Bowyer	35		Captain Bagshaw	70
Capt. Gent	35	Foote	Captain Poole	60
Wm. Laughs	76 Countrymen	Staffordshire		——
Capt. Ashurst	30			130
Capt Handsley	44 Countrymen			
	——			
	220			

& the horse comanded off and on doing little service except those wch by former order were appointed for

Lichfield under Sr: W: B:
Comaund

48

Letter from Sr. Willm. Brereton, Coll. Bowyer and Mr. Vernon to ye Comittee of both Kingdomes touching Ye surrender of Tutbury Castell.

In pursuance of yor Comands wee have treated wth ye Governor, Comanders & officers in Tutbury Castell and received ye same upon condicons herwth sent to yor Honors wch wee humbly conceave wilbee more to yor Honors good likeing and ye publique service then those formerly assented unto by Sr. Jo: Gell, yet wee cannot but informe yor Honors yt notwithstanding yor late Comands by letter to him that his forces should remaine there, Hee after ye receipt thereof did send these orders inclosed to his troopes which occasioned them forthwith to draw off.

And though wee thought not fitt as knoweing it not bee in our power to admitt of Condicons for takeing of sequestracons (wch was much pressed) and because wee apprehended it might bee of dangerous consequence in regard of ye sickness increasing both in ye towne and campe and abroad in ye Countrie to admitt of soe long delay, wee therefore ye rather presumed to send upp theise our humble desires in ye behalfe of Sr. Andrew Kniverton and Sr. Jo: ffitzherbert that theire sequestracons may if thought fitt bee remitted whereunto wee are ye rather induced because ye compos icons of their estates wee humbly conceave will not countervaile ye charge that ye Countrie must have undergone had ye seige beene contynued but a short tyme longer. Hereby you may much oblige us unto you and wee hope without prejudice to ye service of ye Parliam'tt, when they fynde our p'formances goe beyond our undertakings. Notwithstanding wee shall submitt all to yor Honors pleasure, desire yt our endeavours may p'duce anything wch may render us worthy to bee accompted as we shall approve ourselves

Yor Honors most faithfull & most
Humble Servants
W. B.
Hen: Vernon
Jo: Bowyer

Tutbury Apll. 21st
1646

Posscript

Wee did further agree wth ye soldiers yt those wch desire to march for Venice[29] should march without theire armes and have 40s. a man for theire accommodator and those that went to any of ye Kings Garrisons yt are unbesieged, wch wee conceave wilbee few or none, to have 30s. the rest wch wee beleeve wilbee most of them are to have neither armes nor money

---

From Sr. Jo: Gell, Capt. Greens orders to
march away from ye seige of Tutbury
Castell contrarie to ye orders from ye
Comittee of both Kingdomes to Sr. Jo: Gell

I doe order you wth yor troope to march unto Lift. Coll. Hambeltons quarters & d'liver to him ye order yt Lift. Generall Lesleye hath directed to him & others of ye Scotts Officers, itts for ye great good & preservation of our owne Countie wch must not bee neglected utterly & yt service being done then you are to returne to yor service now in hand. This is done by ye approbacon and direction of ye Deputilifts and our Comittee

Jo: Gell

Apll. 16: 1646

49

Articles Agreed upon for ye Surrender of Tutbury Castell
for ye Service of ye Parliam'tt Aprill 20th 1646

1. That al ye fortifications in and aboute ye Castell bee sleighted & ye howse made incapable of beeing made a Garrison and delivered into ye hands of them who had ye keepeing thereof in tyme of peace, & yt Barton Garrison bee alsoe sleighted in like manner soe soone as possible & delivered to ye late owner thereof, hee making his peace wth ye Parliam'tt.
2. That all Comanders Gent & Officers in Comicon may march away wth theire horses, armes & theire own p'per goods and ye Comon Soldiers wth theire swords, armes & p'per goods to any of ye Kings Garrisons unbeseiged, they marching 8 myles a day & carrages to bee p'vyded according and all those yt desire it may have liberties to live at home and enjoy theire estates, submitting to ye Ordinances of Parliam't and to bee secured in theire p'sons and Estates from violence & plunder.
3. That all officers and soldiers yt desire to goe beyond seas may have libertie soe to doe p'voided it bee wthin 6 weeks tyme next ensueing and in ye Interim p'tested doeing nothing prejudicall to ye Parliam'tt and noe oath to bee imposed but an Engagem't never to take upp armes agst ye Parliam'tt.
4. That all yt desire to have theire Sequestracons taken of may have libertie to goe to Compound wth ye Parliam'tt & to have 3 months tyme for yt purpose without interuption & after composicons made & pardon sued out they may have liberty to dispose of theire estates as freely as formerly.

5. That ye sleighting of ye sd. Garrisons shall bee begune tomorrow or upon Wednesday next and yt all those yt are to march from ye sd. Castell according to ye sayd Articles shall begin their march upon Wednesday next.

Signed by Sr. Willm. Brereton & ye rest of ye Comicon on ye behalfe of ye Parliamentt
H: Vernon Jo: Bowyer

Signed by ye Governor and Comiconers for ye Castell
Peter Kniveton
Jo: ffitzherbert
Jo: Gerrard
Wm. Browne

Addiconal Agreem't betweene the Comicons on both sydes

Its further assented unto that all ye soldiers wch will march to any of ye Kings Garrisons unbeseiged & shall have 30s. a man for theire Accomadacon and all those Officers and Soldiers yt desire to live at home shall have leave to live quietly submitting to ye Parliam't and to bee secured in theire p'sons and estates from violence and plunder that ye money to bee payd as above sayd shall ye one halfe thereof bee payd ye same day ye soldiers begin theire march from ye Castell and ye other halfe wthin 7 dayes after, or before they march out of this county and yt 50L bee payd to Lif'tt. Coll. Peter Kniveton wthin 7 dayes next, to bee distributed amongst ye officers in ye Castell as hee shall thincke fitt.

W. B.
Jo: Bowyer
Hen: Vernon
Wm: Browne

Peter Kniveton
Jo: ffitzherbert
Jo: Gerrard

50

An Agreem't betweene Coll. Bowyer Mr. Vernon & Capt. Jo: Gerrard Concerneing ye Venetian Voyage.

Articles Agreed on Betwixt Coll. Jo: Bowyer & Hen: Vernon Esquire and Capt. Jo: Gerrard
Aprill 18th
1646

That such soldiers and officers as shall please to goe along wth Capt. Jo: Gerrard for ye Venetian voyage shall have 40s. a man & 10s. a man upon ye surrender of Tutbury Castell and ye rest to bee put into Coll. Bowyers and Capt. Gerrards hands upon ye march thither and as many as are listed under Capt. Gerrard shall have a weeks tyme to send for or heare from ye Venetian

Embasador whether they may bee entertained or not and during yt weekes tyme to quarter in some parte of Staffordshire, demeaning themselves honestly and doeing yt may prejudice ye Countrie, further it is agreed betweene Coll. Bowyer, Mr. Vernon & Capt. Jo: Gerrard yt if his and ye soldiers intencons bee frustrated in their former resource for Venice to wch they are to march without armes that then Capt. Gerrard wth those soldiers of Tutbury listed under him shall have 10s. addicon to theire 10s. given them at theire departing and giveing upp ye Castell of Tutbury and shall have ye liberty to goe with theire armes to any of ye Kings Garrisons unbeseiged, given under our hands the day and yeare above written

Hen: Vernon Jo. Bowyer
Jo: Gerrard

51

Letter from Sr. Willm. Brereton to ye Comittee of Both Kingdomes touching ye surrendering of Tutbury Castell. To bee delivered if thought convenient.

My Lords and Gentlemen,

Wee have this day according to ye power and directions from yor Honor gone through wth ye Articles for takeing in Tutbury and most humblie informe you yt ye increaseing of ye sickness here in ye towne and amongst our soldiers, wee haveing 18 dead and visited and divers dead suddenly this p'ss'tt day, and ye Countries possessed wth extreame feares thereof by the spreadinge of it abroad and complaineing likewise of ye burthen of ye charge hath enforced us rather to make bold to put a period to ye same (to pr'vent further eminent and apparent danger) then to stay for ye returne of ye further pleasures upon our transmitting them first. There beeing noething comprehended therein wch wee did beleeve you would scruple att. Wee had much debate aboute ye sequestracons. They insisted much upon ye takeing them off, But thereunto wee by noe meanes assentinge all yt wee assumed was to p'vent Sr. Andrew Kniveton & Sr, Jo: ffitzherbert particulars to yor honors to bee p'posed to ye honorable Howse to bee considered wch alsoe wee ye rather make bolde to doe because wee humbly conceaved ye charge (Besydes ye danger) of dyeing heare, would have beene of greater detriment to ye countrie then theire sequestracons advantageous all wch I make bolde to pr'sent and recommend unto yor honors wisdomes not having at pr'ss'tt further to add but my care to dispose of ye forces to ye best advantage in pursuance of yor honors former comands soe soone as wee dare bring them amongst ye rest of our men lest they bring the infection amongst them wherein and in all things I shall ever studie to approve myselfe

My Lords and Gent
Yor Honors most faithfull
and Humble Servantt
W. B.

Tutbury Apll. 20th
1646

52

Sr Willm. Brereton to ye Speaker touching Surrender and taking up Tutburie Castle setting forth the reasons of assenting these Articles although they be tollerable. The Articles are returned before Sat. Ap. 20 1646.

Sr,

Having received severall ltres from ye Comittee of Both Kingdomes directed to yourselfe and others both formerlie and of late to treate about ye surrender of Tutburie Castell (before which I did ye 13th March last place a Leauger under ye Comand of Colonell Bowyer who managed it verrie faithfullie and discreetly) and having this day taken it accordinglie, I cannot allowe myself to omit forthwith to give you thereof, to wch end I have sent, the inclosed Articles. The Conditions given to Ashbie and those tendered by Sr. John Gell to the Castle (though not assented unto by ye Comittee of both Kingdomes) did much encourage ye Enimy to resist upon demands farre higher then those wherin besides wee were enforced to give them ye better Conditions upon these Consideracons wch did much induce us to endeavor ye speedie despatch of this Garrison which were not onelie the Acompts and Cryes of ye Countrey under ye unsupportable burden of ye Charge of maintaining this Leauger and that at Lichfield, and ye daylie Danger of Mutynes quarrells betweene ye Darbyshire and Staffordshire soldiers, but ye Overseinge and dispersing of ye workes both in the Country, Towne and the Leauger, wherein divers died suddenly ever whilst wee were in treaty. Upon ye survey of these in ye Castle (Wherein I was this day) I find there are not above 50, if so manie, or anie at all, that will March away wth theire armes to anie of ye Kings Garrisons unbesieged, if there were anie such Garrison to march unto accordingly. Sr as it is not to be denyed, but ye most of them will submitt or goe for Venice. Wee have sumoned in the Countrie and have this day begun the worke of Demolishinge ye fortificacons of ye Castle, and makeing it Incapeable of being made a Garrison to which Article (wch was insisted upon by ye Enimy) wee ye rather assented thereunto the maintenance of a garrison. There would be an unnfaire charge (and not anie manner of advantage or protecon) to ye Countrey. Soe soone as it may bee convenient and safe to bring these fforces amongst ye rest I shall endeavor to improve all the forces I can possibly spare from Litchfeild for ye further advancem't of your service wch is not more faithfully desired by anie man thenby

Yor most humble Servt.
Wm. Brereton

Tutbury Ap. 21: 1646

The same poste was added to this lre note to ye former lre from Sr. Wm. Brereton, Mr. Vernon, Coll. Bowyer, to ye Comittee of both Kingdomes touchinge those Souldiers yt are to receave mony. 21st Ap. 1646.

53

Letter from ye Comittee at Chester to Sr. Wm
Brereton touching setl. ye Munney in Chester
to ye Gunpowder men.

Honorable Sr,

Wee are much importuned by this bearer, Mr. Guise, Concerneing the powder Worckes, and thincke it may bee of some advantage to this Garrison especially in case of danger. Wee therefore desire yor order to Mr. Brereton to sett him ye Munnes upon such termes as you shall thincke fitt, and wee shall rest

Yor Servants
Jo: Breen
Ro: Gregg
Wm. Davies

Chester 16th
1646

54

The forme of passe granted to Sr. John
Ffitzherbert upon the surrender of
Tutbury attending to ye Articles

Whereas there was an Agreement by the Comissioners for ye Parliam't wth ye Governors of Tutburie Castle to enjoy theire Estates submitting to all ordnances of Parliam't & to be spared in theire Persons and Estates from violence and plunder. And those yt would Compound should have libertie to goe to Compound wth ye Parliam't within three monthes and to have passes for yt purpose. And likewise desire that ye benefit of ye said Articles, these are therefore to Enquire all who it may concerne that ye said Conditions and all ye Clauses therein contained be observed by all and each of you as to ye Person & Estate of ye said.

Given at Tutbury, Aprill 21st 1646.

L're from Colonell Bowyer & Mr. Vernon from
Tutburie touching ye want of money to pay
Ye engage't to ye Souldiers in ye Castle.

Sr,

Since your departure wee have beene considering how wee may performe Condicons on our parte and wee finde that there is but 50L left to discharge our Engagem'ts to ye soldiers whereas there wilbe speedie use of 300L wch wee desire you will please to take care that wee may by ten of ye Clocke twomorowe have it sent unto us otherwise wee shall much doubt of a succesfull proceedinge tomorrow in this business, wherein is engaged together with yours ye honoure of,

Your faithfull friend to serve you
Henry Vernon Jo: Bowyer

Tutbury 21st Aprill 1646
at 7at night

Sr, the truth is this, you have soe left us wth such an inconsiderable finance that we have no hope of performance.

H. Vernon Jo: Bowyer

55

Sr Wm. Breretons Answer to Mr. Vernon
& Colonell Bowyer at Tutbury.

Gentlemen,

I shalbe verie readie to take care there be a full p'formance of Condicons on our part, And therefore in this particular wch you mencon I desired yesterday a liste of ye soldiers wch was delivered mee by ye Governor of ye Castle, wherein I took notice of those that were to receive money by ye Articles and found them to be under foure score that were goeing to march wth Captaine Gerrard, and to anie of ye Kinges Garrisons unbesieged. Now in as much as there are none of ye Kinges Garrisons unbesieged unto wch they might march it remaines to be by you considered what is due upon yt Article in case ainie of them take money and theire Armes and doe not march accordinglie. You know Captaine Gerrards men are to have but ten shillinges apiece when they march out wth their Armes. Those that are to march to ainie of ye Kings Garrisons unbesieged were there any, were to have ye halfe of their money when they march away and ye other halfe within seven daes after they march out. Hereof as I came onely yesterday Captaine Stone and myself considered and resolved that Captaine Stone should yesternighte send away to Stafford for 50L more to be braught upon this day which I hope wilbe p'formed in due tyme and that wee did compute would bee full as much as would be payable this day and were but wee did beleeve the same in safe handes. ffor this end alsoe invested for John Banner from Stafford to take care of ye Armes there, which accordinge to theire owne liste wilbe more then two partes of ye number which I beseech you let be done carefullie and let them be laid up in some Roome under locke and key as alsoe all ye goodes (except those that are ye proper goods of those that march away according to ye Articles), that soe ye same may de disposed of as may be thought fitt, those that belonge to ye Country to the owners and ye rest to publique uses. ffor ye rest of ye monies when I receive an Exact list from you I shall take care for ye same, wherein I doubt not but you wilbe verie punctuall that soe wee may knowe what money to pay and that passes to grante that soe no ecceses may bee committed wherein not doubtinge of your care I conclude, Remaininge

Yor faithfull friend
Wm. Brereton

Elmehurst
Ap: 2 1646

I desire you will send this to Lt. Colonell Leigh at Langley and ye rest that soe there may be accordinglie an Exact List taken.

56

Captaine Stones note to Sr. Wm. Brereton
Touching ye same busines of money.

Sr,

I have sent my man to Stafford who will carry them 50L more this day, and John Tanner to take care of ye Armes. I beleeve as you write, 100L will pay more then by ye Articles are to bee payd at present if they suffer themselves not to be deluded and over worked in ye managing of the busines

Sr, from
Your Honors most humble
Servainte
Henry Stone

Litch'd. Aprill 22nd
1646

57

Peticon of ye Countie of Chesh: to ye
Parliam't in Aprill 1646, About wch Mr.
Manwaringe and Mr. Roger Wilbraham
Sent up to London. Col. Booth and Col.
Jones being gone up the last weeke.

Sheweth

That for ye moste parte ever since Jan 1642, there have beene two Armies maintained upon this small Countie whereby it hath bene soe exhausted that ye inhabitants have little left for theire subsistence. That upon ye Treatie for ye surrender of Chester your Petitioners to save ye Cittie from Plunder engaged themselves to give all ye Officers and Souldiers that served in ye leauger, one monethes pay for theire service which amounted to neare 20,000L all of which is nowe become due unto ye soldiers and above 12,000L under-charged goods of ye best value being Conveyed away when ye King marched out, or soe consealed by ye citizens that monies are verie slowle raised from ye Sequestracons, will fall farre shorte of what was expected to discharge ye same Engagement

That all ye Cheshire horse consisted of neere 600 and 300 dragoones are since ye first of Julie this monthe in arreare besides theire gratuitie the vol-unteery Companies beeing 16 in number, foure months in arreare wherein it is impossible for this impoverished county to give them satisfaction theire necesityes flowing upon them and ye souldyers growing every day more and more Impatient soe that wee were not of longe tyme in more danger of Ruyne by ye Enimy then wee are at this present of spoiling by our owne soldiers and those of other counties to whom wee stande engaged.

That there be some Companies of foote left in the Cittie where the Malig-nants are supernumerary to ye great hazard there of and soe manie foote and dragoones Comanded to Litchfield that north Wales is endangered to be over run by ye enimye that the County has longe suffered through ye want of a member in the Howse of Comons in ye absence of Sir Wm. Brereton.

That both Cittie and County are verrie destitute of a Godly and learned Minister through ye want of Competentie to maintaine churches and of power to establish them in ye places of delinquents and that ye courses of justice are obstructed.

The promises considered, your Debtours humbly Pray that a Consider-able sume of money may bee speedily ordered out of ye Composicons of Delinquents Estates of the County or otherwise toward the discharge of ye great Engagements that lie upon the Country to prevent ye unavoidable ruyne thereof that a Certaine number of Souldiers may bee settled here for ye defence of the Cittie, that a writt may be speedilie issued to ye Sherriffe for ye electing of a knight for the County. That a select Committee may bee appointed by yor Honor for ye settling of ministers in all Chappells and Churches within this city and county, that a worke soe Conduceable to ye glorie of God, and Comfort of his people may not be Retarded by ye absence of one of ye Comittie and yt a Competency for ye minister may out of the sequestration, Tithes belonging to ye deane and chapter (or otherwise) be allowed as in your wis-dome you shall thinke that ye Exchequer and all other Courts in this County may be opened and wee restored to our Antient privileges,

And your Peticoners.

59

Another Petition of ye same date.

That this small countie since the begininge of these warres hath for ye most part maintained seven Garrisons and two Armies by ye vast charge whereof and ye manie Garrisons of ye Enimy where wth it was incompassed ye Countrey hath bene soe disabled to pay those Layes and taxes wee have of necessitie bene forced upon it. That there are verie great sumes due in arreare unto many officers and souldiers of the Countie besides what hath beene advanced upon ye Parliaments propositions. That wee had noe munie left us (when wee had not wherewth to pay our souldiers) to keepe them to goe before and upon dutye dureinge ye longe Leauger of Beeston and Chester but by promising them their arrears upon the Reducement of them nor to quiet the much oppressed and almost ruyned Countrey, but ye unsupportable burthen of free q'ter with want of monies Compelled us unto them by promising them ease when ye Cittie was reduced. That upon Treatie for ye surrender of Chester your p'titioners to save the Cittie from beinge plundered, whereby it would have made verie unserviceable to ye Comonwealth engaged themselves to give all ye officers and souldiers that served in the Leauger one moneths pay as a gratuity for the service which amounted to neer 20,000L all which is now growne due unto ye souldiers and above 12,000L undischarged goods of best value formerlie brought in for security beinge conveyed away when ye King marched out, or soe concealed by ye citizens yt moneyes are verie slowly eased from ye sequestratons and will fall farre short of what was appointed to discharge ye Engagem't for supplie whereof in part wee laid a tax of six hundred upon ye Countye to ease them of the Lancashire horse that would not leave untill satisfied wch was soe contrary to our promises and above ye abilityes of manie partes that it will not be gathered.

That all ye Cheshire horse consistinge of over 600 and three hundred dragoones are since the first of Julie three monthes in arrears besides theire gratuitye the volunteer companies being 16 in number foure moneths in arrears wch doe all of them now presse upon us with much incivility and some threate for theire arreares & will noe longer be fed with promises wherein it is impossible for the impoverished county to give them satisfacon ye Comitee necesityes of coming upon them by the Excessive charge of ye Leauger amountinge to above 80,000L and the souldiers growing every day more and more Impatient, soe that wee were not of longe tyme in more danger of Ruyne by ye Enimy then wee are at present of spoiling by our owne necessitated souldiers and those of other Countyes to whom wee stande engaged. The preausere considered your Petitioners humbly pray that theire former Petiton concerning ye sequestracons of this Countye may be taken into Consideracon and yt a considerable sume of moneye may be speedly ordered out of ye composicons of Delinquents Estates of the Cittye and County towards discharge engagm'ts to prevent theire Iminent Ruyne and Danger

And your Peticoners

61

Peticoners sat in Darbishire, Ap: 1646 for
asserting whereof Captain Greenes and
Captain ffriths troopes were called off dutie.

To ye Right hon'ble ye Lords and others of ye Committee of both Kingdomes.
The humble peticon of divers inhabitants of ye Countrie of Darbie.

Shew,

That whereas this Countrie at present is unfairly oppressed by several great payments to ye leauger at Newarke, at Lichfield and Tutburie & provision for ye Scoch Armie and yet divers of theire horse are quartered amongst us besides ye maintainance of our owne souldiers and other payments by ordnance of Parliam't. And whereas ye present siege at Tutbury hath beene principallee managed by our countrey forces to our great charges and Staffordshire hath but few souldiers there and are at small charge and whereas the present defendants at Tutburie would yeild up yt Castle to Sr. John Gell but will not yeild it upp to others untill they braught to great Extremitie, which is like to prove a worcke of a longe tyme and great expence to our County, the sicknes encreasing there alsoe which may other endanger ye Raiseing of ye leauger or ye spreading that infectious discease to our utter undoinge. Wee therefore most humbly pray that ye Castle may be surrendered to Sr. John Gell upon some reasonable propposition approved by yor Lo'pps,

And your petitioners

The matter of this peticon was not onely false, for ye forces of Staffordshire that were in ye Leauger were double to those of Darbishire who were verie unserviceable & mutynous soldiers, and ye leauger was there placed by Sr. Wm. Brereton, But ye managing thereof very indirect and ye troopes that were appointed by ye Committee of both Kingdomes to attend the service of Tutburie were drawn of by Sr. John Gells orders and imployed it is said to solicite for support to this peticon which was anticipated in ye verie bud by ye delivery of ye Castle to Sr. Wm. Brereton, G'rall of ye field, upon ye Articles of ye 20th March before menconed. The Articles wch were, are indirectly agreed upon and concluded by Sr. John Gells helpe, being wholy disliked by ye Committee of both Kingdomes, who gave a reprehension to Sr. John Gell for his dealing of them who receaved theire Instructions to Sr. Wm. Brereton touchinge ye same, who Imployed Colonell Bowyer to comand that leauger in his absence.

Col. Bowyers letter to Sr. Wm. Brereton
Touching Tutbury Castle.

Sr,

I have almost in all probability brought ye busines to a Period and question not but to Conclude all, God willinge, at your arrival here. I doe forbeare to send you answeres to theire Demands till I see you. For the Conclusion of all depends on your being here I pray you faile not to come at ten o'clocke and be wth

Yor friend & Kinsman
Jo: Bowyer

Tutbury Ap: 18
At 8 at night 1646

For ye hon'ble G'rall, his much honoured
Uncle Sr. Wm. Brereton

Upon ye last lre. From Colonell Bowyer, Sr. Wm. Brereton went to Tutburie and Concluded the Articles before menconed of ye 20th of Aprill. According to wch ye Castle was delivered wherein there were such Armes & goods as were hereafter entald.

63

Letter to Mr. Ashurst and Mr. Swinfen touching
The armes and provisions that were taken in
Tutburye Castle.

Sr,

By my last I could onelie advertise you of our agreem't for ye takeing of Tutburie Castle and send you a Copie of ye Articles. These may give you the further Accompt thereof that yesterdaie those that belonged to ye Castle did according to ye Articles march out. The whole number were about 240 whereof about 140 gave up theire Armes choosing rather then adventure further in ye quarrell where in they have been engaged to live at home and submitt to all ordinances of Parliam't. The rest beinge aboute 140 are march out wth Capt. Gerrard wth little hopes of being received into any of ye Kinges Garrisons but have thought to goe wth Captaine Gerrard for ye Venetian Service and soe to leave us theire Armes soe as then wee shall have all theire Armes. Of provisions of warre wee are hereby furnished wth one Iron Gun carrieing a bullet of about 12 pounds weight, about eighty four musquetts, 17, barreles of powder and match and bullet, 150 pikes, two drumes, some four hand Granadoes and some provisions of victualls, some more of each of these and not of ye worst and some other goods are Embezelled by some desperate men by reason soe meane placed in the castle are supposed to be dangerouslie infected as that nowe durst advertise to bring them together.

The Worckes are demolished and about ye Castle for ye making of them Incapable of being Garrisoned it will be usefull to pull down some of ye towers and walles as well as the out worckes.

I am now returned to Litchfield and am preparinge to drawe off some forces to place before Dudley and for yt end to erect some stronge trenches before yt place (wch I hope wilbe but a short worke) that soe the lesser number may suffice to bee continued there and ye same to be advanced further beyond that place upon ye Enimyes quarters which service cannot be altogether soe expediouslie carried on because wee dare not attempt to bringe up to ye rest, those men that have bene at and about Tutbury where the infecton is, as untill they have rested for some choise tyme in fresh quarters. Att Litchfield our worckes are now in good posture within lesse then halfe a musquett shot of ye Close. Round aboute ye same, yet such end constantly to be approachinge as neere them as may be for our advantage. Wee have played our morter peeces, most whereof are verie small ones. Our former wante of powder retarded the makinge provision of soe many Granadoes as were needful, and I feare the weakness of our powder hath much detracted from the Execucon that might otherwise probably have been done. But I hope the supply of powder that I have long expected and I hope is at hande will prove better. At present I shall delay you noe longer but give you the assurance of my utmost endeavours and dilligence to promote ye publique worke and to approve myself,

Yor Assured friend & Servant
Wm. Brereton

Litchfield Ap: 25th 1646

65

Letter to Mr Speaker by ye same Messinger
to ye same purpose and to Sr. Ralph Ashton
Wm. Ashurst and Colonel Moore.

Sr,

Though there was some liberty Graunted for the Officers and Souldiers that were in Tutbury Castell to march away wth theire Armes to any of the Kings Garrisons unbesieged yett such use was made of ye present opportunitye to possess them wth the knowledge of theire own Condition that as in my last I intymated fewer or none seeme likely to make use of that liberty wch did ye rather embolden us the further to condisend as wee have founde this day according which occasions the further Accompt. That when ye Enimy marched yesterdaie out of ye Castell There was not anie of them went to ye

Kinge but all to theire owne homes for such as desire if they may have libertie to goe for ye Venetian service wth Captaine Gerard (wch are about 120).

The armes left in ye Castle besides manie conveyed away were aboute 160 musquetts, 50 pikes, 2 barrells of powder, one Iron peece carrieing a bullet of about 12 pounds weight and a box of Drakes. There are more armes in some of those roomes that are supposed to be unsorted.

As touchinge ye Condicon of our affaires before Litchfield wee have now perfected our mounts and live about ye Close and are about to erect some other mounts nearer the Close whereby wee may the better discover ye Enimy before as they come out of theire Gates. Wee have tryde our morter peeces and have playde some of our Granadoes wch have done some, but not verie much execucon. As theire may be further occasions you may expect to receave a further accompt and yt my utmost endeavours and dilligence shall not be wantinge to carrie on ye worcke and to approve myselfe in particular,

Ye verie affeconate
friend and humble Ser't,
Wm. Brereton

Lichfield Ap: 23rd
1646

67

Sr. Wm Brereton to Major Zancky for his Troope when some of ye Officers informed that unlesse the Troopes come to Sr: Wm: it Would be dissolved.

Sir Wm. Brereton To Major Zancky Touching ye Troop Serv'd by Quart'm'r Cooper

Sr,

The onelie end and extent of my writeinge for my Troope was no other then ye advancem't of ye service of ye publique, deservinge not to retard but as much as anie may whatsoever to promote ye service of North Wales and ye Generall good of ye kingdome and in particular the promotinge ye comaundes yt lie upon mee not onelie for the Engagement here where wee are, thankes be to God, in a verie good condicon and may spare some forces hence but not sufficient for another dutye.

It is true there were 400 horse of Cheshire assigned to Colonell Mytton for ye Service of North Wales and it is as true both yourself and others may testifie my forwardness to that service and for yt end before my comeing out of Cheshire orders were drawne up assigninge that numbers hither accordinglie. And now by my desiring my troope hither I did not intend to detract from yt comaund. ffor ye number of Horse and Dragoones belonging to yt Comitie are by Resolucon to ye Parliam't

Represented as a burthen to bee neere 900 soe as one troope or two out of them cannot hinder ye other service. This Imploym't I am comanded upon will require all ye force that can be drawne together in these partes of ye kingdome which is a service of great importance and for carrieing on whereof I doubt not but ye Parliam't will make tymely provisions. I shall therefore desire my owne troopes may according to my former lre If he sent for them. march hither to receive orders and if you apprehend it may hinder ye Service if you leave the Regt. then you may send them accordinglie under ye comand of such officer as is at present in Cheife at the head of them. It shalbe my care to see they be provided for wth ye best, and kept together. And had they come sooner they might have bene capeable of sooner receaveing a greater protocol of ye money ye Parlt. hath assigned for this present service, which now must be much losse

And some of ye Comittee of Chesh. writt to Sr. Wm. Brereton that some horse might be spared from Wales If he sent for them.

Who is at pr'sent from
yor verie lo. Friend
Wm. Brereton

Litchfield Ap: 23rd 1646
The Lancashire horse and foote assigned Colonell Mytton are come up unto him I heare.

I doe not desire to Estrange you from the troope and therefore if you please to stay wth ye Regt. if it may be for ye advantage of ye service.

68

Ltre to ye Lords & Com'es at Newarke

Ap: 23, 1646. Richard Clarke a foot post was sent wth a ltre to ye Lords and other Comissoners of ye Parlt. of England at Newarke giving them an acco't of our present Condicon and inclosing the Articles for surrender of Tutbury.

69

List of Armes in Tutbury Castle and
Other materialls sent to Eccleshall Castle.

A true note taken the 24th day of Aprill 1646 of all such amunicon as was delivered into ye handes of Lt. Scot from Tutburie Castle by Henry Deruou Esquire by order from Sr. Wm. Brereton conveyed to Eccleshall Castle and there kept for ye publique service as occasion requires.

Imprimis one great iron peece mounted	
Musquettes and musquetts Bullets	147
Musquett stockes	010
Armee 7 shutes	007
Pikes	040
Gunpowder two barrells	002
Bulletts 2 barrells	002
Match 3 bundells	003
Granadoes 16	016
Drume	002

Receaved by mee Ayber Scott

These were delivered by Lt. Scot (in ye absence of Rd. Blackmore) to Lt. Wolrich, but it seemes the pikes were most broken.

70

Ltre to Sr. Wm. Waller[30] to send a man
to take care of Rydlie and Shocklack
For ye Ladies uses.

Sr,

Since ye returne of yt Gentleman who was sent to take care of Ridley and Shocklash, the profitte whereof ought to be imployed to pay ye Engagemente due to ye Lord Winchesters Daughters there hath not bene yt improvement thereof that might have bene, nor can I hope or expect it unlesse you send some man to be constantlie there to looke after ye managm't thereof, for I assure you I have not tyme nor can looke after the disposing of aynie ones affaires, But doe verie much desire yt all right ought to be done to those deservinge ladyes wch is not more desired by anie man by

Yor Most faithfull friend &
Serv't
W. Brereton

Litchfield Apr 25
1646

71

Ltre to Sr. Wm. Strickland, Mr. Ashurst &
For Mr. Bruen to bee Baron of ye Exchequer

Sr,

Understandinge that the Parliam't is now in a way to open ye Courte at Chester and for yt end have appointed a Comittee to consider touching ye supplyinge the Chamberlaines place and other officers depending upon ye same, I have formerly taken ye boldnes humblee to propounde unto you One whom I conceive to be a verie fitt man for Baron of ye Exchequer, namelie

Jonathon Bruen Esquire whom I have founde to be a man of much faithfulnes and abilitie who hath acted as one of ye Comittee for ye Parliam't within ye Comittee of Chester and bene a great sufferer by reason of his adhering to ye Parliam't service. Whereas I shall earnestly desire your assistance that he may be admitted to ye Imployment in case ye former Baron be Incapeable, who hath continued in the kings Quarters untill Chester was reduced to ye Parliam'ts service. But I shall not enlarge myself nowe then assure you I knowe a man in that Countrye whom you may make use of, more serviceable than the Gentleman I have renounced, who I am confident truly feares God whereby you may much rejoice ye Hearts of ye well affected and much engage

Your verie ffaithfull
friend to serve you
Wm. Brereton

Litchfield Aprill 25th
1646

72

The Intelligence of Peter Warner who
was sent out of ye Close to gaine Intelligence

Sr. Thomas Tilslie,

Whereas it pleased you and ye rest of ye Gentlemen to Imploy mee yor Servant to bring Intelligence if I could learne what Condicon the kinge is in. The truest newes is to be had from Mr. John Harborne who laies two miles from Woodstocke that ye kinge is no wayes able to yeild you anie reliefe.

The kinge being blocked up himself. Sir, as I am a souldier under your comand thinke upon your proved servant & prisoner

Peter Warner

From ye leauger in
Bacon Streete 2 Aprill 1646

Lt. Colonell Gerrard his ltre
to Sr. Tho. Tildesley touching ye
said comand.

Sr,

It hath pleased God to deliver your Intelligencer Mr. Peter Warner, ye late M[aste]r of your fireworkes and doorkeeper of your Counsells into our hands that he may receave according to his activeness and Demeritts, you will herewith alsoe by his note sent you have a briefe Accompt of his journey and therein may perspicuously see your owne and ye rest of ye Gentlemens Condicon who are with you, wch will unavoidable befall you if not speedily prevented. And this he is desired truly to present unto you & them who is,

Yr. Servant
Gilbert Gerrard

Aprill 21 1646
ffor Sr. Tho: Tildesley, Go'r of
Litchfield Close.

73

Sr Thomas Tildesley his Answere to
Lt. Col. Gerrard.

Sr,

Peter Warner was Comanded by mee as a souldier of this Garrison to goe to Oxford. It seemes you have had ye fortune to have a returne of his journey before mee, yet because I have imployed him (though he failed in the action) I shall desire to Exchange him and doubt not but you are sensible of soe manie Civilities from us since you laid out your leauger, in takeing your Engagements for all your soldiers that wee that have taken that you will not refuse this, my proposicon is that you will release him upon my promise either to give you a man equall to him in Exchange or else to send soe much money as Captaine Stone shall demand for the Randsome. I desire that ye more that wee maybe made sensible of ye said Condicon wee are in as you pretend. You gave him severall famous titles as Intelligencer, master of our fireworks and doore keeper of our Counsells, the first it seemes he hath given you the accompt of but never had that Imployment from mee. I never knew anie facultie he had in ye second, formerlie he had beene a doore keeper wch was given him for his subsistence. Now you have a full accompt of ye man. I desire your Answere

Your Servant
Thomas Tildesley

21st Aprill 1646
ffor Colonel Gerrard
at ye Leauger these

74

Lt. Colonell Gerrards reply
touching Warner.

Sr,

Your drumme hath seene Mr. Warner to wch there shalbe noe Civility wantinge, ffor his Exchange I knowe none of our friends in your power to propose for him were hee fit to be Exchanged. And for his Ransome if hee be Redeemable (wch I conceave is not) I shall soe send as I see my Generall propose yor desires unto him in it, and touching his exchange and procure you a satisfactory answere therein wch is all that is in the power of

Yor Servant,
Gilbert Gerrard

Aprill 21 1646

For Sr. Tho. Tildesley kt.
Gov'r of Litchfield Close.

Sr. Thomas Tydesley his ltre to
Sr. Wm. Brereton touching Warners
Intelligence.

Sr,

Accordinge to Engagem't I have returned Warner unto you. Hee has soe ill performed his journey and braught soe bad newes (wch we do not at all believe) yt I had rather he had his quarter with you, then us, yet soe I pressed to release him if he were taken to Right myself, I desire you will propose some reasonable Ransome for him wch I shall pay and then have leave the man to his owne disposall not doubting but he will bringe you better newes then he hath done us.

Sr, I stand engaged to you for ye returne of Major Bywater. The Gentleman is labouring all ye meanes possible for ye procuring of his Ransome. My desire is that you will pardon him two or three daies. I hereby re-engage myself for his returne at that tyme or sooner if you please to demand him. I desire I may heare from you wth ye first concerneing what you have done aboute Captaine Heskith who is respected here before this.

Yr Serv't
Tho. Tildesley

24th Aprill 1646

For Sr. Wm. Brereton Bart. or in his
absence ye next Comander in Chiefe
in ye Leauger.

75

Sr. Wm. Breretons Answere
to Sr. Thomas Tyldesley

[No letter written in book]

76

Major Warners ltre to Sr. Wm.
Brereton.

Honor'ble Sr,

Though my person be a stranger to you yet my Request hath bene presented before whereto though at first you returned a Denyall yet I hope this my second addresse and Importunitie will finde you more favourable. Sr, soe it is that I have bene absent from my owne home in Warwickshire for ye space of three yeares and upwards. Dureing which tyme ye Comittee of Coventry and all other Garrisons belonginge to ye Parlyam't have enjoyed all my Estate to ye value of 1,000L paid besides ye seisure of my personall Estates both within and without doores. I confesse I have ever since made my aboade in one or other of ye kinges Garrisons but how as a sojourner not as a souldier, as a spectator not an Actor. Now is ye offence beinge not of ye Deepest Dye and yt little Reserve of money wch you gave mee to sustaine mee hitherto being quite spent my humble suit is that in Consideracon of ye promise as alsoe intended compassion of ye manie infirmities of my verie old age whereof one to witt an Extreame deafines hath seised upon mee since my last addresse to you. You would be pleased to give mee and my Man Wm. Hans (without whose ayde I am not able to get up into a saddle) your passe to Coventry where though I die prisoner, I shall Reckon you have done mee a great favour. Thus referring all to God & yourself I take leave & rest

Yor most humble Serv't
Georg Warner

For ye Right Hon'ble
Sr. W. Brereton
Barronett

77

Tho. Tyldesleys postscript to
Mr Warners letter

Sr,

I have perused this lre and since it is proceedinge from an old man who hath done well and is nowe wearie of it. I referre both him and ye letter to you wishing you had no better meanes to effect yor Designes

Yor Servant
Thomas Tyldesley

78

Colonell Cootes lre to Colonell Jones
touching his

Sr,

You have professed soe much love to mee and friendship (I hope reallie) as I am ever by those expressions obliged at this tyme to write unto you, my opinions and feares of ye evill issues may happen unto you by your large and undeserved oppressions agt. Sr. Wm. Brereton whom you are soe much lyed to honor by all ye lyes of gratitude that can be expressed for his many Respects from tyme to tyme and rewards to you and yours, many much advise at it and I for my part ingenioulie confesse unto you that I can noe way approve of it, neither can I immagine that a blessinge can follow it.

The Gentlemen of Cheshire who have deserved soe well from you, you may love and honor in that dishonouring him. Ingratitude is a sin notoriouslie offensive to God if not soundly and early repented off and I cannot but professe soe much beleeve as wonder that you could speake any such thinge agt Sr. Wm. Brereton as I have heard you doe, who did with that zeale not onely draw apreh'son wth your owne hande to the Parlt. at ye Leauger at Beeston after my Comeing out of Worrall, for Sr Wm Brereton being sent Comande in Cheife into Cheshire again but should wth yt Eagernes send for mee from Namptwich to Carperley to desire mee that I would gaine as many honors as I could to yt patron I much admire, what diservice Sr W. Brereton hath done since the tyme of your bringing that peticon either to ye State or Kingdome that should cause you vent such expressions agt. Him. If you have bene guiltie of anie such ingratitude unto him lay it to heart and repent, which is expresslie desired by him who desires you to thinke of a reale Peace and remanes,

Your servant
Charles Coote

Litchfield March 15. 1646

79

Colonel Jones did afterwards acknowledge to Colonell Coote his Rashnes in his Expreshons towards Sr. Wm. Brereton and did acq't Colonel Coote that noe man more serv'd & honord him then he did. And that he did intend to goe for Ireland wth ye Lord Lisle, but would never depart the Kingdome while he were friends with Sr. Wm. Brereton. And alsoe Colonell Jones writt to Sr. Wm. Brereton and acknowledgd his rashnes, desired his affecon and that he would passe by what was paste.

80

A Particular of such goods as are layd aside in Chester for Sr. Wm. Breretons use for wch Mr. James Croxton is to pay upon Accompt for John Ashworth.

Sr. Wm. To have soe manie such as he pleased of them upon those Rates being so appraised.

Goodes laide aside for mee in the Ladye Grosvenors House:

One large Greene Carpett 5 yards ½ longe	2. 15. 0
One short Carpett 2yds ½ at	0. 15. 0
One Cubbard Cloath 1 yd ½ at	0. 15. 0
One Cruets	0. 0. 2
One pair of Andiron shovell and Tonges	0. 10. 0
One paire of shooes	0. 1. 0
One coat at	1. 0. 0
One paire of spurrs	0. 1. 0
One paire of boote hose toppes of leather and one Paire of stirrup hose at	0. 4. 6
One paire of good waights	0. 2. 0
One cruets at	0. 0. 6
Foure lockes for doores	0. 4. 0
16 venice Glasses att	0. 10. 8
Foure bottles with sirrupp of Colliflowers and Severall glasses and one paire of tables some tops	0. 13. 4
In the Parlor	
Six backe stools at	0. 18. 0
Two large chaires at	0. 8. 0
One coach chaire at	0. 10. 0
11 Grene sholes at	1. 2. 0
ffive quushens at	0. 8. 0
One Darke carpet, 2 small ones	0. 16. 0
One paire of ffire shovells & tongs	0. 2. 0
In Sr. Wm's Chamber	
One table at	0. 6. 0
One paire of Curtaines & vallance with blew and yellow paire with blew & yellow lace	2. 5. 0
ffoure white blanketts at	1. 6. 0
One fether bed and two bolsters Wt 4. 6d. 2d. Forme 16	
	15. 17. 2
One Cubbard Cloases, one bell 2 stooles one paire Of tongues & fireshovell	0. 8. 0
In ye Roome over the Palts	
One deske of beech wth drawers	0. 13. 4
1 greate Chaire, 31 stooles at	0. 16. 0
One short carpett at	0. 2. 0
In ye Roome besides	
1 Fether bed, 1bolster wt. At 6d. 1L	
4 blanketts at	0. 16. 0
1 quushen and stoole	0. 2. 6

In ye Cock loft	
2 suits at	1. 0. 0
One basquett with Chisells and other Tooles	0. 2. 6
In Sr Wm. Breretons Chamber	
3 stooles at	0. 3. 0
2 bedsteds at	1. 0. 4
1 fether and bolster wt. At 6d.	
1 oulde white Rugge at	0. 6. 6
One blankett at	0. 4. 0
1 greene Rugge and two blanketss	0. 16. 0
1 bed and bolster wt. At 6d. 1L	
In ye Buttery	
6 candle stickes 2 cuppes one salt One grate and small flagon	
wa. at 9d. to	0. 0. 0
1 voydcer, one knife, one brasse candle stick	0. 3. 6
In ye Kitchen	
2 skillets, I ladle at 0. 1. 10	
	7. 5. 0
1 brasse pot, 2 ladles at	
3 cushens at	0. 3. 0
15 curtain rods one long saw 7 some iron	0. 5. 0
In ye Ladyes Chamber	
5 curtaines & one paire of vallances	0. 13. 4
1 counterpaine of Kitterminster	0. 7. 0
1 paire of white blankettes	0. 7. 0
1 paire blanketts at	0. 3. 0
One coubed, 1 wht blankett, 3 course ones	0. 13. 4
1 box stand at	0. 2. 0
2 window curtaines of Kitterminster	0. 6. 0
1 backe stoole, 1 high stoole, 3 lowe stoles of neete works	0. 13. 8
1fire shovell and tongues	0. 1. 0
1 pr. Of great Rackes	1. 0. 0
1 pr. Of lesser Rackes	0. 10. 0
1 fether bed, 2 boulsters & a pillow wt at 6d.	P 11.
2 white blanketts at	0. 6. 0
1 greene Cadop at	0. 13. 4
1 paire of old sheetes at	0. 3. 0
One grate iron	0. 12. 0
1 peece of hanging of ye same ye said shete was of 30lbs.	6. 0. 0
1 Cyprus box wth drawers	1. 0. 0
1 Standish lyned wth mother of pearle	0. 10. 0
	14. 8. 8

83

Mr,. J. Brereton s Note recd. Ap. 25 1646 of
42 Cowes & bullockes, Runts bought
At Wrexham to feed & the Prise thereof:

	£	s.	d.
1 Cowe	1	15	0
2 Runts	4	5	0
4 Runts	8	6	8
6 Runts	12	0	0
2 Runts	4	0	0
2 Runts	4	4	0
4 Runts	8	15	0
2 Runts	4	3	8
2 Runts	4	6	8
2 Runts	4	0	0
	64	16	0
Tole	0	1	4
4 Small Runts	8	0	0
7 more whereof one is a heifer Sterke	13	0	0
	21	14	4
Sume to full	95.	10.	4

Provided by Tho: Wilkinson
in the first end of Aprill 1646

	£	s.	d.
Ten Runts	40	0	0
Ten mons Runts & 29 Cowes	84	0	0

Cheese sent to ye Leauger at Chester
Of Sr. Wm. Brereton

There has been sent to ye Leauger at Chester at severall tymes one the of Cheese from Handforth and Ashton

Yor Honors humble Servt.
John Brereton

Chester 25th Aprill 1646

More cattle baught of Tho: Wilkinson

Honble Sr,

I have received of Thomas Wilkinson 49 Beastes whereof twentie are Runtes ye rest Cowes and hath payd in part for them 100L and there remaines unpaide 25L 15d. Hee will make p'vision for some sheep wth what speed he can

Yr. Dutyfull and obedient Servt.
J: B:

84

Letter from ye Comissioners of ye Parliamt.
before Newarke to Sr. Wm. Brereton.

Sr,

Wee are exceeding glad of youe good successe at Tutbury and doe suppose tht you have given better satisfacion to ye Parliamt. and Comittee of Both Kingdomes then some othes hve done as wee have heard. Wee have little newes in these pates onelie sume of us waited upon ye lord G'rall Leven and the Comissioners from ye Parliamt. of Scotland at Southwell on Munday 20th of the month where wee met with John Gell and did not perceive that Tutbury had bene then soe near ye surrendering up as now wee perceive by your letter it is fullie p'formed. Wee heartily wish you as good successe agst Litchfeilde and Dudley Castle.

On Munday next wee and ye Scoch Com'ders intend to send in a last sumons to Newarke and if they refuse they must expect nothinge but fire and sword. Wee heare ye business in Scotland agt Montrose is in a reasonable good Condition, but wee have noe certain intelligence by reason of the distance. Wee shalbe glad to heare from you still as occasion offers itself as you shall doe from us

Your ready friends to
Serve you
Edward Montagu
Wm. Peirpoint
Edw. Ayscaugh Wm Myne
Anth. Ireby
Tho. Hatcher

85

Sr. Wm. Breretons answere to Mr. Swinfen in
answere to his letter desiring that every County
might pay theire owne men and that ye
3,000L ordered for ye service before
Litchfeilde maybe Imployed to pay provisions.

Sr,

I have this day upon my march betwene Litchfeild and this Towne received your longe ltre by ffrancis Lowe but doe assure you, you are verie much mistaken touching ye Leauger here, the charge whereof is farre below that of Chester. And it is true they buy theire provisions here but it is as true the Countrey brings in money which they should bringe in provisions, whereas Chester dureing the longe leauger there did not onelie bring in provisions in great protocols (but besides) payd great sumes of money and gave free quarter to ye Horse wch were many more of them are here, soe were ye foote also wch were for ye moste parte maintained wth provisions from Cheshire though indeed Staffordshire maintained the other foote. By ye articles it will appeare unto you that I have dealt as effectuallie as is possible to obtayne Cheshire to contribute both money & provisions, and yt you may alsoe see how difficult it is and how ill it is taken. This day wee are marching to Dudley with some forces and the most of the day misspent by reason ye Staffordshire and Shropshire foote refuse to march without money. Soe as if you order ye three thousand for provisions as you mencon, you wholie destroy us and the designe wilbe retarded. I sent also to Shropshire according to yor desire but the answere is returned (as Captaine Turton and theire officers informe us) that they will pay them noe money whilest they contynue there. I have now brought up more then the number of Cheshire men appointed, and more are willinge to come if provisions were made for theire subsistence. I have already taken up some money, otherwise it would have bene of mischevous consequence. Where wee have made some further p'gresse here wee shall give you a further acco't. In ye meane tyme I desire ye will hasten the writte. Colonell Bowyer and Sr. Charles Egerton have given mee assurances they wilbe for Sr. Richard Skeffington and I have laboured likewise. My onely feare is lest it be whilest I stay, and if soe it will occasion a Hazard in ye elecon. Wth many thankes for your lre,. And advice I conclude, restinge

Your assured friend
to serve you
Wm. Brereton

Walsall Ap.27 1646
Postscript

There were foure Shropshire Companies ordered to the service whereof three are gone back for want of money soe as now wee shalbe aboute 200 foote and they have as many in the Castle as wee are informed.

There hath not bene charged upon this county as yet above 20L upon a division and now there is 20L more assessed wch is so small an assess, considering there is noe provision brought in but that is payd for as that I hope it may be borne. But ye necessitie of ye souldiers will not be borne. I beleave theire charge is not much more then ye Enimyes Garrisons w'thin less then one yeare Exacted from ye Countrey.

87

Cessation at Tutbury, Sr. John ffitzHerbert
To go to his Majesty.

Articles agreed upon on ye 24th day of March 1646 between Lt. Colonell Peter Kniverton Comander of his Majesties Garrison of Tutburie Castle and

Colonell John Bowyer Comander in Chiefe of ye forces now at ye saide Castle.

1. That there be cessation of anie hostile Actes betweene ye besiegers and the besieged for twelve dayes. And that Lt. Colonell Peter Kniverton Governor of the said Garrison shall wth all under his Comand keepe themselves within ye sayd garrison & workes, Except there be orders from ye two Comanders in Chiefe.
2. That ye saide Lt. Colonell nor any under his comand shall send out any warrant for Contribucons for men or horse, nor send out any Taske to fetch in any out of ye county dureing ye cessation nor fortify themselves otherwise than they now are.
3. That Sr. John ffitzHerbert, Mr. Hill and Mr. Walthall and theire servants have a passe to goe to his Majesty to knowe his pleasure concerneing the Garrison and to returne to ye Garrison ye tyme above limited for cessacon unmolested.
4. That what provisions or other necessaryes as shall be braught voluntarylie may be received without breach of Articles if appointed by ye besiegers to bee kept by them without breach of Articles.

Peter Kniverton
John Bowyer

88

Sr. John Gells ltre to ye Governor of Tutbury touching
Hostages for his, under same Treaty about ye Articles
agreed by him of ye 6th of Ap: 1646 wch were wholly
Disallowed by ye Comittee of both Kingdomes.

Sr,

I have sent you two Hostages according to agreem't, Captaine Villers & Captaine Bagshawe, and desire to speake with you and Captaine Henry Merry at Wood Howse at Mr. Brockes Howse.

Sr,
Your Servant,
John Gell.
Aprill 4th
1646

For Lt. Colonell Kniverton in Tutbury Castle.

100L a month to bee levied in Staffordshire for Pr.
Maurice, his trayne.

Whereas there is an agreem't that one hundred pounds a month should be levied upon ye Countie of Stafford for ye Entertainm't of my traine & family, these are therefore to require you ye severall & respective Governors of ye Garrisons within that county to levy five & twenty pounds a weeke upon ye Newtralls, Delinquents or what other persons or Estates as you in your districts shall thinke most fitt and most Conduceinge to ye good of his Majestyes service and hereof desire you not to fayle. Given under my hand the fourth of ffeb: 1644 at Bridgnorth.

Maurice[31]

To ye Respective Go: ers
Within ye County of Stafford.

89

Bridgnorth taken. Ltre from Councill of Salopp
to Sr. W. Brereton.

Honoured Sr.,

Wee have received your lre wth ye enclosed articles for ye Surrender of Tutbury Castle wch wee are heartily glad to heare of and wee shalbe glad and joyfull to heare you are in a condicon to blocke up Dudley Castle who undoe all this part of ye Countrey and do send for provisions and plunder w'thin two miles of this towne. Wee send you herein closed the Articles agreed upon betweene us for ye surrender of the castle. Wee are now preparing to draw towards Dudley but wee feare wee shall meete wth some other barrier in ye way our officers and soldiers already beginning to grumble that they should nowe cease to bee under ye Comand of any Leauger. What ye Consequence may be wee knowe not. Wee have placed and settled Colonell Lloyde Governor of this place and have left two or three of his Companies wth him in ye Castle.

Wee heare this morning they have burnt ye Towne of Ludlowe. This is all that wee have at present, but ye tender of our humble services desiring that our old correspondence may bee contynued amongst us, wee rest,

Yor affectionate friends and
Humble Servants
Robt. Clive And. Lloyde
Robt. Charleton

Bridgnorth April 27th 1646

90

Articles for ye Surrender of
Bridgnorth.

Articles agreed upon for ye Surrender of ye Castle of Bridgnorth the 26th day of Aprill 1646 between Sir Robert Howard Kt. of ye Bath, Governor, Sr. Vincent Corbett, Sr. Edward Acton and Sr. ffrancis Ottly Commisioners for ye Kinge & Col. Andrew Lloyd, Colonell Robt. Clive and Robt. Charleton Esqr. Commisioners for ye Parliament.

1. That all Comissioned officers of horse & all Capts. of foote shall march away to anie of his Majesties Garrisons or Armies within forty myles with their Horse and Armes and each of them to have a servant with his horse and sword and theire wearing apparell free quarter for thirtie miles and a safe conduct and not to march less then eight miles a day and anie of ye above said officers laying downe theire Armes to goe home to theire owne habitation.
2. That all Inferior Comission officers shall have liberty to march wth theire swords and ye Comon Souldiers without Armes to anie of his Majesties Armyes or Garrisons within fourty myles as formerly menconed on laying downe theire armes to live at theire owne habitacons for a fortnight and afterward to take ye negative oath if they contynue w'thin this County or lres from home to ye Comittee of ye severall Countyes where they intend to reside and have passes accordinglie.
3. That all Clergiemen, Townesmen and Countreymen w'thin the Castle may have libertie to march to theire owne habitacons provided they lay downe theire Armes and fortnights liberty for ye takeing of ye negative oath and not to live w'thin a mile of ye Parliam'ts Garrisons or otherwise if they shall desire it to march away to any of ye Kinges Garrisons or Armyes.
4. That all wounded and sicke persons w'thin ye Castle shall have liberty to reside in ye Lower Towne or els where until they be fitt for travell and then to have passes to goe home or to any of ye kings Garrisons or Armyes.
5. That Sr. Robert Howard, Sr. Edward Acton, Sr. Vincent Corbett and Sr. Francis Oately wth each of theire horses armes and two men apeece (except Sr. Robert Howard who is to have foure men) wth theire horses and swords and theire masters wearing apparell shall have liberty to march to theire severall habitacons and to continue there for ye space of two monethes, wch tyme they are to make theire election whether they will goe to make theire peace wth ye Parliament or goe beyond sea or to anie of ye kings Garrisons or Armyes and to have accordingly they engage themselves in the meane tyme to doe nothing prejudicial to ye Parlt.
6. That Mr. Howard, Mr. ffisher and Mr. Grosvenor shall march away wth theire horses and swords and one man a peece wth theire wearing apparell and swords to any place within fourty miles.

7. That Lt. Colonell Hosier and Dr. Dewen shall march away without horse and armes to any of ye Kings Garrisons or other place within thirty miles provided it be not within County, and passes Accordinglie.
8. Mr. Mylward, Chaplaine to ye Garrison may have liberty to goe with his horse to his house at Layton in this Countye and to take with him his manuscripts and there to live takeing ye negative oath within one months time or else to march out of this county with the rest.
9. That ye Clerkes of ye Comissioners may have liberty to march as ye rest of ye Inferior officers and to have ye same conditions and to take with them all papers concerneing the Garrison, and theire wearing apparell.
10. That ye lady Oately her children and mayde servants have liberty with theire wearing cloaths to goe to Pitchford or ye Hay and there to live unmolested.
11. That all other women and children within ye castle shall have liberty to goe to theire owne or any of theire friends houses provided it be not within a mile of this garrison.
12. That all Gents, officers and souldiers as well as strangers as others desiring to goe beyond seas shall have passes accordinglie & ltrs to the Comitees of theire severall countyes to afford them the like conditions as the Gentlemen of this Countye upon ye surrender of this Castle here granted.
13. That the Chirugeons of ye castle shall march away and have the same conditions as inferior officers.
14. That ye Gunners and powder men with theire mates may march away as ye rest of ye Comon Souldiers.
15. That noe violence incivility or injury bee offered to any that shall march out of ye Castle but be protected according to the tenor of these Articles and that sufficient Hostages on both sides be given for performance of all and everie the matters here agreed upon.
16. That ye Governor and ye rest of his officers shall doe theire Endeavour to protect & preserve all the ordnance armes amunicon victualls goods bedding provisions and all other accommodators necessarie and belonginge to ye Castle (other then what is allowed to be taken by ye aforesaid Articles) and all these safe and unspoiled to be delivered up together with ye Castle unto ye Comittee or whom they shall appointe and that these articles be confirmed by ye Governor of ye Castle.
17. That if these Articles be assented unto ye Castle to be surrendered tomorrow morning by seven of ye clocke and those who intend to march to Worcester to quarter in the lower Towne or any other Towne w'thin five miles of the Garrison until the returne of ye Trumpeter and officer sent to Worcester provided they come w'thin two dayes.
18. That if anie officers or souldiers shall in any way maliciouslie spoile his

horse or Armes or misdemeane himself who march such misdemeaned shall not be extended further then to ye souldiers offending and upon them justice shalbe done according to ye discipline of warre.

19. That all Comission officers be certified by ye Governor of ye Castle and upon his certificate to be allowed to march accordinglie.
20. That Mr. Edward Latham be delivered to ye mercy of ye Parliam't.

94

Order of ye House of Comons
Touching Bp. of Armagh[32] his
bookes and Library at Chester

Die Veneris 6 ffeb 1645

Resolved

That ye Bi'pp of Armaghs Library of Bookes and Manuscripts at Chester be all Inventoryed or numbered and sent withal haste to ye Parlym't.

Hen. Elsyng for Parl.
Dom. Con.

Mr. Seldon to Sr. W. Brereton
About ye said Library.

Noble Sr,

You were pleased to let us knowe here that you had taken spetiall care of ye Arch bp. of Armaghs library at Chester, the Howse thereupon made the order wch I send you enclosed. How safely or when safely that wch is ordered may be done I presume none can knowe, & w'thout your Judg't. But ye occasion of my putting you to the trouble is for that it hath bene treated here that others perforce are soliciting you here for the bookes or some of them and that there are some addresses made to you concerneing them wch will stand not wth the order of ye House and may easily be answered by shewing it. Your wisedome & Noblenes with such that it were vane to say more of it to you. Onelie give mee leave to subscribe myself

Yr affectionate &
Humble Sert,
Ge: Seldon

Westminster March 11
1645
For ye h'ble Sr. W. Brereton

95

Shropshire Officers lre
for Money

May it please you Sr,

I have waited upon ye hon'ble Comittee of Salop all the last weeke to procure pay from them for ye Shropsh. Force theire positive answere is where we serve there wee must expect pay.

Our request to yor honor is that we may be in a settled condition knowe from whom wee shall have our pay otherwise there is an impossibility of keeping our men together to do any service wch by you is despatched that may satisfie ye souldiers and really p'forme yor hon'ble comands. I request you to determyne some speedy way for their satisfaction and I shall wth the rest of yor faithfull servants through Gods blessinge endeavour to perfect yor operations.

Yor Serv't to Comand
Henry Hunte

Aprill 28th 1646

The State of Dudley Castle
By Capt. Seale Ap: 23 1646

The Number of Souldiers	
Colonel Levesons Companie	60
Lt. Colonell Beaumonts	40
Major Hevingham	30
Captaine Tho. Gifford	20
Captaine ffrancis Coles	15
	165

Troopers	
Mounted	06
Uncounted & unarmed	34
Lt. Col. Gifford mounted	12
Dismounted	18
Officers Horses about	30
	100

They have great store of corne and a corne mill and a powder mill but cannot worke powder. They have but little mault, not to serve them above a fortnight. They have about twelve barrells of powder & good store of match, 40 fadam Deepe a well where may be of ye Castle. A well in ye burnt Towne wch maybe choked by batteringe ye Tower. A guard on ye gate howse wch may be easily surprised by 100 men wch wilbe of the greatest consequence. The Gate house very weeke and may be battered especially where ye drawbridge is. In case ye lower Gate howse be taken. Between ye burnt towne and the New buildinge is the onely place to lay a battery wch may be well undertaken. The mount is not fully finished and may be taken, one nooke of it wilbe presently made defensible agst ye Castle. It will hold 100 men. The Manner of it drawne on the other side, take that & you may batter ye castle & that hath noe guard or centrye in it. There is a necesity of takeing ye gate howse & mount, the first night which beeinge done ye worke canne be difficulte otherwise they may sally forth at theire pleasure. If any place be ruyneable it is ye great Hall or new buildinge.

97

The Lady Dudley her lre from Oxford
to Sr. W. Brereton touching Dudley Castle.

Sr,

Att my Comeinge to Oxford I had an absolute promise my busines should be despatched and sent to mee by Mr. Hevingham, but in regard he was prevented by his passe to returne on soe short tyme he could not stay to see it effected but if you please to give this Gent. your Passe to goe to his Majesties Garrison confident at his returne yt you shall receive an answere according to yor opportunitie.

I am Sr

Yor humble Servante
ffrances Duddley

Upon this Lre and other Information
and Intelligence touching Dudley Castle
there was a passe granted by Sr. W. Brereton
for Mr. Edward Ashcroft of black parke
to goe to his Majestie and returne here
in ten dayes from the present
28th of Ap: 1646. ye date thereof

Intelligence out of Litchfield Close
Ap. 28 1646

Bacon Hill Ap 28 1646

Wm. Pearson borne in Bedfordshire and souldier in ye Close of Litchfielde under Major Hasnet runeing voluntarely from ye Enimy and he says that ye Comanders in ye Close did cause a new sallieport to be made, and begun the worke about a weeke since and have already perfected a running trench towards ye Rayles on Bacon hill, that foure men may march abrest and as the Exaint did confidently report and heare they were fully resolved to make a desperate sally to attempt one of ye mounts & he beleeves tis that wee call Gloucester mount & the tyme would either be Munday night paste or Tuesday night to come. Theire allowance in ye Close is halfe a pounde of bread & half a pound of cheese a day & halfe a pound of beefe. Sayes there is one family shut up of ye shakes and a sentree set at ye doore but noe person as yet dead.

Sayes ye Granadoes have broken six severall tymes wh'n ye Church, but neither anie woman slaine that he knowes of. That ye Enimy doe not now make any powder, That there is as yet noe mutynes amongst them. That upon Saturday next they have intencon to make a sally into ye Cittie at ye Mawes green considering it a fitt time in regard they beleeve the souldiers wilbe disordered by reason of ye fayre. That he verie beleeves they will within a short tyme turne out all theire Horses, sayes of late they have not had any Intelligence and although theire Officers tell them Montrose is in England and the Scots Army joined with him yet they give not credit to them and so he beleeves a small contynuance in ye Close will weary ye soldyers of theire engagement.

G'ralls order upon it.

Upon this intelligence wch read to Sr. W. Brereton who was then at Dudley haveinge drawne some forces thither to besieg ye Castle, Sr. W. Brereton sent fresh orders to Lt. Colonell Gerrard & Major Daniell on ye Bacon hill syde and to Colonell Falksor & Col. Broughton upon ye Cittyside to be verie vigillant & watchfull and to send out a party of five lockes to discover ye dumps workes and to keepe constant intelligence wth him, who will send Adjutant G.rall Louthiane to them as soone as the Mount is begun at Dudley Castle for blocking it up.

99

Order of ye Howse of Comons
refering the ordnance for Chester
to a Co'tee.

Die Veneris ap 17 1646

An ordnance for settling ye Civill Gover'nt of ye Cittie of Chester and of ye county of ye same, was this day read the first and second tyme and upon ye question comitted unto:

Mr. Ashurst
Mr. Crewe
Sr. Gilbert Gerrard
Sr. John Trevor
Sr. John Dauvaroe
Mr. Robinson
Colonell More
Mr. Roger Hodges
Sr. Tho. Luyddringham
Mr. Swinfen
Sr. Tho. Myddleton

Mr. ffell
Mr. Boughton
Sr. Ralph Ashton
Mr. Knightlye
Lt. ffairfax
Sr. Henry Darley
Sr. Tho. Davreu
Sr. Wm. Massam
Sr. John Corbett
Mr. Millington

Mr. Dury
Mr. Rigby
Mr. Recorder
Mr. Shelwall
Mr. Langsom
Mr. Knight and
Burgesses of
North Wales,
Cheshire, Lancashire, Shropshire
& Staffordsh.

This Committee is likewise to consider of a maintainance for ye Mayor of Chester of Dee Mills and of ye Cheshire peticon Chousinge the Chamberlaine of Chester and are to meete tomorrow at two of ye Clocke in ye afternoone in ye starre Chamber and have power to send for Parleys Witneses papers Records

Hen. Elsynge Cler. Parl.
D. Com

100

Orders touching assessing
The country for maintainance
Of ye siege at Dudley, at
Bermincham, By ye Gov'r of
Coventry & Sr. Rich. Skeffington.

This day, Aprill 28th 1646 after ye G'rall Sr. W. Brereton had brought the forces to Dudley and placed them there and given order and set them on worcke to erect mounts or be returned to Birmingham where to meet Sr. Richard Skeffington & Col. Willoughby, Gov'r of Coventry, Att wch tyme this order was made as followes:

Warwickshires Contribute to
Ye sieg at Dudley.

Resolved this day at Bermincham that soe much as hath beene weeklie assessed upon ye Hundred of Hemlinford or any other Hundred eight miles within ye County of Warwickes for ye maintainance of ye Enemyes Garrison at Dudley shalbe henceforth weekly assessed and Payd for ye maintainance of ye leauger before Dudley Castle untill ye said Garrison shalbe reduced unto ye Parliam'ts possession & no longer. And that warrant to ye petty constables to pay in ye sayd Moneyes to Thomas Shawe of Birmingham & he to pay ye same to Cllr. Robert Wilmot, Treasurer of Staffordshire.

Consented unto by Sr. Richard Skeffington and Colonell Willoughby who wrote a copie of ye resolve above written upon ye behalfe of ye committee of Coventry in ye presence of

Sr. Wm. Brereton And Mr. Mainwairinge, high Sheriffe of Staffordshire and alsoe of Captaine Stone.

It was then proposed by them that Sr. Wm. Brereton should send out warrants accordinglie and Colo. Whalleyes Example was sustained as a President.

101

Sr. Wm. Breretons orders hereupon to
Ye County Districts & ye Head Constables.

To ye head Constables of ye hundred of Hemlingford, and to everie of them

Whereas there is and for this two monthes last past hath bene a siege laid before ye garrison of ye Close of Lichfield for ye reducing whereof wch garrison hath bene verie prejudiciall not onelie to ye comittee of Stafford but also to ye Comittee of Warwicke. And ye Reducing ye same wilbe a meanes through Gods Mercy to restore ye tranquillity of ye counties and to free the people there as els where of these burthens that they have undergone by yt Garrison the maintaining of wch sieg hath hither unto bene maintained at ye Charge of ye Countie of Stafford much to ye impoverishing of them and disabling them to Contynue alone without assistance and charge of ye same sieg. And whereas alsoe for ye further settling of ye quiett of ye Countie of Warwicke and Stafford and freeing them of heavy taxation and further one layd upon them by ye Garrison of Dudley Castle. There is now alsoe sieg layd to ye said Castle wch is through Gods assistance in a short tyme hoped to be gained. I have therefore conceived ye good of ye County of Warwicke being thereby most concerned that the Inhabitants of ye county wilbe willinge freelie and cheerfullie to contribute there assistance in helping to beare ye charge of ye seiges that they may goe on wth better assurance of success. Therefore it is thought expedient that all the Constablewickes within you Hundred that live within eight miles from ye borders of ye Countie of Warwicke doe pay weeklie towards ye defraying ye charge of ye said seiges dureing the Investment thereof. The like sumes of money as they have bene heretofore requested charged to ye weeklie heretofore either of ye said Garrisons of Dudley or Lichfield.

These are therefore to require ye, and anie one of you forthwith upon receipt hereof to send forth your warrant as directed to ye severall constables of ye severall Constablewicks w'thin ye said Hundred w'thin the aforesaid Lymitt for ye Levying and Collecting of ye severall sums formerly imposed upon them weekly to be paid to others of ye said garrison. And ye said Constables to pay in theire money weeklie to be taxed wthin theire Constablewick unto Mr. Tho: Shaw of ye Town of Birmingham appointed to receive ye same who is appointed to pay over ye same unto Mr. Robert Wilmot who is thereunto to provide provisions to maintaine the souldiers at ye said leauger thereof. Fayle not as you send or ye part in hand for ye good of ye Countrie. Given under my hande at Birminham 28th Day of Aprill 1646

Wm. Brereton

Ye first weekes pay is to begin from ye date of this war't, and to pay at everie fortnighte. And the first Paym't to be made Upon Tuesday ye 12th day of May next at ye house of Thomas Shaw aforesaid.

104

From ye Gov'er of Dudley, touching
Lt. Col. Beaumonts wife being dead.

Sr,

Lieutenant Colonell Beaumonts wife beinge Deade, I shall take it for a favour if you will permitt us to bury her in ye upper Church of Dudley without interrupcon.

Yor Servant
Tho. Leveson

For ye Comander in
Chiefe of ye Parlt. Forces
Before Dudley.

Answer: Capt. ffradshaw beinge come up with a forlorne hope Returned this answere:

Sr, I cannot at present resolve you of what you wrote to mee in regard ye Generall was not then in ye feilde, but at his returne you may Expect a further Answere. But for myself acquaint you that two of my soldiers were shot when they came to receive your Drum wch I conceive was a dishonourable act and Contrary to ye Lawe of Armes. I hope you can expect noe other from us.

Yor Servant
Hum. ffradshaw

Ap: 28 1646

This was done after ye G'rall had placed ye men in Dudley there & was gone to meete ye Gov'r & Com'tee at Coventry at Birmincham, there returned early tomorrow at Dudley.

105

The G'ralls answere to Col. Leveson
touching interring Mrs Beaumont.

Sr,

Upon my Entrance into the Towne I found your Drum wth a lre desiring to bury Colonell Beaumonds wife in ye upper church, which is such a Civilitie as I will see done, Though I must needs acquaint you that at such tyme as some of my souldiers went to receive him two of them were shot by your men contrary to ye Lawe of Armes. I must demand satisfacton for ye same and further advertise you that there is such wayes destruction taken as will adde to your guilte and rende you in worse condicon by this your fireing of ye Towne.

Your Servant
Wm. Brereton

Dudley Aprill 28th 1646

If you send the names of such
As shall accompany her Interr'mt
You shall receive a passe for them.

106

Lord Pagetts lre to Sr. Wm. Brereton
Promising his voues for Sir Richard
Skeffington.

Honored Sr,

I understand by my wife that you are desirous I should declare my selfe for Sir Richard Skevington who it seemes intends to stand for knight of ye shire for our County. A dubble reason obliges me to a willingness in this particular. The first is the neernesse of blood and longe acquaintance wth from who is everye way worthy and able of further account. Another is my Earnest desire to expresse any civilitye and respect to you for all yor counselling and ffavours to mee and mine and I humbly acknowledg I am most glad of this occasion to serve you and I will doe it wth all Reallity. I have written to my wife about it, charging all my Commity If I be of any Esteeme amongst them to use their utmost endeavours to serve Sir Richard Skevington. Sir, God hath hitherto blessed yor Endeavors in other places. I doubt not by Gods assistance to you in yor deliverance of our Country from further misery and dissention. Thus takes his leave

Yor most affeconate
ffriend to serve you
Wm. Pagett

Whitehall this
17th of Aprill
1646

107

Sr. Wm. Breretons Answere to
ye Lord Pagett.

Right hon'ble and my verie good Lord,

I have received your lre whereby I must acknowledge or lre hath placed wth mee a great obligator in contributing your friends and Tenants votes towards ye elecon of Sr. Richard Skeffington whose worth and faithfulnes to the publique will I hope deserve that high esteeme wch you are pleased to put upon him wch hath I may freely say interested himself as much unto ye offers of all those that are good in the County as any other whatsoever.

I have hereunto sent you our Coppy, the Articles for ye surrender of Tutbury Castle and do hope that had wee a good morter peece and some expert man to manage it there might be a speedy good accompt given of Litchfielde.

Wee have alsoe yesterday possessed ourselves of Dudley Towne and are preparing to erect some workes ag't ye Castle. But hereas yor Lo'p may expect a further Accompt hereafter. In ye meane tyme I subscribe myself

Yor lo'ps most humble
Servant
W. Brereton

Dudley Aprill 29th
1646

108

Lre from ye Comm'ders of ye forces of Col. Morgan at Babington & to Sr. Wm. Brereton at Dudley touching quartering of souldiers.

Sr,

To prevent ye qu'tringe of your souldiers in Kinver or ye adjacent villages assigned to us wee thought fitt to acq't your Lords'p that here is quartered in Kinver under ye Command of Colonell Morgan and by his order aboute 300 horse and foote till further order. This we accompted our duty to Certifie to yor Honor. And soe wee remaine

Yor most humble Serv'ts
John Harrold
Dan Page

The Townes are
Enfield
Over Arley
Sturbridge
Bobington

Sr. Wm. Breretons answere to Capt. Harrald & Capt. Page touching ye same business of quartering.

Gentlemen,

I have received your lre and have thought good to returne this answere. That it will not be posible for us to maintaine the Leauger and allso that at

Litchfeilde if not onely the whole County but neighbour'ing Countyes alsoe doe extend there assistance thereunto. Warwickshire having bene moved thereunto have appointed one of theire whole Hundreds to be contributory and assistant to us. The like must be done by Worcestershire in wch county wee now are. Therefore it is not to be expected that wee should be streightened in our q'ters and that any force could be q'tered neere thereunto but those yt doe duty here. Upon wch consideracon I have thought good to send you this inclosed order wch I cannot doubt but you will afferme and prefere rather to drawe up hither where you may doe service than Remaine in Remote quarters where no service is to be done and whereby the county is disabled from affording us that supply without wch wee cannot maintaine the Leauger. Whereof I doubt not but you wilbe soe sensible as that I shall not need any further to enlarge myself, but remaine,

Your faithfull friend
Wm. Brereton

Dudley Ap.29, 1646

I should not have taken upon mee to have given you this order here had I not bene interested and warranted thereunto by spetiall ordnance of Parlym't. I desire to knowe whether you heare of anie forces moveing up ag't Worcester. If soe I shall know what further orders to give & if Col. Morgan hade bene wth you I could have sent to him, but I heare of his absence.

109

Order inclosed in ye
said lre.

Because there went forces to maintaine the Leauger at Dudley (wherein wee are engaged) you are therefore required either this day or tomorowe to march wth youre foote to ye Leauger at Dudley there to assist to Strengthen that Leauger till further order. And theire shalbe Caire taken of those parts of Staffordshire and Worcestershire out of wch you remove. ffaile not herein as you render this service. Given under my hand at Dudley this 29th day of Aprill 1646.

Wm. Brereton

To ye Comanders of ye foote at
Enfield, Over Arley, Sturbridge &
Babington belonging to Colonell
Morgan.

110

Col. Levesons lre to Sr. Wm. Brereton
touching burying Mrs. Beaumont.

Sr,

I thank you for your civilitie in affording quiet buriall to my Lt. Colonells wife. I have there sent you a list of persons I desire may attend the funerall for whom I desire your passe to come and returne. ffor your men that were shot comeinge to receave my drum it was contrary to my orders, nor doe I know by whom it was done. ffor your advertisement that my fireing ye Towne will adde to my guilt & render mee in a worse condicon, I presume you knowe soe much the duty of a souldier is not to thinke I will suffer an Enemy in plaies advantageous to mee if I can either by sword or fire drive them out and I hope if your siege contynue you will find I am not to be frighted from my resource by ye apprehension of any Change of condicon. ffor ye guilt you mencon I have soe much charity for you that for wch concernes ye Kings Service I wish w'thall my heart your guilt were not greater than that of Sr,

Yor Servant
T. Leueson

Dudley Castle
Ap: 28th 1646

111

Adjutant G'rall Louthian his
Answere (the Generall beinge
gone to meete ye Gov'r of Coventry
about business.)

Sr,

I have received your lre to ye Generall whose absence causeth mee not to answere yours in any particular, But onelie according to his Engagem't I have sent you a passe for ye attendants to ye Corpes, and am,

Your Servant
Francis Louthiane

From ye Leauger before
Dudley Castle
Ap: 28th 1646

List of ye Attendants on
ye Corpes

Robert Noble	Anne Granger
John Ryder	Jane Barnes
Edward Garnett	Eli: Cooke
Thomas Grimsill	Marg: Hardwicke
John Dinton	Martha Guest
James Glover	Catherin Ellis

Col. Morgan to Sr. Wm. Brereton
from Bewdley.

Sr,

yours of ye 23 instant received last night and your other of ye 26th this morneinge, and am verie joyfull that it hath pleased god to give Tutbury into ye hands of ye Parliament. I was engaged to be absent on ye other side of Worcester wth my Horse to prevent what might be ye violence of ye Enemye in those partes from Saturday morneing till yesternight wch was ye reason yor lre sooner received not answered yet in order to what is required in both my Major in my absence comanded about 300 Horse and foote to march to Kinver within two miles of Sturbridge where they are to remane till further order. I doe therefore desire to heare from you that I may resolve what is further requisit to be done therein. Upon Thursdae next I expect Major Smith from London with full Instrucons for ye better advance of ye designe of Worcester which I shall endeavour to prosecute withall possible advantage. For Colonell Birch I understand he hath bene before Ludlow ever since Saturday morning, for anie particulars of his proceedings there, none of consequence hath come as yet to my knowledge. I question not but ye newes of ye surrender of Bridgnorth is come to you, yet am troubled to heare that they have so large an Article as to passe to any Garrison of ye Kinge within thirty miles, you may easily at yor leasure affirm my discovery. I have nothinge more at present to acquaint you wth, but that I am

Your affectionate friende
& verie humble Servt.
Thomas Morgan

Bewdley this 28 of Aprill
1646

112

Sr. Wm. Breretons Answere
to Colonell Morgan.

Sr,

This morneinge about 10 of ye clock I received yours of ye twenty eighth about 2 howers before wch tyme I had received a lre from some of your Commanders at Kinver and other partes intimating that you had assigned them divers grounde thereabouts for theire q'ters, whereupon in regard it wilbe impossible for us to maintaine the leauger I have placed at Dudley, and alsoe that at Litchfield if not onelie the whole County of Stafford but neighbour Counties alsoe doe not end theire assistance thereunto, Warwickshire having upon desire allocated one of theire whole Hundreds to be contributores thereunto and because it wilbe very that our q'ters here should be hemmed up and strengthened by anie forces that performe not dutie here, and beinge here is not that strength wch is needful to carrie on the worke soe expeditiouslie as were to be desired.

Grant unto ye Comanders of your foot there (hearing of your absence and not knowing where you were) to advance hither wth theire foote to assist in the leauger till further order. If they come up accordingly wee shalbe enabled to prosecute this worke more effectually, and ye sooner to fortifie such mounts and trenches as wee intend for blocking up ye castle. Which beinge done wee shalbe able to contribute the more assistance for anie further service that may be comanded as agst Worcester which designe I shalbe readie to promote to ye utmost powers. Concerning which I shall desire to p'take of what you heare of anie forces coming thither that I may prepare accordingly. Though it be soe that liberty is given to ye souldiers of Bridgnorth to march whither they please yet I hope it is in my pleasure to prevent them from marching to Dudley, wch I shall endeavour to doe. Which is all at this tyme wch I shall adde but my respects unto you and ye assurance that I am

Sr, your verie affectionate
Friend and servant
Wm. Brereton

Dudley Ap: 29 1646

114

The G'ralls orders for ye
Horse Guards at Dudley
Ap: 29 1646.

		The Word
Ap: 30th	Captain Hunt	
	Capt. ffradsham	Tamworth
	Capt. Leifield	
May 1st	Capt. Pudsey	
ffryday	Capt. Tuthill	Stafford
	Capt. Barns	
May 2	Captaine fflower	
	Captaine Creed	Coventry
	Major Hawkesworth	

Wm. Brereton

Lre from Lt. Colon. Gerrard & Major Daniell
from Litchfield to Dudley to Sr. Wm. Brereton
of ye Condicon of ye Leauger, this

Hon'ble Sr,

Wee were fullie resolved to give your Honor an accompt of ye Campe, yet protracted ye tyme untill wee doe really apprehend ye workes newly made by ye Enemy and to what end it was done. Upon Munday our Centinells at ye pitt discovered them working at ye edge of ye fields over agst them by ye railes nearest their owne Trench, yet could wee not concience what his Intensons might be except to cast up a breastwork to annoy us in setting up of oure owne mounte, it being directlie opposite. That night wee had tried ye Certentie but that our Carpenters and pioneers would have failed us had there bene anie shot, soe we resolved to gaine tyme in erectinge our owne mount and performed it, blessed be God, without losse of blood.

The same night there came a souldier from ye Close and wee strictlie enquired what theire workes was. Hee answered, About a weeke since they began ye making of a new Sally port under ye Palace wall and from thence a running trench to ye edge of ye hill and there they made a worke to secure theire Trench which wee conceived to be true in regard wee see ye workes like a Horne formeing the other side of their Trench.

Yesternight wee went wthin our Mount & have Rought it verie stronge and before this night that ye Leaveinge a foote pace within wilbe p'fected & wee would to have a stronge guard therein.

Theire worke is not anie disadvantage to us in ye least particular, neither can wee take it from them without losse of many men to night but it beinge soe neere they will regaine & repaire theire grounde tomorrowe. If they come on wth anie other worke, through Gods assistance weele use our best endeavours that prevencon be given. Till then our battery being potent within will make a worke at theire owne doore and wee cannot possibly prevent them. Wee conceive whilst wee keepe our Guard secure and our Enemy soe from getting reliefe or breaking through us wee discharge ye dutie of your Honors Engagm'ts yet in this and all other shall most cheerfully obey your Honors further Comands, Remaining

Yr. Honors Servts
G. Gerrard
W. Daniell

From Bacon Hill
Leag'r
Ap: 29 1646

116

Intelligence out of
Litchfield Close.

The Exam'acon of Thomas Trueman lately a Souldier under Major Orde in ye Close at Litchfield taken ye 29th of Aprill 1646.

Hee sayth that he was borne in Nottinghamshire and entred wth Major Orde, his service, about ten weekes ago and hath contynued in ye Close till this day and now being wearie of yt service by reason of ye scarsity of victualls—haveinge but half a pounde of breade & as much beefe allowed for a man a day and a pinte of beere, thinking yt too small he adventured to come forth to serve for ye Kinge and Parlyam't. hee sayth about a week agoe there was some men Imprisoned for asking for p'vision and yt yester night there was a mutynie in none of ye out guards because some of ye souldiers were comanded to Watch two nights together and were allowed provision but for one day and one night.

Hee alsoe sayth that two horses were killed wth Granadoes wch ye souldiers did make use for provisione of victualls whereof he himself did eate a parte. Hee likewise sayth they killed two horses a fortnight since to make use of it for victualls and that some horses are dead and others ready to die for want of victualls and he sayth it is conceived that the workes wch they are makeinge nowe is to keepe a Centery to secure the men that live in the other worke that is neere to the Close and to secure theire Horses at grasse by the syde of ye Close. Hee sayth that a man was killed in ye saide worke yesterday and an Ensigne shot ye day before, and that ye Souldiers did not know what ye bone fyres were made for ye last Sunday night and for ye other signe of rejoiceing about a fortnight since. It was upon some lres that came from ye Governor of Dudley Castle as Sr. Thomas Tildesley would them, intimating that the King would for certaine speedily reliefe them within another five weekes. Hee further sayth that divers souldiers are willing to come but if they had a opportunity. And he sayeth that ye report of ye comanders thereto about wee hear in ye Close and that there is every Munday a fresh survey taken of all the men that wee provision may be allowed for more men then there is. He sayth yt He: Willers and two souldiers are dead & souldiers are shut up. But whether it be ye sicknes or noe he Cannot tell.

118

Exchange of Mr. Ensor of
Birmincham

Upon ye peticon of ye Towne of Birmincham that Edward Ensor might be released the Generall sent to ye Gov'er of ye Castle that if he would release him he would upon demand doe him ye like courtesie whereupon ye Governor made the returne.

Coll. Leuson to Sr. Wm.
Brereton thereupon

Sr,

Edward Ensor of Birmincham is prisoner here for ye Contrbucon of yt Towne, yet at your request I have sent him to you.

I have prisoner here Robt. Powell belonging to Captaine Hunts Companie in ye Regt. Of Colonell Mackworth, and Thomas Humphreyes in ye Companie of Major Braye, and Edward Crew belonging to Captain Hill at ye Garrison of Chepstowe, Whom I am willing to release for Ensigne Capelwood, taken by ye Countrey then about Kinvar upon Saturday last at night.

Yr. Servt.
T. Leurson

There is due for ye marshall's fees 27s. 6d. from Edward Ensor for which he hath engaged himself to pay it on Saturday.

Sr, I am not at all sorrie that your men shot during the Parley yet I doe not at all charge you wth this nor noe more then I would have you doe mee wth ye like accident was done yesterday.

Dudley Castle Ap: 29 1646.

119

Sr. Wm. Breretons answere
to Col. Leveson

Sr,

The prisoners you mencon are all unknowne to mee, yet because you were pleased upon my request to release Edward Ensor, I will send you Ensigne Caplewood according to your desire. This Ensigne Caplewood served formerly (as I have bene informed) on this side and it was intended to have bene executed by ye same Instance that you Executed Hamilton, one Captaine Backhouse, his troope, notwithstanding I will send (who is now at Wrothley) unto you. There are alsoe some foot souldiers taken with him whom I will release in Lieu of those Country men that were taken at ye same tyme from Kinver and Envill, whose names are under written, and rest,

Yor Servant
W. Brereton

Dudley Aprill 29
1646

John Dickin
James Worsener
Humph. Kettly
Rich. Lucas
John Mytton

120

Sr. W. Breretons lre to ye Comittee at Goldsmiths Hall touching Mr. Burgess of Macclesfield.

Gentlemen,

There is in my Neighbourhood at Chester, Macclesfield an Attorney, one Mr. Burgesse who hath bene a verie great enemie to ye service of ye Parliam't and of late hath made composicon (as I am informed) wth you for his Estate. Besides his beinge a practisioner at Lawe, hee holds a place at Macclesfield as Clerke of his Majesties Courtes of ye Manor and forest and liberty of ye Hundred by reason whereof his Interrest in ye freehold copie holders and other Inhabitants thereof was great. And this gave him a capacitie of doinge greater Diservice to ye State, and was noted to be a Industrious diswader from ye service thereof. This Gentleman pretends an Estate for life in ye Clks place by Patent from ye Earle of Darby then Steward of that maner fforest and libertye wth wch stewardshippe ye Parlt. Hath now Intrusted mee. I have placed under mee one Clke there who has done verie good service to ye publique and suffered much to ye Parlt. Yet I now heare Mr. Burgess is now makinge his addresse unto you to invoke that office into Composicon.

I am Confident you understand ye sense of both Houses concerneing such practitioners yet I thought good to intymate this much unto you concerneing him in particular because I know him to be a verie dangerous Instrument and when the enemy was present in Cheshire there was an Assize held at Chester where myself and verie neere three hundred more were Indicted of High Treason for our service to ye Comonwealth, and he is vehementlie suspected to have beene an Actor therein. I nowe leave him to your grave consideracon and professe myselfe to Remaine

Your most faithfull friend
and servant
W. Brereton

From my Quarters at ye
Leauger at Litchfield
Aprill 30th 1646

121

Names as were indicted
At the Assizes Chesh're
5th ffeb. 1645
Wherein ye said Mr. Burgesse
Is suspected to have bene in Armes.

John More Esq.
Wm Brereton Bart.
Tho. Mydleton Kt.
Peter Egerton Esq.
John Holcroft Armes
Johes Harware Senior Mouldswore
John Hardware Jun. Gent.
John Sadler of Nampwch yeo.
John Dutton de----- ----- yeo.
Philip Mainwaring de peu-----
Thomas Marbury de Marbury Gent.
John Marbury de Marbury Gent.
Edw. Hyde de Northbury Gent.
Wm Tuckett de Whilley Gent.
Peter Ouldfield de Bradwell Gent.
Ralph Hughes de Clune Gent.
John Hughs de Cotton yeom.
Jo. Harrawar de Bridgeman .
Peter Booth de Cogshull Gent.
Hugh Burrowes de Runcorne Gent.
Jo. Ryder de ead yeoman.
Tho. Whitley Gent.
Roger Cheswiss de Chirke Gent.
Jo. Burch de .... yeo.
Tho. Oakes de .... yeo.
Jeffrey Pawler de ....
Randle Houghton de .... yeo.
Johes Wethenhall de Audlym gent.
Johes Brereton de Auger yeo.
Jo. Tapley de Norley Hafband
Thomas Ratcliffe of Wishersea yeo.
Henry Manwaring de ...... A.....
Fr. Page de Es...thaw Gent.
Robt. Davies de Ashton Gent.
W. Davies de ...... gent.
Tho Dawes .... Yeo.
W. Brereton Bart.
Geo. Booth ...... Bart.
Tho. Bromfield de Wilton Gent.
Henry Brooke de Norton ...
Ralph Areerne of Yardoc ...
Robert Gregge de Harshford Gent.
Robert Gregge .... Gent.
Nath. Lancaster .....
Jo. Rathbone de f....by Gent.
Tho. Malsone Gent. De Nampwch Gent.
Tho. Malsome ..... Gent.
Geo. Mallone Gent
Richd. Colborne Gent.
James Garthlee Gent.
Roger Bradley of Bradley Gent.
Tho. N...... of Nanwhich.....
George Eagles de Aston Gent.
W. Edwards N......r
W. Edwards G.... Gent
John Wynne Ironmonger
Robt Neuablee de Antrobus Gent.
John Rutter de Godcroft Gent
Richard Heath de Fra.... Gent.
W. Rutter de ... yeo.
Tho. Banner de ...yeo.
Hugh Minshall de .... Gent
Peter Minshull de ....yeo.
Joseph Hale de Frac..... Gent.
Humph. Johnson de Newton Gent.
Gilbert Ireland of Chester .....
W. Harrison de Minshall Vere.... yeo.
Robert Harrington de Stanthorw yeo.
Tho. Boswell de ead yeom.
W. Walley de ead ..avenham yeo.
Tho. Wally de Shipbrook yeo.
Tho. Axon de Lofthouse yeo.
Jo. Pearson de Stantherw yeo.
Jos. Wright de ead yeo.
Jo. Mytton de Clune yeo.
Raph Beckett de Newton yeo.
Joseph Smallwood de Swifton ...
Fr. D....ell de Darsbury Gent.
W. Tomlinson de Warton Gent.
Jo. Warburton of Great Badsworth Gent.
W. Johnson of ffradoham f...th
Robt. Pike de ead Crew Gent.
Gilbert Gerrard de Crew Gent.
Tho. Fairefax Kt.
W. Fairfax Kt.
Geo. Booth Esq.
W. Marbey of Nearburne Esquire
George Spurstow ....
W. Washe de Mose...
Tho. Cropton de Ravestroft ...
J. Bromhall de Nampwh ....
Richd. Holland A...
Raph Ashton
Robert Leigh Esq.
Jo. Booth de ...
John Leigh de Booth...
Humph. Buckley de Waterest
Tho. Hunt Beere brewer
James Ratcliffe Beere brewer
Hugh Whitney de Ceole Gent.

Jo. Bastocke of ..attenhall Gent.
Mathew Brown de Beryton Gent.
Rob. Duckenfield de Duckenfield Armis.
John Trevore de hert...Gent.
Richd. Jutson de Rushton Gent.
Richard Leicester de Poole Gent.
W. Peartree de Nampwch ...
Edw. Bold de Aston ....
Richard ffowler de Bromley ...
Rich. Oaseler de Needham ...
Peter ....
Tho. Cotton de Aston ...
Robert Wright Baker
John Chesh... de Wick Gent.

132

Copie of a lre to ye Committee at Goldsmiths Hall
touching ye Baron of Kinderton.

Gentlemen,

I am informed by divers that Mr. Venables, Baron of Kinderton late one of ye members of your House is aboute to come up touching his composition. Hee was a member of ye House of Comons and verie forward in Revylinge the Parlts. trust and verie verulent in his courses agt ye Parlt.

The reason why I take this freedome is not onely to give you a right sense of ye man in what I knowe but ye Countrey for wch he served. The truth is they are afrayed of his resti'con as knowing him an enemy to reformation and a Tyrant amongst his tenants who now begin to Tremble, being that all his Tenants, or most of them are either out of lease or want but a peace of a yeare. And many rather desire to pay fines and receave their Estates from ye Parliament then to deale wth him. They are verie manie & divers well affected and apprehend themselves (unless you in your discrecon in some measure obstructing him) utterly ruyned. I am sorrie to purport so much of ye fayleinge & fault of a gentleman, my neighbour, but ye pressures of those whom I know well affected to ye Parlt. Extorts it from him who is

Yor most humble Ser't.,
W. B.

Litchfield leag'r
18th Ap. 1646

This Conceived That the fines of his Rent will amount to at least 12000L who are now out of lease this very yeare.

133

Mr. Higinbotham Patent for ye Clerkship
of Macclesfield Court
Durante bene placito.

Sciant presentes et futuri quod Ego Willelmus Brereton de Handford in Comitatu Cestr' Baronettus seneschallus Domini Regis Burgi de Macclesfield in Comitatu Cestr' et manerii et Forresti sin et Curiae libertatum Hundredi sin de Macclesfield predicta Ac omnium Curiarum halmot' Portmote Swainmote visus Franck plegii Curie Barronis et Libertatum manerii Forresti ac libertatem Hundredi predicti spectantium sive pertinentium Constituisse, ordinasse et fecisse delectum michi in Christo Nicholaum Higginbothom Clericum omnium curiarum predictarum Habendum tenendum gandendum et occupandum locum et officium predictum per se ver pr sufficientem Deputatum vel Deputatos suos cum obuo vadis feodis et alliis proficuis loco sive officio Clerici predicti spectantibus sive pertinentibus in tam amplas modo et forma pront aliquo vel aliquibus alius Clerici vel Clericus ante hac habuerunt tennerunt gausi fuerunt vel habuit tenuit aut gausus fuit vel gaudere debuerunt vel debuit durante bene placito mei prefati Willelmi. In cuius rei Testimonium sigillum meum opposui data [**blank**] die Aprilis Anno Regni Regis Caroli nunc Angliae etc. XXII 1646

William Brereton

Translation

Let men now and to come know that I William Brereton of Handforth in the County of Chester, Baronet, Steward of the Kings Borough of Macclesfield in the County of Chester, and of his manor and forest, and of the court of liberties of his hundred of Macclesfield aforesaid, and of all corts of hallmote, portmote, swainmote, view of frankpledge, court baron and liberties belonging and appertaining to the manor and forest and the liberty of the hundred aforesaid, have set, chosen and made Nicholas Higginbothom, beloved to me before Christ, clerk of all the courts aforesaid, to have, to hold, to enjoy and to occupy the place and office aforesaid by himself or by a sufficient deputy or deputies together with income, wages, fees and other profits belonging and concerning the place or office of clerk aforesaid, inn such full manner and form as any other clerks or clerk before this have had, held and have enjoyed or has held or has enjoyed or should have enjoyed during the pleasure of me the aforesaid William. In witness of which thing I have applied my seal dated [**blank**] day of April in the 22nd year of the reign of King Charles now of England etc.

William Brereton

134

Major Bradshawe his lre refusing
the deputy Stewardship of Macclesfield

Sr. Wm Brereton passed a deputacon to Mr. Lightbourne and Major Bradshaw to bee his Deputie Stewards of Macclesfield Court, But Major Bradshawe desired to be excused.

Noble Sr,

I received your lre of ye 23 of this instant by ye contents whereof it seemes to mee that your pleasure is I should intermeddle as one of your Deputies Concerneing ye keeping ye Court at Macclesfield, yourself beinge steward there. I entreat you to give mee leave to Certifie you that my breedynge & bringing up hath not bene as worldly. I am enabled to under goe that place which will need a man of such gifts and understandinge of Lawe as I am not indeed at all. And therefore finding myself altogether unable to execute it as maybe for your Honor, & ruyne our Creditt. I humbly desire you thinke again and appoint some other man more fitt to be your deputye in that place for I cannot accept of it and hope that your Honor will hold me well Excepted in excusing to be imployed in yt wch I am not able to performe. It may please you likewise to understand that the Record and writinge concerning that courte (formerlie recorded by ye Committee of that Hundred) were upon Wednesday last delivered to your servant Rich'd. Higginbotham according to your Honors lre.

Sr. I am and shall thankfullie Remane
Yor Honors humble Servt,
Henry Bradshawe junr.

Wyberley 25th Ap: 1646.

135

Sr. Wm. Breretons lre to Sr. John Cooke touching
Sr. J. Fitzherbert & Sr. An: Kniverton

Sr,

Upon surrender of Tutburie Castle myself and ye rest of ye Comissioners appointed by ye Comittee of both Kingdomes did engage ourselves to write to ye comittee of both kingdomes to move them that they would intersede for ye taking off ye sequestracons of Sr. John ffitzherbert and Sr. Andrew Kniveton, which though wee did not undertake any, nor was anie such thing asserted into ye Condicons, yet it was conceived it would have bene much more Prejudice to ye Country to have maintained ye Leauger untill that could have bene obtained from ye Parlyment then would have doubled the Composicione for theire sequestracons, besides ye Danger of ye sickness extending and dispersing itself both into ye leauger & countrey. A Copie of which lre is hereinclosed sent you . As yet there hath bene noe answere returned thereunto which hath occasioned this address unto yourself, serving for that

Comittee which is the rather sent because I conceive it would be much for ye Honor of ye Parlym't and advantage of your affaires if there were a performance beyond our Engagm't force sent to other strong holdes in these partes that might be perhapps better Inclined thereby soe as herein you may as well do an acceptable service to ye publique as you may much engage

Your verie faithfull friend
and servant
Wm. Brereton

Dudley 30th Aprile
1646

136

Letter to Mr. Ashurst, Mr. Jones &
Sr. Ralph Ashton touching besieging
Dudley Castle.

Worthie Srs.

Upon Tuesday April 21 Tutburie Castle was delivered into our hands. And upon ye 26th of the same monthe I tooke ye Warwickshire and Leicestershire Regiments of horse and some Staffordshire and Shropshire foote and marched towards Dudley intending yt day to have possessed ourselves of ye Towne. But ye Shropshire foote mutyned for want of pay soe alsoe due Captaine Portes Companie. Whereby it came to Passe wee were disappointed of ye halfe of ye number intended for yt Designe which occasioned us to take up our quarters that night wth our ffoot that night at Walsall, and wth a strong guard of Horse placed before ye Castle, ye Enimy was kept in until the next morneinge (Tuesday) When wee expected ye rest of ye ffoote to come up unto us, wherein alsoe wee were disappointed, notwithstanding wth those fewe foot wch were wth us, in all were fewer then 200, wee marched forward and about 11 of ye Clock possessed ourselves of ye Towne of Dudley without anie losse save onely two men slain and one horse killed. Att wch tyme ye Enimy set fire in foure or five severall places in ye Towne at once, which pleased God soe to destraine as it did not much harme there being not manie more howses burned then those wherein the fire begun and some of those next adjoining to them. The grounde being not penetrable (the most of it beinge like stone), wee were Constrained instead of making Trenches, to erect High walls and brestwokes of Stone wherewith wee were accommodated by ye Conveniency of ye Stone of ye Church wch the Enimy themselves demolished. ffrom which breast workes wee intend to make a strong Trench to ye Priory for wch end Owere Pyoneers are already at worke. Wee have alsoe fortified the Priory and placed therein a stronge Guard (these three Companies of Shropshire foote who formerly muytned beinge come up to us ye next day). Concerneing whom I cannot omitt one Remarkeable Passage of divine providence, wherein ye lord was pleased to manifest his Justice to them and his mercy to us. They had bene verie mutinous and outrageous upon theire march (as those use to be who are soe ill payd) and Comitted severall misdemeanours, mortally wounded a yonge man at Wedgbury because he did not soe soone as they expected discover unto them the next Ale howse which was neighbour fitt to bee concealed from them who had tasted too much stronge Liquor before. They were no lesse careless and some upon theire Guarde presuming upon the strength of theire walls and workes, and stragglinge abroad, and were fishing some Ponde within ye viewe of ye Castle whereof ye Enimy takeing notice and advantage, ye Centrees beinge asleep and manie of those upon dutie negligent and ye rest wth matches unlyted, entred ye Howse and surprised them upon theire guarde before they could make resistance, wounded two of them mortallie and tooke five prisoners & were indeed possessed of all theire guard and Armes, had not our foote from ye maine guard bene verie ready to release them and ye Leicestershire horse lead by Colonell Hacker upon one guard and ye Governor of Leicester, his troope wth Cornet Paget upon another guard made hast unto theire rescue soe as wee lost noe more then onely two men mortallie wounded and foure taken, and had full play upon ye Enimy up ye hill in theire Retreat but knowe not what executon was done which as it cannot but be acknowledged to be a great mercy that the guard was not Cutt off (as yt att Litchfeilde first placed upon Bacon hill wch Certenlie was Designed and expected by ye Enimy) soe wee hope it wilbe a warninge to make them more carefull and diligent and more Reformed seeing they observe Gods hand upon them. Whereof some of them are already verie sensible. I hope alsoe it may be of good use to ye rest to make them more Circumspect because the Enimy is soe active and desperate. Notwithstandinge I doubt not but through Gods assistance a good accompt may be given both of Dudley and Litchfeilde, concerneing wch I desire your advice what is fittest to be done in case the Kinge be come to London as wee heare it confidently reported. If ye Leicester Gunner yt played at Belvoir and that morter might be ordered to Litchfeilde I doubt not but ye Close might be had much sooner. How as Gods tyme wilbe best till wch tyme I desire wee may waite wth patience and alsoe neglect noe meanes that may hasten ye same. ffor which end ye utmost Endeavor shalbe used of him who is and shall always Remaine

Your verie much
obliged friend to serve
you Wm. Brereton

140

Lre to ye Comittee of both Kingdomes
(& another of ye same to ye Speaker)
touching besieging Dudley.

My Lords and Gentlemen,

After ye surrender of Tutburie part of my care was first to sequester such of that leaguer for a tyme as wee feared might support others and to imploy ye rest and such as wee could spare elsewhere for ye Reduceinge of Dudley Castle in further pursuance of your Honors first Instruccon for these partes. To where wee made speedie march hither and upon Tuesdaie last possessed ourselves of the Towne wth ye losse onlie of two men dead and one wounded. But before ye Enemy was forced from ye Towne they set fire in five severall places in ye Towne at once which yet ye providence of ye Lord soe overuled as wth some easie care and hazard it was soone stoped from proceeding much further then the first or next houses in any of ye places. The next worke was Imediatelie to fall upon Entrenching where we could and otherwise erecting breastworkes of ye Materials of ye Church wch ye Enemy had Demolished.

There was also a Ruynated Priory equally distant from ye Towne and from ye Castle (within a halfe musquetts shot) which wee made use of as one of ye Guard. Where this day ye Enemy sallieng out in an unespied way were Entred ye place. But our Horse and foote from theire severall Guards Imediately beat them off and rescued the most of our men without anie further harm than the dangerous wounding of 2 of our men & taking five prisoners (but no Armes) and those men alsoe I have already received. This losse I hope wilbe liable to begett double Dilligence and spiritt both in yt partie and throughout ye whole Leauger. The best accompt whereof (as of all your comands and Trustes) as God shall enable, you shall upon all occasions still receive from,

Your Honors most ffaithfull
and humble servant
W. Brereton

Dudley Ap. 30 1646

141

From Colon. Leveson to
Sr. Wm. Brereton

Sr,

I have sent unto you the three prisoners I menconed and shall desire my Ensigne may be sent tomorrowe for those men of Envill, prisoners here. I cannot as yet release them.

Yr. Servt. Leveson

Dudley Castle Ap 29 1646

Answer: Sr,

You sent out 3 men last night wch I desired not. Not knowing who they were nor how they were taken. I desired onelie ye Countrey men wch I named, wch may justlie challenge theire release for your Ensigne in regard they took a time wch is my desire still, or if not all, to send out Richard Luke of Kinver being but a poore simple man.

ffor ye men you tooke this day I shall send those you writt for if they be in our custody. But hereafter I shall take it for noe courtesie to send mee such men, such as desire not exchange. Your Ensigne and men are sent for from Wrotesly, wch when they come shall be returned you by,

Yor Svt.,
W. Brereton

From ye leag'r before
Dudley Castle
30th Aprill 1646

142

A lre to ye Gov'r of
Dudley Castle

Two of those seven men you sent are soe Extremely wounded that they were Carryed down upon Barrows and are noe better then dead men as I am informed. And since ye signeing hereof I understand that Joseph Davies was one of our souldiers as by his owne confession appears therefore I have detained him.

Gov'r of Dudley's lre wch is
answered by ye last.

Sir,

I have taken seven of your men whom I send you disireinge you wilbe pleased to release and send mee hither Joseph Davies, Wm. Reskavy and Tho. Ward, prisoners at Wrotesley, George Wood prisoner at Rushall and Robt. Everill prisoner at Coventry

Yr Sert.
Leueson

For Sr. Wm. Brereton

The Lo: Ashley to Sr. Wm. Brereton desire Libertie for his Man to goe to Bridgnorth to enquire after writings Conc: his Barrondry.

Sr,

Your Centuryes having often this night tould the Centuryes of this Garrison that Bridgnorth is delivered upp Causeth mee though a stranger to you to send this letter to desire you to doe me the favour to lett a servant of mine passe with any Drum or Trumpetts of yours to Bridgnorth to enquire if hee can find what is become of some Writeings of mine that were left in the Castle in Sr. Lewis Kerks tyme. Sr. they are writings only that Concerne my Barrondry which Cannot any way advantage any Body but my selfe and posterity that yt encourageth mee to desire this at your hands is that in the Instructions for the Comittees for Sequestrations of Delinquents Estates, the 12th Instruction gives comaund to all Sequestrators in these words, you are to take care for the safe keeping of the deeds, Evidences & Writeings of all Delinquents and for preserving of their Howses Tymber trees and fruit trees from Waste and Destruccon. Sr. if you shall please to do mee this favour or to lett my Man goe to Stafford and acquaint Mr. Backehouse where hee left these Pattents and give Mr. Backehouse leave to goe to take care of them your Civilitie will much oblige mee, and I will passe you my honour & faith, that my servant if soe Liccenced by you hall neither carrie letter nor Messuage of anything but concerneing these Writeings, nor Sr. shall I desire them into my hands but that they may bee in any Gentlemans hands if that should cause any difficultie; Sr. your care to observe the direccons of Parliament I doubt not will bee one motive to you to doe mee this favour. Sr, my Brother Benjamin Weston in being much your Servant may be another motive, a likewise the Civilitie will oblige mee to bee

Your humble Servant
Walter Aston

Lichfield Close
Thursday May 1st
1646

Sr. Wm. Breretons answere to the last

My Lord,

It is most Certaine Bridgnorth is delivered upp, and for your further satisfaction therein, as alsoe if possiblie you can heare of those Writeings you specifie in your letter, I shall send a Drum with your Lor'ps to nominate some Gentleman in whose hands you shall desire them Intrusted, which shall likewise bee assented to, by

Your Lor'ps humble Servant
Wm. Brereton

May 2nd 1646

144

Sr. Tho: Tildesley to Sr,. Wm. Brereton
touch: Captaine Dyott.

Sr,

As I have formerlie declared to Capt. Stone my Resolution still is that I will either have the performance of Capt. Stones engagement to procure (or endeavour'mt) Capt. Dyotts Release, or else I expect as hee is a Soldyer the returne of the three Ensignes for I never Release them for any other.

For the other motion of Capt. Heskith I desire first to knowe your possitive Answere whether hee bee at Libertie or noe, if hee bee, I shall propose a Reasonable Exchange for those I have Released, Relying upon yor promise your Answere is desired by

Your Servant
Tho: Tyldesley

1st May 1646

Sr. Wm. Breretons Answere thereunto

Sr,

I am altogether a Stranger to these proceedings betwixt you and Capt. Stones touching the exchange of Capt. Dyott, and shall therefore deferr the further Answere thereunto till Capt. Stones his Returne which will not bee long. As for Capt. Hesketh I have not Received any Answere Concerning him, though I sent to Chester to that purpose and will nowe send alsoe again for further satisfaccon that soe there may bee a perfprmance of what was promised by,

Your Servant
Wm. Brereton

2nd May 1646

145

An accompt of ye race at Tutbury and allowance
Due to ye Surveyors & yeomen. Received from Mr. Vernon
May 2 1646.

Ould breedinge Mares in fole	24
Oulde breedinge Mares wch Barren	10
ffoles nowe 4	10

ffoles nowe 3		05
ffiles nowe 2		07
ffiles nowe one		14
	Tot. of mares	70

Taken Ap 28 1646

Stoudd coaltes now three	11
Stoudd coaltes nowe 2	14
Stoudd coaltes nowe 1	12
	37

Surveyors ffees

From ye King yearely about £40 or £53. 13. 4

Horses	6
Allowance in keeping of Oxen	12
Cowes	12
Bull	01

Yeomans fees

From ye King annation		6. 0. 0
Allowance in keeping of Runt	20	
Oxen	06	
Bull	01	
Bullock	08	
Mares	08	
Sheepe	40	

146

Major Phillipps and Major Grayes Parolls

These may Certifie all whom it may concerne in ye service of ye Parliam't that I have given Major Phillipps now prisoner at Ecleshall his p'oll for a months tyme from the date hereof to goe to Conaway in Wales after ye expiracon of wch month hee is to returne into the Parliam'ts Quart'rs and to surrender himself prisoner to mee att my Quarters and all whom it may concerne are to p'mitt him to pass and repass accordingly without lett. Given under my hand 4th May 1646.

Sr. Wm. Brereton

The like for Major Grey for 6 weeks to goe for Worcester.

Both of them alsoe gave bonds interchangeably each for other for paym't of a months pay at ye end of their parolls for their Ransoms.

Major Phillipps as major of Horse &
Major Grey as major of foote.

Lre from Colonell Leveson desiring a passe
for a second Messenger to goe to ye kinge.

Sr,

If you have yet received your Generalls answere concerneing ye passe to sende to ye King, I desire you will let mee know it, if not that you will send mee a passe for a Gentleman to goe to your Generall to treat wth him for it.

Your Servt.
Leueson

For Coll. Stone

147

Somons of Dudley

Sr,

I perceive you desire libertie to send a second messenger to ye Kinge. You Cannot but be sufficientlie informed of ye Kinge's present condicon by ye former messenger that is returned and therefore I shall not thinke fitt to admitt anie further delay but doe hereby require you in ye name of both Howses of Parliam't to deliver up ye Castle with all ye Armes & amunicon and other warlike provisions therein to mee for ye use of ye Kinge & Parliam't ffor ye Effectinge whereof commissioners may be agreed upon on both partes to treat whereof if you now accept you may Expect such condicons for yourself and souldiers as may be fitt for you to receave & wee do grant. But if further delay be used you might looke for noe better (but worse) then those that haveinge used hon'ble termes when they were tended were afterwards constrained to accept farre worse, you cannot but know that Oxford is besieged and that noe reliefe can come thence or from anie other place. Att nyne of ye Clocke tomorrowe Morneing I expect your Positive Answere. And rest,

Your Servant
W. Brereton

Dudley May 6 1646

For Colonell Leveson Gov'r of
Dudley Castle, these

148

Lre to Capt. Greenwood & Capt. Watson
to demolish Tutbury Castle

Gent,

Upon ye Surrender of ye Garrison of Tutburie it was referred to your Care to see ye same dismantled soe as it should be incapable of being hereafter made a Garrison. What is therein done I knowe not but have wholie depended upon you and must still relye upon your care therein. And to this end have sent this to desire you or ye one of you to goe hither and to lodge in one of ye Towers untill ye same be done sufficientlie & made not to be Garrisoned. The country wilbe verie willinge to assent thereunto. I desire yt some twenty musquetiers maybe taken alonge to contynue in ye castle till it be effectuallie done and that there may be noe need of delay in ye dispatch thereof least such bad effects ensue as wilbe too late hereafter to remedie. Let ye musquetiers be sent hither forthwith under some careful officer. Whereof now that I have given you this Intymason I doubt not but you wilbe verie active herein as knowing of what dangerous consequence it may be to suffer any delay in ye confidence whereof and expectacon of hearing from ye how it goes on I remain

Yor assured friend
Wm. Brereton

Dudley May 6 1646

149

Sr. Wm. Breretons second leter to Capt. Watson
and Capt. Greenwood to demolish Tutbury Castle.

Gentlemen,

Yesternight I writ unto you to desire one of you would Constantly Reside and lodge in some part of Tutbury Castle with twentie Musquetiers to take the Chardge and Care of seeing the same soe demolished as to make it uncapeable of being engarrisoned hereafter. It was some Intelligence I Received that woried mee to write that letter and therein to desire noe delay might bee comitted which being confirmed to mee I have thought good the place being of soe greate Concernm't to send these lines to desire that you will not faile in this Trust reposed in you according to the inclosed (which is a Coppie of the Letter yesterday sent). If you have not Musquetiers to spare then you may send this order to Coll. Bowyer. Herein depending on your Care I Remaine

Your assured friend
Wm. Brereton

Dudley May 7th
1646

To Col. Bowyer for the same purpose

Sr,

Upon some Intelligence I have Received I thought fitt and accordinglie writt to Captaine Greenewood and Captaine Watson to take especial care to see the Castle of Tutbury speedily and soe effectuallie demolished as that it may not hereafter bee engarrisoned, and have appointed them to place therein at least twentie musquett'ers untill the same bee sufficiently done. Now in case they have not Musqueteers to spare I desire you will send twentie of yours (with some Careful officer) of those that were Ordered for Litchfield to Continue there till this worke bee done. That this worke bee done you are engaged with myself not only as it is of General Concernement, but as you were jointly intrusted by the Parliament in that Treatie and to see the Articles on the behalfe of the Parliament performed. I shall therefore in regard my employments deteine mee this way I desire that you will make it your speciall Care that noe delay may be made in the effectuall execucon thereof, least that danger ensue which will bee hereafter too late to remedy, Whereof now that I have given you this advertisem't I depend on and doubt not of your care therein, the Country will upon Comaund willingly assist. I am

Your Assured to:
Uncle W:B:

Dudley May 7th 1646

150

Post to this one I have sent to Capt. Greenwood or Capt. Hardstaffe to be constantly there & desire your care that it be not neglected.

Order for 20 musqt. to be placed in Tutbury Castle until it be demolished.

It is ordered that Colonel Bowyer or his Lt. at Litchfield doe upon sight hereof send twenty musquetiers, good fire men wth Amunicon and provisions of victualls under ye comand of a Corporal & faithful officer to Tutbury Castle there to remaine untill the said castle be made ungarrisonable and till further order from mee. And in case of danger to defend & keepe the saide towers agst. all opposicon till further order for ye service of ye Parlt.

Given at Dudley
W. Brereton

May 7th 1646

Capt. Greenwood or Capt. Hardstaffe are appointed to take Charge hereof.

151

Letter to Sr. Tho. Fairfax[33] touching the King wth ye Scotch Armie

May it please your Excellencie,

Upon my march this daie from the leauger at Lichfield to ye leauger agst Dudley I received a lre from Darbie from Captaine Hope who is a verie honest man and comands a Troope of Horse in ye Derbyshire Regt. whereby I am informed confident'le that his Majestie was yesterday wth my lord Leven in ye Scotch Armie a mile from Newarke. The advertisem't whereof is of such high Concernem't both to ye publique and yourself that (How best your Excellencie may have received earlier Intelligence) I could not but apprehend it a part of my dutie to give your Excellencie notice thereof besides my desire and readines to apprehend all opportunitie whereby I may approve myselfe

Your Excellecies most
humble servant
Wm. Brereton

Dudley May 6 1646

This lre was sent from Dudley on May 6 and May 7 in ye morning these following lres were received

---

From ye Gov'r and Comittee at Leicester
To Sr. Wm. Brereton.

Hon'bl Sr,

Wee are to give your thoughts this Interruption in your worke to let you knowe our Intelligence runs thus, that wee received a lre from Colonell Grey wch speaks this language.

That the lords did wish mee to write unto you to let you knowe that this day newes came unto them of Colonell Rositers sent that ye King this morning was in Southwell and there was wth him a Frenchman whose name I have forgotten, and within one hower and halfe after came word again that he went out of Southwell wth a Troope of Horse and at ye Townes end there did meete a Regt. of Horse soe ye lords desire you would be carefull in the Towne and Countrie and if possible you care to inquire of his motions and to let them, and ye Parliam't know, and likewise they would have you send word to theire Garrisons in the South partes and let them knowe alsoe. The treatie goes on well and I hope that Newarke wilbe ours w'thin this three or fower daies. This being in hast I rest

Yor friend & Serv't
Tho. Grey

Sr, with this Intelligence wee present you wth our service and as our advertisem't are more you shall have it from

Noble Sr,
Edward Cradock, Major John Needham
Tho. Haselrig ffran. Hacker
Fran Smalley
Rich. Ludlam
Wm. Stanley

Sir Thomas Fairfax, son of Lord Fernando Fairfax, took the surrender of the Royalist garrison at Oxford.

153

From ye Com'tee of ye Parliam't of England
at ye Leauger at Newarke touching K.
being at Southwell

Sr,

Wee are this morneinge about ten of ye Clocke credibly informed that ye Kinge and three others wth him came hastily to Southwell this morning about 7 of ye Clocke at lighted at ye House of Mon'r. Mentrell ye ffrench Agent who hath bene at Southwell this month (ever since he came from Oxford) About twelve this day two of the Scotch Comissioners came to us from ye Towne acquainted us of the Kings comeinge. Wee are nowe goinge to meete wth them to consider thereof. Thees desire you that what horse you can possibly spare may be sent this way to be in readines upon all Events.

Your affectionate friends
and Serv'ts.
Edw. Montague
Wm. Perrpoint
Fra. Myne
Edw. ....

From Colo: Rositers Tent
at ye Leauger before
Newarke 5th May 1646

Wee have since ye writinge hereof
that ye King was conveyed wth
a troope of Horse out of Southwell
and that a Regt. of Horse were ready
to receive him at ye Townes end
and wither he is marched wee
cannot tell

Anoth. Lre by
Tho: Hatcher.

154

Sr. Wm. Breretons answere to ye
Lords & other Com'rs at Newarke

My Lords and Gent'n,

Yours of ye 5th Instant I received this morneinge and am sorrie that I was forced yesterday to part wth ye Warwickshire Horse, ordered to be disbanded. But I shall immediately hasten after them to see if I may prevent it, the better to enable mee to performe your desires (our Cheshire horse beinge not wth mee, but ordered for North Wales) And our Leauger here and at Litchfeilde being over weake already. But to ye utmost if I am able I shall everie way endeavor. ffor wch purpose as I sent ye Intelligence of ye Kings motions yesterday (before this of your Lo'ps came to mee) unto ye Parliam't and to Sr. Tho. ffairefax, his Excellency, by other wayes, soe have I alsoe sent to Strengthen ye principal places within my verge, and still to the utmost of my power to be carefull and Circumspect herein, and all things els whereby I may approve myself

Yor Lo'ps most humble & faithful
Servt.
Wm. Brereton

From ye Leauger at
Dudley
May 7th 1646

I beseech yor Lo'ps let mee heare yet further from you anie occasion require that soe I may yet further be serviceable to yor lo'ps.

155

The G'rall upon the former Intelligence of ye Kings beinge at Southwell sent lres to ye Governor of ye Castle of Chester, the Deputy Governor (in ye absence of ye Gov'er) of Chester and to ye Comittee there, and alsoe to ye Governor of Namptwch (and to Colonell Brookes to look to Holte Castle), desiring them respectivelie to take care theire Garrisons be furnished wth provisions, and workes repaired. And ye Castle of Chester and the Mount fortified and the forces kept on their guard and in readiness upon all Events.

Col. Levesons answere to ye
Somons Yesterday

Sr,

You wilbe pleased to send mee a passe by my Drum for ye safe passage to you and returne backe, of Lieutenant Colonell Beamont and Major Christopher Heveningham. You shall by them receive an Answere to your demands.

Yor Servant,
Leueson

Dudley Castle 7th May 1646
For Sr Wm. Brereton

Sr Wm. Breretons Answere

Sr,

I have according to your desire sent herewith a passe for Lt. Colonell Beamont and Major Heveningham whose comeing forthwith accordingly is expected by,

Yor Servt.
Wm. Brereton

156

The passe that was sent

These are to require you and everie of you upon sight hereof to Permit Lieuten't Colonell Beamont and Major Heveningham to passe this day from ye Castle of Dudley to mee, to my Quarters in Dudley Towne and thence to returne into ye said Castle without anie manner of violence or interrupcon. Given at my Quarters in Dudley Towne this 7th of May 1646

Wm. Brereton

To all Colonells and other officers and
souldiers belonging to this leauger & to
all others to whom it may come &
Concerne in the Parl'ts. Service.

Sr. Wm. Breretons lre to Sr. Tho. ffairfax
from Coventry

May it please your Excellency,

Soe sone as I received ye welcome newes of ye reduceing of Banburie and of your Excellencies settleing before Oxford, I thought fitt to communicate the contents of ye inclosed as not knowing anie other Expedient whereby ye desires of ye Countrie may be satisfied then by applieing such a strength of Horse as in your wisedome shalbe thought meet, ffor by our engag't before Dudley those forces assigned unto mee are nowe then sufficientlie taken and wee are put upon much harder dutie by ye late discharginge of those serviceable Warwickshire Troopes wch otherwise might have bene assistant to us in our Leag. agt Dudley soe as I could not spare any horse noe occasion is and as it shall please God to prosper us in our designes in these partes It shalbe reported to yor Excellencie by

Yor most humble Servt.
Wm. Brereton

Coventry May 8 1646.

157

2nd order for levying money in Hemlingford
Hund: for ye Leauger at Dudley.

To ye high Constable of ye Hundred of Hemlingford
& to everie one of them.

Whereas you have formerly received a war't from mee of ye 28th day of Aprill directed to you for ye assisting, collectinge and receaving of such fines of moneyes as have bene weeklie required or payd to the Enemy Garrisons of Litchfield or Dudley from such places as lye within Eight miles of ye borders of ye County of Warwickshire within your Hundred for the maintenance of ye Leaugers before ye said Garrisons. There being some Inconveniency found in the same. These are to will and require you to send out your warrants to all the Constables within your Hundred at what distance said, to paye in the Monies on the day, and laid at the place assigned in your former warrants. Hereof faile not as you render the service in hand and ye good of your Country. Given under my hand at Birmingham ye 7th day of May 1646.

Wm. Brereton

158

Newarke Surrendered. Lre from the Com'te
to Sr. Wm. Brereton

Sr,

This last night ye treatie concluded and ye Sconces of Newarke w'thall ye ffortes, sconces and provisions of warre are to be surrendered into our Hands on Saturday next exceptinge onelie ye Horses, Armes and goods of all the officers of ye Garrison. But ye Troopers and foote are to March without Horses and Armes (saveing theire Swords) to any of ye Enemyes Garrisons unbesieged or unblocked up. And all Gentlemen & Clergie and others that are accepted to travell are to have passes beyond seas or otherwise are at liberty to live at home submitting to all ordinances of Parlym't. This is ye substance of ye Articles wch tyme will not permitt us to send you a transcript of. Wee heartily wish ye like success to yor Endeavours and doe assure you wee shall not be wanting in giving you our best assistance. Wee have here one Mr. Gardiner, a verie skilfull friend whom if you have occasion to use, or anie of our forces or Artillerie here, wee shall upon a lre thereof send them unto you. The Kinge is still at Lt. G'rall Leslie's Quarters at Kelham and wee find ye Scots willing to march northwards as that this night they drewe out ye Isleland.

Yor assured friends
Edw. Montague
Wm. Pierpoint
Arth.
Tho. Hatcher

Balderton 7 May

For ye hon'ble Sr. Wm. Brereton
Baronett these wth speed.

159

Answere My Lords and Gentlemen

I have noe sooner this night received ye most Glorious Newes of Newarkes surrender for wch I returne most humble thankes as alsoe for your Care & noble offer of assistance. I have thought good herein closed to send you ye Articles whereupon Banburie was this day to be surrendered. And that this day alsoe wee have ordered hereunto a treatie for Dudley Castle, whereof I will not faile to give you a further Accompt according as wee shall make a further progresse therein. Litchfield remaines still verie obstinate, but if you please to assist us with Mr. Gardiner & (if he be not ye same) wth ye Leicester man who played the Granadoes at Belvoir together wth two of ye greatest morter peeces for them and shells accordinglie, soe manie as you can spare, I doubt not but Litchfield Close wilbe speedily delivered alsoe which as yet they are ye rather encouraged to hold out though our Granadoes doe execute and breake through ye leades and Roofe of ye Minster (where theire Magazine lies and whereunto ye most of them retire when our morter peeces play.) yet they are not able to penetrate thorowe the Ancient stone roofe into ye Bodie of ye Church wch is theire onelie refuge and place of safetie. And whereas you are pleased to offer your best assistance of forces I shall most thankfully Embrace that Motion espetiallie of ffoot, who ye sooner they come to us the more serviceable they may be and more Considerable to ye further Designes comanded by ye Comitee of both Kingdomes in these parts and in the perfecting that worke whereunto yourselves have contributed soe much and whereby you have engaged the whole Kingdome and none more in particular then,

Yor most humble Srvt,
Wm. Brereton

May 8th 1646.

161

Sr. Wm. Breretons lre to ye Comittee at Evesham
To meet touching ye design agt. Worcester
May 9 1646
The lre to Colonell Morgan

Gentlemen,

I am soe sensible of ye manie engage you have Placed wth mee as that I desire to lay hold upon all opportunities whereby I may approve my readiness to serve you. Whence hither unto I have bene disabled by ye other pre engagements but now having received intelligence from ye Lords Comons Comissioners at Newarke that this day Newarke is to be delivered up upon verie hon'ble Conditions. And the Kinge is in the Scotch Armie. That ye

Scotch are already marching northwards. Soe as I cannot doubt as some others doe but that wee shall fairly conclude wth them when the messenger alsoe came upon theire Returne northward. They have alsoe tendred mee theire utmost assistance wch I doubt not wilbe hastened unto mee. Soe alsoe some other foote are ordered from Banbury and I hope Dudley wilbe noe longe worke. If therefore it were soe that I could meete wth some of ye members of ye Comittee & Colonell Morgan upon Tuesday, Wednesdaie or Thursday next, upon wch of these daies you & he shall appoint (Giveinge mee tymelie notice thereof), in ye meane tyme at Dudley or Litchfield, I will there, if ye Com. Permitt, give you meeting and wee may then Consider and Conclude howe the further Comandes of ye Comittee of both Kingdomes for reducing of Worcester may be pursued, wch is not more desired by anie man then by

Yor most ffaithfull friend
& Servt.,
Wm. Brereton

Dudley May 9th 1646.

162

Sr. Wm. Brereton lre to Sr. Thomas Fairefax touching surrendering of Newarke
Wherein was inclosed the former lre from ye Lords & Comons concerning it.

May it please your Excellencie,

I have received intelligence from ye Lords and Comons Comissioners at Newarke that they have concluded upon conditions for ye surrender of Newarke this day according to ye termes of ye lre the copie whereof is here inclosed sent to ye and my former sent yesterday may noe wayes discompose or dysturbe your Excellencies other proceedings and engagements whereof now that I have given you Intymacon I shall not thinke fit to enlarge myself anie further than to assure you that I am and will always Remaine

Your Excellencies most
ffaithfull and most humble
servant,
Wm. Brereton

Dudley May 9th 1646

For his Excellencie Sr. Tho.
Fairefaxe, these

163

Order of ye Co'tee at Yorke touching Mrs Egerton
Taking of ye Sequestracon of Rd. Egerton

Whereas ye mannor or Lo'p of Allerston in ye Countie of Yorke and divers Messuages, land and Tenements and Hereditaments there being ye Inheritance of Richard Egerton Esquire, were lately sequestered for ye delinquencie of ye said Richard Egerton, now for as much as it appears by ye Evidence of one Mr. George Parker made and taken before Mr. Page, one of ye Masters of his Majesties high Court of Chester ye 28th day of August last paste that ye said Mr. Egerton longe before ye tyme of his supposed Delinquencie to untill ye first day of November in the 13 yeare of his now Majesties Raigne did by Indenture of lease of yt date for valuable consideracon therein expressed Grant, bargaine, sell, Devise & to favour unto Sr. Wm. Brereton Bart. and Arthur Aldburgh Esqr., ye said Manor Lo'p and premises amongst other things for ye terme of three score yeares from ye day of ye date of ye said Indenture. And by another Indenture of Lease bearing ye date ye 27 of Nov in ye 14 yeare of his said majesties Raigne for good & valuable Consideracons in yt Indenture menconed and more espetiallie for yt ye said Sr. Wm. Brereton and Arthur Aldburgh had at ye Instance and request of ye said Mr. Egerton undertaken and engaged themselves for ye Paym't of divers greate sumes of money being ye proper debts of ye said Rd. Egerton and to ye end that they ye said Sr. Wm. Brereton and Arthur Aldburgh might have sufficient wherewith to pay and discharge ye same & to secure and save themselves harmless and Indempnified ye said Rd. Egerton did grant bargaine sell devise and to favour,

Let ye said manor and Lo'p amongst other things to ye said Sr. Wm. Brereton and Arthur Aldburgh for ye terme of ten yeares from ye tyme of ye sealing of ye last menconed Indenture. It is therefore ordered that ye said manor or Lo'p of Allerston and premises aforesaid not beinge sequestrable for ye present for ye Delinquencie of ye said Mr. Egerton shalbe discharged of ye said sequestratons wch is hereby declared to be voide and that ye sequestrators shall from henceforth permitt and suffer ye said Sr. Wm. Brereton and Arthur Aldburgh Esquire or theire assignes quietlie to enjoy ye said mannor or Lo'p and premises according to ther Lawfull Interest and Estate therein and to receive ye Rents issues and profitts thereof accordinglie untill further order to ye Contrary and to restore and Pay to Sr. Wm. Brereton and Arthur Aldburgh or theire assignes all such Rents and sums of money as they have received and taken by Colour of ye said Sequestracons and are nowe Remaineing in theire......

ffinis

166

From Mr. Eaton to Sr. Wm. Brereton

Noble Sir,

God is with you of a very truth, and hee hath helped you and hee hath honoured you, and hee hath stopped the Mouthes of Detractors and put to shame Your Adversaries and hath Rescued your life from imminent dangers and still thinks fitt to use you in honourable services to his name. And those that feare God Rejoyce in it, and sound out the prayers of the Lord for it, and others gnash their teeth at it. As for mee, the presence of Gods grace and power with you is a matter of thanksgiving unto God from mee, and my prayers shall bee that hee would still deliver you and honour you, that you may live to honour him. Sr. I beseech you adhere to God still and his Cause, and truth, and honour those that feare the Lord, and lett Vile Persons bee more and more Contemned in your eyes, and entrust the Godly for they being faithfull to God will bee soe to you, when as others serving you for their owne ends will prove treacherous unto you and to advantage themselves will turne Enemyes to you, you have experience of it, but they have not, they cannot hurt you because God hath and will uphold you soe long as your wayes please him. Sr. I have Condemned myself for neglecting soe long writeing to you. Your honouring of God and serving of Christ in the Cause of the Gospell (though you had never shewed Countenance to mee) must needs engage mee in what I am to you, howe much when you are pleased to owne mee even to the stirring upp of envy in others, Sr. my purpose is to Travell to London about a fortnight or three weekes hence, and to waite upon you in my way thither, and to bee to you as you shall dispose of mee one Sabboth day. In the meane tyme I beseech you accept the tender of humblest service from

Yor honors much engaged &
Greatly devoted Servant
Samuel Eaton

Duckenfield the 20th
of Aprill 1646.

167

Colonell Jones intencons for Ireland
desiring Sr. Wm. Breretons assistance

Sr,

I intend for Ireland If I may get some of my arrears of England and be secured for ye rest if you wilbe pleased to further me in it. It will pleasure mee much and be advantageous to you wch I shall make appeare when I waite on you. For ye meane tyme desire to approve myself

Your Servant
Mich. Jones

London May 6 1646

For ye Ho'ble Sr. Wm. Brereton Barron't
Commander in Cheife at Litchfield
these present

Sr. Thomas Fairefax to Sr. Wm. Brereton

Sr,

I returne you many thankes for your advertisement of ye Kinge beinge come unto ye Scotch Army. I had a little before ye same tyme intelligence from Newarke and London and shalbe glad to understand from you as occasion shall require of anie thing of concernment that you conceive may happen. I am now engaged wth my Armie before Oxford and hope verie shortlie to be securelie Intrenched before it. Wishinge you good success in these engage-m'ts you have undertaken, I remaine

Your verie affeconate
friend and Servt
Tho. Fairfax

Wyddington
May 8th 1646

168

Exam'con of a trooper that came out of
Ye Close, May 6th 1646.

John Terrington a trooper under Sr. Jervis Lucas, a souldier in ye Close came from ye Enimy to our Leauger. Exa'ed sawth that a Granadoe fell into Captaine Turnpennes Howse and had not ye Magazine bene removed the night before it had bene blowne up and did blowe upp a great deale of Match. That another Granadoe light upon ye grounde and blewe upp two Peeces of Plate, and that another fell within six yardes of Sr. Thomas Tilsleyes lodginge Roome. That ye Townesmen have noe allowance but finde themselves.

169

Accompt wth Mr. Pott

Due in August 1644	20. 00. 00
Att Martlemas 1644	16. 00. 00
Att Mydsomer 1645	16. 00. 00
Att Martlemas 1645	16. 00. 00
Att Mydsomer 1646	16. 00. 00
	84. 00. 00

Payd by Mr. Pott to John Eaton for my use at three severall tymes in 1644 & 1645, 12L. Thes challengeth due to him to be abated for quartering Scotch

Reformadoes and others and for all other charges, Leves, taxes, Contribucons and assesm't since beginning of these Warres 38. 14. 8

Remnanet 16. 00. 00

As concerneing the thirte eight pounds abatement I am content to referre ye same to two honest men indifferently chosen for ye deciding thereof as they shall see fitt and reasonable which is assented unto on both sides at Dudley 9th day of May 1646 upon Condicon that ye accept halfe yeares rent due at mydsomer next followinge be paid in some Reasonable tyme. John Eaton to be first consulted withal to knowe whether there was but twentie pounds in arrears in ye Month of August 1644.

John Pott

Dudley, May
wth Tho. Aldersey.

A scornefull letter out of ye Close
between Joseph and Zachery Kirke

Brother Zachary,

I desire you to get Licence of Colonell Stone for my sister Eliz. To come to my wife to speake wth her from mee and to hurrie backe again. I shall Remaine

Yr. Thankfull Brother
Joseph Kirke

Answere

Sr, In regard you have written a datlesse, answers you must have this answere to noe purpose that your request shall not be granted by

Bacon hill Leauger

Brother Joseph,

Your dateless lre without direccon argues your manie destructors, emptie stomackes and light heads that you cannot have any answere to purpose, Concerneing your sister Elizabeth either from your neighbours or from

Your brother Zachary Kirke

170

Sr. Andrew Kniveton
Lre to Sr. Wm. Brereton

Hon'ble,

The late meeting at Addiston for ye Ashbie Gentlemens Composicons beinge put off till Munday next by ye Governor of Leicester, Sr. Richard Skeffington, I shall humbly intreat your lre to them in my behalfe according to yt noble offer you were pleased to make when I last had ye honor to waite on you. Sr. any favour that you shall be pleased to doe mee in this particular I am confident can neither be disservice to ye Parliam't nor any wayes retard your Generall proceedings but shall ever oblige me to appeare in all my accons

Yr. Most humble and thankfull
Ser't
Andrew Kniveton

171

Sr. Wm. Breretons lre to Sr. Rich. Skeffington & Col. Needham on Sr. And. Knivetons behalfe.

Gent,

Though wee thought not fitt by anie meanes to Condicon in ye Articles for ye surrender of Tutbury for takeing off ye Sequestracons of anie (though it was much insisted upon for most of ye Gentlemen in ye Castle) yet I did promise to endeavour to effect ye Remitting ye Sequestracon of Sr. Andrewe Kniveton (who was indeed ye Governour of ye Castle and had a great interest in ye Souldiers & Commanders there) And for that end have presented my Humble desires in ye Comittee of both Kingdomes whose answere is appointed. And though it should be soe that this should not be granted I shall earnestlie desire that he may receive more than ordinary favour soe farre as is consistent wth your Trust which I hope may be noe disservice to ye Parliam't because our performances beyond our undertakings may have an influence of good upon those who have not yet submitted and may holde out anie pt. Of ye Countrey to farre greater charge (besides trouble) then ye value of ye Composicons of manie Estates which I leave to your Consideracon and remain

Yr. Very faithfull friend
and Serv't.
W. Brereton

Litchfield May 9 1646.

172

Letter to ye Speaker of ye house of Comons from Sr. William Brereton touching ye surrender of Dudley Castell. Another letter to ye same Effect to ye Co'tee of both Kingdomes, to Sr. Henry Vane, Mr. Rich. Oldhouse inclosing the Articles.

Honorable Sr,

These lines are sent to give you this Accompte yt in further pursuance of my first Orders and Instructions from the Comittee of both Kingdomes for Reduceing of Lichfield and the Garrisons in these partes. Upon Tuesday Aprll. 27th Wee came before Dudley Castell: who opposed our entrance and alsoe in theire Retreate set the towne on ffire in five severall places at once to ye endangering of ye Whole towne. The Townesmen giving little Assistance to ye quenching of theire owne Howses. But our Soldyers put upon all ye Difficultie and Hazard thereof and yett all wth ye losse onelie of a few more Howses then they sett. The fire in and onelie of two men of our owne. When wee first Entred ye towne wee Rescued out of ye markett place manie Hundreds of Cattell wch ye Enimy had taken from ye neighbourhood upon the Approach of our fforces, all wch we restored to the severall owners. Our first care then was to place our Guards as neere and as Comodiously to the Castell as could bee to secure our men in ye towne and to Blocke upp ye Castell. To this End Wee Brought in ye Countrie and Sett our men to worcke w'thout Delay Errected stronge Brest Worckes of Stone in such places as wee could not Entrench, placed a strong Guard att ye Priory wthin little more then halfe Musquett shott of ye Castell and made Brestworckes of stone betweene ye Towne and Castell from ye great church (wch was burnte by ye Enimy) all along to ye priory. Soe soone as our Worckes and mounts were in good forward I sent upon Wednesday last May ye 6th, a Summons into ye Castell and Thursday they sent out two Gentlemen to desire a passe to ye Kinge wch was Denyed but they were Content to Treat and a Sessacon from Hostillitie was agreed upon, and upon these Inclosed Condicons the Castell is to bee Surrendered upon Wednesday next. Wherein wee did ye Rather a little Condiscend in some particulars to them both by reason they are soe strongly provided and have beene soe shorte a tyme Besieged in ye place soe stronge and Impregnable, and wee had almost Concluded before any Intelligence of takeing of Banbury or Newarke came to our hands. Whereunto I was ye rather Induced to yt End those fforces may bee disposed of for such further service as by ye Comittee of both Kingdomes is for my bee ordered yt soe there may by Gods blessing an End to this Warre wch is not more desired and Endevored by any man then my selfe who am,

Yor faithfull friend &
Humble Servant
Wm. Brereton

173

Articles agreed upon the tenth of May 1646 between Lt. Col. Beaumont, Major Christopher Heveningham and Mr. John Giffard deputed on the behalfe of Col. Leueson Governor of the Castle of Dudley and Col. Stepkin, Lt. Col.

Hunt and Captaine Stone, Commissioners appointed by Sr. Wm. Brereton Commaunder in Cheife of the Forces imployed for the Reduceing of the said Castle touching the surrender thereof.

1. Imprimis that all Gentlemen with their servants and all officers in Commission shall march away with their Horses and Armes soe that they exceed not the number of thirtie. And all Comon Soldyers that will march to any of the Kings Garrisons unbeseiged without their Armes. And all such as will live at their owne Howses to have protections (submitting themselves to all Ordinances of Parliament) and all Gentlemen Soldyers and others to carry with them their owne proper goods and noe more.
2. Item they shall have two Monethes tyme to Consider whether they will live at home or departe the Kingdome and in that tyme freely to passe into any parte of the Kingdome without Molestation or Arrest for any hostile Act or debt, soe farr as in our power, and to have passes to that purpose, provided in the meane tyme they doe nothing prejudiciall to the Parliament.
3. Item that in the end of two Monethes all that will live at their Howses shall enjoy their goods and estates without plunder or Molestation (submitting to all Ordinances of Parliament and giving engagements not to beare Armes against the Parliament). And such as will goe beyond Sea to have passes accordinglie and Convenient tyme allowed them to travell to any Porte Towne to take shiping with passes accordinglie.
4. Item that noe Oath shall bee imposed on any Officer or Soldyer that shall chuse to goe to the said Garrison dureing ye tyme of their March.
5. Item that a sufficient Convoy shall be appointed for such as will March away, and Carriages provided for their goods and not to bee forced to march above tenne myles a day and to have free quarter in their March, and care taken that noe abuse bee offered to their Persons or any of their owne proper goods diminished.
6. Item that all Prisoners in this Countie belonging to this Garrison shall bee released and likewise all Countrey Men and Sodyers in the Castle sett at Libertie.
7. Item that the Governor shall on Wednesday next 12 of the Clocke deliver upp the said Castle with all the Ordinance, Amunitions, Armes, Victualls, Provisions, Goods, Bedding and all other Accomodations necessary and belonging to the Castle (except what is allowed by the aforesaid Articles) and all those safe and unspoiled unto the said Sr. Wm. Brereton or whom hee shall appoint for the use of the Parliament.
8. Item that (the Parliament giving Order) the Workes, Walles and Towers of the said Castle shall bee sleighted and made incapable of a Garrison.

9. Item that all goods in the Castle that lawfullie Canne bee Claymed and owned by any of the Countrey shall bee Restored.

Item that all wounded Soldyers shall have libertie to Remayne in the Towne till they are cured and then have passes according to the Articles.

John Beaumont Peter Stepkin
C. Heveningham Robb. Hunt
John Giffard Hen: Stone

175

Letter from Col. Morgan touching meetinge

Hon'able Sr,

I have receaved yours of ye nynth of this instant and returne you humble thankes for your good newes of ye surrender of Newarke wch presentlie sent into Hartlebury Castle with a sumons unto wch I received a Civill Answere and am of great hope to reduce that place in a short tyme and doe greater wth ye Body of my Horse and foote at Amberslye, and doe intend this day to send a Partie unto Holt Castle for ye securinge of these Parts or the further side Worcester Severne from beinge spoiled by ye Enemy untill such tyme as addiconall forces can bee gotton for ye reducing of Worcester. Sr, if you please at your owne convenience to take ye paines to ryde to Amberslie or Hartleburgh I shall be glad to waite on you and three or foure of ye Committee at Evesham wilbe ready to attend you there or in anie other place where you will appointe if you please to give mee notice thereof wch is all at present, but that I am

Your humble Servt.
Tho. Morgan

Amberslie ye 10th of May
1646

For ye hon'ble Sr. Wm. Brereton at
Dudley or Litchfeilde

176

Sr. Wm. Breretons answere to
Colonell Morgan

Sr,

If it were soe wth mee that I had noe more worke and Imployment elsewhere I might ye rather and wth lesse manouvering have given meetinge at Amberslie or Hartlebury as you appointe but in regard of my severall Engagements & comand elsewhere I cannot be dispensed withal And therefore if yourself and some of ye Comittee of Evesham thinke fit to meete at Dudley upon Wednesday next by 12 of ye Clocke wee may consider about ye Carryinge on that worke agst Worcester wch noe man desires more to promote and advance according to ye Comande of ye Committee of both Kingdomes but

Your friend and
Servant
Wm. Brereton

Litchfeild May 11 1646

177

Letter from Generall Points to Sr. Wm. Brereton
of takeing Newarke

Sr,

Having this opportunity I should doe no lesse then salute you and offer you an Accompt of ye surrender of Newarke wch was yielded on ye 5th of May and entred by those under my Comand upon the 8th upon these condicons. They march out wth there swords only all Horses Armes & Amunicon were delivered up for ye use of ye Parliament, onely the Generall and the officers of Horse and foote and the noblemen, Clergie and Gentrie march out wth theire horses and Armes and all theire proper goods, and have libertie to live at theire own Howses submittinge to all Ordinances of Parliam't. Sr, I am,

Your Servant
Sydenham Points

March 9th May 1646.

For ye Hon'ble Sr. Wm. Brereton

An answere was sent to this lre to Generall Points by Richard Elcocke and in liewe thereof impartinge the newes of & including the Articles for Surrender of Dudley Castle to Sir Wm. Brereton according to ye before menconed Articles.

178

Sr. Wm. Breretons lre to Sr. Thomas Fairefax
touching taking Dudley

May it please your Excellencie,

I cannot but apprehend it a part of my duty to give your Excellencie an acc't. of our affaires and proceedings here. Our batteryes at Litchfield are formed and begun to play agst theire highe mister steeple that much annoyed us in o'r mounts and Campe. Dudley Castle wee have concluded upon and are to enter on Wednesday nexte whereby wee shalbe somewhat prepared (according to our former orders) to advance towards Worcester. Which is all for p'sent I have to informe your Excellency of for the better orderinge your owne affaires and Comandinge Sr,

Your most ffaithfull
friend and humble
Servant
Wm. Brereton

Litchfeild May 11th 1646

Letter to the Lords &
Comons at Newarke.

Another lre to this purpose was written to ye Lords and Comons Comissioners of ye Parlt. Of Englande, And alsoe desiring that ye forces they be pleased to promise to send in there lre to Sr. Wm. Brereton might be speeded up to goe agst. Worcester.

179

An order for the west part of Pirehill
Hundred touching Eccleshall Castle.

Whereas by an ordinance of Parliam't dated 1643, ye west parte of ye division of Pirehill hundred was assigned for ye maintanance of ye Garrison of Eccleshall Castle, And ye troopes of Horse of Capt. Stone and Captaine Pudsey which have bene hither unto Constantlie maintained out of the weekly pay of ye said division, And whereas nowe by ye mercie of God the Country is much freed from those Partes severall whereof are reduced & others blocked up, It is therefore ordered that there be noe more souldiers there contynued, Then wilbe necessarily sufficient to maintaine and defend ye said castle, for wch end it is conceaved that twelve or fifteen wilbe a number competent for ye keeping thereof. And that ye rest of ye foote souldiers therein be forthwith sent under ye Comand of Sergeant Cole to strengthen ye Leauger at Dudley there to observe such orders as they shall receive from ye Comander in Chiefe at that Leauger. And it is further ordered that there be noe further sumes of money imposed upon those partes by vertue of ye saide ordinance then shalbe sufficient to maintaine such competent number as aforesaid untill further danger, and that no greater charge be Contynued upon that part of ye said Hundred then is imposed upon the rest of ye County.

Wm. Brereton

Dated 6th May 1646.

180

The Maner of the Kings comeing to Newarke
To ye Scotch Armie represented by a lre of
Col. James Chadwickes.

The King came verie privately yester night wth three horsemen and a guide unto wyddowe Clarkes in Southwell into ye Roome where the ffrench Agent lay, about six of ye Clocke in the morneinge, and Thomas Rippon a Baker first discovered him as he Rydd in ye Streete. Then I rid post to our Lords and Comons and Carryed the first and strange Intelligence to them. I found them in ye Island neere Newarke Bridg. They gave mee Direccon to goe back wth speed and to endeavour to discover what I could, which I did, and by yt tyme ye Kinge had broken fast and a Troope of Horse came about twelve or one of ye Clocke. He tooke horse and ridd openly to Kellum where as yet hee is. I went post the second tyme to our lords and Comons to give them notice that his Majestie was come to ye Leauger, and in that Interim ye lords and Comons of Scotland had writt to our Lords & Comons to ye verie same purpose and desired a meeting to consult what was to be done, and they did meete and are met again this Morneinge and as it is Credibly reported here, there is a good Correspondence. As I went the second tyme to ye lords and Comons I went by the Tent where the Treaty was, and sent to desire Colonell Hutchinson to speake wth mee to whom I imparted the Newes to ye end he might makeinge best use of it, who I am Confident did soe. Hee then told mee they were come to a Conclusion of all things for ye surrender of Newarke save onelie some Puncttilliors off Honor Concerneing the Enimyes march wch were not fullie Concluded on wch he desired mee to signifie to ye lords & Comons wch I did. The newes this day is that albeit ye Kinge doth not well like ye Scotch Ministers Prayers, yet he hath written to ye Governor of Newarke to deliver up ye Towne to ye lords & Comons of both Kingdomes. The Kinge came as it is reported by a Color of a Passe made by the Speaker to Ashburneham for him and one Servant and a Guide to passe soe as the Kinge wth his haire Cutt and meanly horsed and Cloathed came as Ashburnehams Servant, these came by Byngham. This is all for ye present. 6th May 1646.

King Charles I fled to the Scottish army besieging Newark.

Since this written it is Credibly reported to mee by asure Reporter that the Lord Generall wth much Respect and Modesty tould his Majestie that he hoped his Majestie was not come hither wth anie purpose to divide them and the Parliament and thereupon tendred the Nationall League and Coven't. Whereupon his Majesty startled, and ye Generall upon some other discourse told his Majestie that if Newarke did not yeilde presentlie he should see ye Towne fired about his Eares, or to that effect.

James Chadwicke

182

Articles for ye Surrender of Banbury.

Articles agreed upon ye 6th day of May 1646 by Captaine Grancote, Captaine Baylie deputed on ye behalfe of Sr. Wm. Compton Gov'nor of ye Castle of Banbury and Colonell Whetham, Colonell Bridges, Lt. Col. Matthewes & Lt. Colonell Castle, Comissioners appointed by Colonell Whaley, Comander in cheife of ye forces imployed for ye Reduceing of ye same Castle touching surrendering thereof.

1. Imprimis that ye said Governor and Sr. Spencer Compton and the Major wth everie of them one servant & theire Armes wth six of theire owne horses, shall have libertie to march away to what places they thinke fitt. The Captaines, each of them his owne horse and sword. The rest of the officers wth theire swords, and private souldiers without Armes in like sort to march away to such places as theire passes shall direct.
2. That all officers and souldiers of ye said Garrison shall have liberty to march away wth theire wearing apparell and halfe theire moneye soe as they give a true and just Accompt thereof.
3. That Sr. Wm. Compton wth all the officers and souldiers shall have pases to goe to any place wthin ye Kingdome and Principallity of Wales not beleaguered (the Cittie of London excepted) and the said Colonel Whaley shall endeavour to procure passes to all such persons of ye said Garrison to goe beyond ye seas as shall desire ye same.
4. That all officers and souldiers of ye said Garrison shall have free quarter in theire march to ye severall places appointed by theire passes soe as they remaine not above one night in a place.
5. That all officers and souldiers of ye said Garrison may freelie passe to the places appointed without anie oath imposed upon them by ye said Colonell or anie other.
6. Item that the said Colonell Whaley upon the surrender of ye said Castle shall take such care for ye restitution of such goods belonging to ye Country now in ye said Castle as to ye said Colonell Whaley shall seem just and equall.

Itm that the said Governor nor any officer nor souldier of ye said Garrison shalbe molested for anie debts or Actes done by anie of them untill the tyme limited in theire passes shalbe expired.

That all officers and souldiers in ye said Garrison being sicke or wounded together wth Mr. Woodall, Chyrugeon to ye sayd Castle and his Mate shall have accomodation in ye Towne of Banbury or neere thereunto while they be recovered and afterwards shall have passes granted as others of these Articles and the Chirugeon to departe wth each of them one case of Instruments unmolested.

Item that Carriages be provided by ye direction of ye said Colonell Whaley for ye conveying such things as are to be carried away by vertue of these Articles to such places as the said Sr. Wm. Compton shall thinke fitt, the same being not distant ten miles from Banbury.

Upon which consideracon the said Sr. Wm. Compton doth engage his Honor to surrender ye Castle of Banbury in the condition it now stands with Canons, Colors, Armes, Amunicon and all things (not contained in ye Articles) without any Embezelm't whatsoever to ye said Colonell Whaley for ye use of ye Parliam't on Friday morneinge next beinge the eigth day of this instant May, at 9 of the Clocke att which tyme the said Armes are to be delivered to such Persons as Colonell Whaley shall appointe, in the halfe noone before the Castle gate and Hostages to be sent out for ye performance thereof.

Finis

185

Sr. W. Breretons 2nd Sumons of Litchfield
Close beleaguered by him.

Gentlemen,

Your rejecting my first Sumons at such tyme as you could not but see Gods hand everywhere agst you might have deprived you of further senders of mercy. But such is ye Clemency of ye Parliament, whose servant I am, that to prevent ye further effusion of blood and ye Ruyne of your selves and all those Gentlemen and others wth you I have sent you this second & last sumons And hereby demand and Require you to surrender ye garrison and Close of Litchfield with all ordnances, Armes, Amunicon, Provisions of Warre and all other goods whatsoever into my hands for ye use of ye Kinge and Parliament.

What I informed you in my last sumons Concerninge Sir Ralph Hopton[34] and his Armies submission to Sir Thomas ffairefax, the defeat of Sir Jacob Astley and ye deliverence of Exeter I canne now doubt but you beleeve.

This as true that since that tyme ye Garrisons of Barstable, Dunster, Woodstocke, Ruthin, Bridgnorth, Aberistwith, Tutbury, Banbury, Newarke and others are delivered, and Dudley Castle agreed to be yelded up tomorrow.

And Oxford wth ye Rest either Streightly Beleaguered or blockt up, and His Majesty in Person come to our Army.

You Cannot therefore but apprehend yourselves in a desperate condicon and that there is a vast difference betweene ye Condicons you might have Expected when I first Summoned you and those I can now grante soe ye longer you persist in your Obstinacy adding to ye Expence of Tyme Treasure & Blood ye greater wilbe ye Accompt and Inegm't upon your selves and those wth you.

I give you untill tomorrow at foure of ye Clocke in ye afternoone to advise, at wch tyme I expect your finall Answere

Remaininge,

Your Servt.
Wm. Brereton

From our Campe on Bacon Hill
May 12th 1646

To Sr. Tho. Tildesley and Col. Bagott in Litchfeild Close, these.

187

The fall of ye High Steeple
in Litchfield Close

May 12th 1646.

[**See page 250**]

188

Letter for a day of Thanksgiving in Staffordshire

Sir,

The longe delay of publique thankesgiveing for ye mercyes of ye Lord in freeing part of this Countie from ye Pressures of Tutburie would have some Compensacon now in speeding ye same duty for his increasing mercies in freeing this other part from ye annoyance of Dudley. I shall therefore desire your concurrent assistance herein that in both our names you would be pleased to send throughout or to such Places of ye Countie as you see fittest to enjoine the setting apart of some day next weeke, Tuesday or Wednesday as you shall appoint for publique thanksgiving to God for his great Mercies towards us (and the whole County)in Reduceing the said Garrisons. A worke I know that you wilbe forward in your selves and to see and cause affected as

Your assured loveing
Friend & servt.
W. Brereton

Dudley Castle
May 13 1646

For the hono'ble and verie worthy
Friend, Edw. Mainwaring Esquire
high Sheriff of Staffordshire.

189

Order Concerneing Eccleshall Castle and for
the ease of the Country

Whereas by an Ordynance of Parliament dated 1643, the Weste Parte of the division of Pyrehill Hundred was assigned for the mainetenance of the Garrison of Eccleshall Castle (and myself made accompteable for the same by the said Ordinance) which hath been hitherto accordinglie disposed of for the Constant maintenance of that Forte belonging to the said Castle. As alsoe the Troopers of Horse of Captaine Stone and Captaine Putsey have been Constantlie paid and maintained out of the same Allotment.

And whereas nowe by the mercie of God the Countrey is much freed from those Enemyes Garrisons which did annoy & disturb those partes, the most whereof being Reduced and others blockt up. It is therefore Ordered that there bee noe more Soldyers Continued at the said Castle of Eccleshall then will bee necessary for the defence thereof; And that the rest of the Foote Soldyers bee forthwith sent unto mee to bee disposed off as may bee most usefull for the Service of Parliament. And that there bee noe further sumes of Money imposed upon the said division by vertue of the said Ordinance then shall bee sufficient to maintaine such a Competant number as aforesaid untill further danger or further Order, And that noe greater then is imposed upon the rest of the said Countie of Stafford. Dated at Dudley Castle May 13th 1646.

Wm. Brereton

Letter from the Committee of Sallop to Sr.
Wm. Brereton for money for his souldiers

Ho'ble Sr,

Wee acknowledge our thankefull engagements for the Continuance of your favour in imparting unto us the late Occurrences at Newarke. Wee hope the Surrender of that place and his Ma'ties Returne will much facilitate what Remaynes to bee dunne of the worke wherein wee have all soe longe laboured; Wee doubt not but in fewe dayes wee shall bee able to give a good Account of Ludlowe. This day wee expect the Enemyes Answere to our last Sumons (Sr. Wm. Blackstone and Lt. Col. Godfrey being now returned from Oxford)

And wee imagine what wee shall Receive from them will bee to purpose, unlesse some Colde and faintly hopes (wherewith they are possessed) of the Kings being gone into Scotland begett in them an inclination to some further fruitless delayes.

Wee heare our Soldyers (in service with you) are much discontented for want of pay, you knowe it hath not formerly been the Course with us, to put you to pay your Soldyers whilst they have been in the publique Service in this Countie, and wee hoped the burdon and Chardge of accomodation for those of ours with you, should most properlie have been borne by those places which Receive the present fruite and benefitt of their Service, nevertheless wee should have done our Endeavours were our Countrey in a Condicon to answere our desires, but it is growne generally soe poore and indigent that wee see at present noe possibilitie of raising meanes here for that purpose; wee therefore humbly desire you will please to take them into your thoughts for their present supplies, whereby they may with more alacritie persist in doeing you service to which end, that they may prove effectuall Instruments are the heartie wishes of

Your most humble Servants
Robert Clive
And: Lloyd
Robt. Charlton

Salloppe 12th May 1646.

Wee have at this instant received intimation from our Soldyers in your service that they have not yt accommodator as others though put to more hard duetie; Wee desire you please to take their Condicon into your Consideracon.

190

Letter from Sr. Wm. Brereton to Mr. Ashurst &
Mr. Swinfen touching the surrender of Dudley Castle.

Sr,

This day the strong Castle of Dudley was delivered unto mee whereunto Wee entered aboute One of the Clocke. The Condicons for the surrender whereof were sent unto you by the last, which I shall not now repeat but shall give you this further Accompt touching this place; That it is one of the strongest Houldes both by situation and Fortification that wee have seene in this kingdome, Not to bee approached, nor I believe undermined nor scaled, nor battered & noe advantage was omitted for the further strengthening thereof. They left us neere twelve Monethes provision of Victualls, twenty Barrels of powder and neere 400 Armes.

There marched out of the Castle neere 300 Foote of the Common Soldyers, besides Horse, and neare 40 Reformade Officers Marched out with their Horses and Armes; They were well furnished wth Beere and plentifullie with Water, soe as if that God (which by the sounding of Rammes Hornes and seaven tymes Campassinge the Walles of Jericho braught downe those strong Walles) had not alsoe taken away their Courage and divided them amongst themselves, this might have been a tedious and expensive worke and one of the last Reduced Garrisons in the kingdome, I desire the whole honor and glory may bee ascribed to God with whom it is as easie to deliver upp the strongest as the weakest Houls. Untill such tymes as Litchfeild and Worcester bee Reduced without doubt this Castle may bee serviceable to bee Continued a Garrison. To which end Captaine Toothily (whoe was Governor of Rushall) is for present placed therein, with his foote company and Troope of Horse; And truly I doe much feare (if the Walles should bee sleighted and this castle demolished which is in exceeding good Order and Repaire) that (if there should bee a powerfull Enemy in the Field) there might bee such Workes and Fortifications made in the topp of the Hill where the Castle now Stands, which might as much annoy and oppresse the Countrey as formerlie; Therefore I should not dare to advise the dismantling & demolishing thereof, though it will bee some Chardge to the Countrey to Maintaine the same, and indeed Worcestershire must either Contribute to the Chardge or it will bee insupportable for Staffordshire alone to beare that burden, seeing the Castle stands in Staffordshire but the Towne in Worcestershire which may bee equally advantaged and secured thereby.

Therefore it is most necessarie that there bee some fitt establishment extending into all the severall Counties within six miles all which may bee equallie secured & Advantaged by the protection and benefit of this Garrison, which may bee maintained in the meane tyme with a smaller Chardge & a farre lesse number; touching which I have soe much enlarged myself, as that I shall not think fitt to add any more then the faithfull Respects of,

Your assured Friend & Servant,
Wm. Brereton

Dudley Castle May 13th 1646.

This day Col. Morgan and the Governor of Evesham & some of the Worcestershire Committee were with mee in the Castle to consider and advise about the carrying on the Worke against Worcester, whereunto I hope to bee able to contribute in some good Proportion (if there bee a Performaunce of that assistance which is promised). Notwithstanding they should Remayne Obstinate in the Close; But if that should bee Reduced (whereof I doe not despaire) there would bee a verie considerable Force applied hence; Concerning which you may expect a further Account by the next.

192

Articles for the Surrender of Newarke

Articles agreed and concluded the 6th May 1646 betweene the Comiss'ers hereunto Named, Authorisede by the Committee of Parliament of both Kingdomes of England and Scotland on their parte, And the Comiss'ers hereunto written, Authorised by the Governors of Newarke, Lt. Gener'll to his Ma'tie of the Countreys of Nottingham, Lincolne and Rutland and Governors of the Towne and Castle of Newarke of the other parte touching the yielding and surrendering of that Garrison and the Castle, Forts and Sconces thereunto belonging to the Comittee of both Kingdomes for the use of the Parliament of England.

That the Towne and Garrison of Newarke with the Castle Forts Sconces, Ordinances, Morterpeeces, Armes, Amunition, Provisions and necessayes of Warre not hereafter excepted, bee surrendered on Saturday next at 10 of the Clocke into the hands of the Comittee of both kingdomes to whom they shall appoint for the use of the Parliament of England.

1. That the Governor of the said Garrison shall March away wth his Servants, Horses, Armes and proper goods to any Garrison hee shall name not besieged nor blocked upp, or to his owne Howse, there to Remayne unmolested, submitting to all Ordinances of Parliament; And alsoe that the said Governor shall have libertie upon desire any tyme within three Monethes to passe beyond Seas, and to have passes for himself & Serv'ts accordinglie.
2. That all officers in Comission or that have been formerly in Comand shall March away with their Horses, Armes and proper goods, the Comon Soldyers of Horse and Foote with their Money, Cloathes and Swords to any Garrison not besieged or blocked upp or to theire owne Howses as they shall make Choyse of, and those that have no money, to have free quarter in their march, and not to march above 10 Myles in one day unlesse they please, and to have Convoy and Carriage provided for carrying away their Goods (Hostages being given for the Returne of the Convoy and Carraiges) and such goods as cannot be Removed, the owners shall have libertie to dispose of them.
3. That all such Officers and Gentlemen nowe in the Garrison whoe shall desire to departe out of this kingdome, shall upon signifieing thereof to the Comittees of both Kingdomes any tyme in three Monethes, have passes to that purpose for themselves and Servants, ingageing themselves dureing their stay, to doe noe disservice to the Parliament.
4. That all such Officers and Soldyers as by Reason of sicknesse or otherwise are not able to March out at the same tyme appointed shall have libertie to stay in the Towne, or some other Convenient place till they bee recovered,

and such as are not able to provide Maintenance for themselves, shall have Care taken for them.

5. That all Noblemen and Gentlemen in the said Garrison shall have libertie to March forth of the Towne with their Horses and Armes, and their knowne Meniall Servants with their Horses and Swords to their owne Howses, there to Remayne without Molestation submitting to all Ordinances of Parliament, and to have libertie to Carrie away their owne proper goods then or ant tyme within 3 Monethes and to have passes for themselves & servants to goe beyond seas upon desire 3 monethes, and in the meane tyme to ingage themselves to doe nothing to the disservice of the Parliament.
6. That all Clergie Men in the Garrison that have libertie with their Horses, Servants and their owne proper goods to March to any Garrison not blocked upp, or not besieged, or to their Howses, there to Remayne unmolested, submitting to all Ordinances of Parliament.
7. That the Mayor, Aldermen and Inhabitants of the said Garrison shall notbee molested in their Persons, Priviledges, goods or Estates, submitting to all Ordinances of Parliament & enjoy the same libertie, and to have the same protection as all other Townes have which are in the power of the Parliament.
8. That the Ladyes, Gentlewomen, Wives, Widdowes, Children and Servants belonging to any of the persons mentioned in the former Articles, or any other shall have libertie to March forth of the said Garrison with their Coaches, Horses and proper goods as in the 6 Articles, And if any of them by Reason of sicknesse or any other just Reason Cannot March forth, then they shall have libertie to stay there till Recoverie, and then to departe unmolested.
9. That all Prisoners now in the said Garrison, Castle or Forts, or any other Prisoner of Warre taken by either Partie since the seige beganne forthwith upon signeing these Articles bee sett at libertie unless they bee detrayned for Criminall Offences not as Soldyers.
10. That all Persons comprised within these Articles grounded upon the Summons of the 27th of Aprill which begott the Treatie, bee Recomended to Compound with the Parliament for their Estates as coming inn before the 1st of May, soe as they doe effectually prosecute such Compositions within twoe Monethes next ensueing the date hereof.
11. If any Persons above Menconed shall vyolate the said Articles or any parte of them, they shall loose the benefit of the said Articles.

That for the performance of the said Articles, Hostages bee mutually given, and that a Cessation of Armes bee Continued by both sydes till the tyme of surrender according to the said Articles. And that Guards and Convoyes bee appointed to protect the Gentlemen and Soldyers in their March from violence.

Signed by us the Comm'ders	Signed by & Authorised by
for the Lord Bellasis	the Committee of both kingdomes

195

Letter to Captaine Swinfen Relating the Kings coming to the Scotch Army from Oxford May 1646.

Cousen Swinfen,

For your satisfaccon concerning the deliverence of Newarke, of the Articles I have sent a Coppie unto you, which may spare my further Relation touching that particular.

For the kinges coming hither, you may believe (as wee are therein satisfied) that hee came the last Lords day in the night about 2 of the Clocke the next morning out of Oxford, none being privy thereunto but Sr. Thomas Glenham the Governour; hee came only out with Mr. Ashburnham and his Man, by the passe of the Speaker of the Howse of Comons, which Mr. Ashburnham had been (it seems) long labouring for, for himself, his servant and a guide; When his Ma'tie came to Uxbridge, in his way to London, hee tooke his opportunitie to turne his Horse out of the way towards London, towards St. Albans; Mr. Ashburnham askt him his meaning and told him hee went out of the way; His Ma'tie answered, Well goe you whither you will, but for my part I am resolved to Cast my selfe upon the Scotts Army and thither will I make speede as fast as I canne; Hee came to Stamford in the Monday night, and rested at the George about 4 howres, from thence hee came to Southwell (the headquarters of his Exellencie the Earle of Leven, Lord Generall of the Scotts Army) on Tuesday Morning presently after six of the Clocke, into an Inne, and into a lowe Parlour where was quartered a young Gentleman whoe was a French Agent to the Lords and Comons of Scotland, Resident here; This Agent had sent out a servant of his to bee a guide to the place where his Ma'tie should light, hee came in halfe an hower before the King, with his Horse all bloudy with spurring, and extremely reeking and presently tooke a fresh Horse and Rode backe, when shortly after hee returned accompanied with three more; The King comeing into the Frenchmans Roome (under my Quarter) some of the Townesmen well knew his Ma'ties person, and one being very Confident it was hee, Came to my Landlady and tould her hee would lay his life that it was hee, she came hastily to my howse Chamber and tould mee the king was in the Howse, whereupon presently I sent for Col. Chadwick (my associate here) and acquainted him with it, and intreated him (myself being very ill) to post over the Trent to the English Leauger and to Relate what wee had heard (and found probable) to the Lords and Commons of the Parliament of England there Resideing with the Army which desired by them to bee further confirmed to them with all expedition; His Ma'tie after his coming Rested some 3 or 4 howers upon a Bedd, then Dinner was called for an hower after; One of the L'ds of the Comittee of Scotland tould mee they had sent post over to our L'ds and Comons that the king was here; By that the king had dined, there was a regiment of Horse drawne out into Southwell Streete, about one of the Clocke on Tuesday his Ma'tie came into the Inne yarde, tooke Horse and with divers Lords rode in the Front of the Regim't downe to Kelham a Mile from Newarke to the Leiut. Gener'lls Quarters, which was surrendered to him being nere the Scotts Leauger but on the north side Trent; Their Army lying in an Iland betweene the mayne River & the towne of Newarke, there Ma'tie Rested. Tuesday and Wednesday; Upon Thursday the Articles for the Rendition of Newarke being perfected the Towne was free for any to enter, all the Posts being opened about twoe of the Clock in the afternoone. The Scotts Army having notice of some scandalous speeches raised of them by the Malignant partie in the Countrey, that though Newarke were taken yett they would not bee gott out of the Countrey, but meant to possesse it at their pleasure and would prove as Jerusalem Hartichocks in a Garden as alsoe to preserve their Army from the infeccon of such as should come forth of Newarke the same hower the Ports were opened, had Orders from the Lord Generall (as strict it could bee) to March in that very hower; In halfe an hower they were in an Orderlie March, and were gone about 4 or 5 Myles before it was known to our Army on the South side Trent, that they were Risen; All the Horse (except a Reare Guard) marched before, the King, the Generall and the Lords; after them the Foote, then the Reareguard of Horse; The King verie Cheerfull in his March; Soe that many feares in the countrey are very well appeased and satisfied. The Countrey cleared and Yesterday at Noone, not a Scott left in the Countrey, As we heare, they intend to march with out Stoppe to Newcastle, and there to stay till they heare from the Parliam't and then to proceed according to agreement betwixt the Parliament and them; Thus Cousen have I punctuallie Related all passages, which I could observe or heare; The Relation of the kings turning at Uxbridge this way, was from his owne Mouth at supper, Thus I having noe more, I only subscribe myself,

Your kinsman and
Friend to serve you
Thos. Salusbury

Southwell
10th May 1646

197

From the Deputie Lts. & Comittee at Chester to
Sr. Wm. Brereton touch: the leauger at Hoult.

Honorable Sr,

Wee this day received your letter touching the sending of Adjutant Louthians Company at Hoult for the strengthening of that Leauger and preservation of Broxton Hundred, And before the Receipt of it wee had thoughts to have done it, but the Guards of this Cittie are soe many and the Companye left here soe few that they have been put upon every third Nights duty, and none Could be spared hence, and therefore by the advice and with the Consent of all or most of the Gentlemen of qualitie in that Hundred, wee have provided pay for Captaine Breretons Company, whoe (being something full) have undertaken to keepe the Bridge and Farndon Church where they now are, and are about to build a Mount in the face of the Castle on Cheshire side, and with the helpe of some Horse doubt not but to keep Broxton hundred safe, which is to the good Content of the Neighbourhood there and as there shall bee occacon all assistance wee are able shall God willing bee given to that Leauger, and to the preservation of that Hundred as you desire.

Some Horse are of late taken out of Denbigh Castle and are joyned with the Forces of Flint Castle soe that the Horse there are said to bee 140 or more, which have done some haste of late and doe put the country into some feares. It is much desired that wee would afford the assistance of some Forces for the blocking upp of that Castle which wee are very willing and desirous to doe soe farre as wee Canne possiblie but doubt wee cannot spare any Foote to send thither but shall send some Horse.

It much troubles us that wee Cannot send provisions to the Leauger at Litchfield, nor make such present pay as wee desire to the Staffordshire Soldyers for their service at Chester, though wee use our utmost endeavours, Yett moneys come in slowly, fewe coming to buy goods of late, and the six Asizes (for which you and the Deputie Lts. gave order before you went hence) being Refused or Neglected to bee paid in many parts of the Countie especially at Namptwch and in those partes; Wee therefore desire you to move the Staffordshire Gentlemen and Comaunders that they will yett a while longer forbeare their & their Soldyers moneyes wch shall bee hastned to bee made ready for them with all speede possible, Wee have already borrowed greate somes of money that remayne yett unpaid, and alsoe most of the Moneys of the ingagement due to Col. Mittons Forces as well as to the Staffordshire remayne unpaid, and alsoe some other Moneyes to others which are continually called for and wee much perplexed about them, And wee desire your advice and Discern how to raise Moneyes for this discharge thereof and to continue some way or meanes for that purpose. Wee are glad to heare the good newes of the delivery upp of Dudley Castle soe soon, Wee add noe more but that wee are

Your faithfull Friends and Servants

	Hen: Brooke vic:
Will: Massie	Tho: Stanley
Robt: Gregge	John Legh
James Gartsyde	Henry Birkened
Rich: Leicester	Will: Davies

You writt to some of us touching Sr. Hugh Calveleyes Chaplaine, none comes to us with any information against him, wee desire you will certifie us of whome to enquire.

Chester May 16: 1646.

199

A Noate of Cattell Laid into Weston Demesne at tenne shillings a Beast For the whole Ley. May 1st 1646.

Laid in 4 Yeare oulds for John Smith of Bruewood at 1s. a weeke 20s. The lay
1 Cowe for Robt. Scott of Aston
1 Yeare Ould for the same Man
4 Yeare Oulds for Wm. Tayler of Brockhurst
3 Yeare Oulds for Thomas Cotton of Weston
2 Weanings for Wm. Locke of Weston
6 Yeare Oulds for Wm. James of Brewewood
16 Yeare Oulds for Tho: Ley of Brewewood
2 Oxen for Rich: Paddie of Byterton 1s. a weeke
3 Yeare Oulds for Roger Jones of Billington
2 Cowes for John Humpatch of Billington
9 Twinters for the same Man
11 Yeare Oulds for the same Man
4 Weaneings for the same
2 Twinter Coults for the same
3 Yeare Oulds for John Riley of Billington
4 Yeare Oulds for Francis Burne of Billington
4 Twinter Heiffers for Mrs Talbot of Stafford
2 Yeare Oulds for Henry Cartwright of Byterton
1 Weaneing for the same Man
4 Yeare Oulds for Humphrey Vall of Copnall
2 Twinters for the same man
4 Yeare Oulds for Roger Bromley of Copnall
2 Twinter Bullockes for John Paddie of Byterton
2 Yeare Oulds for Smith of Season
1 Twinter Heifer for the same man
May 4th 3 Twinters for Wm. Hand of Whiston Crosse
2 Yeare Oulds for the same man
3 Weaneings for the same man
4 Yeare Oulds for Roger Fox of Stableford

3 Weanings for the same
1 Yeare Ould Coult for the same
4 Weaneings for Benjamin Gibbines of Stableford
2 Yeare Ould Coults for the same Man
2 Twinter Heifers for John Fennihouse of Longner
2 Yeare Ouldes for the same man
2 Weaneings for the same Man
4 Twinter Heifers for Ward of Mitton
2 Steers for Wm. Nightingale of Shackerley
1 Cowe for Roger Tranter of Horesbrooke at 6d. a weeke
5 Yeare Oulds for Harris of Norton
2 Yeare Oulds for Robt. Bird of Tongue
3 Yeare Oulds for Wm. Blackmore of Blimhill
2 Yeare Oulds for Marie Elesley of Weston
2 Cowes foe Ed. Sawyer of Weston
2 Yeare Oulds for Brumfeild of Shackerley
2 Yeare Oulds for Walter Haughton
2 Weaneings for the same Man
3 Twinter Heifers for Wm. Shutt of Brinton
1 Weaneing for Locke Ley
May 7th 2 Yeare oulds for Humphrey Vall of Copnall
2 Weaneings for the same
May 8th 1 Bullocke for John James of Littleton
1 Twinter for Edward Blackmore of Littleton
1 Yeare ould for Ed: Parkes of Aston
1 Yeare ould Coult for Wm. Lettel of Aston
3 Twinters for Wm. Adams of Walleston
2 Yeare Oulds for the same Man
3 Twinters for Rich: Allsopp of Wallaston 1s. a weeke
2 Yeare Ouldes for Wm. Leeke of Wollaston
2 Bullockes for Henry Bab of Weston at 1s. a weeke

A Noate of Beast layd into the Cowe Hey

3 Cowes for Harris of Norton at 1s. 6d. a weeke
2 Cowes for Robert Numan at 1s. a weeke
4 Yeare Ouldes for Jefferie Sanbrooke 1s. a weeke
1 Cowe for Widdowe Tunkes at 6d. a weeke
May 14th 4 Oxen for Fowler of Brockton at 2s. a weeke
1646 4 Oxen for the Millner of Lidiat Mille 2s. a weeke

The Whole number of Beast in the Park

Whole Beast 14
Twoe yeares Ould 37
Weaneings 24
Coults 06
Whole Beast in ye Cowe hey 16

201

From the Comittee for the kings Revenue
Concerning the Race at Tutbury

Sr. Wm. Brereton,

These are to desire you to take into your Care the oversight and ordering of his Ma:ties Race at Tutburie; In Regard Sr. John Fenwicke at this tyme is soe farre remoate who as (wee are informed) hath a Legall right to the Custodie of the Race: and that you will send unto us a Noate of what Horses and Mares are now Remaining there: And soe we Rest

Your very loveing Friends
Northumberland
H. Vane Hen: Mildmay
Denis Bond
W. Ashurst

Dated at the Comittee
of L'ds & Comons for his Ma'ts
Revenue sitting at Westminster
the 5th day of May 1646

201

Letter from Sr. Tho: Fairefax to Sr. Wm.
Brereton May 10th 1646 giving thanks
for ye newes of surrender of Newarke

Sr,

I Received yours from Warwicke Certifieing the newes of the Articles being agreed to for surrender of Newarke. I returne you many thankes for your tymely advertisement thereof; The Governor of Leicester about the same tyme Confirmed yours; I Canne add but little from hence in Returne; In a shorte tyme I hope wee shall bee securely Intrenched before Oxford and March with a good Force to assist in the Reducement of other partes of the kingdom; The Forces that were before Banbery are Ordered to March to assist in the Reduceing of Worcester. I am Sr.,

Your most humble Servt:
Tho: Fairefax

May Xth 1646
Heddington

Letter from Sr. Thos. Fairefax 13 May
Touching Worcester

Sr,

I Received your Letter of the 11th Instant, and blesse God for your good successe before Dudley; I wish you the like at Litchfeild, that you may bee at libertie with your full strength to attend Worcester, that Col. Morgan may be imployed in Walles for the Reduceing of Ragland about which I am much solicited. Having sent a Summons the other day to Oxford they Returned a Modest Answere with a Request for two to come forth and speake with mee (which being graunted) their Message was to have leave to send to the kinge wch being denyed they Returned yesterday and are this day Come again to the Headquarters with a possitive Answere Concerning the Summons, Having noe more to trouble you with at present, I Rest

Your humble Servant
Tho: Fairefax

Heddington
May 13th 1646

202

Letter from Sr. Wm. Brereton to Sr. Tho: Fairefax
15th of May touching the Answere sent to his
Second summons out of Litchfeild Close

May it please your Excellence,

Since my last to your Excelence I have Received an Answere to my second Sumons to Litchfeild Close wherein they discover soe much obstinacies which makes mee more doubtfull that the whole Forces there Cannot bee employed soe speedily as were to bee desired against Worcester: Some say they were in a high mutiny the last night in the Close but I Cannot give the Certaintie thereof but doe Confidently believe the Comon Soldyers have been kept in Subjection by meere falsities and untruthes. It shall bee my endeavour to undeceive and Rectifie them. In pursuance of former Comaunds from the Comitee of both kingdoms to endeavour the Reduceing of Worcester, I have intended the Forces that were imployed against Dudley, and those that are to bee sent unto mee by Order of the Lords and Commons at Newarke upon Reduceing that place, and alsoe that canne bee spared hence should bee imployed against Worcester for the Expediteing whereof noe endeavour of myne shall bee wanting, But till Litchfield bee Reduced I cannot believe there can bee sufficient strength applied to Carrie on that worke if Col. Morgan bee otherwise disposed off, Howsoever what may bee your comaunds shall bee obeyed by

Your most humble Servant
Wm. Brereton

Litchfeild
15th May 1646

203

The Cheshire Comaunders at Litchfeild touching
want of Moneyes for their Soldyers there

Honorable Sr,

Were wee not absolutely inforced by the necessitie of our Soldyers, wee should very unwillinglie have given you these ensueing expression of our Condicon, and were wee not assured that your Honor is fullie acquainted how long wee have been ingaged under your Comaund, and what Continued subsistence our selves and soldyers have Received this paper had been too little to sett downe, and your honors Affaires too waightie to looke over.

Wee have been imployed in this Leauger of Litchfeild Close & the tyme of our Respective engagements as alsoe our duty and extraordinary working is fullie knowne to your honor. Wee have not allotments as divers here, soe wee cannot in the least particular furnish our Men with present necessaryes. Our Comaunds are uncomfortable and performed with a great deale of trouble, and wee Reallie acquaint your honor that some of our Men have deserted our Colours, the rest in a Mutenous Condition because their Cloathes are worne and they have noe assurance of subsistence to furnish themselves for the future. Wee desire your honor to take what wee speake into your thoughts, and supplie our Companies with Moneyes very speedily, least our utmost endeavours prove ineffectuall for the keeping our Soldyers diligent and observant to yor Comaunds in this service. Wee leave it to your honors discretion Remayning

Your honors humble Servants

From Bacon Hill Campe

Wm. Daniell — John Rathbone
Edward Glegg — Thomas Walley
Godfr: Gimbart — John Leadbeater
Symon Finch — Hugh Bertles

204

Letter from Generall Poynts to Sr. Wm. B.
May 14th 1646 conc. the Scotts marching
Away with his Ma:tie towards Newcastle

Noble Sir,

I Received yours and Returne you this as well to Congratulate your good successe, as to yeild you the best Accompt I can of what you desire; The Scotts are Marched with his Ma:tie to Newcastle, where its thought they were last night; The Scottish Com:s and ours were on Tuesday last to meete at Bawtrey where ours Came, but the other only sent them a letter to excuse their neglect, And their Reason, because they were informed Leiftenn:t Generall Cromwell and my selfe were advancing in the Reare of them, upon what grounds this suggestion was framed I cannot tell, but onely that I am now Marching towards Yorke; Wee hope the best, God graunt there may bee noe other Cause.

Sir I am deeplie engaged by your Civilities, and ambitious of nothing more then to meete in oppertunitie to expresse myself,

Your most ready Friend
and Servant
Sednham Poynts

Wentbridge
XVIII May 1646

Richard Broke was sent backe to Colonell G:rall
May 18th wth thankes and desiring further to partake
of affaires touching ye king and ye Scotch Army
and of ye state of Enimye in Scotland

205

Letter from Mr. Wm. Brereton of Cogshill touching
his claime to Lands in Blymhill & Brainton belonging
to Mr. Egerton and passed over by him to Sr. Wm. Brereton

Cogshill 28th Aprile 1646

Sr,

I doubt not but you have heard how it pleased Sr. Randle Brereton to passe his estate over unto his brother Richard and his Heires males and for wante of suche issue did his brother Sir Thomas Brereton and his heires males and for wante of such issue unto mee and my heires males. By force of wch same leeas Mr. Richard Brereton and after him Sir Thomas Brereton enjoyed for theire severall lives, And both of them Dieinge without issue male, the estate is now fallen unto mee. ffor parte of ye Lande I founed as ye sale, and those I questioned not, but for Staffordshire lands I founed in anie thinge, but intend, God willing to prosecute my owne Right. I latelie sent over to informe myselfe howe and by whom ye said lands are helde and I finde some Tenements lyinge in Blymhill & Braineton to be in your poss'ion by some Estate past from Mr. Egerton. My desire is rather to serve you then Contend wth you whom I soe much honor which causeth mee to acquaint you wth this business beinge Confident yt your wisdome and justnes is such and ye Cause soe manifest that you will not endeavour any opposicon. I humbly crave your Answere by this bearer. And it shall be my desire ever to manifest myselfe your servant and to pray for your health and happienes whilest I am

Wm. Brereton

206

Mr. Higinbothoms lre to Sr. Wm. Brereton
Touching the Earle of Darbies Composicon
For the Office of Forrester of Macclesfield and etc.

Sr,

I found in one box wch I looked into since the Records of Macclesfeild Courte were put into my hands, a copie of an order of ye Comissioners for defective titles, 20th February 1639 for ye Earle of Darby, his composicon for ye office of fforester of ye fforest of Macclesfeild and ye Stewardship, and of ye lands, Ground meadowes and Pastures of Saltersford Harrop, Codiliffe, Wilbourough, Muggilry and Shuttlington and the severall pastures in ye fforest held under 5l. p.a. and by Grants from Hen 6 & Edw 4th

It might be worth searching above to see what proceedings were upon this order. I never understood howe it was helde before and if the Composicon were not perfected to fall in wth ye Comittee of ye Revenue and if perfected, to farme it and keepe it in possession as intended parte of your 1500 pound Conferred by Ordinance

Your honours obedient
Servante
W. Higginbotham

29th Ap. 1646

207

Sir Wm. Brereton 3 or 4 lre to Sir W. Waller
One concerneing Ridly & Shocklaiy to send one
Downe to improve the lands

Hon'ble Sr,

I have sent three or foure at least former lres to let you knowe it would not be anie default assuringe if ye Estate of Shocklish Ridly this yeare be not improved as were to be desired for ye advantage of those therein Concerned there is one John Egerton a younger brother of Mr. Richard Egerton who having an Anuity or Rent Charge of 90 pound upon ye lande. I hath by reason of some default come in a tumultuous manner wth some twenty souldiers and viewed ye ground (since my coming out of Cheshire) to ye great discourag'mt not onely of ye Ten'ts but others to have any thinge to doe wth or lay out anie moneies upon the yeare (albeit I offered him that he should take his choice of grounds to yt value or if ye lands were let without interupcon and disturbance that he should receive his Anuity out of ye first monies) That wch therefore I shall propound as ye fullest and onely expedient is that your servant might be sent downe again and that if you thinke fitt a processe might be sued forth agst Mr. Egerton to ye value of 1000 ls. Whereby I hope ye like courses may be prevented for ye future.

All wch I referre to your Consideracon and remaine

Sr. your most faithfull & affectionate friend
& Servt.
Wm. Brereton

May 18 1646

208

A pass Granted to Sir Henry Skipw'th wch was written under a copie of ye Articles for surrender of Dudley Castle

These are to require all whom it may Concerne to permitt Sir Henry Skipwith knight and Barronet (who was a member of ye Garrison of Dudley Castle before ye Reducon thereof) to pase and repasse according to ye Broad Articles above written, and to receave ye Cerfitt of ye rest of ye Articles accordinglie without molestacon doinge nothinge prejudichall to ye Parl't. according to ye Intencon thereof. Given under my hande at Litchfield. May 19 1646

W. Brereton

A Bond from Sr. Wm. Brereton to save Mr. Manwayring and Mr. Broughton harmless from a bond of 600L. wherein they stand bound with the said Sr. Wm. B: to Mrs. Sarah Wentworth

Noverint universi per presentes me Willm. Brereton de Hanford in Com'te Cestr. Bar:t teneri et firmiter obligar Edward Manwarying Jun. De Whitmore et Edward Broughton de Langden in Comit Stafford Armiger in Mille et ducan libris bene et leytes Monet Ang:t Solvend eisden Edward Manwarying et Edward Broughton out cord Aler vel eod Certs Attornat Heredibus Executor Administr vel Assignat suis me Hered, Executor Administ et Assignat meos firmit per presentes sigitt meo sigitt du duodecimo die May Anno Regni Regis Caroli nunc Angli: Vicessimo secundo 1646.

The Condicon of the above written obligator is such That whereas the above Named Edward Manwarying and Edward Broughton stand bounden togeather as suretyes with the above bounder Sr. Wm. Brereton In one Certaine Bons or Bill Obligatory bearing date with these present in the sume of six hundred pounds for the payment of three hundred pounds of lawfull English money unto Mrs Sarah Wentworth of the Cittie of Coventrie her Executors or Assignes at and uppon the fourteenth day of November next ensueing the date hereof (which said some of 300L the said Sr. Wm. Brereton hath borrowed of the said Mrs Sarah Wentworth for the present supply of the wants of thes Soldyers now in the Leauger at Litchfeild. If therefore the above bounden Sr. Wm. Brereton, his Executers Administrators or Assignees doe and shall well and truly save defend and keepe harmless & indemnified the above named Edward Manwayring and Edward Broughton, theire Heires, Executers, Administrators and assignes of & from the said Bond or Bill Obligatory, That then this present Obligacon to bee utterly void and of none efect, or Asc. the same to stand, Remayne and bee in full force and vertue in the lawe.

Wm. Brereton

Sealed and Delivered in
The presence of us
R. Skeffington
John Bowyer
Mich: Byddulphe

209

Sr. Tho: Tyldesley his letter to Col.
Bowyer May 16: 1646

Sr,

According to your desire Mrs Terricke shall meete Mrs Birche at the place appointed by you; there is now a Drum with us, uppon a proposition that Col. Snead shoulde meete Major Daniel this after noone, to which I have given my consent and upon Receipt of Mr. Gerards Passe they shall all come together; I am as desirous to meet you, but this scurvie punctilio of Governorshipp will not give leave, but I can truly subservite myself,

Your Friend and
Servant
Thomas Tyldesley

16th May 1646
Sr, I doubt not but you will doe mee the
favour to deliver this inclosed according
to the direction.

Yours, Thos: Tyldesley

Remember mee to Mr. Birche & give him
thanks for his Civill visits to mee when
I was in Eccleshall.

210

From ye Comittee at Evesham touching
assistance agst Worcester

Sr,

Upon ye Returne of those Gentlemen that were sent by us to waite upon you and Colonell Morgan at Dudley Castle wee were not then sufficiently

The ruins of Dudley Castle from an eighteenth century engraving.

informed to returne a speedy answere according to our Intensons untill wee had conferred wth Colonell Whaley concerneinge what diaconal forces might be spared and expected out of Oxfordshire which wee finde to be farre short for ye carrieing on soe great a werke as ye Cittie and Garrison of Worcester and Madderfield wch you and ye Comittee of Salop unto whom wee have now addrest ourselves wilbe pleased to contribute speedily to our assistance. Wee onelie desire you wilbe pleased to spare us those horse and foote that were imployed for ye Reduceing of Dudley Castle if you shall thinke fitt to spare us anie from ye Leauger before Litchf'ld. Sr, wee know your great interest and prompt Intymacon to advance ye publique wilbe a sufficient motive, still to pursue ye weightiest affaires and in what place ye greate honesty invite. Therefore wee shall desire to recommend the premises to your Consideracon and ourselves to ye contynuance of your love and favour, and rest

Your humble Servants
Thomas Rous
Jo: Hawkes Wil: Moore
Tho: Cooke Edw: Yonge

211

Sr. Wm. Breretons Answere to ye Gov:r
& Comittee at Evesham

Gentlemen,

I have received your lre and will not faile to Contribute my utmost assistance for ye advancem't of ye worke you are aboute. And to this end will give order to ye Shropshire foote that were at Dudley to prepare to march unto you so soone as some others can be made readie to send wth them for they are not above seven or eight score wch all ye foote that were there except some Staffordshire foote that are constantlie Imployed here in the Siege. But I hope a considerable number of foote may be elsewhere spared and obtained wch shalbe without delay applied to your assistance from whom if I may after learne what progresse you make I may be ye more serviceable unto you whereby I may confirme you in ye beliefe that I am and will always remaine

Your faithfull and affectionate
friend to serve you,

Litchfield May 21st 1646 Wm. Brereton

211

Sr. Wm. Brereton to ye Comittee of Salop touching
Electons & touching settling Pious ministers.

Gentlemen,

I cannot but Congratulate wth you and blesse God for your late prosperous success in reducing Bridgnorth and Ludlowe, whereby your whole countie is cleered. I cannot doubt but your nexte werke to establish Pious, faithfull and diligent Preachers and to make those of such able and conscientious members to serve you in Parliam't as may be most serviceable unto your countie to which I am soe much a welwisher and have endeavo'rd to doe you the best service I was able, And therefore can doe noe lesse then mynde you thereof at present and assure you thereunto to my former advice and Request that you would please to recommend Mr. Wm. Steele to Brudgnorth or Ludlowe who is a verie able faithfull Pious man, and would be most serviceable to you whereby as you may doe mee a great Courtesie soe you may do yourselves and your country well Right and I who have neglected noe opportunity to doe you service shall thereby apprehend myself further engaged to approve myself

Your verie faithfull & thankfull Friend
& Servant
Wm. Brereton

Litchfeild
May 22nd 1646

212

Sr. Wm. Breretons lre to ye Comittee of Salop
for assistance for Worcester

Gentlemen, I have heard, though not from yor selves of Gods goodnes to you in delivering up Ludlowe, for wch I desire alsoe to be thankefull wth you. And if soe your forces be at Libertie I shall not doubt but that your forces that were ordered by ye Co:tee of Both Kingdomes and alsoe by a late ordinance of Parliam't under my Comands may be now disposed of to some wch your forces nowe wth mee and such as canbe spared and collected elsewhere to carry on ye worke agst Worcester wch I cannot but beleeve you wilbe as forward to promote as canbe desired and whereunto if you please to contribute anie forces those of yours now with mee are fittest to be formed wth them. I have received some lres from Sr. Thomas Fairfax intimating that Colonell Whaley wth ye forces that were before Banburie are ordered to assist Worcester. I have alsoe this day received a lre from ye Comittee at Evesham desiring that at least ye forces that were at Dudley and yours maybe despatched that way. I desire to knowe when your forces may march that these and alsoe such as can be hence spared may be formed wth them soe as they may be most Improved for ye advantage of ye service, wch is not more desired by anie man then by

Your assured friend
to serve you
Wm. Brereton

Litchfield
May 21 1646

I desire yor speedie answere that I may knowe ye better how to frame my Course.

I would Endeavour if knew your tyme to procure ye Leicester forces to meete you and those that were at Dudley, Droitwich or thereabouts.

214

Letter from Mr. Rushworth secretarie to Sr. Tho: ffairfax touching Oxford being upon Treatye

Sr,

The Generall received your lre. Hee was not verie well at present to write. The treaty began yesterdaie. I see noe likelihood of anie thinge but a surrender. With this great Place all ye out Garrisons will desire to be Involved. Some heareinge of ye Treatie have already done it. A fewe daies will secure ye others. Wee goe on wth our Werkes notwithstanding the Generall excepted onely against Sir George Byron wch they admitted of this is all I have at present to informe you of

Sr,
Your most humble Servt
John Rushworth

May 19 1646

For ye hon'ble Sir Wm. Brereton Barro't
Commander in Cheshire
at Lichfield.

A note of such Armes as were taken
in Dudley Castle

One case of Iron Drakes	
One Brasse Peece	
Musquetts & Carbines	242
Pikes and Halberds	52
Cosletts	11
A Boate or Tunne weight of Match	
Barrels of Powder	21
One little Iron Peece	
Greate store of Bulletts and lead	
One Drume	

Wee Cannot yett give your honor an Accompt in Regarde wee find more that was hidden but I hope speedily to give you an Accompt of much More

John Tanner

215

Sr. Wm. Breretons Answere to Mr. Rushworthe
Secretarie to Sir Thomas ffairefax

Sr,

I have received yours dated May 19 and am verie sorrie to heare Sir Thomas ffairefax is indisposed and hope his distemper may not be longe able to detaine him from his publique services wherein the Lord hath made him soe successful and no man desires more his further progress then myself, who do ye rather Demure upon my preparations towards Worcester to yt end It may be ascertained what may be ye issue of your Treatie at Oxford, What being surrendred I knowe not. Whether Sir Thomas ffairefax may thinke fitt the reducing of Worcester ye fullest worke and Imployment for that Armie and there force untill I heare further from you (wch I desire much) though I shalbe as much expeditious here as is possible in Reduceing this place wherein they Remaine verie obstinate, yet I shall not thinke fitt to be soe forward but rather to attend your request and according to your Intymations I shalbe much guided by ye speedie conveyance whereof you may much engage

Your verie faithfull friend
Wm. Brereton

Lichfelde May 22 1646

Lre from ye Co:tee of Darbie
touching forces

Sir,

Wee have received a lre from ye Lords and Comons at Newarke of ye 10th instant desiring our foote might be speedily sent to your assistance at Litchfeld. Wee have willinglie consented thereunto and have intimated as much in our answere to ye lre of Lords and Comons. Onelie it remaines that Sir John Gell compleates the business, And soe wee Remaine

Sir your humble servants
G. Benett Maior
Sam Sleigh Edw. Cooke
Jo. Munday Thomas Saunders
Rau. Clarke ffra Munday
Rob. Morewood Ro. Wilmot
Wm. Wooley

216

The Earle of Rutlands lre to Sir Wm. Brereton
Touching Sir Gervas Lucas Gov'r of Belvoir Castle

Sr,

In ye besieged of Lichfield you have one Lucas late Governor of Belvoir Castle and if you have not heard how Injurious he was to ye Comonwealth and Trecherous to mee Colonel ffrancis Harker can give you a full Accompte. He hath speedinglie enriched himself by ye Ruyne of divers well affected persons. And I have bene noe small sufferer by him. Sr possibly you may convenient fitt to berate him yourselfe. My requeste is (being importuned by manie others) that if it may bee noe prejudice to ye publique busines he maybe left in such a Capacitie as you Conceive most Convenient for giveing satisfacon by Lawe or otherwise. I have desired Colonell Harcker (my good friende) to attend you herein And shall heartily pray for your good successe in this and all other your undertakings. I am

Sir
Your affecconate friend
and servante
Rutlande

Exeter House 18th May
1646

To ye Right Honble Sir Wm. Brereton
Comander in Chiefe of ye Armie
For ye Service of ye Parliam't
Before Litchfeld

these

217

Orders from Sir John Gell to Capt. Bagshawe &
Captaine Poole to March to Litchfield. May 18th 1646

Captaine,

Your orders to send your Lieuten't wth your Companie and those of Captaine Poles Companie formerlie at Tutbury unto ye Leauger at Litchfield there to receave orders from Sir Wm. Brereton untill the Close there be reduced and after you are to returne wth your Companie unto Derbye there to receave orders from

Your Colonell Jo: Gell

May 18th 1646

To Captaine Bagshawe

Captaine your assistance beinge soe urgent you may leave your Comand in Chief wth your Lieut. until your returne wch is soe ordered to be

John Gell

May 18 1646

For Mr. Bronby order for their returne

Whereas ye Companie of Captaine Bagshawe & Capt. Pole were ordered by Sir John Gell to march to Litchfield and after ye reducem't of yee Close to returne to Darbie. Now for yt the assistance of these forces may be els where imployed for greater advantage of ye publique and there being as manie forces in ye Leauger at Lichfield as can by that Country be able to maintained and wee hope by Gods assistance able to make good ye Leauger I have therefore thought fitt to appoint the said Companies to returne into Darbieshire till further order

Wm. Brereton

May 23rd 1646

218

Articles for Surrender of Hartlebury

Articles of agreement concluded upon the 15th of May 1646 by Colonell Bromwich, Lt. Colonell Turton, Captaine Dormer upon ye behalfe of Colonell Morgan, Governor of Gloucester as of ye one parte and Lt. Colonell Skipwith, Captaine Guntre and Captaine Martin Sandys on ye behalfe of Captaine Sandys Gov'r of Hartlebury Castle on ye other party for ye surrendering the said Castle for ye use of ye Parliam't

1. That ye Castle wth all fortificacions, Armes, Artillerie, Amunicon and millitarie provisions to be surrendered unto Colonell Morgan tomorrowe by twelve of ye Clock without any spoile or destruction for ye service of Parliam't.
2. That ye Governor and all field officers belonging to ye said garrison shall march forth wth theire owne horses, armes, each of them wth two servants and theire horses and swords and everie Captaine in Comision wth his horse and Armes and each Captaine, two servants wth his horses, and all other officers in comision wth theire horses and swords.
3. That all troopers and common souldiers shall march out of ye said Garrison without Armes.
4. That all Gentlemen and souldiers that desire to goe beyond seas shall have passes accordinglie and two monthes tyme given them to accommodate them by going to theire owne or friends howses or to anie of the Kings Garrisons not besieged or blocked up — Raglande Excepted, provided dureing that tyme they do nothinge prejudichall to the Parl't.
5. That all private souldiers of horse and foote wch are willing to lay downe theire Armes shall have libertie to goe to their owne homes and there quietly to remaine without molestacon provided they doest nothinge prejudichall to ye Parl't.
6. That noe officers nor souldiers, nor anie other persons whatsoever shalbe reproached or have anie disgracefull speeches or affronts given them in theire march out of ye said Castle, or have anie of theire persons wronged or molested.
7. That all prisoners noe in the said Garrison forth with be released & set at liberty upon the signeing of these Articles and all Country men wch are now prisoner in the said Castle for not paying theire contribucon shalbe set at liberty and in case anie person in the tyme of theire imprisonment have bene forced to give bond or otherwise engage themselves for paym't of anie sumes of money That all such bonds and engagem't be delivered up and made voide.
8. That the Governor nor noe field officer shall march forth of the said Castle wth above 50 L. nor Captaine wth above 20 L., Lt. Not above 10 L. nor Cornet or Ensigne with above 5 L. nor any private Trooper above 20s.
9. That if anie person comprehended in these Articles doe breake anie one of them he shall lose ye benefitt of them all.
10. That Colonell Morgan doe give assurances yt all officers and souldiers under his comand really endeavour that all others in the service of ye Parlym't shall duelie and exactly observe these Articles and if they or any one of them doe violate or infringe ye same, upon complaint made, justice may be done or reparacons made.

11. That noe oath, Coven't or protestacon shalbe imposed upon anie person comprehended in these Articles provided they aske nothing prejudicall to the Parliam't.

Wm. Skipwith	Jo. Bromwich
Gilbt. Gentery	Rich Turton
Martin Sandys	Ensor Dormer

These are Articles are Confirmed
By mee, Thomas Morgan

221

Additional Articles

1. In ye first Article that there may be a longer tyme given for Gentlemen and officers to stay in the Castle to dispose of themselves wch wilbe untill Colonell Sandys his house be freed from quarter.
2. In ye second Article Colonell Sandys is Lymitted for himself and two servants wch I desire may be all his servants and horse not exceeding the number of six as alsoe a passe for beyond seas for himself, ten men & horses and three months tyme to provide for theire journey.
3. In ye third that the Comon souldiers may march away wth all theire weareing apparell that you wilbe pleased at the laying downe theire Armes to allow two shillings a peece for the common souldiers and 10s. a peece for all sergeants and corporalls.
4. That in all the Articles where the Governor & Officers are concerned and that Gentlemen may be included.
5. That all officers and Gentlemen may carrie away theire wearing apparell and likewise theire Serv'ts.
6. That the Governor may have free libertie to dispose of all his owne howse hold stuffe and also of those Bookes of his owne & other Gentlemens.
7. The Governors six beds and three suits of hangings and his Lt. One bed and furniture and the prisoners yt are upon exchange to beset at libertye.

All these I doe freely condescend unto if the Articles be agreed by you.

Tho. Morgan

222

Col. Morgans pass to the Gov'r of Hartlebury
upon surrender.

Thomas Morgan Colonell and Comander in Cheife of all ye Parliam'ts forces in ye Countyes of Gloucester, Monmouths'r And Comander in Cheife of all the Parliam'ts forces before ye Castle of Hartlebury And Governor of ye Cittie and Garrison of Gloucester.

These may certifie all whom these may in any way Concerne that Captaine William Sandys late Governor of ye Garrison of Hartleburie having surrendered the said Garrison into my hands for ye service of ye Kinge and Parlt. I doe therefore desire that according to my Engagem't expressed in the Articles agreed upon in the surrender of ye said Garrison that the same Captaine Wm. Sandys may passe from ye Castle of Hartlebury to Kelham in Nottinghamshire or to anie other places in the Parlt. Quarters there to remaine quietly for ye space of three monthes Dureing wch tyme neither himself, Servts, Hors nor goods shall by anie meanes or under any pretence whatsoever be molested upon or violently taken away but fullie to enjoy the benefit of ye said Articles Provided he Asks nothing prejudishall to the Parlt. Given under my hand & seal at Hartlebury Castle May 17 1646.

Tho. Morgan

To all friends and soldiers in
Service of ye King and Parlt and
To all others whom it may concern.

223

Mr Steven Andersons lre to Sr. Wm. Brereton
Touching restoring 2 horses to Capt. Wm. Sandys

Honoured Sir,

I have bene by Litchfelde and at Sir John Skevingtons to have enjoyed ye honor of kissing your Hand. But faleing of my Intencon of haveinge the opportunity I cannot omitt in this way to present my service to you & likewise to begg your past favour to this Gentlem; a Person to whom I am highly obliged in giving of him your best ayde for the recoverie of his horses that were last night taken out of his Quarters by some of Captaine Hunts men at Wolverhampton. Sir I know you wilbe highly sensible of ye violator of our Articles and contribute your best in his repaire

Shall ever be acknowledged by
Your Humble Servt
and Kinsman
Stephen Anderson

Sr. Wm. Breretons lre thereupon
To Captaine Hunt.

Captaine Hunte,

The late Governor of Hartleburrie Castle and some other good friends of myne in his Behalfe have importuned mee to procure two Horses restored unto ye said Captaine Sandys wch were ye last night taken out of his Quarters in Wolverhampton by one of your trooper boyes, wch if it were done is soe unworthy and dishonourable an Acte and soe much wounds the honour and Justice of ye Parlyam't as may not be endured. There being nothinge more hatefull then violation of Articles and Agreem'ts nor any thing more insufferable then that such actions as these should passe unpunished there being nothinge more sacred then the performances of Coven'ts and Engagemts of the nature whereof I hope you will be soe sensible as that I shall not neede to take anie further cares to doe this Gentlman Right and vindicate ye hand of ye Parlam't in assurance whereof I remaine,

Your verie Loveing
friend,
Wm. Brereton

Lichfielde May 23
1646

224

Money paid to Capt Gerrard in full of the 40s. a
sum due to his men according to ye Articles
of Tutbury, May 23 1646

In regard ye souldiers that were in Tutburie Castle and were according to ye Articles to March wth Captaine Gerard for foreigne service & in ye meane tyme to quarter in Staffordshire, contynue still in Stafford shire as a great burthen to ye Country. It was this day ordered by Sr. Wm. Brereton and ye rest of ye Comitte at Lichfield that whereas there was 40s. a man to be paid to ye said souldiers (who are as are by Captaine Daniell Watson whom ye G'rall appointed to muster them one hundred & eleven) wil amount to 222 L. whereof ye said Captaine hath received of Captaine Stone 55 L. 10s. of Colonell Bowyer 27 L. and of Richard Shelsoe by appointment of Sr,. Wm. Brereton 20 L. in all 102 . 10s. that the Head Constable of Totendslow Hundred should pay unto Captaine Daniell Watson ande Captaine Villers 119 L. 10s. Wch makes up the whole due to ye said Souldiers) out of the monies assessed upon that Hundred towards ye maintainance of ye leaugers of Litchfield, Dudley & Tutbury wch tyme ye said Sir Wm. Brereton writt orders to Captaine Watson and Captaine Villers (inclosing ye said order for 119 L. 10s. to be paid by ye Head Constable) to pay ye money according to ye said Souldiers upon theire marching out of the County and to pay part of the money to take theire Armes according to ye Articles and to send the same to Litchfield wth a perfect list of ye names of the said Souldiers.

225

Sr. W. Breretons lre to Capt. Hunt to restore
Capt. Sandy's Horses.

Captaine Hunt,

Yesterdaie upon ye information given mee that some of Troope namely one Symons a Trooper boy had (in violacon of ye Articles agreed upon for ye surrender of Hartleburie Castle for ye service of ye Parliam't) taken two Horses from Captaine Sandys late Governor of ye said Castle from his quarters at Wolverhampton. I did write affectionatlie to you to cause ye said restored. Now by this bearer his servant I have thought good to send these lines to desire you whereof upon anie pretence whatsoever deliver these horses but cause them restored accordingly to the Articles. There can be nothing of greater indignity to the Parlt. then breach of Covenant and if these horses be not founde out and given back accordingly the Parlyam't must be made acquainted thereof. But I have always had and still resceive soe good an opinion of you that as I beleeve it was without your privily that ye same horses were soe taken I shall not need to enlarg myself not doubting but you wilbe so sensible of honor herein as that you will see it done

Your verie Lo friend
Wm. Brereton

May 24 1646

226

The Committee of Shropshire theire lre to Sr. Wm. Brereton touching assistance for Worcester

Honored Sir,

You may be Confident of our readiness to serve you wth all ye forces wee have, haveinge soe manie reasons induceing us thereunto. But truelie our souldiers have received so manie discouragements in Shropshire and at Litchfield that wee have cause to feare they will not be comanded out of the County without some assurance of pay and accommodations befittinge souldiers wch they are informed is denyed those wch are now wth you. Ludlow is not yet reduced. Yesterday wee received ye Articles for ye surrender of ye Castle upon ye last of the monthe if it be not relieved in ye interim. The Articles are verie hard on our parte and too tedious nowe to Copie out haveinge soe short a tyme to returne yor answere onely wee shall give you the short touch that ye Enemy is to march away upon as hon'ble termes as anie ever did that wee have heard of. This wee are informed Chiefely by some Interrupcons wch happened by diversity of Comande And ye place was well fortified beinge one of ye most stately Castles in this part of ye Kingdome and victual led for twelve monthes. Just 36 peeces of ordnance 37 barrelles of powder wch onlie are to be left behind. This much wee Certified ye Committee at Evesholme in returne to a lre from them. The truth is the Countie is most ruyinated having wholie come under the old Contributon these three years and not able to pay ye arreares due to our souldiers much lesse to contynue them longer in pay soe that wee are requested to make speedy Reducement of them to halfe the number wch wee have constantly maintained according to our former Engag'mt to the Countrey wch wee are constantlie solicited to performe already yet if you have anie service to comand our forces wee shall keepe them together untill your designes be effected if you please to take Care for payment of them otherwise wee must be enforced to part wth 500 foote as well comanded men as any are in these Parts besides divers Troopes of Horse. Sir you may assure yourselfe that nothinge wilbe wantinge in us to approve ourselves

Your most humble servants
And. Lloyde Robt. Clive
Robt. Charleton

Salop May 22 1646
at 3 in ye afternoone

227

A Certificate of Mr Addams, his sufficiency
for the Ministrie

We the under subscribers doe unanimously testifie that wee have knowne the Bearer hereof Mr. Randall Addams, for divers yeares to bee a Man of high esteeme for his Soundnesse of Doctrine, Pyetie, Learning, good life and Conversation in the eyes of all these with whome he oft conversed hoe walked strictly and conscientiously in the wayes of Godlinesse And therefore we could not deny that which wee owe to the truth and him, to witt the Testimony to the best of our knowledge of his unblameable life and Conversation, Pyetie and learning by which he hath ever endeavoured to promote the wayes of Godliness as witnesse our hands this 30th of March 1646.

Tho: Temple, Joshua Hoyle, G. Hamilton
Edw. Danstervile
Stanley Gower

228

Order for Mr. Addams to have the
Medietie of the Rectory of Wallesey

Whereas the Medietie of the Rectory of Wallesey in the Countie of Chester hath been enjoyed as a pluralitie by Doctor Snell, a Delinquent untill his Estate was sequestered And that the Parrishoners of Wallesey aforesaid have peticoned for Mr. Rand. Addams to officiate there and bee their Pastor (the place being vacante) whoe is an approved Orthodox Divine, and whose losses have been greate in Ireland by the present Rebellion there. Wee have therefore in prosecution of the Ordinance of Parliam't of the 26th of March 1644 Appointed for placeing of Ministers in the Roome of Delinquents or Scandalous Ministers and such as have deserted their Ordinarie place of Residence; nominated, put and appointed the said Mr. Randle Addams to bee Pastor, and officiate at the Church of Wallesey aforesaid, in the Roome, Place and Stead of the said Doctor Snell, And to take, Receave & perceive to his owne use the said Medietie of the said Rectory of Wallesey, and of the profits and Revenue thereunto belonging in as large and Ample Manner as the said Doctor Snell hath used to doe, or of right might Receive the same. Given under our hands the twentie fifth day of May 1646.

Wm. Brereton

The Certificate of Dr. Hoyle, Dr. Hamilton
Dr. Temple, Mr. Gower and Mr. Dunstervile
Of Mr. Adams the conversacon and ability to
Dispence ye worde of God and ye peticon
Of a well affected in habits of ye same.

229

Sr. Wm. Brereton to Mr. Swinfen touching
Sparing forces to Worcest'r & want of money

Sr,

Thee Committee of Lords and Comons at Newarke sent unto ye Comittees of Leicester, Nottingham and Darbie, and some others to desire that theire foote might be ordered hither to observe my orders. The Committees of Eveshome have sent unto mee for ye assistance of what forces can be spared to strengthen ye sieg ag'st Worcester where they are much overstretched as I have heard and to whom I am not able to Contribute more then ye forces that were employed ag't Dudley wch are soe miserable as that they would not be anie waies usefull untill those from Lincolne, Leicester and Darbie come up unto mee. Some whereof are in readiness (those of Leicester) expecting ye comminge and accesse of ye rest in tyme I can contribute little or nothinge towards Worcester whereof I desire the Worcester Gentlemen, Sergeant Wilde and Galloway may be possessed and made aware as alsoe if they intend that siege ag't Worcester to be Carreyed on wth successe there must be some provision of money be made for I am much distressed here for want thereof. The Shropshire foote Mutinied when they were to have marched ag't Dudley to whom I was Constrained to promise and pay the greatest parte of ye money brought down by Mr. Sympcox soe as now I am constrained & have upon my owne personall security made provision of money to pay those Cheshire soldiers also (for whom there is no provision elsewhere made) one monthes pay for want thereof they are in soe much want and distresse without shoes stockings and Lynnen that Adjutant Louthiane told mee on Saturday last that he would not obtaine them that might upon .... untill I had presented a day for their satisfaccon whereupon I was Constrained to promise theire paymt upon Saturday or Munday next. Some of them are gone backe others sicke and I can doe noe lesse then give you this Intymacon that I feare much that if my Comands determyn and that I receive hence the Cheshire foote may not be Contynued upon their service wch may be the more grievous & hazardous by ye occasion of ye Sicknes wch doth extend and dispense though as yet none of our souldiers have bene seised upon by the infeccon (blessed be God) onelie one of the souldiers was brought unto ye Campe last day out of a Howse in the towne wch was presently suspected to be infected, whereupon ye souldier, one of Captaine Clegs was returned speedily. The morter peeces from Leicester are come hither and expert further but we want shells. They in ye Close remaine still obstinate expecting (as it is thought) better Condisons from Others when my Imployment is determined. Therefore it shalbe necessarie that some speedie resource be taken and made known unto us. Until then I cannot hope for any better answere from them.

In the meane tyme I herinclosed send you ye muster rolls, And wth my prayers to God to direct & guide you I remaine

Your most assured friend
& Serv't.
Wm. Brereton

Litchfeld May 25 1646

231

A stronge sally out of ye Close made

On may perceive neere if **[torn page]** Cheshire foote yet is desperate sally and advanced both Horse and foote as farre as to our workes in the Remootest place from ye Close in that parte of ye line wch is neere unto Stowe Church. They were beaten backe wherein there was lost on our parte Lt. Miller, Capt. Thorne his Lt. Belonging to Coventry who was a very valiant man and is much to be lamented, Two or three more of yt Companie were slaine & wounded. ffive or six of Captaine ffinch his firelockes wounded. Captaine Rachbornes Drummers thigh and Arme broke in shivers by a drake bullett and severall others wounded, but what otherwise was done upon ye Enemy I can't yet informe you but that there were stronge parties sallied out both of Horse and foote and engaged with them whilest wee skirmished wth them and beat them backe. The Enemy from ye toppe of ye Pallaces and from theire Towers and walls did much injury and gall our men. I hope wee shall make good use of the attempt of ye Enemyes and it shalbe thereby directed if it be possible without unavoidable denger to erect another mount neerer unto them to keepe in and restraine theire cattle from graseinge under ye walles neerest to ye Close. They made a second sally this Evening wth Colours. I hope to bee better provided for them

232

Examinacon of John Bust who came out
Of ye Close May 19 1646

John B [**torn page**] at
Nasbie and comeing this
present day forth of ng examined sayth
that the last summons sent into the Governor was not read or made knowne to the soldyers. That the allowance to ye soldyers is not lessened to them above halfe a pound of bread in a weeke since the beginning of the Leauger; That its Reported there is betwixt seven and eight hundred Soldyers in the Close besides Women and Children; that there are three Sally Ports beside the greate Gate which is Barrocaded upp, One into the Mount before Damm Street, One neere the drawe Bridge goeing towards the Swan, The third leading into the newe Worke next Bacon streete; That the Newe Worke is Triangular & with Pallasadoes about, saveing the end next Stowe Church which is not yett finished; That the Enemy hath Intelligence of the bringing upp of our great Gunnes, and thereupon are Lyneing the Wall about tenne foote thicke, the whole Wall being distributed among the Companies for the effecting of it; That it is not yett finished within the Close; That the hand Grenadoes shott by them, were shott by a Morterpeece made of Leade, and that the Enemy hath gathered some of our Granadoes about 40 pound weight which burst not, and are Casting a Morter of Leade to Returne them uppon us; That the Granadoes have Ruined the Howses of the Lord Aston, Henry Hynd, Mr. Martins, Mr. Turpennyes, Mr. Williams, Mr. Robinsons, One neare the Viccarage, One Gentlemans nere the Ashtree, The Gardenhowse nere the Pallace, Morris his howse the Smyth, a Smiths shoppe nere Sr. Tho: Leighs and parte of the Lord Astons Stables; That yesterday the Gentlemen were borrowing Moneyes of the Inhabitants & Cittizens for the satisfaction of the soldyers.

John Bust

Pages 233 and 234 are missing in the original letter book

235

Sr. Wm. Breretons answere
to Mr. Rushmore

Sr,

I have receaved your lre and give you manie thankes for your intelligence. In Liewe whereof these may acquainte you that this day the Enemy made a verie bold and a verie stronge sallie both wth Horse that were in verie good charge and foote. But advancing neere to our workes and line neare ye Poole side towards Stowe Church where after some hot skirmishing beaten back and had noe cause to insult. Wee had one Lieutenant and some souldiers slaine by that from ye Towers of ye Close and battlements of ye Pallace in pursuate of ye Retreating Enemy. I hope the sally may be of good use to us and that wee may be guided where to erect a newe mount nearer ye Close if it may be possible done wthout unavoydable Danger of great losse by reason ye Enemy hath such comand from ye Towers. Our line and mounts already rounde aboute ye Close are on Bacon Street syde within halfe musquett shot of ye Close and ye Cittie side Close to ye Poole side within pistol shot of theire Drawbridge. I would have desired to have contributed more considerably towards ye Designe agt. Worcester then we are able.

I have ordered three companies of Shropshire foote that were at Dudley to march unto ye Leauger wch is all wee can for present spare.

Some horse I could better spare but perceive they are not soe needfull neither much desired by ye Committee at Evesham. I have written to ye Comittee of Shropshire to send all ye foote they can spare now that theire county is cleered to assist agt Worcester but have not ye assurance of anie by reason I hearte they are upon Reducem't of theire forces and intend to discharge and disband five hundred well disciplined foote for want of revenue to pay them by reason that countie hath bene soe much oppressed thereunto by double contribucon and ye like. I have provided and have here two Demi Cannon, two Culverings and foure other peeces to batter theire Houses, but for the morter peeces that came from Leicester and wanted shells and some materialls nothing shalbe omitted that may eppreciate this worke and put an end to ye distruccon, wch is in ye power of

Your assured faithfull
friend,
Wm. Brereton

Litchfield
May 25th 1646.

236

Sr. Wm. Brereton and ye Committee at Litchfield
To ye Committee at Coventry to send money

Gentlemen,

Such is our extreme wante of money, haveinge received little or none from ye Parliam't though ye Parliam't hath appointed 3000 L. for this service, soe that wee are in great distresse. There is noe doubt to be made but there wilbe good payment though not in our tyme. Wee have used all possible meanes for a supplie but cannot prevaile. Some of our Souldiers have bene at least 12 weekes without pay, and ye country is not able to make provision of victualls for ye Leauger much more valuable then pay and unlesse you please to helpe us to a supplie wee knowe not how to carrie on this worke haveinge founde it verie difficult to bringe ye souldiers to doe dutie for divers nights past and ye Enemy we finde much engaged & desperate in theire salleyes and Attempts wherein though wee have suffered some late losse yet wee hope they have noe great cause to insult and Tryumph agt when wee hope wee shall make some further progress and neerer approaches if wee can but keepe our souldiers. Soe as wee may be able to give you a better accompt of this place for wch end noe opportunity and endeavour shalbe omitted wch may be attained & performed by

Your verie faithfull
Friend and Servant
Wm. Brereton

Litchfield
May 26th 1646.

Gent. The sume desired is 500 L. wch wee will engage ourselves for repayment either soe soone as the monie is paid to us from ye Parliam't or at six months end

Wm Brereton
Phil. Jackson

Leicester Barbour
Jo: Sympson

238

Comittee at Leicester to Sr. Wm. Brereton
touching Granadoes & returne of their Horse

Sr,

Wee received this morneinge severall lres from you and for ye shells you write of. Wee have sent to Nottingham about them and shall willinglie Concurre to ye utmost of our ability for ye furtherance of that important service. In regard of spetiall occasions wee have given order to all our Horse to returne speedily to us. And therefore desire your favour therein. Wee believeing that theire Contynuance wth you may now be spared. Wee have seven shelles left here for our morter peece wch wee will send presentlie unto you. Wee have sent your warrant to ye presentlie to attend ye Commete of warre by ye appointed

Wee are Sir
Your affectionate Servts.

Leicester
25 May 1646

Tho: Hasilrigg Jo. Browne
ffr. Smalley
Jo. Swinfen W. Stantry
Ric. Ludlam

Copie of ye order

In pursuance of ye order of ye Comittee at Leicester you are hereby required to march wth all ye Leicestershire Horse unto Leicester there to receive further orders from ye Committee

Wm. Brereton

Lichfield May 26 1646
To Maior Mayn

239

Lre from ye Co'tee at Evesham to Sr. Wm.
Brereton desiring assist. of foote agt. Worcester

Sr,

Colonell Whalley is now entrenching himself in ye most convenient places to annoy ye Enemy that can be taken within Cannon shot of ye Cittie but in regard of ye strength of the enemy the foote that he hath here are little enough to make two quarters on our side of the Cittie and Garrison to blocke it up round soe as the Enemy may to keepe from provisions will require foure such quarters at least. Therefore we earnestlie intreate your assistance by procuring you what foote possibly may be spared from Stafford, Leicester, Nottingham or Shropshire. Wee need not say any thinge of ye great Concernm't the reducing this place would be to ye publique or of ye ruyne of this poore County. The Enemy hath made two or three sallyes, not much operacon on either part. Last night about 200 foote and 50 horse came neere our pioneers but were beaten of and forced in again wth some losse. Sir your Publique spirit in this bleeding kingdome gives us assurance of your helpe at this present. Wee desire to heare from you upon all occasions and remaine

Your affeconate friends &
Servants

Himlipp House
May 26 1646

Tho: Rous
Edw. Smith
Hen: Hunt Tho. Mylward
W. More

240

Sr. Wm. Breretons Answere

Gentlemen,

I have received your letter wherein you desire some asistance of foote wch I should be ready to affoard if the stubborne people were reduced or that I could possibly spare anie from hence but I can assure you that ye Enemy are soe strong in ye Close and soe enraged that they have of late made some gallant sally & wherein though wee have sustained some great losse yet they have noe cause to insult and tryumph.

Wee are purposed wthin two daies to make further use of our morter peeces and cannon and if it please God to give us good success Evreway be applied to your assistance and considerable strength wee can obtaine anie encouragm't and satisfacion for our souldiers some whereof have received noe monie since they came hither. I have sent inclosed an order for ye Shropshire foote that were at Dudley who are all that can be spared hence and could have sent you some Darbieshire foote but Sir John Gell's orders to his foote were either to serve at Litchfield or to returne backe to Darbie.

As there may be further occasion I will not faile to doe you the best service I am able and to communicate to you accordinglie and shall desire alsoe to heare from you to whom I will not faile to approve myself

Your verie faithfull
friend and servant
Wm. Brereton

Litchfield
May 27 1646

241

Order to ye Shropshire foote

It is ordered that Captaine Heslain, Captaine Hunte, Captaine Mainwareinge wth theire Companies of Shropshire foote doe forthwith march to ye leauger before Worcester to asist to ye strengthening that leauger and to receive orders from the Comander in Cheife for further order.

Wm. Brereton

Lichfeild May 26 1646.

Order to send all the Wives into the
Close, May 26: 1646

Litchfeild 26th May 1646

Whereas many Prisoners have come out of the Close to speake with their Wives, and by that meanes doe gaine intelligence from them to the greate prejudice of this Leauger & it is therefore Ordered that for the future preventing hereof a list bee taken of the names of all the Wives of those that are in the Close that they may bee speedily sent into the Close to their Husbands and not permitted to come out again and if they or any shall dare to come out of the Close the Officers of that Guard are Required to shoote them or otherwise to bee answerable for the same at a Counsell of Warre. Given under my hand the day above written.

Wm. Brereton

The Mayor of the Towne is to take
Care that out of every Company in ye Towne
One Officer bee Chosen to see this Order to bee
speedily put in Execution, and to take Care
that under pretence hereof noe plunder bee
Comitted in their Howses, and to give an
Accompt in Writeing of the Names of those
that are sent in.

242

Letter sent into the Close to the Lady
Dyett by all the Women of Litchfield

Good Madam,

The Miseries and vexatious Occurants (the woefull effects of Warre) that hath of late befallen us are such as forceth us to make a Relation of them unto your Ladyship, as to our noble and Compassionate Friend that will Comiserate though you Cannot helpe us, And it will bee some ease to our grieved Mindes if you will be pleased to entertaine the unburdening of them into your Lady:sps Consideracon and to take a viewe of our many Miseries being deprived of the fruition of our Husbands the only stay and Comfort of us and of our families, and having our Howses fitted with Soldyers, our Land untilled that should mainteyne of Families for future and paying Weekely soe great assessments towards the Mainteyning of the Army as wee are not able long to subsist under; besides some of us having our Howses that were empty defaced and pulled in peeces, in wch munble the glorie of our Cittie, wee meane your own faire Habitation doth exceedinglie suffer, the Roomes being everie day more and more pulled downe; Wee would not intimate these our griefes unto you were there either hope or helpe or Reparation, for then it would bee both Comfortable and honorable for our Men to continue in their Resolutions, but seeing wee can expect nothing in the progresse but a Continuation of our Miseries, nor any Reparations in the Conclusion, wee thinke it would bee happie for us if the tyme of a good agreement might bee hastened, least deferring till necessitie cause it the end as well as the progresses Concluded with our Ruine; Wee acknowledge it presumtion in us to take upon us to give Councell to Men of Wisdome in tymes of warre though that wise and Valliant Warriour of God the Prophett David (1 Sam: 25) both accepted and pronounced a blessing upon a Womans Councell at such a tyme, And indeed our intentions thus farre extend to desire your Lady:spe to intimate to such of our Husbands as shall at any tyme present themselves unto your Lady:p our present and much feared Miseries, especially to your owne most Worthy Husband whoe wee conceive is best able in his wisdome to helpe us all & that both hee and they may use their best endeavours to free themselves and us from those Miseries which wee feare some Men from Sinister ends and desperate engagements seeke to bring them to, And as a Motive further to engage your Lady:p to the more effectuall performance of our desires; wee Represent unto you that Newarke, Banberry, Hartleberry and Ludlowe are lately Surrendered, Oxford, Worcester and (for ought wee knowe) all other Garrisons of the Kings in England besieged, and soe farr off from any hopes of helpe from him, that the king himself for safetie hath cast himself upon the affection of his Native People. And wee Conceive it canot bee against the Rules either of honor or Wisdome for us to followe his example, upon good Condicons to seeke our own safetie alsoe which hath been his Ma:ts Comaunds to divers Garrisons that have sent to him, and whom hee hath been unable to succour, And wee conceive his Action and Example herein Carries with it the nature of a precept at least a sufficient direction, but wee Cease further to bee troublesome to your Lad:p beseeching the Lord soe to direct your Lady:p that by your meanes and some other happie Instrument wee may attaine some freedome from our daylie Miseries and a happie end of them.

243

Letter out of the Close from Mr. Hill
to his Wife in the Fryers

Indeo epes mea

My dare sweete Ursula,

There Cannot bee a greater blessing on Earth befall mee then to heare of your welfare which would bee Completed to the highest pitch if soe God were pleased wee could enjoy one the others mutuall societie, his leisure must bee expected, and I doubt not but hee will Continue to give us more patience to endure the worst of Afflictions which noe may shall move or stagger mee and I hope your Resolves are Correspondent & never grieve at but undergoe what cannot bee altered; Grange is not yet Returned into the Close. The Rest of the things you mencon in the Letter I have Received and somewhat else the Palyis etc.; The plague or any other disease is within us, is not about us it may bee I am and soe have been since my hither coming in as good health as ever, and I hope shall continue; The heate of the weather will make mee Cautilous in taking much Tobaccoe; God blesse with health & happinesse you and

Your truly loving Husband
John Hill

May 4th: 1646

Fato patientia Major

244–5

Pages 244 and 245 are blank

246

The first summons sent into Litchfield
Close by Sr. Wm. Brereton, Aprill 13th 1646
Directed to Sr. Thomas Tyldesley and Col. Bagot.

Gentlemen,

I have hitherto forborne to Sumons you to the end you might as much despaire of escape as of Releife, and have not before tenders of Mercie put in execution any destructive Attempt knowing the Parliament (whom I serve) desires rather your Reducement then your Ruine; It Canne be noe newes to imparte to you the totall defeate given to your only Field Army in this kingdome (late under the Comaund of Sr. Jacob Ashley) within a short tyme after the submission of Sr. Ralph Hoptons Army to Sr. Thomas Fairefax in the West, besids the Surrendering of Exeter which (though perhaps unknowne to You) is most true, whereof I make Mention not to Seduce or Tryumph ov'r you, but to bring you to a right understanding of your present Condicon. I have now sent this Sumons to demaund for the use of the king and Parliament the Close of Litchfield, with all Armes Amunition and other Warlike Provisions your speedie surrender whereof will pre vent further effects of Hostilitie, And your selves and those Gentlemen of qualitie and others with you, may Receive Honor:ble Conditions, but if your obstinacie deprive you & them thereof, the guilt (which must necessarily bee answered for) is your owne and you must expect worser Condicons hereafter. Your Possitive Answer is Required by 4 of the Clocke this Afternoone by

Your Servant
Wm. Brereton

From our Campe on Bacon
Hill, Aprill the 13th : 1646

Answere to the first Summons

Sr,

Though your Summons hath been long expected the Answere shall bee shorte. Wee will keepe this Garrison (God willing) with our lives and Fortunes for the king our Leige Soveraigne by whom wee are intrusted; This is the Resolution of the whole Garrison together with

Your Servants
Thomas Tyldesley
Hen: Bagot

Litchfeild Close
Aprill 13th 1646

247

The Second Sumons sent into the Close
by Sr. Wm. Brereton 12th of May 1646
directed to Sr. Thomas Tyldesley and Col. Bagott

Gentlemen,

Your Rejecting my first summons at such tyme as you Could not but behold the hand of God every where against you might justly have deprived you of further tenders of Mercie; But such is the Clemencie of the Parliament (whose servant I am) that to prevent the further effusion of blood and the Ryuine of your selves and all those Gentlemen and others with you, I nowe send you this second and last Sumons, And hereby demaund and Require you to surrender the Garrisoned Close of Litchfield, with all Ordinance, Armes, Ammunicion, Provisions of Warre and all other goods whatsoever into my hands for the use of kinge and Parliament.

What I informed you in my last Sumons Concerning Sr. Ralph Hopton and his Armies submission to Sr. Thomas Fairefax, the defeate of Sr. Jacob Ashley and the deliverie of Exeter I cannot nowe doubt but you believe.

It is as true that since that tyme the Garrisons of Barstable, Dunster, Woodstock, Ruthin, Bridgnorth, Aberistwicke, Tutbury, Banbury, Newarke, and others are delivered, and Dudley Castle agreed to bee yielded upp to Morrowe, and Oxford with the Rest either straightlie Beleaugered or blockt upp, and his Ma:tie in Person Come to our Armie; You Cannot therefore but apprehend yourselves in a desperate Condicon, and that as there is a vast difference betwixt the Condicons you might have expected when I first summoned you and those I canne nowe graunte; Soe the longer you persist in your obstinacie (adding to the expence of tyme, treasone and Blood) the greater will bee the Accompt and Judgement upon yourselves and those with you.

I give you untill foure of the Clocke tomorrowe afternoone to advise at which tyme I expect your finall Answere, Remayning

Your Servant
Wm. Brereton

From our Campe on
Bacon Hill May 12th 1646

Sr,

You shall to Morrowe Receive an Answere from
Your Servants
Thomas Tyldesley
Hen. Baggot

12th of May 1646

248

Sr. Thomas Tyldesley and Col. Bagot their
Answere to Sr. Wm. Breretons second Summons

Sr,

Yesterday being the 12th of May Wee Received your second Sumons wherein you Require us partely by persuasions & partly by Menaces to surrender into your hands the Close of Litchfeild with all Ordinance, Armes, Amunition, Provisions of Warre and all other goods whatsoever for the use of king & Parliam:t but you neither produce nor affirme that you have any Warrant or authoritie from the king and Parliament to enable us to deliver it, or you to receive it, which you might easily have procured (if the king and Parliament had been thereunto consenting) since the king (as you write) is come in Person to your Army, and you have daylie intercourse of intelligence wth the Howses of Parliament; unlesse perhaps the kinges Consent bee little Regarded by you whoe in your letter professe yourself (only) a Servant to the Parliament without any mencon of dutie or acknowledgment of service to your lawfull Soveraigne.

For our Partes as wee knowe that noe Governors or Comaunders of any of the kinges forces canne without manifest guilt of High Treason deliver upp the same without his Ma:ts Consent, unlesse they bee thereunto forced or necessitated, which (thanks bee to God wee need not to feare) soe being as sensible as your selfe of the Miseries of a Civil Warre, wee shall not keepe this Garrison an hower after wee are assured it is his Ma:ts pleasure it shall be delivered, And wee must tell you nothing makes us more diffident of your Relation of the accord betweene the Kinge and your Partie, then your outrages and Barbarous violence utterly to deface and destroy the Lords House one of the most Auncient Monuments of Christian Pietie in this kingdome, being a Thousand years ould within eleaven & the Cheife Ornament of this countrey, which being noe way advantageous to your designe Renders you odious to all good Men As for the submission of the Lord Hoptons Armie and the Surrender of the many Garrisons men coned in your letter, wee knowe not upon what ground or Reason it was done. Lett them answere for themselves, if they have done anything unworthily (which wee Canne never believe especially of soe gallant & honor:ble a Person as the Lord Hopton) they shall bee examples for our detestation, not imitation, who had Rather suffer for our loyaltie then prosper by perforce the expence of Blood and Treasure must bee cast upon yor Account whoe are the Assaylants, doe the wronge and endeavour the Ruine of his Maj:ties loyall subjects, not upon ours, whoe stand only upon a just defence of our Soveraignes Rights, our owne Persons and Estates, a defence which the Lawe of God and Man Comaunds, and wee must observe unlesse wee will bee Accessaries to the Ruine of our Maister and our selves.

And what heavie Judgement soever you intend against us and those with us for our Constant Loyaltie which you tearme Obstinacie, know Sr It is our Resolution rather to suffer evell at your hands then doe it with our owne, Rather to bee Martyrs, and Rather to offend them that Canne but kill the Body then him whoe canne destroy both soule and body in Hell.

Whereas you say wee Cannot but behould the hand of God every where against us, Wee Conceive Fortunate Successe to bee noe good Argument of a just Cause, for that hee that hath Right hath many tymes Sinnes for which God justly permitted him to bee scourged by his Enemyes, and at last casteth his scourge into the fire, as hee oft tymes did to his owne People by the Philistines, and to the Christians by the Turkes and Saracens. And though afflictions bee many tymes the portion of Gods Children, yett this is our Comfort that Gods Judgements beggines in the Howses of his servants and ends in the Howses of his Enemyes, And wee heartily wish that a true sight and sence of your Errours may avert Gods Judgement from you, whoe impute ye efficiencie of that to the God of Heaven, which belongs to the God of this World, whoe hath blinded your mindes, and is the author of Averice, Ambition, disloyaltie, Crueltie &c.

Sr. The many particulars of your Letter and weight thereof occasioned this length which wee hope you will Pardon in them whoe have noe other end then to acquitt themselves & satisfie you (as well they could) and to expresses themselves as indeed they are his Ma:ts Loyall Subjects and

Your Servants
Thomas Tyldesley
Her Bagot

From the Close in
Litchfield this
13th of May 1646

250

Letter to Mr. Ashurst Mr. Swinfen at
London touching batteringe down ye
Greatest of the three stepples of the
Minster at Litchfield

Sr,

Soe soone as wee were Furnished with any Considerable proportion of Amunition which was noe more but a tunne of powder and a tunne of Match, Wee made the best use thereof erecting a Batterie neere unto our next Mount to the Close, and plaid foure or five dayes freely upon their highest Spire steeple out of which they had most galled and annoyed us even from the very highest Windowes (which were not many yards belowe the Weather Cocke) whence they had done much execution both in the Towne & Campe and elsewhere noe lesse then 8 or 10 slayne & wounded upon May day last wch was their faire day though it is true most of them were their owne Friends. This was that spire which was most beautified and adorned wth colours, scarfes and other ornaments on all sydes even from ye Bellfrie to the Toppe almost of the Spire especially on May day last, herein their Ladyes and Grandies (as was Reported) were accommodated with Lodging not knowing where to bee soe much secured from the danger of our Morterpeeces, which begin to bee more formidable among them, And this was Conceived to bee the most safe and Convenient place for the disposing of theire Magazeene.

Wee had noe more then two Gunnes a Demy Cannon & Demy Culverin both which wee had noe more than 60 shott a peece or thereabout wth twentie for each are Remayning and with the expence of lesse then 7 or 8 Barrells of powder wee braught downe (May 12th about eleaven of the Clocke) this loftie proud spire, which was the highest and most Comaunding of these three stately Spires which did belong to this Minster which (it is believed) were erected in Resemblance of the Popes triple Crowne, and if soe this downefall may bee ominous and prognostic a further downefall; The effect whereof was almost like that of Sampson pulling downe the House (which did greate execution) at his death; Soe here the fall of this spire did mightie execution as well upon the Chauncell wherein was their .... Service and Organs placed as alsoe on the other side of the Steeple upon that parte of the body of the Minster wherein Pulpitt stood, and those fewe sermons which were made; Into b......... which there was greate breaches as though the Lord were purpose Reckon for that Hypocrisie, prophanesse and Ignorance which hath been therein nourished and practised; This Spire was the greate Ornament of that Grose structure which now looketh very nakedly. It was conceived that this downefall would alsoe humble theire loftie proud spirits in the Close, upon which consideration I sent this second summons herein enclosed, whereunto I received this Answere, whereby you may perceive that they doe still obstinately persist to the further Chardge of the Countrey and to bring upon themselves Certain Destruction.

The Lord direct and guide you in all your greate Transaccons and send you a speedie and blessed Peace, for which noe man desires to bee more thankfull then

Your very faithfull Friend to serve you
Wm. Brereton

Litchfeild May 14th 1646.

252

May the 23: 1646

An abbreviate of the Names of the severall Cap:ts their L:ts and Ensignes with the Number of the other Officers and whole Companies whoe are nowe engaged in the seige against Litchfeild Close, Mustered by Lt: Col. Hunt in Cheshire side the Leauger the day above said.

92 Major Danyell, Lt: Heath, Ensigne Witten, 3 Sergeants 2 Drums, 3 Corporalls, 1 Gentleman of Armes and 92 Comon Soldyers

48 Captaine Booth, 1 Sergeant, 1 Drum, 2 Corporalls and 48 Comon Soldyers

33 Captaine Leadbeater, Lt: Norbury, Ensigne Bennett 1Sergeant, 1 Drum, 2 Corporalls & 35 Comon Soldyers

These twoe make but one company and officers are allowed accordingly

60 Captaine Rathbone, Lt: Browne, Ensigne Wettmough 3 Sergeants, 1 Clarke, 2 Drums, 3 Corporalls & 60 Comon Soldyers

36 Captaine Walley, Lt: Bostocke, Ensigne Bradford, 2 Sergeants 1 Drum, 2 Corporalls & 36 Comon Soldyers

76 Captaine Finch, Lt. Madden, Cornett Sydes, 2 Sergeants 1 Drum, 3 Corporalls & 76 Comon Soldyers

65 Captaine Gimbert, Lt: Turner, Cornett Thomson, Quarter maister Bentley, 12 Sergeants, 1 Drum, 3 Corporalls & 65 Soldyers

52 Captaine Birtles, Ensigne Cartwright, 2 Sergeants, 1 Drum 2 Corporalls, 1 Clarke & 52 Comon Soldyers

69 Captaine Glegg, Lt: Swettneham, Ensigne Ball, 3 SergeantsThese twoe make 1Clarke, 2 Drums, 3 Corporalls & 69 Comon Soldyers

36 Captaine Monke, Lt: Pargiter, 2 Drums, 2 Corporalls and 36 Comon Soldyers

567 The number of Capts: other officers & private Soldyers, Capts: 10, Lts: 8, Ensignes 8, Sergeants 18, Clarkes and Quarterm:ts 4, Drums 14, Corporalls 25, Comon Soldyers 567

Trayned Bands, Besides Col. Croxtons Companye about 140} 270
Lt: Col Gerrards Compan y about 130

837

253

Sr. Wm. Breretons Answere to Col. Bagot

Sr,

Beinge at our Campe when yours of this day came directed to Adjutant Generall Louthiane I have thought good to returne this speedie answere that Colonell Cropton, Lieut. Col. Gerrard and Captaine Stone shall accomodate you meeting to those you advocate at ye place appointed and for yt end shall send this inclosed for yor comeing forth and returne of your comts and Expect from yourself and Sir Tho: Tildesley a passe accordingly for those if Anie above names

Your Servant
W. Brereton

ffrom or Campe on
Bacon Hill
May 28 1646

254

Sr. Wm. Breretons passe inclosed
in ye ltre

These are to require and comand you upon sight hereof to permitt the Lord Aston, Sr. Rich. Diot and for John Drake this day to come forth of ye Close and to meete at ye old workes between our Mounte and ye Close and to Treate with Colonell Cropton, Lt. Colonell Gerrard and Captaine Stone according to Instruccions and to returne thereunto into ye Close without violence or molestacon. Given at our Camp on Bacon hill the 28 of May 1646

Wm Brereton

To all Cols. And other officers & Souldiers
In the leauger for ye Parlts Service. To
Whom this may come.

255

Monie Borrowede by Sir Wm. Brereton
for ye Service of ye forces of Chesh. At
ye leauger at Litchfield that are not
otherwise provided for wch bonds
were given

300Ls Mar. 12 1646 Sr Wm Brereton borrowed of Mrs Sarah Wentworth of Coventry three hundreth pounds and gave bond in himselfe

256

Letter from Sr. Thomas Tyldesley
To Sr. Wm. Brereton touching the
Women sent into the Close

Sr,

Your last nights nightworke (which might well bee ashamed of the light) is an Act soe much Barbaritie, soe remote from nature, Lawes, Christianitie, and soe dangerous to your Soules, That we Cannot suffer you to sleepe in it another, and pray you may not harden your hearts to consumate it; for our parts wee are secure that neither the blood of those Innocents (if shed) can bee layd to our Chardge, nor dare wee faile to lett you understand to whom it must bee imputed.

You have turned out of their habitations sundry poore Women and their Innocent Children (whom you should Rather have Releived) upon us, that are now freed from all obligations to Receive the Harbourlesse, or feede the hungrey.

It is not unsuspected alsoe that Gods visiting hand is upon them (which if being true) their Howses are fittest for them as is by lawe appointed, and wee have noe better Warrant to entertaine them, then to bee desperate & tempt God.

Our Resolution is neither to Receive these, nor any other you are unchristianly Resolved to expose to Death. Wee are all absolved from the duety, and all sinne that may growe by the neglect of it, and advise you to thinke upon it seriouslie with a beleife of a tyme when God will make Inquisition for blood, And soe wee Recommend them to your Reception, or other disposall upon more Christian thought. And wee further wish you to thinke of the visited of sublunary affaires, and that your partie may bee Capable; For though wee will not Menace to bee your Imitators in soe bad an example & yett wee will not for our better discharge omitt to tell you, that there has been knowne many an Adonibezech in the World, and the Just God hath his wonderfull just Retaliations, and soe having done our duty both to the miserable exposed, and your Soules, Wee pray God to keepe you from soe Merciles, unreasonable and Wilfull a wretchednesse as you are Acting upon these Innocent Women, whoe (upon our engagements as wee are Gentlemen and Soldgers) have not done anything this Seige prejudiciall to your Cause by Intelligence or otherwise that wee knowe of, if this may not satisfie you we shall send twoe or three Gentlemen to meete the like number of yours to discusse the businesse by word of mouth, least this extreamitie should bee occasioned by some mistake. In the meane tyme Remayning

Your Servants

Thomas Tyldesley
Her. Bagot

Lich. Close
28th May 1646

257

Lt: Col. Gerard his answere thereunto in
ye absence of the Generall

Gentlemen,

In the absence of my Superior Comaunders I have perused yours of this day directed to my Generall Comaunder in Cheife of this Leauger which is full of bombast language of one of you, much like a wilde bull in a nett, and (according to your accustomed manner) grosely abusing the sacred Word of God, by which you and all your Complices must one day bee judged. And for soe much of your paper as is worthie to bee Considered of, I returne you this Answere. That if you so farre wish ye welfare of your selves and those deluded Persons with you as to Certifie mee that you desire to send two or three Gentlemen to meete the like number of ours for the surrender of Lichfeild Close and the submission of your selves and those with you to the Justice of the Parliament. I shall then Recommend your desires of that nature (if it bee not too late) unto my Generall, and bee Ready to doe you and all with you any friendlie office therein, otherwise I shall Rather suppresse your follie (in thinking wee will receive your friends backe into our Quarters, or Retaine those not yett sent in to you) then answere your expectacon in the least measure more then to assure you that I am and will bee

Your daylie Watchman
in this Leauger
G. Gerard

May 28: 1646

258

Petition to Sr. Wm. B: and Adjutant Gener:ll Louthian
By the women which were sent into the Close

To his Excellencie Sr. Wm. Brereton Barron:tt and Major Adjutant Louthian.
The humble Petition of the Miserable unfortunate Women of Lich. Whose Names are Subscribed.

That by Reason of your strict Comaund last night given to thrust us out of our Habitations upon the Garrison of the Close of Litch. And the vyolant Carriage of your Soldyers to the great endangering of our Lives. Wee are enforced to Lodge in the Cold open Ayre, and there likelie to perish for want of Releife to sustaine nature which all the Garrison absolutely denying us either admittance, sustenance or other necessaries to defend us from the Cold or hunger whereby some of us are already much endangeed in our healthes and are likely to come to some untimely and miserable end if not otherwise Remedyed and helped.

May it therefore please you out of your Christian Charitie to give us (Relying only upon your mercie) leave to Repaire into the countrey to prevent our perishing for lacke of food and lodging, that soe our Innocent blood may not untimely bee taken away by this lingring kind of death and most grieving suffering

And wee shall ever pray for your
health and happinesse

Ursula Hill
Anne Pyddocke   Katherine Burbry
Anne Cowsie   Frances Sate
Elizabeth Baker   Elizabeth Stubes
Judith Ballard

259

Adjt. Louthiane, his Answere to the foregoing
Petition

Gentlewomen,

If your Husbands and their Comaunders in Cheife will not shewe you Mercie, you must know the greatest Mercie yt can be shewed from us is to execute Justice upon you and all your Complices which you shall find if you presume to come within viewe of our line, and they Continue in theire Rebellion and obstinacie; Only this for your Comfort that the Lady Bagot, Mrs Snead, Mrs Scrimshawe and Mrs Archibald with many more of your sex and opinion soe soone as they can bee apprehended shall bee sent unto you for your Consorts by

Your Servant
James Lothian[35]

I hope you will bee as dere to your
husbands as Mrs East was to hers, and as
Mrs Ward is to the Governors whoe would
not suffer her to come forth to live with
her husband being one your owne Partie
and late Comissarie at Tutbury, but after
conference had with him Caused her to bee

guarded backe by twoe Captaines into the
Close.

Lady Bagots letter to Sr. Wm. B: or in his
Absence ye next Com:der in Cheife.

Sr,

All the favour I can gett of the Close is this, to gett a Drumer to come to begg the favour from you that I may safe come to you my selfe with a Drum to acquaint you with what Answere I Received from them.

Your Servant
Arden Bagot

28th of May.

Adjt: Louthiane his answere thereunto
In absence of the Generall

Lady,

Your Answere I desire not, you must remayne where you are till those within the Close submitt themselves to the Justice of the Parliament, yet if there bee a desire to meete upon a Treatie with three Gentlemen on either Partie, I will upon the Receipt of the names of such as Colonell Bagot shall nominate, send them safe passe, and the names of such as my Gener:ll will send to meete them, If I Receive the like from Col. Bagot; And this never the sooner for Sr. Thomas Tyldesleys false Rumors shott forth of the Close yester night upon an Arrowe, I have noe more Madam, but that I am,

Your Servant
James Louthiane

May 28: 1646.

Here this Letter Book ends

Conclusion

As Fairfax rode back to the siege of Oxford, the King and two companions, his chaplain and his Groom of the Bedchamber, departed the city. For a week there was nothing. No one knew where the King was. Then on 6th May 1646, the House of Commons learned in a letter from their army besieging Newark, that the King had given himself up to the Scottish besiegers there. The Commons became anxious as to what the Scots might then do. They requested that the King be handed over to the custody of the Parliamentary garrison at Warwick. As they waited a reply, word reached them that the Royalist garrison at Newark had surrendered to the Scots upon the orders of the King. The Scots, their mission now completed, then left Newark and marched north with their "prisoner." In London, the Committee of Both Kingdoms, the Scottish members largely side-lined, feared that the King would make a deal with the Scots to continue the war. As the Covenanters reached Newcastle-upon-Tyne, a Parliamentary messenger with a letter of protest caught up with them. The Scots defended themselves in that they were unaware that the king was coming to them. But now, as the King was in their power, the Scots sought what was in their national interest, the establishment and recognition of the Presbyterian church. The priority for the English, if they could exercise any influence over the Scots, was to curtail the King's military power as a means of preventing his re-establishing his authority. As a gesture of good faith to the English, the King ordered the garrison of Oxford to surrender. But Charles was a duplicitous man, prepared to compromise himself in order to retain power. He adopted a policy of divide and rule amongst the English and Scots, playing for time, while negotiating to bring over an Irish army to link up with Montrose, and thus continue the war. The allies, while not completely trusting each other, knew that they must reach an agreement acceptable to both nations. Talks between them began. The King, still at Newcastle, ordered the surrender of his last garrison at Worcester as a further gesture of goodwill. From Jersey, on the 25th June 1646, the Prince of Wales sailed into exile in France; and by thus doing kept alive the potential of further war.

On 30th July, the Commissioners from Parliament reached Newcastle, there to discuss terms with the King. The Scots put pressure on the King that if he refused the terms offered, then the English would depose him and set up another government. If that were so, then he could not reign as King in

THE
CONFESSION
OF
Richard Brandon

The Hangman (upon his Death bed) concerning His beheading his late Majeſty, CHARLES the firſt, King of Great Brittain; and his Proteſtation and Vow touching the ſame; the manner how he was terrified in Conſcience; the Apparitions and Viſions which apeared unto him; the great judgment that befell him three dayes before he dy'd; and the manner how he was carryed to White-Chappell Church-yard on Thurſday night laſt, the ſtrange Actions that happened thereupon; With the merry conceits of the Crowne Cook and his providing mourning Cords for the Buriall.

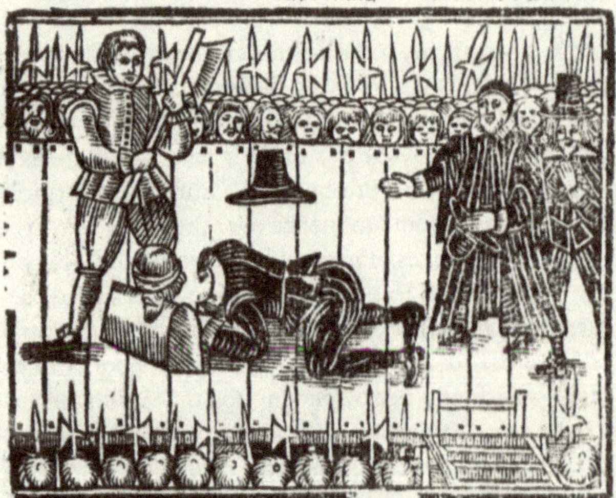

Printed in the year Year, of the Hang-mans down-fall, 1649.

The execution of Charles I from a contemporary booklet.

Scotland. Already there was talk in London that the King would be replaced by the Duke of Gloucester, his six-year-old son, or by a republican government. The King however was fully aware that in London there were growing tensions between the Independents and the Presbyterians. Could they form a new government without him? With the war ended though, Cromwell reassumed his Parliamentary duties, and became the figurehead for the Independents. He also retained leadership in the New Model Army. Cromwell had become an important man. In the autumn of 1646 the Scots proposed to sell the king to the English for the amount of back pay owed to their soldiers, on the proviso that any agreement would ensure the King's honor and safety. While the Committee of both Kingdoms agreed to this, the Commons in Parliament declared that the King should be disposed of as both Houses of Parliament thought fit. On Christmas Eve, 24th December, the King attempted to escape, but was immediately recaptured. On 2nd January 1647 the Commissioners from Parliament arrived at Newcastle, led by the Earls of Northumberland and Pembroke. The King agreed to go with them to take up residence at Holmby House, a country mansion in Northamptonshire.

In the months that followed tensions grew between Parliament and the New Model Army. Parliament attempted to send the army to Ireland to crush the rebellion. The army mutinied, refusing to go until they had received their back pay. Charles sought to gain advantage by playing one side off against the other. In the end the army seized the King, and placed him under their jurisdiction, in Carisbroke Castle on the Isle of Wight. In 1648 there followed a series of disparate risings in support of the King. These risings are now known collectively as the Second Civil War. The Covenanting Scots invaded England but were decisively beaten at Preston on 17th August by the New Model Army commanded by Oliver Cromwell and General Lambert. In late August Colchester, the last of the Royalist centers of support, surrendered to Sir Thomas Fairfax after a decisive and bloody siege. In Parliament the Independents were in agreement that as long as the King lived there would be rebellions. He was brought to London, and on 1st January 1649, was put on trial for levying war against his people. While the King refused to accept the authority of the court, proceedings against him continued. On 27th January Charles was condemned to death as a "tyrant and a traitor who had shed the blood of his own people." Three days later he was beheaded on a scaffold erected outside of the Banqueting House in Whitehall.

The Prince of Wales now became Charles II. Exiled in Holland he made plans to continue the war by invading England by way of Ireland; but Cromwell ruthlessly put down all opposition in Ireland during 1649–50. Charles then turned for support to the Scots, who demanded what they had from his father, a Presbyterian state. Charles agreed, and the Scots raised an army with the intention of invading England on his behalf. After a series of forced marches the New Model Army invaded Scotland and decisively, and with equal ruthlessness, defeated the Scots at the Battle of Dunbar on 3rd September 1650. Charles, now in Scotland, had himself crowned King at Scone on 1st January 1651. He raised another army and invaded England, reaching as far south as Worcester, the city that had been so loyal to his father. Cromwell marched to meet him, and on 3rd September destroyed the Royalist army. Charles fled the field and eventually escaped back to the Continent.

In Parliament Cromwell became exasperated at the excesses of the ruling body and their intolerance in religious matters. He seized power, and in 1653 became Lord Protector—King in all but name. It was a Protectorate based on military power. The country was divided up into areas controlled by military commanders. As a politician Cromwell was surprisingly moderate in his views, given his previous history. He preferred stability and supported the established order.

At the conclusion of the war Parliament rewarded her champions. Sir William Brereton was given a London residence, the archiepiscopal palace of Croyden, in order to carry out his duties in the Capital. In the administration of the country Brereton was appointed to the Council of State, overseeing both civil and military matters. Within his home county of Cheshire he was appointed Chief Forester of Macclesfied Forest and Seneschal of the Hundred of Macclesfield. In February 1651 the Calendar of State Papers reveal that he was active in the accessing and provision of timber for the navy. Reflecting his love of books he also administered the pictures and library of St. James' Palace. Brereton also supervised the removal of religious ministers who refused to acknowledge the supremacy of the Parliamentary Government, from garrison towns.

In 1651 following Prince Charles' abortive attempt at regaining the throne, Brereton was appointed to the Ordinance Committee, charged with re-equipping the trains of artillery. He was also given responsibility for the commissioning of officers for the Regiment of Dragoons. In September, following the defeat of Prince Charles' Royalist army at Worcester, Brereton was put in charge of the disposal of the Scottish prisoners. Many were sent off to the West Indies as slaves.

Under Oliver Cromwell's Protectorate Brereton became Militia Commissioner for Cheshire, and later Surrey, ensuring that the local militias were trained and armed. Harking back to his time as a soldier, in September 1655, he answered the petition of the widow of Captain Thomas Grant, who had served under him, and who had lost his life at the Battle of Rowton Heath. Grant, who came from County Cavan in Ireland, had also fought under the Earl of Essex, and was wounded at Edgehill. His widow Elizabeth requested

£528 due to him in unpaid salary. Brereton endorsed her request and forwarded it on for payment.

Cromwell died on 3rd September 1658. He was succeeded as Protector by his son Richard. Richard was a weaker man, and found himself unable to control the conflicting surge of Puritanism, Royalism and anarchy that broke out. He abdicated in May 1659, and spent the rest of his days in obscurity. Into the power vacuum strode George Monk, Commander in Chief in Scotland. He had originally been a Royalist. Monk was captured at the Battle of Nantwich in 1644, and after briefly being held prisoner, was released on license. As a professional soldier, having fought in the Thirty Years War on the Continent, Parliament sought his service, but Monk, being an honorable man refused as he had sworn an oath of loyalty to the King. Following the beheading of Charles I Cromwell persuaded him to join the New Model Army, and under Cromwell's Protectorate Monk rose to high rank. Now he marched south in late 1659, ostensibly to restore order in England. He formed an alliance with the more moderate elements in the city of London and those few Members of the House of Commons who had sat in the Long Parliament. In the great uncertainty that followed, in the spring of 1660, Charles II opened negotiations for his return as King. He issued his Declaration of Breda, a manifesto of moderation in religious and political matters in his defense. The country needed a head of government and following the declaration, the Convention of Parliament as it was then called, issued an invitation to Charles to return as King.

With the prospect of the Restoration of the Monarchy close at hand, Brereton removed from his state residence into shared lodgings at Whitehall. Brereton survived the Restoration, and died peacefully in his bed in his fifty-seventh year, on 7th April 1661. His body was taken north for burial in the family chapel at Handforth in Cheadle. On the way though, while the carriers were attempting to cross a river in flood, the coffin was swept away and never recovered.

Chapter Notes

Introduction

1. The ambiguity of the year is because in seventeenth century England the start of the year began on 25 March rather than 1 January. The date has to do with the conception of Jesus Christ, giving him nine months exactly before birth. So the date 1642–3 covers the first three months of 1643; 1643–44 covers the first three months of 1644; and so on.

Chapter 1

1. The Ottley Papers, Shropshire Archaeological Society, Vol. VIII, 1895, p. 277.
2. Clarendon, *History of the Rebellion*, 1843, p. 348.
3. Thomason Tracts (hereafter T.T.) E75 (9).
4. T.T. E10 (4).
5. A True Relation...T.T. E7 (25).
6. Vicars, God's Ark...p. 84.
7. Calendar of State Papers Domestic (hereafter C.S.P.D.) 18 Jan. 1644–5. N.B. in the 17 century the new year began on 25 March. So, the 18 Jan. 1644–5 above, is in reality the 18 Jan. 1645.
8. Shrewsbury taken...T.T. E270 (26).
9. Letters from Sir William Brereton...T.T. E10 (4).
10. Brereton Letter Book B.M. Add. Ms. 1131, fol. 145.
11. Oxford Historical Society, Vol. LV, and Transactions of the Lancashire & Cheshire Antiquarian Society, Vol. LXIII.
12. Clarendon, p. 350.
13. Trans. Lancs. & Cheshire Antiquarian Soc. Vol. LXIII.
14. Chetham Society, Vol. I.
15. Civil War in Lancashire and Cheshire, Chetham Papers, Vol. 2.
16. Clarendon, p. 348.
17. God in the Mount, p. 260.
18. C.S.P.D., 1643–4, p. 26.
19. Letter to the House of Commons, Saturday, 4 March 1642–3. Birmingham Public Libraries Civil War Collection (hereafter BPL).
20. Warburton, *Elliot, Prince Rupert and the Cavaliers*, Vol. 2, p. 132.
21. Letter to the House of Commons...
22. Ibid.
23. The Letter to the House of Commons states that Lord Brooke was shot through the eye, while a Royalist letter from James Audeley to Lady Dyer (11 March) refers to Brooke being shot through the mouth.

24. Lord Brooke's Regiment with a list of the officers is given in a Parliamentary tract of 1642 entitled The List of the Army Raised under the command of his Excellency, Robert Earle of Essex...T.T. E117(3). Brooke's "Purple Coats" were theoretically 1,200 strong, plus officers. The Regiment was at the battle of Edgehill where it suffered heavy losses. Captain Thomas Fox who was sent to Sir John Gell, was probably commissioned into the regiment after the battle. In addition Brooke's army was reinforced from the garrisons of Warwick and Coventry.

25. Captain Thomas Fox.

26. A True Account of the raysing and imployeing of one foote regiment under Sir John Gell, from the beginning of October 1642, untill the middle of February 1643. BPL.

27. A Perfect Diurnall of some Passages in Parliament, March 1643. BPL.

28. Sutherland Papers Vol. 2, fol. 69. The Dunrobin MSS. Staffs Record Soc. 1936.

29. Special Passages in Parliament, 21–28 March 1643. BPL.

30. A Letter from Sir William Brereton, quoted in Stebbing Shaw's *History of Staffordshire*, Vol. 1.

31. A Relation of the Military Service of Sir John Gell. BPL.

32. Dunrobin MSS.

33. This disposition is based on the reference that the Royalist canon on its "first shott killed six of their men and hurt four."

34. Mercurius Aulicus. BPL.

35. Dunrobin MSS. The distance would be about 400 yards.

36. Shaw, Vol. 1, Brereton Letter.

37. Dunrobin MSS.

38. Brereton Letter. "These came on with great resolution and boldnes, and in very good order. Some say there were six score, others judge there were 200 in front when they came up and charged our horse."

39. Gell.

40. Dunrobin MSS.

41. Clarendon, *History of the Rebellion and Civil Wars in England.*

42. Dunrobin MSS.

43. Gell.

44. Dunrobin MSS.

45. Ibid.

46. Ibid.

47. See Introduction Note 7.

48. There are two versions of this skirmish at Warrington. The Royalist version appears in Mercurius Aulicus, 1643, p. 179, and the Parliamentarian, Providence Improved, 1643, p. 116. Though each is a biased account, the basic narrative is as written.

49. Stebbing Shaw, *The History and Antiquities of Staffordshire*, Vol. 1, p. 53. Shaw quotes from the now missing "2nd book...endinge in Julie 17, 1643," formerly in the possession of J. Wright of Stafford, in 1795.

50. Providence Improved, p. 117.

51. No. 51, 29 May–5 June.

52. Vicars, God's Ark over-topping the World's Waves, p. 18. BPL.

53. God in the Mount, p. 411. BPL.

54. A Perfect Diurnall of some Passages in Parliament, 7 Sept. 1643, No. 8.

55. God's Ark, p. 63.

56. A True Relation of a Great Victory obtained by the Parliament's Forces against the Cavaliers neere Chester, 17 and 18 October 1643. T.T. E7 (7). It would appear that Mytton was probably using the seventeenth century equivalent of shrapnel in his small canons.

57. Clarendon (1826 edit.) Vol. IV, p. 427.

58. Denbigh MSS, Ottley Papers, Salop Arch. Soc. Trans. Vol. VIII (Second Series).

59. C.S.P.D., 1644, p. 322.

60. A True Relation of Two Great Victories obtained of the Enemy, August 30, 1644. T.T. E7 (25).

61. Burning Bush Not Consumed, p. 16.

62. Ottley Papers.

63. C.S.P.D., 14 Sept. 1644, p. 457.
64. Perfect Diurnall, Sept. 9–16 1644.
65. C.S.P.D., 14 Sept. 1644, p. 458.
66. Letters from Sir William Brereton, Sir Thomas Middleton, Sir John Meldrum of the great Victory (by God's providence) given them, in raising the siege from before Mountgomery castle, 24 Sept. 1644. T.T. E10 (4)
67. Ibid.
68. C.S.P.D., 2 Oct. 1644, p. 5.
69. Wedgwood, C. V., The King's War 1641–1647, p. 279.
70. Perfect Diurnall, No. 67, 4–11 Nov. 1644.
71. C.S.P.D., 15 Nov. 1644, p. 126.
72. C.S.P.D., 18 Jan. 1645, p. 259–60. The skirmish before Chester is also recorded in Burning Bush, pp. 97–8.
73. Harleian MS. 2125.
74. Shrewsbury taken, a copie of Sir William Brereton's letter to the Parliament. T.T. E270 (26).
75. Shrewsbury taken...
76. C.S.P.D., 16 March 1645–6.
77. Ibid., 17 March 1645–6.
78. C.S.P.D., 1644–5, p. 435.
79. Ibid., p. 365.
80. Brereton Letter Book, B.M. Add. MSS 11331 folio 5.
81. C.S.P.D., 1645, p. 402.
82. Ibid., p. 471.
83. Brereton Add MSS 11331 folios 78, 81–4 and 92–5.
84. C.S.P.D., 1645 p. 402.
85. Brereton Add MSS 11331 folio 145.
87. A Great Fight at Newarke...BPL.
88. C.S.P.D., 1645–6 p. 369.
89. A True Relation by Colonel Morgan...T.T. E329 (8).
90. This and the following correspondence are taken from the Diary of Henry Townsend, edited by J. Willis Bund, and published as Worcs. Hist. Soc. Vols. 31–2, 1915–20.
91. Ibid. p. 102.

Chapter 2

1. Severall Occurences that have lately happened...Worcs. Record Office 899:31 BA36691/1 (VIII).
2. Diary of Henry Townsend, Worcs. Hist. Soc., Vols. 31–2, 1915–17.
3. Staffs. Record Office D260/M/F/1/6f.8.
4. Rushworth's Parliamentary Chronicles, Vol. 6, p. 276.

Chapter 3

1. The surname has been struck through, making it illegible.
2. Left blank for later insertion of a name.
3. Sydenham Poyntz, born at Reigate, Surrey in 1607, was apprenticed to a London draper, but ran away to become a soldier in the Netherlands. He fought under Count Mansfield and was present at the battle of Breitenfeld in 1631. Changing sides he fought at the battles of Lutzen and Nordligen under Count Wallenstein. Poyntz returned to England c. 1644, and took service in Parliament's army. He was appointed commander of the Northern Association army in May 1645. He defeated the king's cavalry at Rowton Heath near Chester in September 1645, and

under Lord Leven took part in the siege of Newark in November 1645. In the debates between Parliament and the army in 1647, Presbyterian Members of Parliament looked to him for support against the Independents in the New Model Army. He was suspected of plotting to ally the Northern Army with the Scots, and was replaced as its commander. In London he raised the militia against the Independents, but was forced to flee the country with the arrival of the New Model Army. During the Second Civil War Poyntz supported the King in his alliance with the Scots, and was commissioned Major-General. Following the defeat of the Royalists at Preston, Poyntz sailed to the West Indies with the Presbyterian, Lord Willoughby of Parham, where they declared for the King in the colonies. Parliament sent a force under General-at-Sea, George Ayscue, and the rebellion was put down. Willoughby returned to England, but Poyntz disappeared, allegedly fleeing to Virginia.

4. Edward Montagu (1625–72) was the eldest son of Sir Sydney Montagu, and cousin of Edward Montagu, Earl of Manchester. With the outbreak of war he supported Parliament, and was appointed a colonel in the Eastern Association army, under his cousin. He took part in the storming of Hillesdon House in March 1644, and the capture of Lincoln in May. He was at the siege of York, and fought at Marston Moor and second Newbury. In 1645 Montagu's regiment was absorbed into the New Model Army. He took part in the battle of Naseby and the storming of Bristol. Under the Self Denying Ordnance, he being M.P. for Huntingdonshire, he was stripped of military command. In 1648, following Pride's Purge, he withdrew from Parliament. He was elected to the "Barebones Parliament" of 1653, which surrendered its powers to Cromwell. Under the Protectorate Montagu was elected to the Council of State, and acted as a diplomat. In 1656, despite any previous naval experience, he was appointed joint General-at-Sea with Robert Blake, in an expedition against Spain. In 1657 Montagu was in the faction that offered Cromwell the crown. As a loyal supporter, Cromwell appointed him to the Upper House. He was also appointed to the Privy Council. In his role as General-at-Sea he commanded the fleet in the joint Anglo-French attacks on Mardyke and Dunkirk. Following the capture of Dunkirk in June 1658 he was presented to the French King, Louis XIV. In March 1659 Montagu commanded the fleet sent to the Baltic during the war between Sweden and Denmark. Following the collapse of the Protectorate, with Cromwell's death, General Monck occupied London, and Montagu was dispatched to Scheviningen in the Netherlands, to convey Charles II back to England. As a reward he was made a Knight of the Garter and created first Earl of Sandwich. Montagu died aboard his flagship, the Royal James, at the battle of Solebay, during the Third Dutch War, in May 1672.

5. John Belasyse (1615–89) the son of Thomas Belasyse, first Viscount Fauconberg of Henknowle, was born at Newburgh, in the North Riding of Yorkshire. He was brought up a Roman Catholic, and spent much of his early life in France. He served in the King's Lifeguard in the Bishops' War of 1639–40, and was thereafter elected M.P. for Thirsk. At the outbreak of the war Belasyse accompanied the King and commanded an infantry regiment at the battle of Edghill (October 1642). He took part in Prince Rupert's storming of Bristol, and fought at the battle of Newbury. In January 1644 he was appointed Governor of York. Following an unsuccessful campaign against Lord Fairfax's Parliamentary army, he was captured at Selby, and imprisoned in the Tower of London until January 1645. He was released in an exchange of prisoners, and the King created him Baron Belasyse of Worlaby. Belasyse fought at Naseby, was appointed commander of the King's Lifeguard, and in October 1645 was appointed Governor of Newark, in place of Sir Richard Willis. From November 1645 to May 1646, Belasyse defended his charge against a combined Parliamentary and Scottish army, until ordered to surrender by the King. His next two years were spent in exile on the Continent. He served under the Prince of Conde at the siege of Mardyke. Returning to England he was arrested on suspicion of attempting to raise a Royalist army against Parliament. Released, he was arrested once more in 1659 because of his involvement in Booth's Uprising, betrayed by Sir Richard Willis, whom he had replaced as Governor of Newark. After the Restoration Belasyse was appointed Lord-Lieutenant of the East Riding of Yorkshire, and Governor of Hull. He also served as Governor of Tangier from 1665 to 1666. He was forced to resign all offices due to his Catholicism, following the Test Acts of 1673. Belasyse was imprisoned in the Tower from 1678 to 1684 on suspicion of involvement in the Popish Plot. He was eventually cleared of all charges in May 1685, and served as First Lord of the Treasury under James II. Belasyse died at Whitton, Middlesex, in September 1689.

6. Thomas Tyldesley (1596–1651) was born at Morleys Hall, Astley, in the parish of Leigh, Lancashire, the son of Edward Tyldesley. He became a soldier, and served in Germany during the Thirty Years War. Returning home he raised regiments of horse, foot and dragoons, for the King, and fought with distinction at the battle of Edghill. He was involved in the storming of Burton-on-Trent, rewarded with a knighthood, and made a brigadier. Tyldesley commanded under the Earl of Derby at the successful siege of Bolton, and in 1645 was appointed Governor of Litchfield. He surrendered Lichfield Close in obedience to the King's royal warrant on 10 July 1646. In 1648 he was given command of a division in the Royalist army besieging Lancaster. The siege was lifted by the approach of a Parliamentary army, who brought the Royalists to battle just outside of Preston, totally defeating them on 17 August 1648. Captured, Tyldesley was obliged to go beyond the seas within six months. He went to Ireland, then to the Isle of Man, where under the Earl of Derby, he took part in Charles II's unsuccessful campaign of 1650–51, to regain the throne. At Wigan Lane in Lancashire, on 25 August 1651, Derby's small army was confronted by a Parliamentary army under Colonel Robert Lilburne. In the ensuing skirmish Tyldesley was killed.

7. Thomas Leveson, Governor of Dudley Castle. His name also appears as Lewison, and Lusen. He was the son of Sir Walter Leveson, a Roman Catholic, and prosperous merchant in Wolverhampton. The family made their money in the wool trade, then diversified into industry. They owned land at Cheslyn Hay, and in 1636, having succeeded his father, Thomas Leveson received permission to mine for coal and lead. At the outbreak of the Civil War Leveson, assisted by his workforce of local miners and nailers, seized Dudley Castle for the King. At Christmas 1643, Leveson supplied Sir Thomas Holte of Aston Hall, with troops, after fears that Parliamentary supporters in Birmingham, assisted by soldiers from Coventry would seize the house as a garrison. After a short but bloody siege, Leveson's men were forced to surrender. From his base at Dudley, Leveson raided several local towns, including Birmingham, where in one raid he drove off 300 head of cattle. In March 1644 Leveson supplied 100 horse and 200 foot for the relief of Newark. After his surrendering of Dudley Castle, Leveson went into exile at Bordeaux, in France. He came under the patronage of the Prince Conti, who gave him two thousand livre for entertaining. Leveson died on 8 September 1652, and was buried in the church of St. Purgett. He left behind him furniture and two horses, which were sold to pay his funeral expenses.

8. John Swinfen (1612–94), was born at Swinfen near Lichfield, the son of Richard Swinfen. He was elected Member of Parliament for Stafford in 1640. At the outbreak of the war he sided with Parliament. In 1645 he was appointed Commissioner for Compounding in Staffordshire. He also served on the committee for the ejection of "ignorant and scandalous ministers." Like Brereton he leaned towards the Presbyterians, and fell out with the Independents, for which he was excluded from Parliament by Pride's Purge in 1648. He was elected M.P. for Tamworth in 1659, but was not allowed to take his seat. Following Monck's temporary seizure of power prior to the Restoration, Swinfen was returned as M.P. for Stafford, and took his seat in Parliament. He was re-elected M.P. for Tamworth, and sat in Charles II's first Parliament from 1661 to 1678. Swinfen remained in politics until his death on 12 April 1694.

9. Stow-on-the-Wold battle, 21 March 1646. At the opening of 1646 King Charles ordered Jacob, Lord Astley, Lieutenant-General of the Royalist forces in the west and the Marches, to draw out as many men as could be spared from his garrisons to form an army, which was ordered to link up with the King at Oxford. Royalist plans fell into Parliamentary hands, and Colonel John Birch, Parliamentary Governor of Hereford, was ordered to rendezvous with Colonel Thomas Morgan, Governor of Gloucester, at Evesham. The combined force, approximately 2,300 men, then prepared to intercept Lord Astley. Sir William Brereton, Major-General of Cheshire, Staffordshire and Lancashire, was ordered south from Lichfield to take command of the Parliamentary army. He set out with 1,000 horsemen. Astley meanwhile crossed the Avon at Bidford, shadowed by the Parliamentary army of Morgan and Birch. By 9 P.M. on 20 March, Astley was at Broadway. Between 1 and 2 A.M. on the morning of 21, Brereton with 800 of his 1,000 horse joined with Morgan and Birch. It was agreed that Morgan should command the Parliamentary army and attack Astley's force in the rear as they approached Stow. As Morgan's skirmishers located Astley's force, they discovered that they were drawn up in battle array on high ground, about half a mile west of the village of Donnington. As daylight broke the Parliamentary force attacked. The left wing of the Parliamentary army was checked, and driven back,

but the right wing under Brereton totally routed and drove off the Royalist left. Now without cavalry support, the Royalists were driven back towards Stow. Morgan meanwhile rallied the left wing, who rejoined the battle. The Royalists were now totally routed, and withdrew up the hill into Stow, where the killing continued. Some 200 Royalists were slain in the village itself before Astley surrendered. All the Royalist officers of foot were captured, including Sir Charles Lucas, as were 1,700 common soldiers. These were rounded up by Colonel Fleetwood and his force of 1,000 horse, who arrived shortly after hostilities had ceased. With his last army in the field defeated, the King slipped out of Oxford on 27 April 1646, and surrendered to the Scots at Newark.

10. Anthony Booth of Cheshire, a maternal relative of Sir William Brereton.

11. George Booth (1622–84), nephew of Sir William Brereton. He was the second son of William Booth of Dunham Massey, and like Brereton was brought up by his grandfather, Sir George Booth. He attended the Inner Temple in 1637, but fled to France in 1639 after quarrelling with his grandfather over his marriage to Catherine Clinton, daughter of the Earl of Lincoln. After Catherine's death in 1643, Booth married Elizabeth Grey, daughter of the Earl of Stamford. Booth had returned to England with the approach of Civil War and became a leading supporter of Parliament in Cheshire. He took up a commission and fought at the siege of Chester in 1645. He was elected M.P. for Cheshire in 1646, but was excluded from sitting in 1648 following Pride's Purge. In 1654 Booth was elected to the First Protectorate Parliament, and in March 1655 was appointed a commissioner to assist the Major-Generals in Cheshire. He was elected to the third Protectorate Parliament of 1659 and that of the "Purged Parliament" of May 1659. He worked hard for the restitution of the former Presbyterian M.P.s expelled in Pride's Purge, but failing, became involved in the restoration of the monarchy. In the summer of 1659 Booth led an insurrection in the north, and succeeded in seizing Chester. The rebellion was short-lived, the insurrectionists were defeated by Major-General Lambert's army at Winnington Bridge on 19 August. Booth was captured and imprisoned in the Tower of London. He was later released on bail by General Monck, and subsequently was elected to the Convention Parliament which invited Charles II to return as king. Following the Restoration Booth was created Lord Delamere. He died in August 1684.

12. For Skefingham read Skeffington. Sir Richard Skeffington of Coventry was the son of Sir William Skeffington, and brother-in-law of both Brereton and Michael Biddulph, M.P. for Lichfield. He was a member of the Committee of Both Kingdoms and was himself elected to Parliament as M.P. for Staffordshire in 1646–7.

13. Spencer Compton, 2nd Earl of Northampton (1601–43). He was knighted in 1616, and granted the title of Lord Compton when his father, Sir William Compton, was elevated to the peerage as the first Earl of Northampton. The younger Compton married Mary Beaumont, a cousin of the Duke of Buckingham, and accompanied Prince Charles (later Charles I) to Madrid in 1623 in an attempt to arrange a royal marriage with the King of Spain's sister. He became a close and personal friend of the future king. Upon the death of his father in 1630, Compton succeeded to the title as second Earl of Northampton. During the Thirty Years War, Compton served under George Goring, fighting for the Elector Palatine. He was present at the battle of Vlotho in 1638. Returning home, he raised troops for the King in the Bishops' War of 1639–40. At the outbreak of the English Civil War the King appointed him Commissioner of Array for the counties of Warwick, Northampton and Gloucester. Northampton fought at Edghill in October 1642, and later captured Banbury for the King. After the capture of the Royalist garrison of Lichfield by Sir John Gell, in March 1643, he joined forces with Henry Hastings to prevent Gell and Brereton from capturing Stafford. At the ensuing battle of Hopton Heath he was killed by a blow to the head. He was buried at All Hallows Church, Derby, but was subsequently later reburied at the Northampton's ancestral home at Compton Wynyates in Warwickshire.

14. Michael Jones, son of Dr. Lewis Jones, Bishop of Killaloe, Ireland, was a student at Lincoln's Inn at the outbreak of the civil war. Returning home he took service in the King's army. With the cessation of hostilities in 1643, by now holding extreme Protestant views, he traveled to England and joined Parliament's cause. Jones distinguished himself as a very capable cavalry leader. He took part in the defeats of the Royalists at Tarvin, Malpas, and the repulse of Lord Byron before Beeston Castle. In September 1645 he assisted Poyntz at the victorious battle of Rowton Heath. In November of that year with Colonel Mytton, he defeated at Denbigh, the

troops sent by Sir William Vaughan to relieve Chester. The following month he routed another relieving force, capturing its commander, Sir William Byron. Upon the surrender of Chester Jones was appointed its Parliamentary Governor. In 1647 he returned to Ireland as commander in chief to put down a rebellion. He defeated General Preston at Dungan Hill, in August, routing his horse, destroying his infantry and capturing all his artillery and baggage. More than 2,000 officers were captured, and over 3,000 of the enemy were killed. Lack of money prevented Jones from completing the task of subduing the Irish. In 1649, Lord Ormonde, the Irish leader went on the offensive. He captured the English garrisons of Drogheda and Dundalk, and on 19 June laid siege to Dublin. In July 1,600 foot and 600 horse arrived from England to raise the siege. On 2 August Jones counter-attacked and fell on Ormonde's camp at Rathmines, capturing 1,800 prisoners. On 15 August Cromwell landed at Dublin to take charge, and Jones as Lieutenant-General, became his second in command. He took part in the capture of Wexford and the start of the siege of Waterford. Jones then took ill with a fever, and died five days later on 19 December 1649. [See also the letter on folio **167.**]

15. Hierome Zanchy from Cambridge, was Colonel of Brereton's own troop of horse. He was taken prisoner at Hanmer on 30 June 1643, but was part of an exchange of prisoners in October of that year. Zanchy fought at Tarvin and at Malpas in August 1644. He was in the Parliamentary force that defeated Lord Byron at Beeston on 18 January 1644–5, and was commissioner for General Mytton at the surrender of Caernarvon Castle in June 1645. At the end of the war Zanchy was appointed Senior Fellow of All Souls' College, Oxford. With the outbreak of further rebellion in Ireland, he was sent there as Colonel of Horse. In December 1649 he defeated Colonel Wogan at Passage, and in the following March captured Dundrum, being wounded in the shoulder. In February 1651–2 Zanchy's men stormed Bellitan and captured FitzPatrick's stronghold. Reporting to Parliament on 12 April 1652, he recorded that in his campaign he had killed above 400 Irish, hanged above 50 in accordance with Cromwell's Orders, as well as capturing some 350 prisoners. In all he lost but one officer, Captain Ball, and 5 common soldiers. Returning to England Zanchy was made "Seal Keeper," but in October 1653 he returned to Ireland. In August 1659 he returned to England with the Irish Brigade to put down Sir George Booth's rebellion. He allied himself to General Monck and was instrumental in bringing about the Restoration of the monarchy.

16. John Gell was born at Hopton Hall in Derbyshire, sometime about 1593. In 1635 he was appointed Sheriff of Derbyshire. In 1642 Gell was created a Baronet, but at the outbreak of the war he supported Parliament's cause, and was commissioned by the Earl of Essex to secure Derby. In 1643 he was ordered to take charge of the siege of Lichfield following Lord Brooke's death. Gell joined with Brereton in a plan to capture Stafford. On the way they clashed with a Royalist army led by the Earl of Northampton, at Hopton Heath. In 1643 Gell was appointed commander of Parliament's forces in Derby, Stafford and Warwickshire. Rivalry between Gell and Brereton, as is indicated in the Letter Book seems to have originated about this time. Gell's loyalty to Parliament came under suspicion when he failed to obey an order to join with Fairfax in the campaign culminating in the battle of Naseby. At the siege of Tutbury Castle Gell offered the defenders such favorable terms as to once more bring his loyalty into question. Brereton was given command of the counties of Warwick and Stafford in his place. In 1650 Gell was found guilty of plotting against the Commonwealth, and was imprisoned in the Tower until 1652. Thereafter he lived quietly in London. Charles II forgave him his part in the war and granted him a minor position at court. Gell died in October 1671.

17. Tutbury Castle, Staffordshire, was garrisoned for the King by General Hastings. He was later succeeded as Governor by Sir Andrew Kniveton. A brief siege by Parliament's forces in 1643 was thwarted following a mutiny. The King visited Tutbury at Whitsun 1645 on his way to Leicester, and again in August on his way to Ashbourne. Brereton's successful siege of Tutbury was begun on 30 March 1646; the castle surrendering on 20 April.

18. Hervey Bagot, son of Walter Bagot, was born at Blithfield, Staffs, on 8 February 1590. He was appointed Sheriff of Staffordshire, and in 1623 created a Baronet. Following Prince Rupert's capture of Lichfield Close in 1643, Bagot was seconded to the garrison. His estates were Sequestered by Parliament in 1644.

19. Thomas Mytton (1597–1656) of Halston Hall, Colonel, and Parliamentary Governor of Wem in Shropshire. A very active soldier, he relied heavily on intelligence to defeat his ene-

mies. In January 1644, at Ellesmere, he captured Sir Nicholas Byron, who was en route to Shrewsbury seeking arms. In June 1644 Mytton and the Earl of Denbigh assaulted and took Oswestry Castle. Later that summer, along with Sir Thomas Middleton, they lay siege to Dudley Castle. The siege was raised by Lord Wilmot, following a brief but effective skirmish at Tipton Green, wherein Mytton came close to being captured. In February 1644–5, Mytton and his men took Shrewsbury for Parliament. In May 1645, as a reward, he was made Parliamentary Commander in north Wales. On 9 August 1646, Mytton, with an army of some 4,000 men, assaulted and captured the town of Conway, in north Wales. Overwhelmed, the Royalist garrison withdrew into the castle, which fell after a siege of three months. On 15 March 1647 Harlech Castle, the last Royalist stronghold fell to Mytton, effectively ending the first civil war. In 1648, following a Royalist insurrection, Colonel Mytton brought Sir John Owen of Clenenny, to battle at Llandegai, Caernarfon, and defeated him. The Parliamentary army then went on to capture Beaumaris in Anglesey, putting an end to the revolt.

20. John Birch, eldest son of Samuel Birch of Ardwick, Lancashire, was born on 7 April 1616. His father was a carrier by trade. At the outbreak of the Civil War John Birch was a prosperous merchant in Bristol. He is first recorded as a captain in Parliament's army at the siege of Bristol. Traveling to London he raised a regiment in which he served as colonel under Sir William Waller. He was wounded in the assault upon Arundell, but recovering returned to command, and was present at the battle of Alresford, the blockade of Oxford and the battle of Cropredy Bridge. With the establishment of the New Model Army he briefly served under Fairfax and Cromwell.. He was appointed Governor of Bath, and took part in the storming of Bristol. By a clever stratagem he and Colonel Thomas Morgan, Governor of Gloucester, captured Hereford. Birch was appointed Governor of the captured city. Birch took part in the last battle of the first Civil War, at Stow-on-the-Wold, defeating Lord Astley.

21. Henry Stone of the Windmill, Walsall, was a Plymouth merchant who inherited his uncle's property in Staffordshire. At the outbreak of the war he was appointed a Captain of horse, but later was seconded to the Parliamentary Committee for Staffordshire, and supplied Brereton with much military intelligence. At the end of the war he was appointed a Justice of the Peace, a position he retained until the Restoration. Thereafter he contented himself with charitable works.

22. Thomas Morgan, second son of Robert Morgan of Llanrhymny, gained military experience serving in the Low Countries under Bernard Saxe-Weimer during the Thirty Year's War. He appears to be that Major Morgan skilled in siege warfare, listed in March 1644 as fighting in Lord Fairfax's Parliamentary army. Then a colonel, he took part in the siege of Lathom House later that month. On 18 June 1645, Morgan then a colonel of dragoons, was appointed Parliamentary Governor of Gloucester, succeeding Sir Edward Massey. During October 1645 forces commanded by Morgan captured Chepstow Castle and Monmouth. On 18 December that same year, in conjunction with Colonel Birch, he captured Hereford. Birch was subsequently appointed Governor of that city. In March 1646 Morgan, with Birch and Brereton, defeated Lord Astley at Stow on-the-Wold. Morgan captured Hartlebury Castle in May, and Raglan Castle in August 1646. Following the end of the war he retired to his wife's estates in Yorkshire, but in 1651 took up his commission once more and joined Cromwell's expedition to Scotland. He was seconded to General Monck's command, but when Commonwealth forces north of the Tay following the Glencairn Uprising of 1652–3. With Monck once more in command in Scotland, Morgan defeated Major-General Middleton's Scots-Royalist army at Dalnaspidel, near Loch Garry on 19 July 1654. Morgan was promoted to Major-General in February 1655. Two years later he was appointed second in command to Sir John Reynolds in the English army sent to Flanders as allies of the French in a war against Spain. Morgan was appointed Governor of Mardyke. He led the successful attack on the Spanish forts around Gravelines in April 1658, and commanded the English army at the Battle of the Dunes on 4 June. Returning to England, Morgan was knighted by Cromwell's son, Richard. Morgan supported Monck in the restoration of the monarchy, and held Scotland when Monck marched south to London to establish control. For his loyalty he was granted a Baronetcy by Charles II. Appointed Governor of Jersey, he died at St. Hellier in April 1679.

23. Charles Fleetwood (c. 1618–92) Born at Aldwincle in Northamptonshire, the third son of Sir Miles Fleetwood, he attended Emanuel College, Cambridge then studied law at Gray's

Inn. At the outbreak of war he was appointed to the lifeguard of the Parliamentary Earl of Essex. By May 1643, he had become a captain, and fought at the first battle of Newbury, where he was wounded. About this time he first met Cromwell. Fleetwood was given command of a cavalry regiment in the Eastern Association, under the command of the Earl of Manchester. He retained command when the regiment was transferred to the New Model Army. Fleetwood fought at the battle of Naseby in 1645, and thereafter campaigned in the west country and was at the siege of Oxford in 1646. In May 1646 Fleetwood was elected to the Long Parliament as M.P. for Marlborough in Wiltshire. He was later appointed Governor of the Isle of Wight, but in 1651 he returned to active service, and fought under Cromwell at the battle of Worcester, in which Charles II and his Scottish army were defeated. The following year Fleetwood married Cromwell's daughter, Bridget, the widow of Henry Ireton. Fleetwood was appointed Lord Deputy of Ireland, but was recalled in 1655, where he was appointed Major General during the rule of the Major Generals. Fleetwood was opposed to Cromwell becoming King, and protested at his dissolution of the Second Protectorate Parliament. Following the death of Cromwell, Fleetwood was instrumental in expelling Parliament on 13 October 1659, which prompted General Monck to march south with his army, in opposition. Fleetwood was deprived of Command, and following the Restoration was barred from holding public office. He died at his Stoke Newington home in October 1692.

24. Henry Ireton (1611–51) was born at Attenborough, near Nottingham. He was educated at Trinity College Oxford, then studied law at the Middle Temple, in 1629. He then returned home to run the family estate. At the outbreak of the Civil War he was nominated captain of a troop of horse raised in Nottingham. He fought at Edghill under the command of the Earl of Essex. In July 1643, as a major in Colonel Thornhaugh's regiment, Ireton took part in the Parliamentary victory at Gainsborough. Here he came to the notice of Cromwell. When he became Governor of the Isle of Ely, he invited Ireton to become his deputy. Both men shared the same religious beliefs. Ireton was promoted to Quartermaster -General in the army of the Eastern Association. He fought at Marston Moor in July 1644 and at Second Newbury in October. In 1645 Ireton was given command of a regiment in the New Model Army. At the battle of Naseby he was wounded, and briefly held prisoner, before managing to escape. Recovering from his wounds he took part in the siege of Bristol in September 1645 and was present at the surrender of the Royalist Lord Hopton and his Western Army at Truro, in March 1646. He was also present at the siege of Oxford in the spring and summer of 1646. On 15 June Ireton married Cromwell's daughter, Bridget. Ireton entered Parliament as M.P. for Appleby, and soon came into conflict with the Presbyterian element within the Commons, who were intent on disbanding the army so that they could come to their own settlement with the King. In concert with Cromwell and Lambert, Ireton, it is said, directed Independent elements within the army to seize the King, then held prisoner at Holmby House in June 1647. In the Putney Debates between the army and Parliament, Ireton settled the army's material grievances, thus defusing their political aims. In the process he secured the loyalty of the army. In the Second Civil War of 1648, Ireton, along with Fairfax, was sent to suppress the Royalist rising in Kent. They took Canterbury on 8 June 1648 and laid siege to Colchester. Upon the Royalist surrender of the town, leading Royalists, Sir Charles Lucas and Sir George Lisle, were executed as a deterrent to others. It was Ireton that initially demanded, on behalf of the army, that the King should be brought to trial. When opposition arose in Parliament, Pride's Purge, initiated by Ireton, saw the King's sympathizers, removed. Ireton was appointed a Commissioner of the High Court of Justice, which tried the King, and found him guilty. He was one of the 59 signatories of the King's death warrant. As Major-General Ireton accompanied Cromwell in his pacification of Ireland. He was present at the infamous storming of Drogheda and Wexford, in the Autumn of 1649.In joint command with Colonel Michael Jones he captured Inistioge and Carrick, and in February 1650 captured Ardfinnan Castle. With Cromwell's departure from Ireland Ireton was appointed Lord Deputy in his place. He embarked on a campaign of English colonization, depriving the native Irish of their land and rights. This led to a further uprising by the Catholic Confederation. In the summer of 1651 Ireton laid siege to the Catholic stronghold of Limerick. During the siege Ireton contracted a fever and died, on 26 November 1651. His body was returned to London and buried in Westminster Abbey, but was disinterred at the Restoration, and as a regicide, was hanged in a gibbet at Tyburn.

25. Henry Vane (1613–62) son of Sir Henry Vane, courtier and Secretary of State to Charles I, was educated at Westminster School and Magdalen College, Oxford. In 1635 he traveled to the Massachusetts colony in New England, where he was favorably received by the Puritan colonists. While there he negotiated the purchase of Rhode Island and as Governor, was instrumental in the establishment of Harvard College. Returning to England, through the influence of his father he was appointed to the post of Treasurer to the Navy. Vane was knighted by King Charles on 23rd June 1640. In November 1640 Vane was elected to the Long Parliament as M.P. for Hull. Following his involvement in the impeachment of the Earl of Strafford, the King dismissed Vane and his father from office. Vane embraced Parliament's cause during the Civil War, and was reinstated as Navy Treasurer. Vane was looked upon as one of the leaders of the "War Party" in Parliament, and was instrumental in setting up the Committee of Both Kingdoms, for whom he often acted as spokesman. Vane advocated the reform of the army, removing the Earl of Essex as commander by introducing the Self-Denying Ordinance in December 1644. He was instrumental in the formation of the New Model Army of 1645. Vane's influence in Parliament waned as the Presbyterian gained influence. He refused to sit as one of the King's judges, and totally disassociated himself from his execution. With the rise to power of Cromwell, Vane was appointed to various prestigious positions, including a seat on the Admiralty Committee, where his skilful management was seen as an important contribution to the defeat of the Dutch in the first Anglo-Dutch War. Cromwell dissolved Parliament in April 1653, and Vane withdrew from Government to write. In 1655 he published *The Retired Man's Meditations.* His first major work, *Zeal Examined*, published in 1651, had advocated complete liberty of conscience in matters of religion. Increasingly his writings criticized the Protectorate, and Vane was arrested and briefly imprisoned. Following Cromwell's death, Vane was elected M.P. for Whitchurch in Hampshire. Following the Restoration, Vane was one of 24 non-regicides excluded from a general pardon. He was brought to trial in June 1662, on a charge of High Treason. Charles II observed that Vane was too dangerous to live, and accordingly he was found guilty. Henry Vane was beheaded on Tower Hill on 14 June 1662.

26. Arthur Haselrig (1601–61) was the eldest son of Sir Thomas Haselrig, Baronet, of Noseley, Leicestershire, and succeeded his father in 1630. Haselrig held strong radical political and religious views. He was an outspoken critic of the King's personal rule, and was brought before the court several times for non-payment of taxes that he considered illegal. After his first wife died he married Dorothy Greville, sister of Lord Brooke, in 1634. Through Brooke, Haselrig met Lord Saye and Sele, and other leading Puritans. Haselrig sat in the Short and Long Parliaments, where he became associated with John Pym, and other radicals opposed to the King. Haselrig played a significant part in the impeachment of Lord Strafford, and was one of the five M.P.s whom the King attempted to arrest in January 1642. At the outbreak of the war Haselrig raised a regiment of Horse for Parliament, equipped at great expense, as fully armored cuirassiers. They became known as the "Lobsters," and fought in the army of Sir William Waller. Haselrig and his regiment fought at Lansdown, and eight days later at Roundway Down, in 1643. His regiment was decisive in the defeat of the Royalists at the Battle of Cheriton, in March 1644. When Parliament adopted The Self-Denying Ordinance, Haselrig resigned his commission and became a leading figure in the Independent faction in Parliament. Recalled to military duties in December 1647, Haselrig was appointed Governor of Newcastle. Following the outbreak of the second Civil War Haselrig recaptured Tynemouth Castle from the Royalists. In 1650 he accompanied Cromwell on the Dunbar Campaign. Haselrig broke with Cromwell in 1653, after the expulsion of the Purged Parliament and Cromwell's accession as Lord Protector. In 1658 Haselrig was party to the petition calling for the abolition of the Protectorate. This led Cromwell to dissolve Parliament. Following Cromwell's death in September 1658, Haselrig refused to support his son Richard, and his attempts to bring the army under Parliamentary control by calling for the impeachment of Colonel Lambert, led to Lambert and a military junta closing Parliament and dissolving the Council of State. The members of the Council appealed to General Monck for support. While Monck and his army marched south, Haselrig rode to Portsmouth to secure the naval base for Parliament. He was warmly welcomed, and a force sent by the junta, was persuaded to join Parliament's cause. At the end of December 1659 Haselrig marched on London with three regiments, to restore the Purged Parliament. Only after Monck had secured London did Haselrig come to realize that it was Monck's intention to restore the monarchy. Following

the Restoration Haselrig was imprisoned in the Tower of London, where he died in January 1661, before he could be brought to trial for treason.

27. William Purefoy (c. 1580–1659) was born at Caldecot, Warwickshire. He was educated at Cambridge and Gray's Inn. As a young man he traveled around Europe, and spent time at Geneva where he became a devout Calvinist. Returning to England he was elected M.P. for Coventry in 1628. He became friendly with Lord Brooke and other leading Puritans. Purefoy was elected to the Long Parliament as M.P. for Warwick. Upon the outbreak of the Civil War he raised troops for Parliament's cause, and held command in Lord Brooke's Midland Association Army. Following Lord Brooke's death at Lichfield, Purefoy saw active service as the colonel of a cavalry regiment in Lord Essex's army. Due to his age he was seconded to administrative duties for the county of Warwick, and in Parliament. Purefoy was appointed to the High Court of Justice that tried King Charles in 1649, and was one of the signatories to the death warrant. During the Interregnum Purefoy held a number of positions in Government and local politics. He opposed the offer of the crown to Cromwell, and became more associated with the Republican Commonwealth, controlled by Parliament. At the outbreak of Booth's rebellion Purefoy secured Coventry for Parliament. William Purefoy died in August 1659.

28. Henry Vernon of Hanbury, was a member of the Parliamentary Committee of Staffordshire. He was the son of Sir Edward Vernon, and held estates in Stafford, Derby and Cheshire.

29. This is a reference to the Venetian Republic's war with the Ottoman Empire. The war began in June 1645 when the Ottomans invaded Crete, formerly a Venetian possession, in retaliation for a series of pirate raids. Sultan Ibrahim assembled a navy of 400 ships and over 100,000 soldiers and invaded the island. He quickly captured the town of Canea, but political division at home forced the army to return to Turkey. The call went out from Venice for soldiers, in what was seen as a crusade against the infidel. Reinforcements, including 33,000 mercenaries from the German states arrived, as did smaller numbers from most European countries. The Venetians blockaded the Dardanelles in 1648, leading to the over-throw of the Sultan. An Ottoman fleet that evaded the blockade in 1651, was defeated off Naxos. In June 1656 the Venetians inflicted a crushing defeat on the Ottoman navy off the Dardanelles. The Ottoman fleet was rebuilt and the blockade was broken in 1657. Renewed efforts to retake Crete were made by Fazil Ahmet Pasha during the1660s. Quarrels between the Venetians and their allies in the Crete garrisons, led to a withdrawal of troops, forcing the Venetians to relinquish control of the island.

30. William Waller (c. 1598–1668) was born at Knole House, Kent, the son of Sir Thomas Waller, Lieutenant of Dover Castle. He was educated at Magdalen College, Oxford, then traveled in France and Italy. In 1617 he joined a company of English volunteers fighting in the army of the Venetian Republic. In 1620 Waller was part of Sir Horace Vere's expedition to the Palatine to rescue Elizabeth of Bohemia. Here he met Ralph Hopton. After the defeat of the Bohemians at the battle of White Mountain, in 1620, the two men escorted Elizabeth and her children through the snow to Frankfurt. Waller was knighted by James I in 1622, he married Jane Reynal, and upon her death married Anne Finch, daughter of the Earl of Winchelsea. Her father was a devout Puritan, and this influenced Waller's thinking. In 1640 Waller was elected to the Long Parliament, and at the outbreak of the war he gave his support to Parliament. He raised a regiment of Horse, and in one of the earliest engagements of the war, captured Portsmouth, with its important naval base. The next month Waller fought at the Battle of Edgehill, where his regiment was routed by Prince Rupert. Like Cromwell, he realized that if they were to win, then the army had to be well-trained, with professional officers commanding, rather than relying on the outdated and ill-trained county militia, led by Grandees, who commanded simply because of their position within society. In the months that followed Edgehill, Waller captured Farnham Castle, Winchester, Chichester and Arundel Castle. In 1643 Waller was appointed Major-General in the West. His success continued. He captured the port of Bristol, Malmesbury, and scattered Lord Herbert's newly recruited levies at Highnam. Waller then went on to capture Ross-on-Wye, Monmouth and Chepstow. He now suffered a series of defeats. Prince Maurice checked his advance at Ripple Field in April 1643, and then Waller faced his old friend, Ralph Hopton, Royalist Commander in the West, who narrowly defeated by him at the Battle of Lansdown in July 1643; then eight days later on 13 July, at Roundway Down. Waller put his defeats down to lack of support from his commander, the Grandee, Earl of Essex who was known to be in favor

of a negotiated settlement with the King. In October 1643 Waller was appointed Commander of the newly formed Southern Association Army. He besieged Basing House, but was forced to abandon it when he discovered that Hopton was advancing on London Waller marched to its defense, and Hopton abandoned his march. In the spring campaign of 1644 Waller defeated Hopton at the Battle of Cheriton on 29 March. The victory was confirmation of Waller's belief in a well-trained, professional army. Unfortunately Waller was still under the command of the Earl of Essex, who ordered him to shadow the King's army, while Essex himself sought glory in what proved to be a disastrous western campaign. Waller, with an inadequate force to face the Royalists in battle, had no choice when confronted, and was defeated at the Battle of Cropredy Bridge on 29 June 1644. With Essex's army defeated at Lostwithiel on 2 September, and his own force weakened, Waller was unable to prevent the King and his army from returning to Oxford. All he could do now was to link up with the Earl of Manchester to prevent the Royalists from marching on London. This they achieved at the Second Battle of Newbury in October 1644. During the spring of 1645, with Oliver Cromwell as his second in command, Waller continued his campaign in the west. In London, Parliament responded to Waller's suggestion that the army should be reorganized on a national basis, and staffed by professional officers. They proposed a New Model Army. Under the Self-Denying Ordinance, that accompanied the proposal, Lords and M.P.s in the army were obliged to resign their commissions. Waller himself became subject to the Ordinance. He now took up active politics once more, sitting on the Committee of Both Kingdoms, a body that directed the war. With the war coming to a close Waller became identified with the Presbyterian faction in Parliament, and when the army occupied London, Waller was forced to withdraw from the House. As tensions between the army and Parliament escalated, Waller and his family fled to Holland. Returning to England the following year he took his seat once more in Parliament, but at Pride's Purge he was ejected once more, and imprisoned for the next four years for conspiracy. After his release from prison in 1652, his wife having died, he married his third wife, Lady Anne Harcourt. During the Protectorate Waller developed Royalist sympathies, believing that the restoration of the monarchy was the only way of uniting the country. He was arrested for complicity in Booth's Uprising of 1659, and spent ten weeks in the Tower. Upon his release he was elected M.P. for Westminster in the Convention Parliament, which led to negotiations for the return of Charles II. After the return of the King, Waller retired into private life, where at Osterley in Middlesex, he died in 1668.

31. Prince Maurice (1621–52) was the son of Frederick V, Elector of the Palatinate and Elizabeth, the daughter of James I, King of England and Scotland. Maurice's military career began in the Dutch army of the Prince of Orange, and later in the Swedish army under General Banier. In August 1642 he and his elder brother Rupert traveled to England to fight for their uncle, Charles I. Maurice was commissioned colonel of a regiment of cavalry, and fought at the battles of Powick Bridge, Edgehill and Brentford. In March 1643 he was given independent command when he led an army of 2,000 men in a harassing campaign against Sir William Waller in the Welch Marches. He successfully maneuvered Waller into battle, and defeated him at Ripple Field in April 1643. Maurice then commanded the cavalry in the Marquis of Hertford's Western Army. At the Battle of Lansdown in July 1643 Maurice's cavalry was driven from the field by Haselrig's "Lobsters." Pursued by Waller, Maurice and 300 cavalry succeeded in escaping to Oxford. Aided by Lord Wilmot and Sir John Byron, Maurice at the head of 1,800 Horse, succeeded in defeating Waller at the Battle of Roundway Down. Maurice then joined his brother Rupert in the successful assault of Bristol. He was given command of the entire Western Army, and tasked with reducing the remaining Parliamentary garrisons. Maurice assisted the Earl of Carnarvon in the task, but letting his men plunder the captured towns, forced Carnarvon to resign his commission in disgust. In September 1644 rejoining King Charles, he assisted in the defeat of the Earl of Essex at Lostwithiel. At the Second Battle of Newbury, Maurice's cavalry were routed by Waller in a flanking attack. A year later at Naseby, Maurice fought on the right wing alongside his brother. Maurice was briefly appointed Governor of Worcester, but following Rupert's surrender of Bristol, he rode to join him at Newark, defending him before the King. Maurice and Rupert were at Oxford at the time of its surrender, and were banished from the country by order of Parliament. Maurice returned to the Prince of Orange's army, but in 1648 joined Prince Rupert and the Prince of Wales in a series of unsuccessful naval expeditions against Parliament's navy. In a ship named the "Defiance," Maurice sailed to the West Indies in 1652.

He was lost at sea during a storm near the Virgin Islands. 32. James Ussher (1581–1656), Archbishop of Armagh, was the son of Arland Ussher, clerk of the Irish Court of Chancery, and was born in Nicholas St., Dublin. He attended the Free Latin School, Dublin, and at the age of 13 was one of the earliest scholars to enter Trinity College, following its foundation on 9 January 1593–4. He graduated with a B.A. in 1597, and was made a Fellow in 1599. Ussher was ordained a priest in 1601. He made his first journey to England that same year with a gift of £1,800 to buy books for Trinity College. In London he met Thomas Bodley, then collecting books for his Oxford University foundation. In 1606 Ussher returned to England in search of books, and met William Camden. In 1607 Ussher was appointed Professor of Divinity at Trinity. He was appointed to the See of Meath and Clonmacnoise in 1622, and that same year preached before the House of Commons at St. Margaret's, Westminster. The following year Ussher was granted indefinite leave for the completion of his work on the antiquities of the British church, published as "Britannicarum Ecclesiarum Antiquitates." On 22 March 1624–5, he was appointed Archbishop of Armagh. He spent increasingly more time in England, though did preach in March 1640, at the opening of the Irish Parliament. In 1642 he went to live at Oxford, occupying the house of John Prideaux. Following the outbreak of the war Parliament confiscated his library, then deposited in Chester. The books were redeemed by George Seddon for a nominal sum, but by then a substantial amount of his correspondence had disappeared. At the beginning of 1647 Ussher was appointed, by Parliament's sanction, preacher at Lincoln's Inn, London. Ussher died on 21 March 1656. Cromwell ordered a public funeral for him at Westminster Abbey.

33. Thomas Fairfax (1612–71) born at Denton in Yorkshire, was the son of Ferdinando, second Lord Fairfax. He was educated at St. John's College, Cambridge, then spent three years in the Low Countries in the army led by Sir Horace Vere. He returned to England in 1632, and in 1637 married Anne Vere, daughter of his former commander. During the First Scottish War he commanded a troop of 160 dragoons, and was knighted by the King on 28 January 1640. At the opening of the Civil War both father and son were prominent among the supporters of Parliament in Yorkshire. Fairfax served under his father in the first few months of the war, but in January 1643 the younger Fairfax recaptured Leeds for Parliament. Two months later he suffered his first setback, when he was defeated by General Goring on Seacroft Moor. Fairfax and his men were acting as the rear guard to the main army led by his father, marching from Selby to Leeds. On 21 May Fairfax had his revenge when he captured Wakefield. With 1,500 men he stormed the town, held by a Royalist force twice their number, and in the process took General Goring himself, 28 colors and 1,400 men prisoner. This victory was followed by a major setback when Father and son were defeated at Aldwalton Moor on 30 June. Sir Thomas' right wing was driven from the field, and fled to the safety of Bradford. When Bradford itself was besieged, Fairfax and his troop cut their way through the Royalist forces and rode to Leeds where Fairfax found his father safe. On 11 October 1643, Fairfax with 20 troops of Horse, fought alongside Cromwell and Lord Manchester at the successful Battle of Winceby. On 29 January 1644 Fairfax defeated Lord Byron and his English troops recalled from Ireland, at Nantwich in Cheshire. He took 1,500 prisoners. He participated in the victory at Selby in April 1644, and at Marston Moor, where he commanded the right wing, consisting of 55 troops of Yorkshire cavalry and 22 of Scots: 4,00 men in all. In August Fairfax was wounded at the siege of Helmsley Castle, when he was struck by a musket-ball in the shoulder. While he recovered Parliament undertook the reorganization of the army. On 21 January 1645 Fairfax was appointed commander in Chief of the New Model Army. At Naseby on 14 June 1645 Fairfax brought the King to battle and defeated him with a loss of all his infantry, artillery and baggage. He retook Leicester for Parliament, relieved Taunton and defeated Goring, who had been part of an exchange of prisoners, at Langport in Somerset on 10 July. Bridgwater fell to him a fortnight later, then Bristol, after a three week siege. On 18 January 1646 Fairfax captured Dartmouth, and in the next month defeated Ralph Hopton at Torrington. On 14 March Hopton's army surrendered to Fairfax. Several further successful sieges followed, until Parliament's final victory. In November Fairfax received the thanks of both Houses of Parliament. With the King defeated, Parliament set about the reduction of the army. The soldiers objected until they had received their back-pay, resulting in much discussion between the two. At the end of July 1648 the army marched on London. Fairfax managed to restore order and discipline. Early in September he was able to report that 6,000 foot and 2,00 horse were ready to serve in Ireland, if their arrears of pay were settled. The remaining

mutinous regiments and the Levellers were suppressed. Fairfax was very much aware though that until the abuses and disorders were redressed, there would be discontent in the army. At the outbreak of the Second Civil War General Lambert was sent north to check the march of the Scots; Cromwell was sent to the west to suppress insurrection in Wales, while Fairfax held London and the south-east. The Kentish Royalists were crushingly defeated by him at Maidstone on 2 June, and on 13 June Fairfax laid siege to Colchester. The defenders held out for 75 days before surrendering. Royalist leaders, Lucas and Lisle, were executed for their part in the rebellion. With the rebellion suppressed the King was now brought to trial. Fairfax was appointed one of the King's judges, but refused to officiate at the trial. In fact he did all he could to prevent the King's execution. Relations between Fairfax and Parliament became strained. In the summer of 1650 he was called upon to lead the army against the Scots, and agreed, but only on the proviso that he would do so only if the Scots invaded England. He would not attack Scotland. In the end he resigned his commission. For the rest of the Commonwealth and the Protectorate, Fairfax lived in retirement at Nun Appleton in Yorkshire. In the last days of the Protectorate Fairfax entered into negotiations with Monck. On 30 December 1659, Fairfax seized York. That same day Monck crossed the Tweed and marched on London. At the Restoration, Charles II rode into the Capital on a horse provided by Fairfax. Thereafter Fairfax took no further part in public life. He died at Nun Appleton on 12 November 1671.

34. Ralph Hopton (1596–1652) was born at Witham in Somerset and was educated at the local grammar school, Lincoln College, Oxford, and the Middle Temple. He went abroad to gain military experience, and took part in Sir Horace Vere's expedition to rescue Elizabeth of Bohemia. During this campaign he befriended William Waller, and served alongside him in Elizabeth's lifeguard. Upon his return to England he was elected M.P. for Shaftsbury in 1621. Hopton married Elizabeth Capel Lewin in 1623. The following year he returned to Europe and gained further military experience in the following year when he served as a lieutenant-colonel in Sir Charles Rich's regiment on Count Mansfeldt's expedition to the Palatinate. Hopton was knighted by King Charles I when he came to the throne in 1625. He was elected M.P. for Bath, but upon the death of his father in 1636, he temporarily gave up the House of Commons and served as a Justice of the Peace as well as Deputy Lieutenant of Somerset. With the outbreak of the Bishop's War in 1639 Hopton returned to military life as Captain of the King's Lifeguard. With the return of peace, Hopton was elected M.P. for Somerset. He was very much a Royalist, and defended all of the King's policies. He was briefly arrested by order of the House of Commons in March 1642, but released from the Tower two weeks later. With the coming of war Hopton rode into Cornwall at the head of 160 horse and dragoons. He gained the support of the leading Cornish Royalists, and mobilized the militia. Hopton now raised a volunteer army, and in January 1643 confronted a Parliamentary army at Braddock Down, and defeated it. In May he defeated the Earl of Stamford at the Battle of Stratton, near Bude, leaving the west country in the hands of the King. With Prince Maurice and the Marquis of Hertford, Hopton then defeated his former comrade and friend, William Waller at the Battle of Lansdown, in July 1643. The day after the battle Hopton was seriously injured when an ammunition wagon accidentally blew up. Refusing to surrender command, he withdrew his forces to Devizes, where he was joined by Lord Wilmot. The two then inflicted a decisive defeat on Waller at the Battle of Roundway Down on 13 July 1643. With Prince Rupert, Hopton was present at the storming of Bristol. The King appointed him Lieutenant Governor of the city, and ennobled him as Baron Hopton of Stratton. In September 1643, his wounds now completely healed, Hopton was appointed Commander of the Royalist Forces in south-western England. The King ordered him to advance upon London, and as he did so he captured Arundel Castle in December 1643. At Cheriton in March of the following year, Hopton was driven back by Waller. In July 1644 the King's army pursued the Earl of Essex into the west. Hopton succeeded in encircling Essex, and defeated him at the Battle of Lostwithiel. In August Hopton was appointed General of Ordnance. In the spring of 1645 Hopton laid siege to Taunton, but was obliged to raise it at the approach of a superior Parliamentary army. Following Parliament's success at the Battle of Naseby, Fairfax marched into the West Country. The Royalists retreated to Exeter, before him. In early 1646 the King appointed Hopton Commander-in-Chief of the Western Army. By now though his army was greatly diminished. At Torrington in February 1646 Fairfax decisively beat him, and after securing the escape of the Prince of Wales, Hopton surrendered his army to Fairfax at Truro on 14 March 1646.

Hopton was permitted to go into exile, and rejoined the Prince in the Channel Islands. Charles then continued on to France with his mother, and Hopton traveled to the Hague in July 1648. After the execution of Charles I, Hopton was appointed to the young King's privy council. Still in exile, Hopton died at Bruges in September 1652. Following the Restoration his body was returned to the parish church of his ancestral home in Somerset.

35. James Louthian was a professional soldier, probably with experience from the Thirty Years War. He was a Scotsman, recruited by Brereton to train recruits at the outbreak of the Civil War. As a major, he fought with Brereton, as an officer of foot, at Nantwich and Middlewich in 1643. Louthian was captured in a skirmish outside of Nantwich on 17 December 1643, but was part of an exchange of prisoners soon after. He had experience of explosives, using a petard to blow in the doors of the church at Middlewich, and at the siege of Hawarden Castle in 1645, was responsible for under-mining the castle. Louthian was at Brereton's siege of Chester, as a colonel of Foot, while Michael Jones was colonel of Horse. Louthian and Jones, along with Colonel Mytton attacked and defeated at Denbigh, the Royalist army led by Colonel Vaughan, intent on relieving Chester. Louthian was at the siege of Lichfield, taking command in Brereton's absence. During the Second Civil war, in 1648, he was commanders of one of three regiments of Foot raised in Cheshire, and later after the Royalist defeat at Preston, served under Mytton in suppressing a rising in north Wales. He was at the Battle of Beaumaris, on 1 October 1648. After the war he retired to become a land owner in Cheshire.

Bibliography

Manuscripts

British Library: Brereton Letter Book Add MSS 11331.
Staffs. Record Office: D260/M/F/I/6 Letter concerning the yielding of Dudley
LII.B Contributions to the Garrison in the Close.
Worcs Record Office: 899: 31 BA3 6691/1 (VIII): News out of Staffordshire...
899: 31 BA3 159/1 (XXXIX): Sir Thomas Fairfax, his summons sent into Oxford ... and the copie of the Articles for the Surrender of Dudley Castle 1646.

Books

Ashley, Maurice. *Cromwell's Generals*. London: Jonathan Cape, 1954.
Bellett, The Rev. G. *The Antiquities of Bridgnorth*, 1856.
Childs, John. *Warfare in the Seventeenth Century*. London: Cassell, 2001.
Clarendon, Edward, Earl of. *The History of the Rebellion and Civil Wars in England*, 1843.
Dickinson, William. *History of Newark*, 1819.
Firth, C.H. *Cromwell's Army*. London: Methuen, 1962.
Gardiner, S. R. *History of the Great Civil War*, 1886.
Harwood, The Rev. Thos. *The History and Antiquities of the Church and City of Lichfield*, 1806.
Hemingway, J. *History of Chester*, 1831.
Hyde, Edward, Earl of Clarendon. *History of the Great Rebellion*. London: Oxford University Press, 1967.
Lomax, T. G. *A Short Account of the Ancient and Modern State of the City & Close of Lichfield*. Lichfield, 1819.
Noake. *Worcestershire Nuggets*, 1889.
Ormerod, George. *History of Cheshire*, 1819.
Ricraft, Josiah. *Survey of England's Champions*, 1649 (reprint 1818).
Shaw, Stebbing. *History and Antiquities of Staffordshire*, 1801.
Warburton, Elliott. *Prince Rupert and the Cavaliers*, 1849.
Webb, John. *Civil War in Herefordshire*, 1879.
Webb, Robert. *Memorials of the Civil War*.
Willis Bund, J.W. *The Civil War in Worcestershire*, 1905.
Young, Peter. *Marston Moor 1644*. Kincton, UK: Roundwood Press, 1970.
_____. *Naseby 1645*. London: Century Publishing, 1985.

Contemporary Civil War Tracts

T.T. = Thomason Tracts, British Library
B.P.L. = English Civil War Tracts Collection in Birmingham Public Library

Articles for the delivering up of Lichfield Close, 16 July 1646 (B.P.L.).
Barrife, Lt. Col. William, Militarie Discipline, 1643 (B.P.L.).
Copies of the King's Letter, and Generall Order for the Surrender of all his Garrisons T.T. 341 (6).
Crusoe, John, The Arte of Warre 1642 (B.P.L.).
A Great Fight at Newarke...T.T. E327 (19).
Great Fight at Newarke...Also the manner of taking the City of Lichfield 1645 T.T. E527 (19).
Letter to the House of Commons...4 March 1642–3 (B.P.L.).
Letters from Sir William Brereton...Mountgomery Castle, 1644. T.T. E10 (4).
Mercurius Aulicus (B.P.L.).
Perfect Diurnal of some passages in Parliament, 1643 (B.P.L.).
Perfect Occurances of Parliament, 1645–49 (B.P.L.).
Severall Occurences that have lately happened at Warwicke, Coventry, Northamptonshire and Oxfordshire, 1642 (B.P.L.).
Shrewsbury Taken. A copie of Sir William Brereton's letter to the Parliament. 1645. T.T. E270 (26).
Shropshires Misery and Mercie T.T. E75 (9).
Special Passages in Parliament, 21–28 March 1643 (B.P.L.).
True Relation by Colonell Morgan...Stow, 1645 T.T. E329 (8).
A True Account of the raysing and imployeing of one foote regiment under Sir John Gell (B.P.L.).
A True Relation by Colonell Morgan T.T. E329 (8).
A True Relation of a Great Victory obtained by Parliament's Forces...neere Chester T.T. E7 (7).
A True Relation of Two Great Victories obtained of the Enemy; the one by Sir William Brereton T.T. E 7 (25).
Vicars, John. England's Worthies, 1647 (B.P.L.).
_____. Vicars Parliamentary Chronicles.
_____. Vicars Parliamentary Chronicles: Vol. 2 God in the Mount.
_____. Vicars Parliamentary Chronicles: Vol. 3 God's Ark Over-topping the World's Waves.
_____. Vicars Parliamentary Chronicles: Vol. 4 Burning Bush Not Consumed (B.P.L.).

Journals and Periodicals

Archaeologia, Vol. 33, 1844.
Calendar of State Papers (Domestic) 1642–59.
Dictionary of National Biography (various).
Journal of Chester Archaeological Society, New Series, Vol. 25, 1923: Siege of Chester.
Journal of the House of Commons, Vols. III–V.
Lords Journals, Vols. VI–VIII.
Staffs. Record Soc., Vol. 1: The Committee at Stafford, 1643–45; Sutherland Papers, 1936.
State Papers (Committee for Compounding) G. Vol. 100.
Surtees Society, Vol. 124, 1915.
Trans. of the Lancs. & Cheshire Antiquarian Soc., Vol. 63, 1952–3: The Early Life of Sir William Brereton. Vol. 67, 1957: Sir William Brereton's Siege of Chester & the Campaign of Naseby.
Trans. of the Salop Arch. & Nat. Hist. Soc., 1896: The Ottley Papers.
Worcestershire Historical Soc., Vol. 31–2, 1915–20: Diary of Henry Townsend.

Index

www.ingramcontent.com/pod-product-compliance
Lightning Source LLC
Chambersburg PA
CBHW021812110726
47902CB00006B/1748
9780786472697